New Perspectives on

Microsoft® Office Outlook® 2003

Introductory

Robin M. Romer

THOMSON
COURSE TECHNOLOGY

Australia • Canada • Mexico • Singapore • Spain • United Kingdom • United States

New Perspectives on Microsoft® Office Outlook® 2003—Introductory

is published by Course Technology.

Managing Editor:
Rachel Goldberg

Senior Product Manager:
Kathy Finnegan

Senior Product Manager:
Amanda Young Shelton

Senior Product Manager:
Christina Kling Garrett

Product Manager:
Brianna Hawes

Associate Product Manager:
Emilie Perreault

Editorial Assistant:
Shana Rosenthal

Marketing Manager:
Joy Stark

Developmental Editor:
Katherine T. Pinard

Production Editor:
BobbiJo Frasca

QA Reviewers:
John Freitas, Christian Kunciw, Burt LaFountain, Danielle Shaw, Marc Spoto

Composition:
GEX Publishing Services

Text Designer:
Steve Deschene

Cover Designer:
Nancy Goulet

Preface

Real, Thought-Provoking, Engaging, Dynamic, Interactive—these are just a few of the words that are used to describe the New Perspectives Series' approach to learning and building computer skills.

Without our critical-thinking and problem-solving methodology, computer skills could be learned but not retained. By teaching with a case-based approach, the New Perspectives Series challenges students to apply what they've learned to real-life situations.

Our ever-growing community of users understands why they're learning what they're learning. Now you can too!

See what instructors and students are saying about the best-selling New Perspectives Series:

"The New Perspectives format is a pleasure to use. The Quick Checks and the tutorial Review Assignments help students view topics from a real world perspective."
— Craig Shaw, Central Community College – Hastings

"I have used books from the New Perspectives series for about ten years now. I haven't been able to find anything else that approaches their quality when it comes to covering intermediate and advanced software application topics."
— Karleen Nordquist, College of St. Benedict & St. John's University

www.course.com/NewPerspectives

Why *New Perspectives* will work for you

Context

Each tutorial begins with a problem presented in a "real-world" case that is meaningful to students. The case sets the scene to help students understand what they will do in the tutorial.

Hands-on Approach

Each tutorial is divided into manageable sessions that combine reading and hands-on, step-by-step work. Screenshots—now 20% larger for enhanced readability—help guide students through the steps. **Trouble?** tips anticipate common mistakes or problems to help students stay on track and continue with the tutorial.

Review

In New Perspectives, retention is a key component to learning. At the end of each session, a series of Quick Check questions helps students test their understanding of the concepts before moving on. And now each tutorial contains an end-of-tutorial summary and a list of key terms for further reinforcement.

Assessment

Engaging and challenging Review Assignments and Case Problems have always been a hallmark feature of the New Perspectives Series. Now we've added new features to make them more accessible! Colorful icons and brief descriptions accompany the exercises, making it easy to understand, at a glance, both the goal and level of challenge a particular assignment holds.

Reference

While contextual learning is excellent for retention, there are times when students will want a high-level understanding of how to accomplish a task. Within each tutorial, Reference Windows appear before a set of steps to provide a succinct summary and preview of how to perform a task. In addition, a complete Task Reference at the back of the book provides quick access to information on how to carry out common tasks. Finally, each book includes a combination Glossary/Index to promote easy reference of material.

Student Online Companion

This book has an accompanying online companion Web site designed to enhance learning. http://www.course.com/downloads/newperspectives/office2003/.
This Web site includes:
- Student Data Files
- Microsoft Office Specialist Certification Grid

Certification

This logo on the front of this book means that this book has been independently reviewed and approved by ProCert Labs. If you are interested in acquiring Microsoft Office Specialist certification, you may use this book as courseware in your preparation. For more information on this certification, go to www.microsoft.com/officespecialist.

Review

Apply

Reference Window

Task Reference

www.course.com/NewPerspectives

New Perspectives offers an entire system of instruction

The New Perspectives Series is more than just a handful of books. It's a complete system of offerings:

New Perspectives catalog
Our online catalog is never out of date! Go to the catalog link on our Web site to check out our available titles, request a desk copy, download a book preview, or locate online files.

Coverage to meet your needs!
Whether you're looking for just a small amount of coverage or enough to fill a semester-long class, we can provide you with a textbook that meets your needs.

- Brief books typically cover the essential skills in just 2 to 4 tutorials.
- Introductory books build and expand on those skills and contain an average of 5 to 8 tutorials.
- Comprehensive books are great for a full-semester class, and contain 9 to 12+ tutorials.
- Power Users or Advanced books are perfect for a highly accelerated introductory class or a second course in a given topic.

So if the book you're holding does not provide the right amount of coverage for you, there's probably another offering available. Go to our Web site or contact your Course Technology sales representative to find out what else we offer.

Instructor Resources
We offer more than just a book. We have all the tools you need to enhance your lectures, check students' work, and generate exams in a new, easier-to-use and completely revised package. This book's Instructor's Manual, ExamView testbank, data files, solution files, figure files, Tutorial Projects, Rubrics and Annotated Solution Files and a sample syllabus are all available on a single CD-ROM or for downloading at www.course.com.

How will your students master Microsoft Office?
SAM (Skills Assessment Manager) 2003 helps you energize your class exams and training assignments by allowing students to learn and test important computer skills in an active, hands-on environment. With SAM 2003, you create powerful interactive exams on critical Microsoft Office 2003 applications, including Word, Excel, Access, and PowerPoint. The exams simulate the application environment, allowing your students to demonstrate their knowledge and to think through the skills by performing real-world tasks. Designed to be used with the New Perspectives Series, SAM 2003 includes built-in page references so students can create study guides that match the New Perspectives textbooks you use in class. Powerful administrative options allow you to schedule exams and assignments, secure your tests, and run reports with almost limitless flexibility. Find out more about SAM 2003 by going to www.course.com or speaking with your Course Technology sales representative.

Distance Learning
Enhance your course with any of our online learning platforms. Go to www.course.com or speak with your Course Technology sales representative to find the platform or the content that's right for you.

www.course.com/NewPerspectives

About This Book

This book offers a case-based, problem-solving approach to learning Microsoft® Office Outlook® 2003.

Students will learn how to send and receive e-mail, manage contacts, plan tasks and schedule the Calendar, manage their Inbox, integrate Outlook with other applications and the Internet, and customize Outlook by creating forms and modifying the Outlook interface. Three appendices cover using Outlook with Microsoft Exchange Server, using Business Contact Manager, and synchronizing Outlook with PDAs. In addition, an Outlook Feature Guide demonstrates how Outlook uses color for various tasks.

Acknowledgments

It's a pleasure to work with the Course Technology team again. Christina Kling Garrett, Senior Product Manager, thanks for shepherding this book through its third revision. BobbiJo Frasca, Production Editor, thank you for your follow up on all the production details. I appreciate the efforts of the Quality Assurance group; a special thanks to John Freitas for taking the Exchange screenshots for Appendix A.

A very heartfelt thank you to Katherine T. Pinard—developmental editor extraordinaire. Thanks for all your work to make sure everything was ready to go and on schedule, and your willingness to check and double-check the details. Your input has helped to make this a better book.

Also, thank you to the reviewers for their time and suggestions on this edition: Debi Griggs, Bellevue Community College; Theresa Savarese, San Diego City College; Judy Law, Howard Community College; and Kathryn Striebel, MiraCosta College.

A big thank you to my son, Jake, for taking a few extra-long naps when deadlines loomed. And, most especially, thank you to my husband, Brian Romer. Your love and encouragement makes everything possible.

Robin M. Romer

Table of Contents

Appendix A   OUT A1

Using Outlook with Microsoft Exchange Server . . . . OUT A1

Appendix B   OUT B1

Using Business Contact Manager . . . . OUT B1

Appendix C   OUT C1

Synchronizing Outlook with Personal Digital Assistants . . . . OUT C1

New Perspectives on

Microsoft Outlook 2003 Introductory

Read This Before You Begin: Tutorials 1-6

To the Student

Data Files

To complete Outlook Tutorials 1, 2 and 5, you need the starting student Data Files. Your instructor will either provide you with these Data Files or ask you to obtain them yourself.

The tutorials require the folders shown in the next column to complete the Tutorials, Review Assignments, and Case Problems. You will need to copy these folders from a file server, a standalone computer, or the Web to the drive and folder where you will be storing your Data Files. Your instructor will tell you which computer, drive letter, and folder(s) contain the files you need. You can also download the files by going to *www.course.com*; see the inside back cover for more information on downloading the files, or ask your instructor or technical support person for assistance.

If you are storing your Data Files on floppy disks, you will need five blank, formatted, high-density disks for this book. Label your disks as shown, and place on them the folder(s) indicated.

▼**Outlook 2003 Data Disk 1**:
Tutorial.01 folder
Tutorial.02 folder
Tutorial.03 folder
Tutorial.04\Tutorial folder
Tutorial.04\Review folder

▼**Outlook 2003 Data Disk 2**:
Tutorial.04\Cases folder

▼**Outlook 2003 Data Disk 3**:
Tutorial.05\Tutorial folder
Tutorial.05\Review folder

▼**Outlook 2003 Data Disk 4**:
Tutorial.05\Cases folder

▼**Outlook 2003 Data Disk 5**:
Tutorial.06 folder

To the Instructor

The Data Files are available on the Instructor Resources CD for this title. Follow the instructions in the Help file on the CD to install the programs to your network or standalone computer. See the "To the Student" section above for information on how to set up the Data Files that accompany this text. You are granted a license to copy the Data Files to any computer or computer network used by students who have purchased this book.

System Requirements

If you are going to work through this book using your own computer, you need:

- **Computer System** Microsoft Windows 2000, Windows XP or higher must be installed on your computer. This book assumes a complete installation of Outlook 2003. You must have also have Internet access and an e-mail account/address you can use to send and receive e-mail messages. In addition, installation of Microsoft Office 2003 Professional (Word, Access, Excel, and PowerPoint) is required to complete certain sections and exercises.

To complete the Instant Messaging steps in Tutorial 5, you will need a Passport account. To complete Appendix A, you must be using Outlook with Exchange Server. To complete Appendix B, you must install Business Contact Manager.

Install on First Use: You may be required to insert the Microsoft Office 2003 CD-ROM the first time you try to use certain features of Outlook. Follow the instructions on the screen to install the feature.

- **Data Files** You will not be able to complete the tutorials or exercises in this book using your own computer until you have the necessary starting Data Files.

www.course.com/NewPerspectives

Objectives

Communicating by E-Mail

Sending and Receiving Messages

Case

The Express Lane

The Express Lane, founded in 1998 by Alan Gregory and Lora Shaw, is a complete and affordable online grocery store in the San Francisco Bay Area, specializing in natural and organic foods. Unlike traditional grocers, The Express Lane does not have a storefront where customers come to shop. Instead, it stores both packaged goods and fresh produce in its warehouse. Customers place orders through the company's Web site. The Express Lane staff confirms the order by e-mail, packs the requested items, bills the customer's credit card for the cost of the groceries plus a $10 service fee, and then delivers the groceries to the customer's front door on the day and at the time selected by the customer.

Alan focuses on the supplier end of the business, ensuring that the warehouse has the proper stock, locating new suppliers, and preparing budgets. Lora focuses on the customer end of the business, which includes finding new customers, responding to customer comments, and processing customer payments. To coordinate these activities, The Express Lane relies on **Microsoft Office Outlook 2003**, a personal information management program used to perform a wide range of communication and organizational tasks, such as sending, receiving, and filing e-mail; organizing contacts; scheduling appointments, events, and meetings; creating a to-do list and delegating tasks; and writing notes. In this tutorial, you'll use Outlook's e-mail to send information about increasing an order to a supplier.

Student Data Files

▼**Tutorial.01**

▽ Tutorial folder

Sales.xls

▽ Review folder

Tea.doc

▽ Cases folder

Amendments.doc

Session 1.1

Exploring Outlook

Outlook is organized into six main components, as described in Figure 1-1. With these six components, you can perform communication, scheduling, and organizational tasks to help you work efficiently and effectively. As you work with these components, you create items such as e-mail messages, appointments, contacts, tasks, journal entries, and notes. An **item** is the basic element that holds information in Outlook, similar to a file in other programs. Items are organized by and stored in **folders**. Unlike other folders in Office programs, which you can view and open in Windows Explorer, Outlook folders are available only within Outlook.

| Figure 1-1 | Outlook components |

Component	Description
Mail	A message/communication tool for receiving, sending, storing, and managing e-mail. The three most commonly used Mail folders are the **Inbox** folder, which stores messages you receive; the **Outbox** folder, which stores outgoing messages you have written but not sent; and the **Sent Items folder**, which stores copies of messages you have sent. You can also create other folders to save and organize e-mail you've received and written.
Calendar	A scheduling tool for planning your appointments, events, and meetings.
Contacts	An address book for compiling postal addresses, phone numbers, e-mail and Web addresses, and other personal and business information about people and organizations with whom you communicate.
Notes	A notepad for jotting down ideas and thoughts, which you can group, sort, and categorize.
Tasks	A to-do list for organizing and tracking items you need to complete or delegate.
Journal	A diary for recording your activities, such as talking on the phone, sending an e-mail message, or working on a document.

Outlook also has a special page, called **Outlook Today**, that displays a summary of activities scheduled in the Calendar folder, items on your to-do list in the Tasks folder, and the number of unread messages in your Mail folders.

Starting Outlook

Before you can use Outlook, you need a **user profile**, a group of e-mail accounts and address books or directories and the data files that Outlook uses to store e-mail messages and documents. You can add several e-mail accounts to one profile. If you use Outlook on multiple computers, you will need to set up a profile on each computer. Although a person can have more than one profile, typically you need only one. When several people share one computer, each person should have his or her own profile to ensure that each user's Outlook information remains separate from other users' information.

The next set of steps walks you through the process of setting up a new profile. You need to do this only once. If you are working on a lab computer, a profile may have already been set up for you. If you are unsure whether you need to create a profile or have permission to do so, check with your instructor or technical support person.

To set up a profile:

1. Click the **Start** button on the taskbar, and then click **Control Panel**. The Control Panel window opens.

2. Click **User Accounts** to open the User Accounts window, and then click the **Mail** icon. The Mail Setup – Outlook dialog box opens.

3. Click the **Show Profiles** button. The Mail dialog box opens, listing the profiles that are already set up on your computer.

   Trouble? If your profile name already appears in the list, you do not have to create a new profile. Skip to Step 7.

4. Click the **Add** button. The New Profile dialog box opens so you can enter a name for your profile.

5. Type a name for your profile in the Profile Name text box, and then click the **OK** button. The first dialog box for the E-mail Accounts Wizard opens, prompting you to create an e-mail account for your profile.

6. Click the **Close** button, and then click the **OK** button in the dialog box that opens to confirm that you want to create a profile without an e-mail account. You'll create an e-mail account later in this tutorial.

   Outlook creates a data file for your profile, and in a moment your profile name appears in the Mail dialog box.

7. Click the **Prompt for a profile to be used** option button in the Mail dialog box. Each time you start Outlook, a dialog box will open, enabling you to select your profile from a list of existing profiles. If you have only one Outlook profile, you could choose the option to Always use this profile. See Figure 1-2.

Mail dialog box ◀ **Figure 1-2**

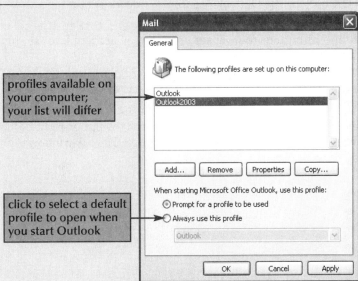

profiles available on your computer; your list will differ

click to select a default profile to open when you start Outlook

8. Click the **OK** button to close the Mail dialog box, and then click the **Close** button ⊠ in the upper-right corner of the Control Panel window to close it.

Once you have a profile, you can start Outlook. As with most other programs, you can start Outlook in several ways: use the Start menu, click the Outlook button on the Quick Launch toolbar (if displayed), or click the Outlook icon on your desktop (if shown).

To start Outlook:

▶ **1.** Click the **Start** button on the taskbar to display the Start menu, point to **All Programs** to display the All Programs menu, point to **Microsoft Office**, and then point to **Microsoft Office Outlook 2003**.

Trouble? If you don't see Microsoft Office Outlook 2003, look for it in a different submenu, on the All Programs menu, or in the pinned items list on the Start menu. If you still can't find Microsoft Office Outlook 2003, click the Launch Microsoft Outlook icon on the Quick Launch toolbar or double-click the Outlook icon on the desktop and skip Step 2. If none of the above is available, ask your instructor or technical support person for help.

▶ **2.** Click **Microsoft Office Outlook 2003**. The Choose Profile dialog box opens so that you can select your profile from the list of existing profiles.

Trouble? If Outlook opens without displaying the Choose Profile dialog box, then Outlook opened the default profile set in the Mail dialog box. To see the Choose Profile dialog box, you need to modify the settings in the Mail dialog box. Click File on the menu bar, and then click Exit to close Outlook. Complete Steps 1, 2, 3, 7, and 8 in the previous set of steps, and then repeat this set of steps.

▶ **3.** Click the **Profile Name** list arrow, and then click your profile name.

Trouble? If you don't see your profile name on the list, you need to create a profile. Click the Cancel button in the dialog box, complete the previous set of steps, and then repeat this set of steps. If you created a profile and still don't see your profile name, ask your instructor or technical support person for help.

▶ **4.** Click the **OK** button. The Outlook program window opens after a short pause.

Trouble? If the Outlook 2003 Startup Wizard opens, click the Cancel button and then click the Yes button. You will set up an e-mail account later so this wizard won't appear the next time you start Outlook.

Trouble? If the Microsoft Outlook with Business Contact Manager dialog box opens, asking if you want to use Business Contact Manager with your current profile, click the Remind me later button.

▶ **5.** If necessary, click the **Maximize** button 🔲 near the upper-right corner of the Outlook window. Figure 1-3 shows the maximized Outlook window with the Outlook Today page displayed.

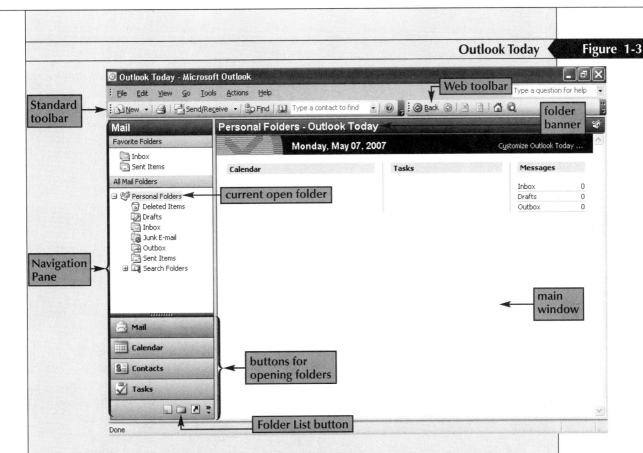

Trouble? If your screen differs from Figure 1-3, just continue with the tutorial. You'll learn how to display different folders and how to hide and display Outlook elements next.

Trouble? If the Send/Receive button is not on the Standard toolbar, there is no e-mail account associated with your profile. You'll add an e-mail account later in this session.

If you have been using Outlook, you see your schedule for the day, your list of tasks, and the number of unread e-mail messages you have. The Outlook Today overview is helpful for seeing the "big picture" to help you begin your day. From there, you can quickly jump to any of the listed items or folders.

The Outlook window contains the usual elements that are familiar to you from other programs for Microsoft Windows, such as Microsoft Word or Microsoft Excel, as well as additional elements that are specific to Outlook. The Outlook window includes the following (refer to Figure 1-3):

- **Standard toolbar.** Positioned below the menu bar, a collection of buttons to frequently used commands that you can click to quickly perform tasks. The toolbar's buttons vary, depending on the displayed Outlook folder. Additional toolbars are available in different folders.
- **Web toolbar.** Positioned below the menu bar to the right of the Standard toolbar, a collection of buttons to frequently used commands for navigating the Web.
- **Navigation Pane.** A central tool for accessing Outlook folders or files and folders on your computer or network; contains buttons to access additional panes.
- **Folder List.** A hierarchy of the Outlook folders that you use to store and organize items; also provides a way to navigate among the Outlook folders. The Folder List is not shown in Figure 1-3; you will work with it later in this tutorial.

- **Folder banner.** A bar at the top of the main window that displays the name of the open folder (Outlook Today in Figure 1-3).
- **Main window.** The display of items stored in the selected folder; this window may be divided into panes. For example, the left pane of the Inbox main window displays a list of e-mail messages in the Inbox, and the right pane displays the contents of the selected e-mail message.

No matter which component you use, these elements of the Outlook window work in the same way. You can display or hide many of these elements, depending on your needs and preferences.

Customizing the Outlook Window

You can use the View menu to change which elements of the Outlook window are displayed. For example, you can hide or display the Navigation Pane and the status bar.

To customize the Outlook window:

1. Click **View** on the menu bar. The list of commands on the View menu appears, including the Navigation Pane command.

   Trouble? If you don't immediately see the Navigation Pane command on the View menu, wait a moment or click the Expand button at the bottom of the menu to display the full menu, if necessary.

   Elements that you can display or hide appear on the menu. Those that appear are preceded by a check mark or have the shortcut icon clicked or shaded to appear pressed in. Clicking those elements hides them or displays them if they are hidden. The Navigation Pane command has a check mark next to it.

   Trouble? If the Navigation Pane does not have a check mark next to it, then it is not currently displayed. Click Navigation Pane and then repeat Step 1.

2. Click **Navigation Pane**. The Navigation Pane disappears from your screen.

   You want to display the Navigation Pane and the status bar.

3. Click **View** on the menu bar. Notice that the Navigation Pane command no longer has a check mark next to it.

4. Click **Navigation Pane**. The Navigation Pane reappears.

5. Click **View** on the menu bar, and then click **Status Bar** to display the status bar, if necessary. Your screen should now match Figure 1-3.

You'll usually use the Navigation Pane to move between the different Outlook components.

Navigating Between Outlook Components

You can click any button in the Navigation Pane to display that folder's contents in the main window. The Navigation Pane contains buttons for the most commonly used Outlook folders—Mail, Calendar, Contacts, Tasks, Notes, Folder List, and Shortcuts. Depending on the size of your monitor, the Notes, Folder List, and Shortcuts buttons appear either as bars with the name of the pane displayed or as icons at the bottom of the Navigation Pane. You click a button to display its content in the Navigation Pane.

You'll use the Navigation Pane now to view the contents of the Outlook folders.

To navigate with the Navigation Pane:

► 1. Click the **Mail** button in the Navigation Pane. The Personal Folders – Outlook Today view appears in the main window. If the Mail button was already selected, the view will not change.

► 2. Click the **Calendar** button in the Navigation Pane to switch to the Calendar folder, and then click the **Day** button on the Standard toolbar, if necessary. The daily planner appears in the main window, and the current month's calendar appears at the top of the Navigation Pane. See Figure 1-4.

Calendar folder | Figure 1-4

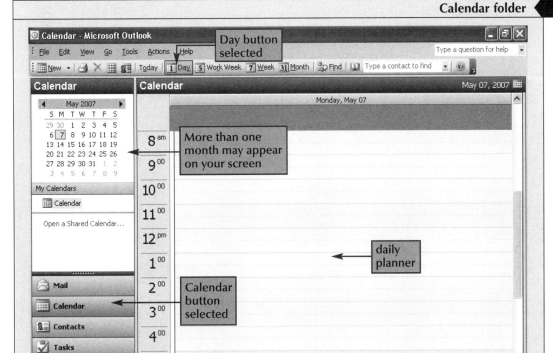

► 3. Click the **Contacts** button in the Navigation Pane to switch to the Contacts folder. The list of contacts is displayed in the main window; if yours is empty, as in Figure 1-5, you will still see letter buttons along the right side that you can use to scroll the contacts list. The Navigation Pane contains the Current View pane. See Figure 1-5.

Figure 1-5 Contacts folder

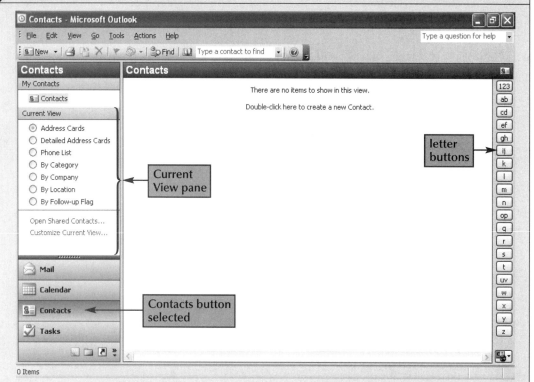

Trouble? If the main window in your Contacts folder looks different than the one shown in Figure 1-5, click the Address Cards option button in the Current View pane in the Navigation Pane.

4. Click the **Tasks** button in the Navigation Pane to switch to the Tasks folder. The tasks list appears in the main window and the Current View pane appears in the Navigation Pane. See Figure 1-6.

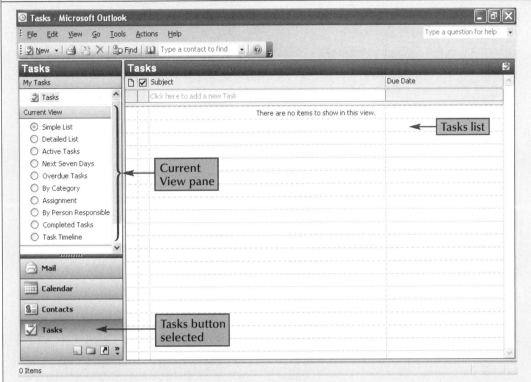

Trouble? If the main window in your Tasks folder looks different than the one shown in Figure 1-6, click the Simple List option button in the Current View pane in the Navigation Pane.

A second way to navigate between folders is with the Folder List. You can click any folder name in the Folder List to display the folder's contents in the main window.

To navigate with the Folder List:

▶ **1.** Click the **Folder List** button 🗀 in the Navigation Pane. The Folder List opens at the top of the Navigation Pane with the All Folders pane displaying icons for each of the folders in Outlook. Many of them are the same as the folders listed in the Mail pane, but there are additional folders as well.

▶ **2.** Click **Calendar** in the Folder List. The Calendar reappears with the current month's calendar in the top pane and the Folder List pane above the Navigation Pane buttons.

▶ **3.** Click **Inbox** in the Folder List. The Inbox folder opens in the main window. If there are any messages in your Inbox, the contents of the selected message might appear in the Reading Pane to the right of or below the main window. If there are no messages in your Inbox, then the Reading Pane will not appear. See Figure 1-7.

Figure 1-7 ▶ Inbox folder

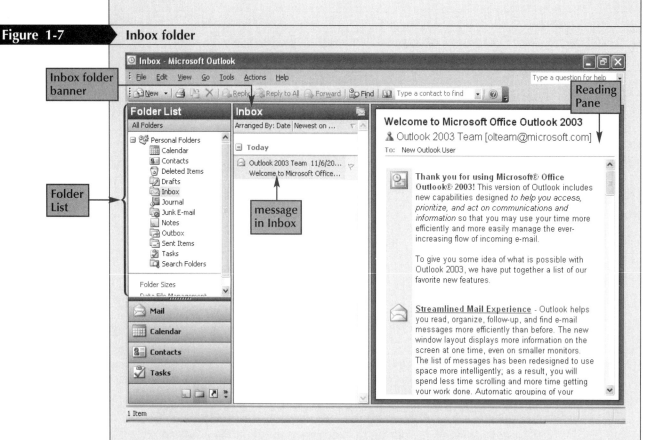

Trouble? If you do not see the Reading Pane and there are messages in your Inbox, click View on the menu bar, point to Reading Pane, and then click Right.

The main window displays the contents of the Inbox folder. You use this view to create and send e-mail messages.

Sending E-Mail Messages

E-mail, the electronic transfer of messages between computers, is a simple and inexpensive way to stay in touch with friends around the corner, family across the country, and colleagues in the same building or around the world. You send messages whenever you have time. The messages are delivered immediately and stored until recipients can read those messages at their convenience. The Express Lane staff uses e-mail to correspond with its customers, suppliers, and each other, because it is fast and convenient. Staff members use e-mail for both internal and external communications.

Before you can send and receive e-mail messages with Outlook, you must have access to an e-mail server or Internet service provider, an e-mail address, and a password. An **Internet service provider (ISP)** is a company that provides access to the Internet. An **e-mail address** is a series of characters that you use to send and receive e-mail messages. It consists of a user ID and a host name separated by the @ symbol. A **user ID** (or user name or account name) is a unique name that identifies you to your mail server. The **host name** consists of the domain name plus its top-level domain. The **domain name** is the name of your ISP computer on the Internet. The **top-level domain** is the broadest category of an Internet address, such as .com, .org, or .edu. Figure 1-8 shows how each of these parts makes up an e-mail address.

Parts of an e-mail address ◄ Figure 1-8

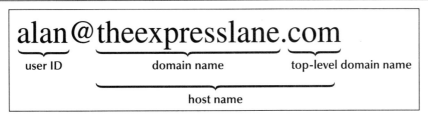

user ID   domain name   top-level domain name

host name

Although many people might use the same host, each user ID is unique, enabling the host to distinguish one user from another. A **password** is a private code that you enter to access your account. (In these tutorials, you'll use your own e-mail address to send all messages.)

Creating an E-Mail Account

You add an e-mail account to Outlook so you can get e-mail service. When you add an e-mail account, you will need to know the type of e-mail server you are using, the name of your incoming and outgoing server, your user name, your e-mail address, your password, and how you connect to your e-mail server. This information is usually available from your network administrator or your ISP. The E-mail Accounts Wizard walks you through the steps of adding or changing an e-mail account to your profile.

If you are working on a lab computer and your instructor has already set up an e-mail account in Outlook for you, so you should read but not complete the next set of steps. If you are using Exchange Server, see Appendix A, "Using Outlook with Microsoft Exchange Server." If you are unsure whether you need to set up an account, check with your instructor or technical support person.

To create a new e-mail account:

► **1.** Click **Tools** on the menu bar, and then click **E-mail Accounts**. The first dialog box of the E-mail Accounts Wizard opens. Here, you choose whether you want to create a new account or modify an existing account.

► **2.** Click the **Add a new e-mail account** option button, if necessary, and then click the **Next** button. The Server Type dialog box of the E-mail Accounts Wizard opens and lists various server types. See Figure 1-9.

Figure 1-9 **Server Type dialog box in the E-mail Accounts Wizard**

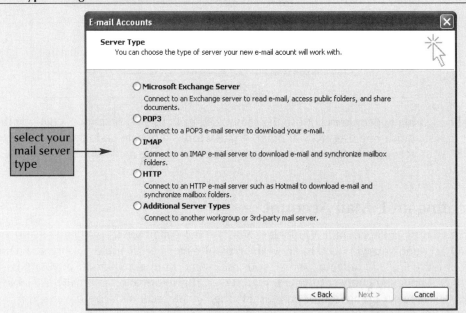

select your mail server type

3. Select the type of server you will use to access your e-mail, and then click the **Next** button. The Internet E-mail Settings dialog box varies, depending on the type of server you selected. Figure 1-10 shows the options when the POP3 server type is selected in the Server Type dialog box.

   Trouble? If you are unsure of what information to enter, ask your instructor or technical support person for help.

Figure 1-10 **Internet E-mail Settings dialog box for POP3 server type account**

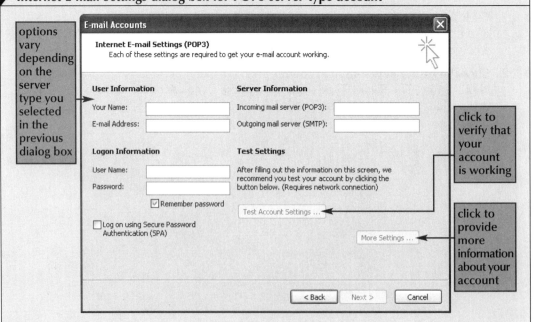

options vary depending on the server type you selected in the previous dialog box

click to verify that your account is working

click to provide more information about your account

4. Enter the requested user, logon, and server information in the Internet E-mail Settings dialog box.

Trouble? If you are unsure of what information to enter, ask your instructor or technical support person for help.

5. Click the **More Settings** button. The Internet E-mail Settings dialog box opens with the General tab on top, so you can enter additional information about your account.

6. Type your name in the Mail Account text box, press the **spacebar**, and then type **E-mail Account**. This is the name by which you will refer to this e-mail account in Outlook.

   Entering a name in the Organization text box is optional. You enter an e-mail address in the Reply E-mail text box only if you want to receive messages at a different address from which you send them.

7. Click the **Outgoing Server** tab. You need to use the options on this tab only if you log on separately to the SMTP server to which you send messages.

8. Click the **Connection** tab, and then click the option button next to the type of connection you will use, such as local area network or phone line. If you connect using your phone line, select the appropriate Dial-Up Networking connection in the Modem section or click the Add button to start the Network Connection Wizard to set up a new dial-up networking connection. See Figure 1-11.

Internet E-mail Settings dialog box **Figure 1-11**

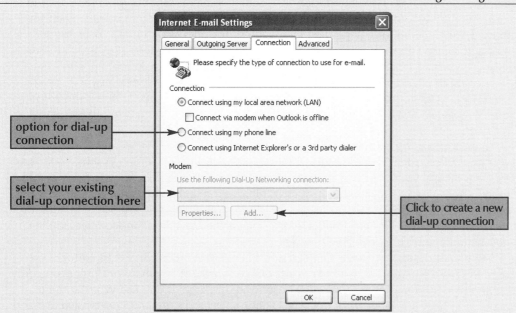

option for dial-up connection

select your existing dial-up connection here

Click to create a new dial-up connection

You won't make any changes to the Advanced tab unless specified by your ISP or server administrator.

9. Click the **OK** button to return to the Internet E-mail Settings dialog box.

   Before you finish, you can test the settings you entered to verify that you can send and receive e-mail messages.

10. Click the **Test Account Settings** button. The Test Account Settings dialog box opens, and Outlook verifies that your e-mail account works.

Trouble? If an error message appears, the test process located an inaccurate setting. Use the information in the dialog box to determine where the problem lies. Close the dialog box, correct the setting, and then repeat Step 10. If you cannot determine which setting caused the problem, ask your instructor or technical support person for help.

▶ **11.** Click the **Close** button in the Test Account Settings dialog box to confirm that the tests were completed successfully.

▶ **12.** Click the **Next** button in the Internet E-mail Settings dialog box, and then click the **Finish** button to set up your account based on the information you entered.

Once your account is set up, you can send e-mail messages. First, you should choose the message format to use to send and receive messages; then you should select the mail editor to use to create your messages.

Choosing a Message Format and Mail Editor

Outlook can send and receive messages in three formats: HTML, Rich Text, and plain text. **HTML** provides the most formatting features and options (text formatting, numbering, bullets, paragraph alignment, horizontal lines, backgrounds, HTML styles, and Web pages). **Rich Text** provides some formatting options (text formatting, bullets, and alignment). With both HTML and Rich Text, some recipients will not be able to see the formatting if their e-mail software is not set up to handle formatted messages. **Plain text** messages include no formatting, and the recipient specifies which font is used for the message. When you reply to a message, Outlook uses the same format in which the message was created, unless you specify otherwise. For example, if you reply to a message sent to you in plain text, Outlook sends the response in plain text, even if you have chosen HTML as the format for messages you send. Although you specify one of these formats as the default for your messages, you can always switch formats for an individual message.

So which message format should you use as your default? HTML is appropriate when you want to enhance your messages with formatting or images, although some recipients may not receive your messages properly. Because you often do not know what program others are using, you might want to stick to plain text. Plain text ensures that all recipients can read your messages, no matter what e-mail program they are using. In addition, the plain text e-mail files are smaller, which means they take less time to travel to their destination and require less storage space.

You can also select between Outlook and Microsoft Word as your **mail editor**, a tool used to create e-mail messages. **Microsoft Office Word 2003** is the word-processing program provided as part of the Office 2003 software package. If you use Word as the mail editor, you have access to all of the Word features and tools, including extensive text and paragraph formatting, tables, automatic checking of spelling and grammar, and AutoCorrect to fix common typos such as transposed letters. The Outlook mail editor provides access to some of these tools, but not all. Be aware, however, that you'll need to wait for Word to start the first time you compose a message in each Outlook session.

You'll set the default message format to plain text to ensure that everyone can read your messages and that they are the smallest size possible. You'll then verify that Word is the default mail editor.

To choose a default message format and mail editor:

1. Click **Tools** on the menu bar, and then click **Options**. The Options dialog box opens.

2. Click the **Mail Format** tab.

3. Click the **Compose in this message format** list arrow, review the options in the list box, and then click **Plain Text**.

4. Click the **Use Microsoft Office Word 2003 to edit e-mail messages** check box to insert a check mark, if necessary. See Figure 1-12.

Mail Format tab in the Options dialog box 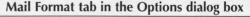 Figure 1-12

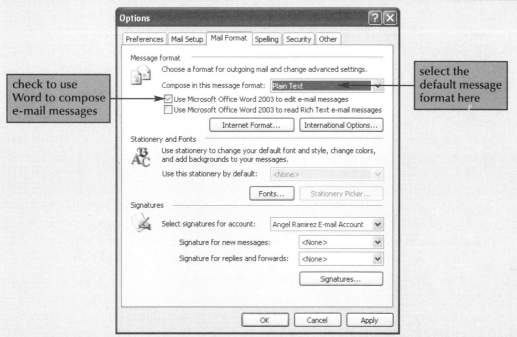

check to use Word to compose e-mail messages

select the default message format here

Trouble? If the Use Microsoft Office Word 2003 to edit e-mail messages check box is unavailable, then you are probably using a standalone version of Outlook. In this case, you'll use the Outlook mail editor to create and send your e-mail messages.

5. Click the **OK** button.

Now each time you create a message, Outlook will use Word as the mail editor and open a new message in plain text format.

Creating an E-Mail Message

An e-mail message looks similar to a memo with separate header lines for the Date, To, From, Cc, and Subject information followed by the body of the message. Outlook automatically fills in the Date line with the date on which you send the message and the From line with the name you entered in the User Name field when you set up your e-mail account; these lines are not visible in the window in which you create e-mail messages. You complete the other lines. The To line lists the e-mail addresses of one or more recipients. The Cc line lists the e-mail addresses of anyone who will receive a courtesy copy of the message. The optional Bcc line lists the e-mail addresses of anyone who will receive a blind courtesy copy of the message; Bcc recipients are not visible to each other or to the To and Cc recipients. You might use Bcc when you send notification messages to a large group of people, such as an address change notification to your entire e-mail list, and you don't want to publicize everyone's e-mail address. The Subject line provides a quick overview of the message topic, similar to a headline. The main part of an e-mail message is the message body.

E-mail, like other types of communication, is governed by its own customs of behavior, called **netiquette** (short for Internet etiquette), to help prevent miscommunications and offending or insulting a recipient. As you write and send e-mail messages, keep in mind the following guidelines:

- **Reread your messages.** Your words can have a lasting impact. Be sure they convey the thoughts you intended and want others to attribute to you. Your name and e-mail address are attached to every message that you send, and your e-mail can be forwarded swiftly to others.
- **Be concise.** The recipient should be able to read and understand your message quickly.
- **Use standard capitalization.** Excessive use of uppercase is considered shouting, and exclusive use of lowercase is incorrect; both are difficult to read.
- **Check spelling and grammar.** Create and maintain a professional image by using standard grammar and spelling. What you say is just as important as how you say it.
- **Avoid sarcasm.** Without vocal intonations and body language, a recipient may read your words with emotions or feelings you didn't intend. You can use punctuation marks and other characters to create **emoticons**—also called **smileys**—such as :-), to convey the intent of your words. (Tilt your head to the left and look at the emoticon sideways to see the "face"—in this case, a smile.) To learn additional emoticons, search the Web for emoticon or smiley dictionaries.
- **Don't send confidential information.** E-mail is not private; once you send a message, you lose control over where it may go and who might read it. Also, employers or schools usually can legally access their employees' or students' e-mail messages, even after a message is deleted from an Inbox.

The adage "Act in haste; repent in leisure" is particularly apt for writing e-mail. For more e-mail netiquette guidelines, search the Web for e-mail etiquette or netiquette Web sites.

Reference Window

Sending an E-Mail Message

- Click the New button on the Standard toolbar in the Inbox or Outbox.
- Type one or more recipient e-mail addresses in the To text box (separate multiple addresses with semicolons).
- Type one or more recipient e-mail addresses in the Cc and Bcc text boxes, if necessary (separate multiple addresses with semicolons).
- Type a topic in the Subject text box.
- Type the content of the message body in the message area.
- Click the Send button on the message toolbar.
- If necessary, click the Send/Receive button on the Standard toolbar in the Inbox or Outbox.

You'll create an e-mail message. Although you would usually send messages to other people, you will send messages to yourself in this tutorial so you can practice sending and receiving messages.

To create an e-mail message:

▶ **1.** Click **Inbox** in the Folder List to select it, if necessary, and then click the **New** button on the Standard toolbar. A new Message window opens in Word in plain text format. If necessary, maximize the window.

▶ **2.** Type your e-mail address in the To text box. You could send the e-mail to multiple recipients by typing a semicolon between each address. Do not add any spaces to e-mail addresses when you type them or your message will be returned.

▶ **3.** Press the **Tab** key twice to move the insertion point to the Subject text box. You skipped the Cc text box because you aren't sending a courtesy copy of this e-mail to anyone.

   Trouble? If the insertion point is not in the Subject text box, then the Bcc text box is displayed or Outlook recognized your e-mail address and inserted your name in the To box as well as your e-mail address. Press the Tab key again to move the insertion point to the Subject text box, and then continue with Step 4.

▶ **4.** Type **Peach Order** in the Subject text box, and then press the **Tab** key to move to the message area. As soon as you move the insertion point out of the Subject text box, the name in the title bar changes to match the contents of the Subject text box.

   You'll type a concise message that includes some intentional errors, which you'll correct in the next set of steps. In the next step, be sure to type the message with the errors shown, including typing "form" before the word "Maklin."

▶ **5.** Type **The Express Lane customers are enjying the peaches form Maklin Produce. Please double our order for the next three weeks.**, press the **Enter** key twice, type **Thanks you,** (including the comma), press the **Enter** key, and then type your name. See Figure 1-13.

Unproofed e-mail message | Figure 1-13

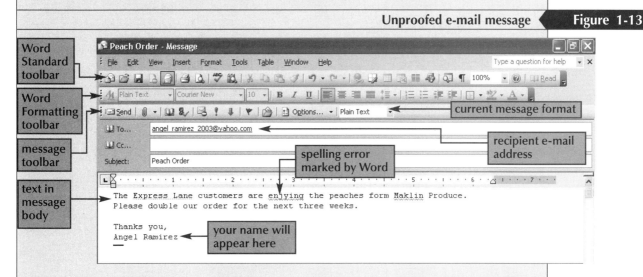

Though e-mail messages may take seconds to create, the time invested in correcting any spelling and grammar errors is well worth it. You don't want a reader to be distracted by the errors and ignore the message you want to convey.

Checking the Spelling and Grammar of Messages

Checking the spelling of messages helps to ensure that you correct any typographic errors before sending your message. If you are using Word as your e-mail editor, the Word Spelling and Grammar Checker reviews the spelling of the subject and body of your message as you type. Any words in your message that don't appear in the Word dictionary are underlined with a wavy red line. Any potential grammar errors are underlined with a wavy green line. You can use a shortcut menu or a dialog box to select to correct the spelling, ignore the word (such as when it is a proper name), or add the word to a custom dictionary that is common to all Office programs on your computer.

If you are using the Outlook mail editor, misspelled words are not underlined or otherwise distinguished. You can use the Outlook spelling checker to review your message text before you send the e-mail or you can choose to start the spelling checker manually to review your message text at any time. There is no button on the message toolbar for checking spelling in the Outlook mail editor, but you can choose the Spelling command on the Tools menu. The Outlook mail editor does not have a grammar checker.

Before you correct the spelling and grammar of your message, you'll verify the spell-checking options that are set in Word. You need to set these options only one time. You'll do this from the Spelling and Grammar dialog box.

To check the spelling and grammar of a message:

1. Click the **Spelling and Grammar** button [ABC] on the Standard toolbar. The Spelling and Grammar dialog box opens.

   Trouble? If you don't see the Spelling and Grammar button on the Standard toolbar, you may be using the Outlook mail editor. Click Tools on the menu bar, and then click Spelling to open the Spelling dialog box.

2. Click the **Options** button in the dialog box to display the Spelling & Grammar tab from the Options dialog box.

3. Verify that the check boxes in both the Spelling and Grammar areas are selected, as shown in Figure 1-14.

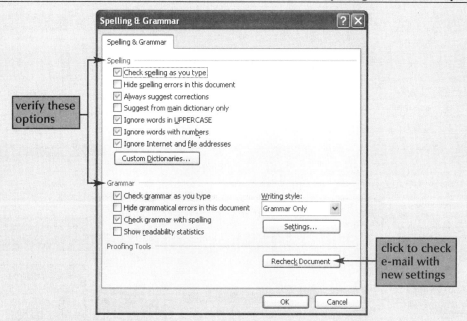

Trouble? If the check box options in the Options dialog box on your screen differ from those shown in Figure 1-14, you may be using the Outlook mail editor. Make sure check marks appear in the check boxes Always suggest replacements for mis-spelled words, Ignore original message text in reply or forward, and Use AutoCorrect when Word isn't the e-mail editor. Then continue with Step 5.

4. Click the **Recheck Document** button, and then click the **Yes** button to have Word review your document with the updated settings.

5. Click the **OK** button to return to the Spelling and Grammar dialog box. The first misspelled word is colored in the Spelling and Grammar dialog box. See Figure 1-15.

Figure 1-15 **Word spelling checker**

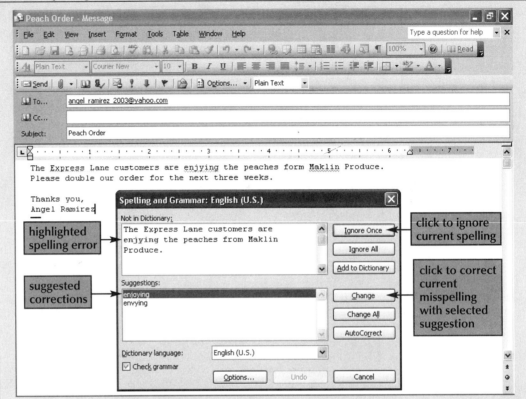

Trouble? If the dialog box on your screen differs from the one shown in Figure 1-15, then you may be using the Outlook mail editor. The dialog boxes function similarly. Continue with Step 6.

Trouble? If your name is selected as the first potential spelling error, click the Ignore Once button (or the Ignore button if you are using the Outlook mail editor), and then continue with Step 6.

6. Click **enjoying** in the Suggestions list box, if necessary, to select the correct spelling, and then click the **Change** button. If this word appeared multiple times in your message, you could click the Change All button to replace all instances of the misspelling with the correct word at one time.

   The word "enjoying" is now spelled correctly in the message and the next misspelled word is flagged. Because Maklin is a proper name, it is correct as is. If you used this name frequently, you could add it to the custom dictionary by clicking the Add button. This time you will ignore the word.

7. Click the **Ignore Once** button. If this word appeared multiple times in your message, you could click the Ignore All button to skip all instances of the word in the message.

   Trouble? If you see an Ignore button instead of the Ignore Once button, then you may be using the Outlook mail editor. Click the Ignore button and then continue with Step 8.

8. Continue to Change or Ignore highlighted words, as necessary. A dialog box opens when Word has finished checking the message.

9. Click the **OK** button to confirm that the spelling check is complete.

You can also set an option so that the spelling in a message is checked automatically before sending it. To do this, click Tools on the menu bar in the Outlook program window, click Options, click the Spelling tab, and then click the Always check spelling before sending check box to check it.

Although the spelling and grammar check is complete, your message is not necessarily error-free. The spelling checker verifies the spelling of individual words, not their usage. Your message may still contain words that are spelled correctly but used incorrectly. The grammar checker will flag some usage problems, such as subject-verb agreement errors, but it will not catch everything. For example, Word did not notice that "thanks you" should be "thank you" because each individual word is spelled correctly. The same is true for the substitution of "form" for "from." The key to a completely error-free message is to proofread your work before sending it. You can edit any text by selecting the word or words and retyping them or by clicking in the word, pressing the Backspace or Delete key to erase incorrect characters, and then typing the correct characters.

To proofread a message:

1. Verify that your e-mail address is typed correctly in the To text box.

2. Verify that the text in the Subject text box is typed correctly.

3. Double-click **form** in the message body, and then type **from** to correct the error in the first line.

4. Click to the right of **Thanks**, and then press the **Backspace** key to delete the letter "s" from "Thanks" in the closing.

5. Verify that the message body contains no other spelling or grammatical errors. This is also a good time to ensure that the content is accurate. Your finished message should match Figure 1-16.

Corrected e-mail message ◀ **Figure 1-16**

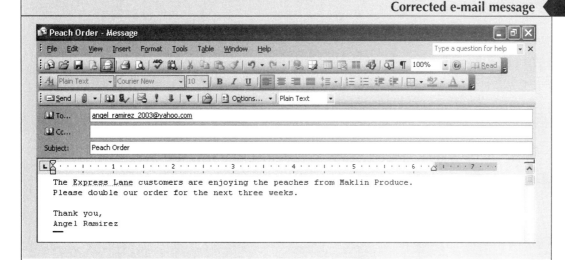

Once you are sure that the message is error-free, you are ready to send it.

Sending Messages

After you finish creating your e-mail message, you move it to the Outbox to send it. How long it remains in the Outbox depends on your connection type and Outlook settings. The message can be sent immediately to its destination (assuming your computer is connected to your e-mail server), in which case you cannot see its brief stopover in the Outbox. The message can remain in the Outbox until you click the Send/Receive button on the Standard toolbar in the Inbox or Outbox. You can also set up a schedule for Outlook to automatically send and receive messages at an interval you specify, such as every five minutes or every few hours.

If you are working **offline** (not connected to your e-mail server), any messages you write remain in the Outbox until you choose to send them. In this case, it is usually efficient to create all of your messages before you send them. You select how messages are sent in the Options dialog box. You'll set this option now.

To change message delivery options:

1. Click the **Inbox - Microsoft Outlook** button on the taskbar to return to the Inbox.

2. Click **Tools** on the menu bar, and then click **Options**. The Options dialog box opens.

3. Click the **Mail Setup** tab. This tab contains the message delivery options.

4. In the Send/Receive area, click the **Send immediately when connected** check box to insert a check mark, if necessary. If you have an always-on connection (such as DSL, cable, or a LAN) or have established a dial-up connection, Outlook will move completed messages into the Outbox and then immediately to your e-mail server.

5. Click the **OK** button in the Options dialog box to return to the Inbox.

You'll send the message now.

To send a message:

1. Click the **Peach Order - Message** button on the taskbar to return to the message.

   Trouble? If there is more than one e-mail account set up in your profile, click the Accounts button on the message toolbar, and then select the account you would like to use to send the message.

2. Click the **Send** button on the message toolbar. The message moves to the Outbox. The Outbox in the Folder List is in boldface and followed by [1], which indicates that there is one outgoing message. See Figure 1-17.

Message moved to Outbox ◄ **Figure 1-17**

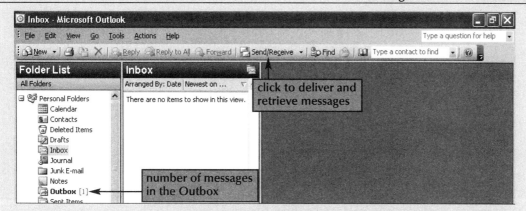

Trouble? If you don't see the message in the Outbox, you are probably connected to the Internet and the message has already been sent. Just read the rest of the steps in this section.

If you are working with an always-on connection, Steps 3 and 4 occur automatically, and you should read but not perform them. If you need to connect to the Internet, you'll need to send the message manually from the Outbox. Although you can send and receive e-mail from the Inbox or the Outbox, you'll switch to the Outbox to deliver this message.

3. Display the **Outbox**. The message appears in the Outbox main window.

4. Click the **Send/Receive** button on the Standard toolbar to send the message. The Outlook Send/Receive Progress dialog box remains open, showing the progress of the message to your e-mail server, until the message is received by your server. After the message is sent, the Outbox is empty and the boldface and [1] have disappeared.

Trouble? If you are not already connected to the Internet, connect now.

Trouble? If Outlook requests a password, you might need to enter your password before you can send and receive your messages. Type your password, and then click the OK button.

Trouble? If you get a message that Outlook encountered a Sending error, and 0 of 1 Tasks have been completed successfully, click Cancel All. Ask your instructor or technical support person for help.

A copy of the message you sent is stored in the Sent Items folder by default, although this option can be switched off. The time your e-mail takes to arrive at its destination will vary, depending on the size of the message, the speed of your Internet connection, and the number of other users on the Internet. When you send a message, your e-mail server identifies its final destination by the host name in the e-mail address.

While sending your outgoing messages, Outlook may check your mail server for messages you have received since you last checked. If you have messages, they will be delivered to your Inbox. The message you just sent to yourself might appear in your Inbox instantly, and you might receive other messages that are unrelated to this tutorial.

As you work in Outlook, there are times you'll want more information about certain features.

Getting Help in Outlook

If you don't know how to perform a task or want more information about a feature, you can turn to Outlook itself for information on how to use it. This information, referred to simply as **Help**, is like a huge encyclopedia available from your desktop. You can access Help in a variety of ways, including ScreenTips, the Type a question for help box, the Outlook Help task pane, and Microsoft Office Online.

Using ScreenTips

ScreenTips are a fast and simple method you can use to get help about buttons you see on the screen. A **ScreenTip** is a yellow box with the button's name. Just position the mouse pointer over a toolbar button to view its ScreenTip.

Using the Type a Question for Help Box

For answers to specific questions, you can use the **Type a question for help box**, located on the menu bar, to find information in the Help system. You simply type a question using everyday language about a task you want to perform or a topic you need help with, and then press the Enter key to search the Help system. The Search Results task pane opens with a list of Help topics related to your query. A **task pane** is a window that opens to the right of the Office program window and provides access to commands for common tasks. You click a topic in the Search Results task pane to open a Help window with step-by-step instructions that guide you through a specific procedure and explanations of difficult concepts in clear, easy-to-understand language.

Reference Window | **Getting Help from the Type a Question for Help Box**

- Click the Type a question for help box on the menu bar.
- Type your question, and then press the Enter key.
- Click a Help topic in the Search Results task pane.
- Read the information in the Help window. For more information, click other topics or links.
- Click the Close button in the Help window title bar, and then click the Close button on the Search Results task pane title bar.

You'll use the Type a question for help box to obtain more information about sending e-mail.

To use the Type a question for help box:

1. Click the **Type a question for help box** on the menu bar, and then type **How do I get help?**

2. Press the **Enter** key to retrieve a list of topics. The Search Results task pane opens with a list of topics related to your query. See Figure 1-18.

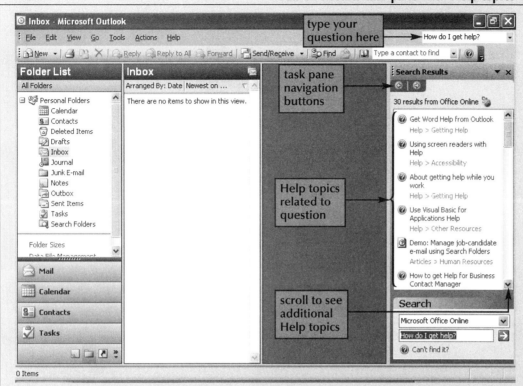

3. Scroll through the list to review the Help topics.

4. Click the **About getting help while you work** link in the Search Results task pane. The Microsoft Office Outlook Help window opens to the right of the Search Results task pane and contains information about the various ways to obtain help in Outlook. See Figure 1-19.

| Figure 1-19 | About getting help while you work Help window |

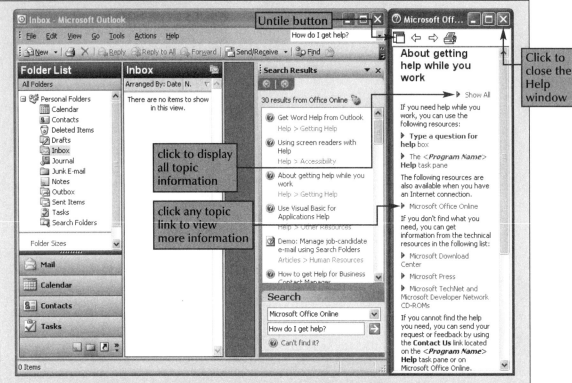

Trouble? If the Outlook program window and the Help window do not appear side by side, then you need to tile the windows. Click the Auto Tile button on the toolbar in the Microsoft Office Outlook Help window.

5. Click the **Type a question for help box** link in the Help window to display information about that topic. Read the information.

6. Click the other links about Help features in the Help window and read the information.

7. When you're done, click the **Close** button on the Help window title bar to close the Help window, and then click the **Close** button on the Search Results task pane title bar to close the task pane.

The Outlook Help task pane works similarly.

Using the Outlook Help Task Pane

For more in-depth help, you can use the Outlook Help task pane, a task pane that enables you to search the Help system using keywords or phrases. You open the Outlook Help task pane by clicking the Microsoft Office Outlook Help button on the Standard toolbar, and then you type a specific word or phrase in the Search for text box and click the Start searching button. The Search Results task pane opens with a list of topics related to the keyword or phrase you entered. If your computer is connected to the Internet, you will also see Help topics stored on **Microsoft Office Online**, a Web site Microsoft maintains that provides access to additional Help resources. The Outlook Help task pane also has a Table of Contents link that organizes the Help topics by subject and topic, as in a book. You click main subject links to display related topic links.

Getting Help Using the Outlook Help Task Pane

- Click the Microsoft Office Outlook Help button on the Standard toolbar (*or* click Help on the menu bar, and then click Microsoft Office Outlook Help).
- Type a keyword or phrase in the Search for text box in the Outlook Help task pane, and then click the Start searching button.
- Click a Help topic in the Search Results task pane.
- Read the information in the Help window. For more information, click other topics or links.
- Click the Close button in the Help window title bar, and then click the Close button on the task pane title bar.

You'll use the Outlook Help task pane to obtain more information about getting help in Outlook.

To use the Help task pane:

▶ 1. Click the **Microsoft Office Outlook Help** button 🔞 on the Standard toolbar. The Outlook Help task pane opens.

▶ 2. Drag to select any text in the Search for text box, if necessary, and then type **send e-mail**. See Figure 1-20.

Outlook Help task pane ◀ **Figure 1-20**

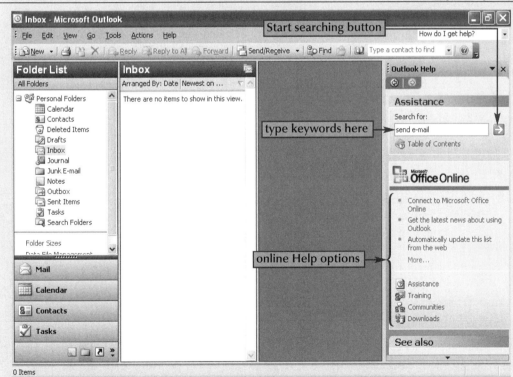

▶ 3. Click the **Start searching** button 🔁 . The Search Results task pane opens with a list of topics related to your keywords.

▶ 4. Scroll through the list to review the Help topics.

5. Click the **Send and receive messages** link to open the Microsoft Office Outlook Help window and learn more about sending and receiving messages. See Figure 1-21.

Figure 1-21

Send and receive messages Help window

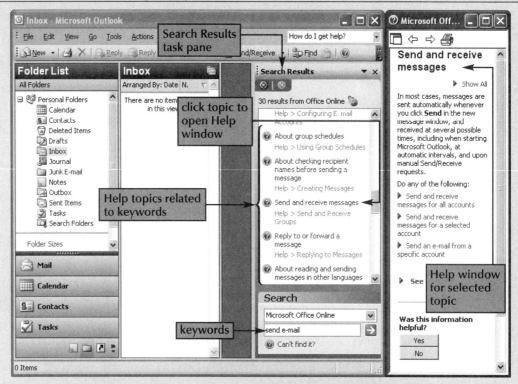

Trouble? If your search results list differs from the one shown in Figure 1-21, your computer is not connected to the Internet or Microsoft has updated the list of available Help topics since this book was published. Continue with Step 6.

6. Click the **Send and receive messages for all accounts** link in the Help window to display information about that topic. Read the information.

7. Click the other links and read the information.

8. When you're done, click the **Close** button ☒ on the Help window title bar to close the Help window. Keep the task pane open.

If your computer has a connection to the Internet, you can get more help information from Microsoft Office Online.

Using Microsoft Office Online

You can connect to Microsoft Office Online from the Help task pane. You can search all or part of a site to find information about tasks you want to perform, features you want to use, or anything else you want more help with.

To connect to Microsoft Office Online, you'll need Internet access and a Web browser such as Internet Explorer.

To connect to Microsoft Office Online:

1. Click the **Back** button  in the Search Results task pane. The Outlook Help task pane reappears.

2. Click the **Connect to Microsoft Office Online** link in the task pane. Internet Explorer starts and the Microsoft Office Online home page opens. See Figure 1-22. This Web page offers links to Web pages focusing on getting help and accessing additional Office resources, such as galleries of clip art, software downloads, and training opportunities.

Microsoft Office Online home page　　Figure 1-22

Trouble? If the content you see on the Microsoft Office Online home page differs from the figure, the site has been updated since this book was published. Continue with Step 3.

3. Click the **Outlook** link. The Outlook Home page opens. From this page, you can learn more about Outlook, check for updates, and access Outlook discussion groups. You can also enter a keyword or phrase pertaining to a particular topic for which you wish to search using the search box in the upper-right corner of the window.

4. When you're done, click the **Close** button ⊠ on the Internet Explorer title bar.

5. Click the **Close** button ⊠ on the Outlook Help task pane title bar to close the task pane.

So far, you have started Outlook and set up a profile and e-mail account. You selected plain text as your default message format and Word as your mail editor. You created and sent an e-mail message. You also learned how to search the Help system. In the next session, you'll retrieve and respond to the message you sent.

Session 1.1 Quick Check

1. What is the difference between an item and a folder?

2. Explain what a profile is.

3. Define e-mail and list two benefits of using it.

4. What is the host name in the e-mail address: "alan@theexpresslane.com"?

5. Why would you select plain text as your message format default?

6. What is a mail editor?

7. List three netiquette guidelines you should follow when writing e-mail.

8. Which folder stores a copy of messages you have written and sent?

Session 1.2

Receiving and Responding to E-Mail

When someone sends you an e-mail message, depending on your setup, either your network server or your ISP's server will receive it. In most cases, messages are moved automatically from your mailbox on your server into your Inbox. If you are using a dial-up connection, you can check manually for new e-mail messages at any time of day or night and as often as you like. Some people retrieve their messages once or twice each day, whereas others check periodically throughout the day. How often you check for incoming messages will depend on your needs and preferences.

In addition to messages from other people, you may also receive notice from a system administrator that a message you sent is undeliverable. This could occur for a variety of reasons—you may have mistyped the recipient's e-mail address, or your server, the recipient's server, or something in between is not working properly. Read the message from the system administrator: sometimes delivery attempts will continue for several days; other times you will need to resend the message after verifying the e-mail address.

Downloading Messages

You check for new e-mail messages by clicking the Send/Receive button on the Standard toolbar in any of the Mail folders. Outlook connects to your e-mail server, if necessary, sends any messages in the Outbox, and downloads any incoming messages that have arrived since you last checked. New messages are delivered into the Inbox. These messages may be removed from your mail server and stored on the computer you are using.

You'll switch to the Inbox and download the message you created and sent earlier. You should also receive a message that was generated when you tested your e-mail account settings. If you are connected to the Internet, whether the connection is always-on or dial-up, the messages may already appear in your Inbox.

To retrieve e-mail messages:

▶ **1.** If you took a break after the previous session, make sure Outlook is running.

▶ **2.** Click the **Mail** button in the Navigation Pane, and then click **Inbox** in the Favorite Folders pane in the Navigation Pane.

3. Click the **Send/Receive** button on the Standard toolbar, and then watch for the new messages to appear in the Inbox. The number of new, unread messages appears within parentheses next to the Inbox folder name in the Navigation Pane. The two new messages you received are the Peach Order message and a confirmation message from Outlook from when you tested your account settings. Your Inbox might contain additional e-mail messages. See Figure 1-23.

Received messages in the Inbox | **Figure 1-23**

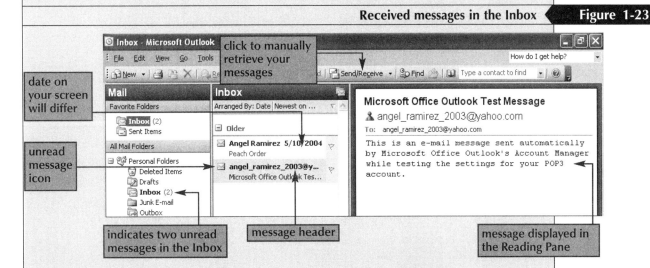

Trouble? If you are not already connected to the Internet, connect now.

Trouble? If no messages appear, your e-mail server might not have received the message yet. Wait a few minutes, and then repeat Step 3.

Once a message arrives, you can open and read it.

Opening and Reading Messages

The Inbox main window is divided into two panes. The left pane displays a list of all e-mail messages that you have received, along with information about the message. The **message header** includes the sender's name, the message subject, and the date the message was received, as well as icons that indicate the message's status. For example, icons indicate whether the message has an importance level of Low ⬇ or High ❗ and specify whether the message is unread ✉ or read ✉ . You can change any column width by dragging the border of a column header with the double-headed arrow ↔ that appears when you position the pointer between columns. To help you locate new messages easily, messages are ordered in the Inbox by date, from newest to oldest.

The right pane, called the **Reading Pane**, displays the contents of the selected message in a memo format. The subject, the sender, the importance level, and all the recipients (except Bcc recipients) appear at the top of the memo, followed by the message content. If a message is longer than fits on screen, scroll bars appear along the edge of the Reading Pane. You can use these to bring the rest of the message into view. You can also open any message in its own window. You can resize the panes by dragging the border between the message list and the Reading Pane left or right.

To read a message:

1. Click the **Peach Order** message in the message list to display its contents in the Reading Pane. In a moment, the mail icon changes from unread [icon] to read [icon], and the message no longer appears in boldface.

   Trouble? If the Reading Pane does not appear on your screen or if it appears on the bottom of the screen, click View on the menu bar, point to Reading Pane, and then click Right.

   Trouble? If the mail icon in the message list does not change to indicate that the message has been read, click Tools on the menu bar, click Options, click the Other tab, click the Reading Pane button, click the Mark items as read when viewed in the Reading Pane check box to insert a check mark, and then click the OK button in each dialog box.

2. Read the message in the Reading Pane.

3. Double-click the **Peach Order** message in the message list. The message opens in its own window. See Figure 1-24.

Figure 1-24 — Peach Order message opened in its Message window

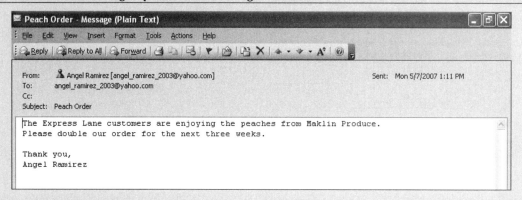

4. Read the message, and then click the **Close** button [X] on the Message window title bar. The window closes.

   Trouble? If a dialog box opens, asking whether you want to save changes, click the No button.

After you read a message, you have several options—you can leave the message in the Inbox and deal with it later, reply to the message, forward the message to others, print the message, or delete it. As with paper mail you receive, it is best to deal with messages as you receive them rather than letting them collect in your Inbox.

Replying to and Forwarding Mail

Many messages you receive require some sort of response—for example, confirming that you received information, answering a question, or sending the message to another person. The quickest way to respond to messages is to use the Reply, Reply to All, and Forward features. The **Reply** feature responds to the sender, whereas the **Reply to All** feature responds to the sender and all recipients; Outlook inserts the e-mail addresses into the appropriate text boxes. The **Forward** feature sends a copy of the message to recipients you specify; you enter the e-mail address in the To or Cc text box.

With both the Reply and Forward features, the original message is included for reference (unless you change the default settings), separated from your new message by the text "Original Message" and the original message header information. By default, any new text you type is added at the top of the message area above the original message. This makes it simpler for recipients to read your message because they don't have to scroll through the original message text to find the new text.

If you're responding to a very long message (or several replies have been exchanged), you might want to delete text that is no longer relevant to the current discussion to keep the message smaller. However, if you delete too much material and send only your response, recipients might no longer recall the context of the message. For example, the message, "We'll change your order as requested," leaves doubt as to what changes will occur because the request for the peach order to be doubled for the next three weeks is no longer included as reference. In addition, the same netiquette guidelines apply for message replies. Responses use the same format as the original message, unless you specify otherwise. In other words, if you receive a message in HTML format, your response is in HTML format; if you receive a message in plain text format, your response is in plain text format.

You'll reply to the Peach Order message. Of course, in reality, you would respond to someone other than yourself.

To reply to a message:

▶ 1. Make sure the **Peach Order** message is selected in the message list, and then click the **Reply** button on the Standard toolbar. A Message window opens with the original sender's name and e-mail address in the To text box (in this case, your name and address) and RE: (for Reply) inserted at the beginning of the Subject line with the current subject still listed. The body of the message appears in the message area below a divider, and the insertion point is above the message, ready for you to type your reply.

▶ 2. Type **You will receive double shipments of peaches for the next three weeks. Thank you for your order.** See Figure 1-25.

Figure 1-25 **Replying to a message**

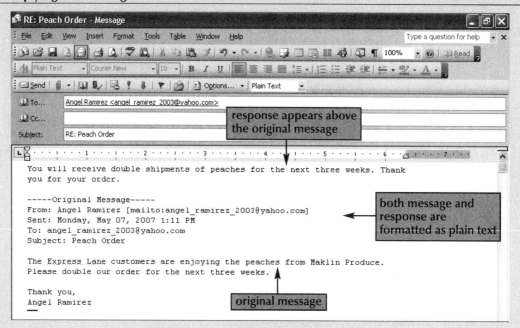

3. Check the spelling of the message, and then send the message. The icon next to the message header in the message list changes to ⌦ to indicate that you have replied to this message.

   Trouble? If the Spelling button is not available in the Reply Message window, click Tools on the menu bar, and then click Spelling.

Next, you'll forward the message to Leslie Katz, the manager at Foods Naturally. Again, you will actually forward the message to yourself. Rather than retyping your e-mail address, you can use the AutoComplete feature to enter the complete address quickly. As you start to type an address in the To, Cc, or Bcc text box, the **AutoComplete** feature lists any e-mail address you used earlier that begins with those letters in a blue box. If you want to use the selected address, press the Enter key; Outlook then places the entire e-mail address in the text box. If you don't want to use the suggested text, continue to type as usual.

To forward a message:

1. Make sure that the **Peach Order** message is selected in the message list, and then click the **Forward** button on the Standard toolbar. This time, the insertion point is in the empty To text box and FW: (for Forward) precedes the Subject line.

2. Type the first few letters of your e-mail address in the To text box. Your e-mail address should appear in a blue box just below the To text box.

▶ **3.** If your e-mail address appears in a blue box just below the To text box, press the **Enter** key to complete your e-mail address automatically. If your e-mail address does not appear, continue typing it until it does, and then press the Enter key.

▶ **4.** Press the **Tab** key three times to move the insertion point to the top of the message area, and then type **Please update The Express Lane account.** (including the period).

   Trouble? If the Bcc text box is visible in your Message window, then press the Tab key four times.

▶ **5.** Check the spelling, and then send the message. The icon next to the message header in the message list changes to 🖼 to indicate that this message has been forwarded.

Alan asks you to file a paper copy of the message for future reference.

Printing Messages and Folder Contents

Although e-mail eliminates the need for paper messages, sometimes you'll want a printed copy of a message to file or distribute, or to read when you are not at your computer. You can use the Print button on the Standard toolbar to print a selected message with the default settings, or you can use the Print command on the File menu to verify and change settings before you print. All default print styles include the print date, user name, and page number in the footer. You'll use the Print dialog box to verify the settings and then print the Peach Order message.

To verify settings and print a message:

▶ **1.** If necessary, select the **Peach Order** message in the message list.

▶ **2.** Click **File** on the menu bar, and then click **Print**. The Print dialog box opens, as shown in Figure 1-26.

Figure 1-26   Print dialog box

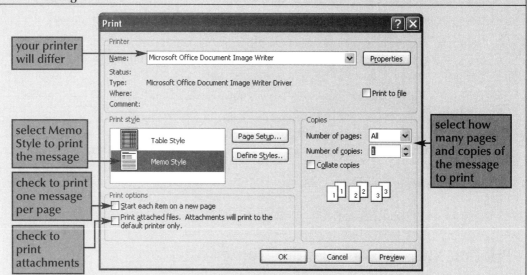

your printer
will differ

select Memo
Style to print
the message

check to print
one message
per page

check to
print
attachments

select how
many pages
and copies of
the message
to print

If you click the Print button on the Standard toolbar, the message will print with the current settings in the Print dialog box.

▶ **3.** Make sure the correct printer appears in the Name list box.

   Trouble? If you are not sure which printer to use, ask your instructor or technical support person for assistance.

▶ **4.** If necessary, click **Memo Style** in the Print style area to select it.

   Memo Style prints the contents of the selected item—in this case, the e-mail message. Table Style prints the view of the selected folder—in this case, the Inbox folder. Other Outlook folders have different print style options.

▶ **5.** Click the **Preview** button in the Print dialog box. The Print Preview window opens, displaying the message in the format in which it will be printed.

▶ **6.** Click the **Print** button on the Print Preview toolbar, and then click the **OK** button in the Print dialog box.

The message prints, and the message appears in the format of a memo.

You might also want to print a list of messages in your Inbox or another Mail folder. To do this, you choose Table Style in the Print dialog box. You'll print the list of messages in your Inbox.

To print a list of messages in the Inbox:

▶ **1.** With the Inbox selected in the Navigation Pane, click **File** on the menu bar, and then click **Print**. The Print dialog box opens.

▶ **2.** Click **Table Style** in the Print style area, and then make sure the **All rows** option button is selected in the Print range area.

▶ **3.** Click the **Preview** button. The Print Preview window opens displaying the list of messages in the Inbox.

▶ **4.** Click the **Print** button on the Print Preview toolbar, and then click the **OK** button in the Print dialog box.

The list of messages in the Inbox prints.

Customizing Messages

There are several ways to enhance e-mail messages that you send from Outlook. First, you can specify that specific text appear on every e-mail message you send. You can also change the default font and style, colors, and backgrounds used in your messages. Formatting options you decide to use will be visible only to those recipients who can view messages in HTML or Rich Text. Rather than change the default message format to HTML, you'll set it for specific messages.

Creating a Signature

A **signature** is text that is automatically added to every e-mail message you send. A signature can contain any text you want. For example, you might create a signature with your name, job title, company name, and phone number. In addition, you can create more than one signature and then use the Signature button on the Standard toolbar to select the signature you want to include in a particular message. For example, Alan at The Express Lane might create one signature that contains a paragraph about how to order groceries for e-mail messages to customers and a second signature that includes the warehouse information for e-mail messages to vendors and suppliers. You can create different signatures for messages you create and messages to which you respond or forward. If you have more than one e-mail account, you can create different signatures for each one. Although you can attach a signature to a message in any format, the HTML and Rich Text formats enable you to apply font and paragraph formatting. For now, you'll create an unformatted signature that includes your name and the company name.

Creating a Signature   Reference Window

- Click Tools on the menu bar, click Options, click the Mail Format tab, and then click the Signatures button.
- Click the New button to create a new signature, type a name for the new signature, and then click the Start with a blank signature option button to begin with a new blank signature. If you wanted to base this signature on an existing signature, you could use an existing one as a template.
- Click the Next button, type the signature text, format the signature as necessary, and then click the Finish button.
- Click the OK button to return to the Options dialog box, and then click the OK button.

To create a signature:

▶ **1.** Click **Tools** on the menu bar, click **Options**, and then click the **Mail Format** tab in the Options dialog box.

▶ **2.** Click the **Signatures** button to open the Create Signature dialog box, and then click the **New** button. The Create New Signature dialog box opens.

3. Type your name in the **Enter a name for your new signature** text box, click the **Start with a blank signature** option button, if necessary, and then click the **Next** button. The Edit Signature dialog box opens with the insertion point in the large text box.

4. Type your name, press the **Enter** key, and then type **The Express Lane**. See Figure 1-27.

Figure 1-27   Edit Signature dialog box

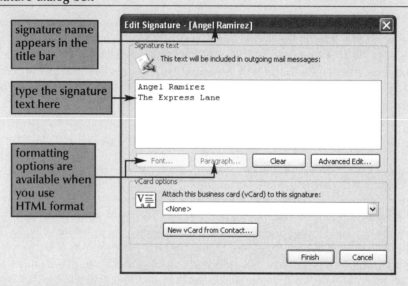

signature name appears in the title bar

type the signature text here

formatting options are available when you use HTML format

If you wanted to add formatting, you could select the text to format, and then click the Font button and change the font and style or click the Paragraph button to change the alignment and spacing. Because you plan to use this signature for both plain text and HTML messages, you won't add any formatting.

5. Click the **Finish** button. The Create Signature dialog box reappears with your new signature listed and selected in the Signature list, and with a preview of the selected signature.

6. Preview your signature in the Create Signature dialog box, and then click the **OK** button to return to the Options dialog box.

You'll add your signature to new messages you create, but not to messages to which you respond.

7. If necessary, click the **Select signatures for account** list arrow, and then click your e-mail account name (your name followed by "E-mail Account" if you set up your account in this tutorial).

8. If necessary, click the **Signature for new messages** list arrow, and then click your name.

9. If necessary, click the **Signature for replies and forwards** list arrow, and then click **<None>**.

▶ **10.** Click the **Apply** button. If you had more than one e-mail account, you could select other signatures for those accounts: repeat Steps 7 through 9, except click the e-mail account you want to use in Step 7. You could also create another signature for this account: repeat Steps 2 through 9, except type a different name in Step 3 and choose the signature you want to use in Steps 8 and 9.

▶ **11.** Click the **OK** button.

Whenever you start a new e-mail message, your signature will appear at the end of the message.

Using Stationery

When you send e-mail, you can select a special look for your message, much as you would select special letterhead paper for your business correspondence. **Stationery templates** are HTML files that include complementary fonts, background colors, and images for your outgoing e-mail messages. The stationery templates that come with Outlook include announcements, invitations, greetings, and other designs. You can also design your own stationery. Be aware that stationery increases the size of messages, so they take longer to send and receive. When you create a message using stationery, Outlook changes the message format for that e-mail to HTML. Stationery uses HTML message format, so recipients whose e-mail programs don't read HTML e-mail won't see the special formatting, but they will still be able to read the text.

Creating an E-Mail with Stationery	Reference Window

- Click Actions on the menu bar, point to New Mail Message Using, and then click More Stationery.
- Select the stationery you want to use, and then click the OK button.
- Complete the To, Cc, Bcc, Subject, and message body as usual.
- Format the text in the message body as desired.
- Send the message.

Alan asks you to send an e-mail message to Daniel O'Brien, a supplier, inviting him to lunch as a thank you for the quality of his produce and the timeliness of his shipments. You'll use stationery to give the message a more celebratory look.

To create an e-mail message with stationery:

▶ **1.** Click **Actions** on the menu bar, point to **New Mail Message Using**, and then click **More Stationery**. The Select a Stationery dialog box opens with the available designs.

You can preview stationery by clicking its name in the Stationery list box. Stationery is listed in alphabetical order, and you can press the first letter of the one you want to move quickly through the list.

2. Type **s**, and then click **Sunflower** in the Stationery list box. See Figure 1-28.

Figure 1-28
Select a Stationery dialog box

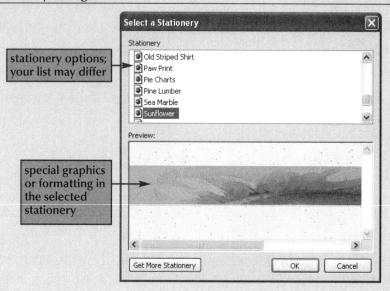

Trouble? If the Sunflower stationery isn't listed, select another design of your choice.

3. Type **i**, and then click **Ivy** in the Stationery list box, if necessary.

Trouble? If the Ivy stationery isn't listed, select another design of your choice.

4. Click the **OK** button. A new Message window opens with the stationery and your signature.

You want to send this message to Daniel O'Brien and copy Alan Gregory.

5. Type your e-mail address in the To and Cc text boxes, type **Thank You** in the Subject text box, press the **Tab** key, type **Daniel,** (including the comma), press the **Enter** key twice, and then type **I would like to express the appreciation of the entire team here at The Express Lane for your company's commitment to high-quality produce and timely shipments. Please join Alan for lunch next Monday to celebrate our two successful years of working together.** (including the period) to create the e-mail message shown in Figure 1-29.

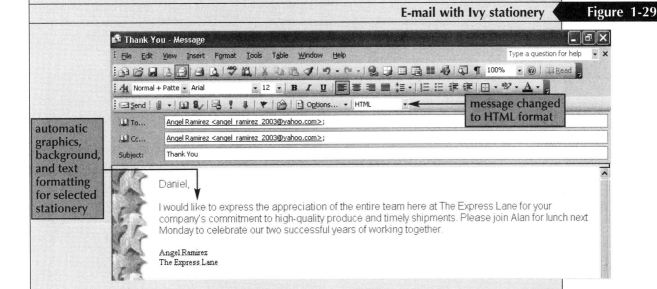

You don't need to type your name because you included it as part of the signature. Before sending this message, you want to add some text formatting.

Formatting a Message

You set up Outlook to use Word as your e-mail editor, which means that you have access to all the formatting features available in Word. For example, you can set bold, underlining, and italics; change the font, font size, and font color; align and indent text; create a bulleted or numbered list; and even apply paragraph styles. You can format e-mail text much as you would format text in a regular Word document. People whose e-mail programs cannot read formatted e-mail will still be able to read the text of your formatted messages in plain text.

To format text in an e-mail message:

► **1.** Select **The Express Lane** in the message body. You'll make this text italic and red.

► **2.** Click the **Italic** button ⚹ on the Formatting toolbar.

   Trouble? If you don't see the Italic button and your toolbars are on one line, click the Toolbar Options button ⚹ , and then click the Italic button.

► **3.** Click the **Font Color** button list arrow ⚹ on the Formatting toolbar, and then click the **Red** tile in the palette that opens.

   Trouble? If you don't see the Font Color button and your toolbars are on one line, click the Toolbar Options button ⚹ , and then click the Font Color button list arrow and click the Red tile.

   Trouble? If the stationery you selected has a red background, select another color so that the text is visible. Use the same color when you complete Step 4.

► **4.** Select **next Monday,** and then repeat Step 3 to change the text to red.

5. Click to the left of your name in the signature, click the **Outside Border** button list arrow ⊞ ▾ on the Formatting toolbar, and then click the **Horizontal Line** button ☰ . Your message should match Figure 1-30.

Figure 1-30 | **E-mail with formatting**

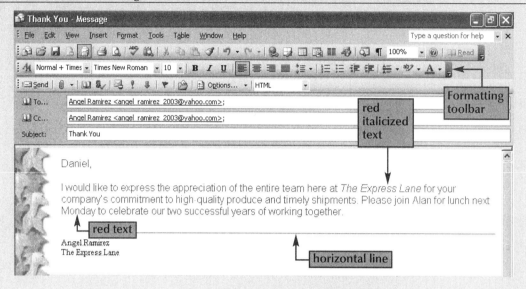

You could add more formatting, but a little goes a long way. Try to be judicious in your use of text formatting. Use it to enhance your message rather than overwhelm it.

Setting Importance and Sensitivity Levels

You can add icons that appear in the message list to provide clues to the recipient about the importance and sensitivity of the message. You can specify an importance level of High or Low or leave the message set at the default Normal importance level. High importance tells the recipient that the message needs prompt attention, whereas a Low importance tells the recipient that the message can wait for a response. Use the importance level appropriately. If you send all messages with a High importance, recipients will learn to disregard the status.

To change a message's importance level:

1. Click the **Importance: High** button 🛈 on the Standard toolbar. The button remains selected as an indicator of the message's importance level. See Figure 1-31.

E-mail with High importance level **Figure 1-31**

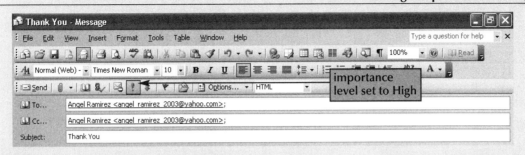

2. Check the spelling of the message, and then send it.

You can also change the sensitivity level for the message from Normal to Personal, Private, or Confidential. This is another way to help recipients determine the content of a message before reading it. To set the sensitivity level, click the Options button on the Standard toolbar in the Message window, click the Sensitivity list arrow in the Options dialog box, and then select the sensitivity level you want for the message. You'll leave the sensitivity set to Normal for this message.

Saving a Message in Another File Format

Because the beauty of electronic communication is the lack of paper cluttering your files, you may prefer to save and store messages as a file you can open, view, and even print from other applications. The Save As command enables you to convert messages from the standard Message Format (.msg) to Text Only (.txt) or HTML (.htm). The Text Only format does not save formatting and can be read by any word-processing program. HTML conserves the formatting of the message, and can be read by some word-processing applications as well as Web browsers.

You'll download and read the Thank You message, and then save it as a Text Only file and an HTML file.

To save a message in other file formats:

1. If necessary, download your messages. You should now have five messages in your Inbox. See Figure 1-32.

Figure 1-32 ▶ **Messages in Inbox**

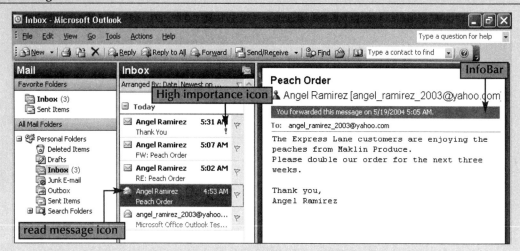

2. Click the **Thank You** message in the message list to select it, and then read the message in the Reading Pane.

   Trouble? If you don't see the HTML formatting, your mail server may not accept messages formatted in HTML.

   The gray bar just above the To line in the Reading Pane is the **InfoBar,** a banner with information about the item. For example, the InfoBar on this message tells you that you forwarded the message and when you did this.

3. Click **File** on the menu bar, and then click **Save As**. The Save As dialog box opens with the message subject in the File name text box.

4. Click the **Save in** list arrow, and then change the Save in location to the **Tutorial.01\Tutorial** folder included with your Data Files.

   Trouble? If you don't have the Outlook Data Files, you need to get them before you can proceed. Your instructor will either give you the Data Files or ask you to obtain them from a specified location (such as a network drive). In either case, be sure that you make a backup copy of the Data Files before you start using them, so that the original files will be available on your copied disk in case you need to start over because of an error or problem. If you have any questions about the Data Files, see your instructor or technical support person for assistance.

5. Edit the filename in the File name text box to **Thank You Text**.

6. Click the **Save as type** list arrow to display the file formats from which you can select. Depending on your setup, you may see file extensions after the file type formats. See Figure 1-33.

Tutorial.01\Tutorial folder included with your Data Files

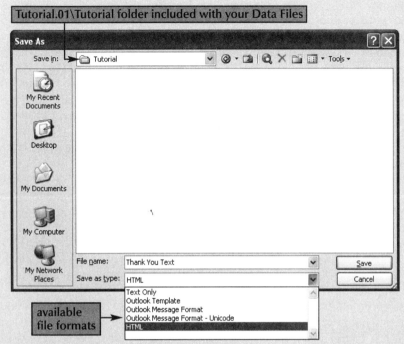

available file formats

Trouble? If your message did not retain the HTML formatting, then the format options available are Text Only, Outlook Template, Outlook Message Format, and Outlook Message Format – Unicode. Complete Steps 7 and 8, but skip Step 9.

7. Click **Text Only** to select that file format.

8. Click the **Save** button. The Thank You message is saved as a Text Only file in the Tutorial.01\Tutorial folder.

9. Save the Thank You message in the **Tutorial.01\Tutorial** folder included with your Data Files with the filename **Thank You HTML** as an **HTML** file.

Saving messages as files rather than printing them can help save paper, toner, and energy.

Working with Attachments

Attachments to e-mail are a great way to share information. An **attachment** is a file that you send with an e-mail message. Attachments can be any type of file, including documents (such as a Word document, Excel workbook, or PowerPoint slide presentation), images, sounds, and programs. For example, you might send an attachment containing The Express Lane's latest sales figures to Alan for his review. Recipients can then save and open the attached file; the recipients must have the original program or a program that can read that file type. For example, if Alan receives a Lotus 1-2-3 spreadsheet, he can open and save it with Excel.

Reviewing Message Security Options

Although attachments are a great convenience, they are also one of the greatest sources of computer viruses. A **virus** is a program that corrupts or damages data on your computer, displays annoying messages, makes your computer operate improperly, or even sends copies of itself in a message to any e-mail addresses you have stored in the Contacts folder. By default, Outlook blocks executable attachments, including .exe, .bat, .mdb, and .vbs files, which may contain viruses. (For a complete list of blocked file formats, see Attachment file types blocked by Outlook in Help.) If you use Exchange Server, then the system administrator sets which file types are blocked. If you try to send an attachment in a blocked file format, Outlook asks you to confirm that you want to send a potentially unsafe attachment. If you decide to send the file, recipients may be blocked from accessing the file by their e-mail programs.

You can see and access message attachments that are not blocked. When you receive an unblocked attachment, be aware of who sent the message. Is the attachment from someone you know and trust? If not, consider deleting the attachment without opening it. If so, consider saving the attachment to your computer and running antivirus software before opening it, because some viruses send infected messages from computers without the owner of the computer being aware of the problem. **Antivirus software**, a type of program that examines files for viruses and disinfects them, provides another way to protect your computer from virus infections.

As viruses become more common and complex, a natural concern may be how secure it is to send messages over the Internet. For normal communication, the Internet is probably just as secure as sending letters through the post office. However, if you need to send and receive confidential or sensitive information, you should consider other ways of securing your messages—authentication and encryption.

- **Authentication** is a system that uses a certificate to enable the recipient to verify the sender's identity and confirm that the message content was not altered. A **certificate**, also called a **digital signature**, is a digital identification used to secure e-mail messages.
- **Encryption** is the process of using a key to convert text into an encoded form that is unreadable except to those who have the key to decrypt it. A **key** is a digital code that encodes or deciphers encrypted messages. Encryption ensures privacy because only the intended recipients who have the key to decipher the message can read the content and attachments of messages.

You'll review the message security options before downloading the message attachment.

To review the message security options:

1. Click **Tools** on the menu bar, click **Options**, and then click the **Security** tab in the Options dialog box. See Figure 1-34.

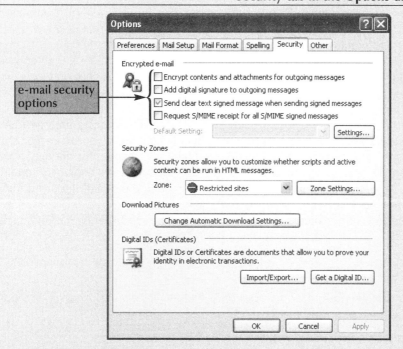

e-mail security options

2. Click the **Question Mark** button ? in the Options dialog box title bar. A Microsoft Office Outlook Help window opens, listing the tabs in the Options dialog box.

3. Click the **Security tab** link in the Help window, and then click the **Encrypted e-mail section** link to expand the list describing the check boxes in that section of the dialog box.

4. Read the description of the options in the Encrypted e-mail section of the Security tab in the Options dialog box.

5. Click the **Close** button ☒ on the Help window title bar to close that window, and then click the **Cancel** button in the Options dialog box to close the dialog box without making any changes.

Messages with attached files display a paperclip icon in the message header in the message list. If you receive a message with a blocked file attachment, you will not be able to see or open the attachment. A paperclip icon still appears in the message list to let you know that the message contains an attachment, and you will see the name of the blocked attachment file in the Reading Pane. If the appropriate program is installed on your computer, you can open any unblocked attached file from the message itself. You can also save the attachment to your computer and then open, edit, and move it like any other file on your computer. Although you can reply to or forward a message with an attachment, the attachment is included with only the forwarded message because you will rarely, if ever, want to return the same file to the sender.

Sending an Attachment

When you attach a file to your message, Outlook makes a copy of the original file to include with the message. It does not create a link between the attached copy and the original. If you edit the original file after attaching a copy to an e-mail message, the changes do not appear in the copy attached to the message.

When you send attachments, be aware of message size; the larger the file, the more time it takes to send and receive. Image files and sound files can be very large. If the attachment is a very large program or document, you should use a program, such as WinZip, to compress it, thus reducing the size of the file. Unfortunately, WinZip doesn't do much to compress graphic image files or sound files.

You should also be aware of recipients' e-mail limitations. Some e-mail and online services don't allow recipients to receive attachments; others accept only one file attachment at a time; still others limit what file types can be received to help prevent the spread of viruses (for example, some organizations no longer allow recipients to receive compressed files). In addition, there may be a size limit for an incoming message.

It is a good idea to include a reference to the attachment in your message. Many times, people write a message and forget to attach the document or file they intended. If the attachment is referenced in the message, then the recipients know you intended to include a file. If they do not receive an attachment with the e-mail, they can reply, asking for the attachment.

You'll send Alan the latest sales figures, which are in an Excel file, as an attachment.

To attach a file to an e-mail:

1. Click the **New** button on the Standard toolbar. A new Message window opens and your signature appears in the body of the message.

2. Type your e-mail address in the To text box.

3. Type **Latest Sales** in the Subject text box.

4. In the message area, type **The attached Excel workbook contains the latest sales figures. It looks like we're on track for this quarter. Let me know if you have any comments.**

   Next, you'll add the attachment.

5. Click the **Insert File** button 🔘 on the message toolbar. The Insert File dialog box opens; it functions like the Open dialog box.

6. Click the **Look in** list arrow, and then change the Look in location to the **Tutorial.01\Tutorial** folder included with your Data Files.

7. Double-click **Sales** in the file list. The file is attached to your e-mail message and the Insert File dialog box closes. See Figure 1-35.

Message window with attachment | **Figure 1-35**

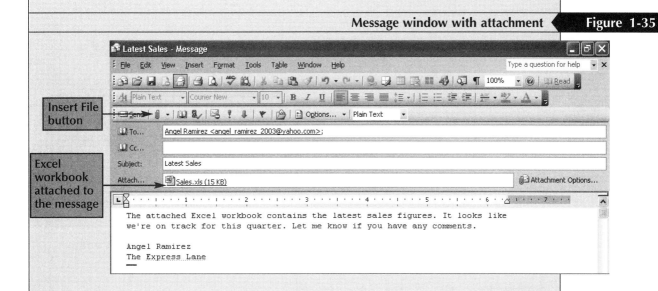

8. Check the spelling of the message, and then send the message.

A message with an attachment may take a bit longer to send because it's larger than an e-mail message without an attachment.

After you receive the message with the attachment, you'll save the attachment and then view it from within the message.

To save and view the message attachment:

1. If necessary, download your messages. Again, it might take a bit longer than usual to download the message with the attachment.

2. Click the **Latest Sales** message in the message list to select it. The message content appears in the Reading Pane. The attachment icon appears below the date in the message header in the message list, and the file icon and name appear in the Reading Pane. See Figure 1-36.

Figure 1-36 **Message with attached file**

filename and size of the attached file

paperclip indicates an attached file

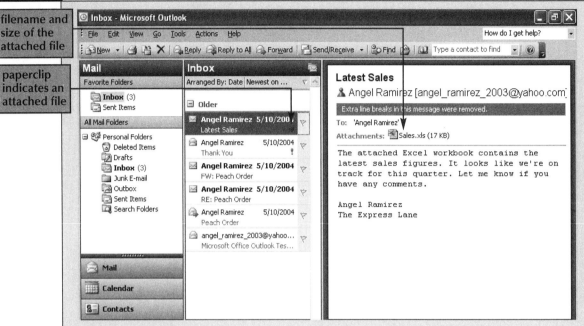

3. Double-click the **Latest Sales** message in the message list. The message opens in its own window.

4. Right-click **Sales.xls**, the attached file, in the Attachments field in the message header in the Message window, and then click **Save As** on the shortcut menu. The Save Attachment dialog box opens, enabling you to select the location to save the attachment.

5. Change the Save in list box to the **Tutorial.01\Tutorial** folder included with your Data Files, edit the filename to **Second Quarter Sales.xls**, and then click the **Save** button to save the attached file. You can work with this file just as you would any other file on disk.

6. Click the **Close** button ☒ on the Message window title bar. The Message window closes.

   You can also save or open the attached file from the Message window or Reading Pane.

7. Double-click **Sales.xls** in the Reading Pane. The Opening Mail Attachment dialog box opens, warning you that you should only open attachments from a trusted source.

   Trouble? If the Opening Mail Attachment dialog box doesn't open, read but do not perform the action in Step 8.

8. Click the **Open** button. The attached file opens in its associated program—in this case, Excel. You can read, edit, format, and save the file just as you would any other Excel workbook. See Figure 1-37.

Sales attachment opened in Excel   Figure 1-37

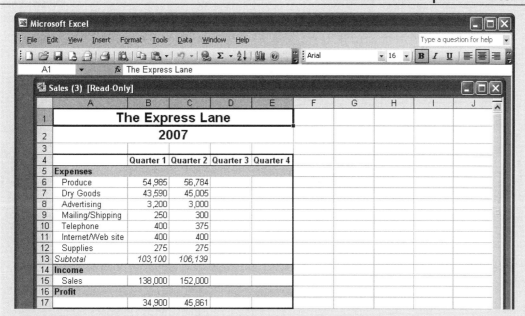

Trouble? If the file opens in a spreadsheet program other than Excel, your computer might be configured to associate the file extension .xls with spreadsheet programs other than Excel. Continue with Step 9.

9. Review the sales figures, and then click the **Close** button ⊠ on the Excel window title bar to close the workbook and exit Excel.

Trouble? If a dialog box opens, asking if you want to save changes, click the No button.

When you no longer need messages or other items, you should delete them to keep your Inbox clear and Outlook uncluttered.

Deleting Items and Exiting Outlook

When you finish using Outlook, you should exit the program. Unlike with other programs, you don't need to save or close any files. Before you exit, however, you'll delete each of the items you created in this tutorial. Items you delete move into the **Deleted Items folder**, which acts like the Recycle Bin in Windows. Items you delete remain in this folder until you empty it. If your instructor wants you to print the messages that you received, you'll print them before sending them to the Deleted Items folder.

To print and delete messages:

1. Click the **Latest Sales** message in the message list, press and hold the **Ctrl** key, and then click the **Thank You** message, the **FW: Peach Order** message, and the **RE: Peach Order message**. The four messages are selected.

2. If your instructor wants you to print the messages you created, click **File** on the menu bar, click **Print**, and then click the **Start each item on a new page** check box to uncheck it, if necessary. Now the four messages will print on as few pieces of paper as necessary to fit all of the text rather than printing on four pieces of paper.

Trouble? If your instructor does not want you to print the messages, skip to Step 4.

Trouble? If the Start each item on a new page check box is greyed out and unavailable, use the default setting.

3. Click the **OK** button in the Print dialog box. The messages print.

4. With the four messages still selected, press and hold the **Ctrl** key, and then click the **Peach Order** message in the message list to select it as well. All the messages you received in this tutorial are selected.

5. Click the **Delete** button ⊠ on the Standard toolbar to move the selected messages to the Deleted Items folder.

6. If you received a confirmation message from Outlook from when you tested your account settings, delete that message as well.

7. Click **Sent Items** in the All Mail Folders pane in the Navigation Pane, press the **Ctrl** key as you select the copies of the messages you sent in this tutorial, and then move them to the Deleted Items folder.

Next, you'll remove the signature you created.

To remove a signature:

1. Click **Tools** on the menu bar, click **Options**, and then click the **Mail Format** tab in the Options dialog box.

2. Click the **Signatures** button, click your name in the Signature list box, and then click the **Remove** button.

3. Click the **Yes** button to confirm that you want to permanently remove this signature.

4. Click the **OK** button in the Create Signature dialog box, and then click the **OK** button in the Options dialog box.

Finally, you'll remove the items from the Deleted Items folder to empty it and exit Outlook.

To empty the Deleted Items folder and exit Outlook:

1. Click **Deleted Items** in the All Mail Folders pane in the Navigation Pane. The items you deleted appear in the folder.

2. Right-click the **Deleted Items** folder in the Navigation Pane, and then click **Empty "Deleted Items" Folder** on the shortcut menu.

A dialog box asks you to confirm the deletion.

▶ 3. Click the **Yes** button in the dialog box to empty the Deleted Items folder.

Now you're ready to exit Outlook.

▶ 4. Click the **Close** button ⊠ on the Outlook program window title bar to exit Outlook.

Alan thanks you for your help. The Express Lane can now fill all of its customers' orders for peaches until the end of the season. As the first-quarter numbers show, a happy customer means a profitable business.

Review

Session 1.2 Quick Check

1. Describe the purpose of the Inbox and the Outbox.

2. What is the difference between the message list and the Reading Pane in the Inbox main window?

3. Explain the difference between the Reply button and the Reply to All button.

4. True or False: When you forward a message, the recipient's e-mail address automatically appears in the To text box.

5. What is a signature?

6. What are two ways to enhance the look of your e-mail messages?

7. What are two potential problems of attachments?

8. True or False: You can save a file attached to a message, but you cannot open it from Outlook.

Review

Tutorial Summary

In this tutorial, you learned about the six Outlook components—Mail, Calendar, Contacts, Notes, Tasks, and Journal—and how to navigate between them. You set up Outlook to manage your e-mail accounts and then created and sent an e-mail message. You learned how to get help in Outlook. You also received, read, responded to, forwarded, printed, and saved messages. You customized your messages with signatures, stationery, and formatting. You sent, received, and saved attachments to e-mail messages. Finally, you deleted Outlook items that you no longer need.

Key Terms

antivirus software	e-mail address	Infobar
attachment	emoticon	Internet service
authentication	encryption	provider (ISP)
AutoComplete	folder	item
Calendar	folder banner	Journal
certificate	Folder List	key
Contacts	Forward	Mail
Deleted Items folder	Help	mail editor
digital signature	host name	main window
domain name	HTML	message header
e-mail	Inbox	Microsoft Office Online

Microsoft Office Outlook 2003	password	stationery template
	plain text	Standard toolbar
Microsoft Office Word 2003	Reading Pane	task pane
	Reply	Tasks
Navigation Pane	Reply to All	top-level domain
netiquette	Rich Text	Type a question for help box
Notes	ScreenTip	user ID
offline	Sent Items folder	user profile
Outbox	signature	virus
Outlook Today	smiley	Web toolbar

Practice

Practice the skills you learned in the tutorial using the same case scenario.

Review Assignments

Data File needed for the Review Assignments: Tea.doc

Lora Shaw focuses on the customer end of the business, which includes finding new customers, responding to customer comments, and processing customer payments. She asks you to help her with customer communication for The Express Lane.

1. If necessary, set up a profile, start Outlook, create an e-mail account and connection, and then display the Inbox folder.

2. Verify that Word is set as the mail editor and that the default message format is plain text.

3. Create a new e-mail message, addressed to your e-mail address, with the subject "Increase Customer Base" and the message "The Express Lane's goal is to double its customer base by the end of the year. I can think of several ways to accomplish this, including: (1) increase advertising in traditional media, (2) offer a rebate or other incentive to current customers who refer friends and family, and (3) enroll all customers who spend at least $100 in a drawing for an all-expenses-paid vacation. Let me know what you think of these ideas." Press the Enter key twice and type your name.

4. Check the spelling of the message, proofread the message, and then send the message.

5. Create a new e-mail message, addressed to your e-mail address, with the subject "Health Benefits of Tea" and the message "I've heard that drinking tea has health benefits. Do you have any information about this?" Press the Enter key twice and type your name. Check the spelling, and then send the e-mail message.

6. Create a new e-mail message, addressed to your e-mail address, with the subject "Welcome New Customer" and the message "Welcome to The Express Lane. We're sure you'll find our grocery delivery service more convenient and cheaper than your local grocery store, not to mention more healthful because all of our foods are certified organic. If you have any questions or comments, feel free to e-mail us." Press the Enter key twice and type your name. Check the spelling, and then send the e-mail message. (*Hint*: Click the Ignore Once button in the Spelling and Grammar dialog box if the Grammar checker flags the word "The" as an error.)

7. Create a signature, using your name as the name of the new signature, and then type your name on one line and the title "Customer Service Representative" on the next line. Use the signature with all e-mail messages (new, replies, and forwards). (*Hint:* Select your name in the Signatures for replies and forwards list in the Options dialog box.)

8. Download your messages. If the Health Benefits of Tea message hasn't arrived, wait a few minutes and try again.

9. Reply to the Health Benefits of Tea message with the text "In addition to being the world's second favorite drink to water, there is growing evidence of a link between tea and disease prevention, particularly cancer and heart disease. Check out The Express Lane's large selection of black, oolong, and green teas. The attached file has some information about teas."

10. Attach the **Tea** document located in the **Tutorial.01\Review** folder included with your Data Files, check the spelling, and then send the message.

11. Forward the Increase Customer Base message to your e-mail address, with the message "Let's meet next week to talk about implementing some of these ideas." Change the message importance level to High, check the spelling, and then send the message.

12. Download your messages, if necessary, and then print the message list in the Inbox main window.

13. Save the Tea.doc attachment in the RE: Health Benefits of Tea message as **Tea Health Benefits** in the **Tutorial.01\Review** folder included with your Data Files.

14. If your instructor wants you to print the messages you received, select the messages FW: Increase Customer Base, RE: Health Benefits of Tea, Health Benefits of Tea, Welcome New Customer, and Increase Customer Base, and then print them.

15. Save each message you received for these Review Assignments in your Inbox as a Text Only file in the **Tutorial.01\Review** folder included with your Data Files, using its subject as the filename.

16. Delete the signature, delete the messages you received and sent for these Review Assignments from the Inbox and Sent Items folders, and then empty the Deleted Items folder.

Case Problem 1

Apply

Apply the skills you learned in the tutorial to send, receive, reply to, and forward e-mails about a tree-planting program.

There are no Data Files needed for this Case Problem.

Green Streets   Green Streets is a nonprofit organization in Chicago that plants trees along city sidewalks, improving the streets' appearance and providing a bit of nature among the concrete blocks. The organization works with private homeowners, neighborhood groups, and local government to encourage them to participate in and support the program. Peter Washington is in charge of responding to all inquiries.

1. Display the Inbox, and then verify that Word is set as the mail editor and that the default message format is plain text.

2. Create a new e-mail message using the Leaves stationery.

3. Address the message to your e-mail address with the subject "Free Trees" and the message "How can you improve your building's appearance, increase your property value, and please residents and tenants without any cost to yourself? Participate in the urban forestry project with Green Streets. You provide the neighborhood. We provide the trees, the labor, and even the city permits. Everyone wins. To find out more about our program, reply to this message." Press the Enter key twice, type your name, and then press the Enter key once more to move your name above the leaf.

4. Select all the message text, and then format the message text as green.

5. With all the text still selected, click the Bold button on the Formatting toolbar.

6. With all the text still selected, click the Align Left button on the Formatting toolbar to align the text with the left margin.

7. Click a blank area of the Message window above the leaf border to deselect the text, check the spelling, and then send the message.

8. Download the message, if necessary, and then reply to the message with the text "Wow. This sounds great. Can I select the type of trees to be planted in front of my building?" Check the spelling, and then send the message.

9. Forward the Free Trees message to your e-mail address and include the response "Pat, have you heard of this program? It sounds too good to be true. I'm requesting more information. When it arrives, let's get together to review it." Change the importance level to High, check the spelling, and then send the message.

10. Download your messages, if necessary, and then forward the RE: Free Trees message to your e-mail address, change the Subject to "FW: Free Trees Response" and include the response "Peter—Please respond to this inquiry with our basic information package and the answer to the question. Thank you."

11. Check the spelling, and then send the message. (*Hint*: Click the Ignore Once button in the Spelling and Grammar dialog box if the Grammar checker flags the word "Please" as an error.)

12. Download your message, if necessary. You will have four messages about Free Trees in your Inbox.

13. Save each message you received in the Inbox for this Case Problem as an HTML file in the **Tutorial.01\Cases** folder included with your Data Files, using its subject as the filename. (If the messages did not retain HTML formatting, or if HTML is not listed as an option, then save the messages as Text Only files.)

14. Delete the messages you received and created in this Case Problem from the Inbox and Sent Items folders, and then empty the Deleted Items folder.

Apply

Apply the skills you learned in the tutorial to send and respond to e-mail messages for a tutoring service.

Case Problem 2

Data File needed for this Case Problem: Amendments.doc

Answers Anytime   Answers Anytime is a unique tutoring service. Students can e-mail specific questions and problem areas to subject experts and receive quick answers. The subject experts reply to students within two hours, either by e-mail message or e-mail message with an attachment.

1. Display the Inbox folder, verify that Word is set as the mail editor, and then change the default message format to HTML.

2. Create an e-mail message, addressed to your e-mail address, with the subject "History Questions" and the message "Please send information about the following: What is the Bill of Rights? When did women receive the right to vote? How does Rachel Carson fit into the environmental movement?" Press the Enter key before each question to place it on its own line. After the third question, press the Enter key twice and type your name.

3. Format the three questions as a numbered list, check the spelling, and then send the message. (*Hint:* Select the list, and then click the Numbering button on the Formatting toolbar in the Message window.)

4. Create a signature with any name you want. In the Signature text box, type your name, press the Enter key, and then type Answers Anytime. Keep the Edit Signature dialog box open.

5. Select the text "Answers Anytime" in the Signature text box, click the Font button to open the Font dialog box, change the Style to bold and the color to red, and then close all open dialog boxes, making sure to use the signature for all messages (new, replies, and forwards).

6. Download your messages, if necessary, and then reply to the History Questions message, using the following text formatted as a numbered list: (1) See the attached document for information about the Bill of Rights; (2) On August 26, 1920, Tennessee delivered the last needed vote and the Nineteenth Amendment was added to the Constitution. It stated that "the right of citizens of the United States to vote shall not be denied by the United States or by any State on account of sex."; (3) I've forwarded this question to Stu Panell, our resident expert on the environmental movement.

7. Attach the **Amendments** document located in the **Tutorial.01\Cases** folder included with your Data Files to the e-mail message, check the spelling, and then send the message.

8. Forward the student's original message to Stu, using your e-mail address, add the response "Hi Stu. Question 3 is yours. Thanks." and then send the message.

9. Download your messages, if necessary, and then save each of the three messages you received in this Case Problem as an HTML file in the **Tutorial.01\Cases** folder included with your Data Files, using its subject as the filename. (If the messages did not retain HTML formatting, save them as Text Only files.)

10. Save the attachment from the RE: History Questions message as **Amendments Sent** in the **Tutorial.01\Cases** folder included with your Data Files.

11. If your instructor wants you to, print the three messages.

12. Delete the signature you created, delete the messages you received and sent in this Case Problem from the Inbox and Sent Items folders, and then empty the Deleted Items folder.

Case Problem 3

Research

Use Help to find out how to save a draft of an e-mail message and how to flag a message for follow-up, and then challenge yourself by creating, saving, formatting, and sending e-mail messages to confirm appointments for a dentist.

There are no Data Files needed for this Case Problem.

Healthy Smiles Dentistry Dr. Louise Schwartz and Dr. Randy Brasiele are partners who practice general dentistry in Montgomery, Alabama. They encourage all patients to come in for checkups and cleanings every six months. Patients schedule their next appointment as they pay for their current appointment. Because patients often forget the appointments they make far in advance, Mollie, the office receptionist, contacts patients a few days before to remind them of their scheduled visit. Mollie wants to use Outlook to send e-mail to patients to confirm their upcoming appointments and to communicate with the doctors' colleagues. You'll help her get started.

1. Display the Inbox folder, verify that Word is set as the mail editor, and then change the default message format to HTML.

2. Create a signature, name it using your name, and then type your name on one line and "Healthy Smiles Dentistry" on a second line. Keep the Edit Signature dialog box open.

3. Select your name, click the Font button to open the Font dialog box, and then change the style to Bold Italic and the color to Purple. Close all open dialog boxes, making sure to use the signature only for new messages.

4. Create an e-mail message with the subject "Appointment Reminder" and the message "You have an appointment scheduled for tomorrow at Healthy Smiles Dentistry. If you need to reschedule your appointment for any reason, please contact us. Thank you." Do not enter an e-mail address in the To text box. Check the spelling of the message.

5. Switch back to the Outlook program window, and then use the Type a question for help box to find out how to save a draft of an e-mail message. (*Hint:* Click Save a message in the list of options that appears.)

Explore

6. Use what you learned to save the message as a draft. (*Hint:* Switch back to the Message window, click the Close button on the Message window title bar to close the Message window. and then click the Yes button when asked whether you want to save the changes to the message.)

7. Create an e-mail message addressed to your e-mail address with the subject "Referral" and the message "Dr. Randy Brasiele is referring patient Timmy Larson to you for possible orthodontic work. He has a severe overbite that could be corrected with braces." Check the spelling, and then send the message.

Explore

8. Display the Drafts folder, and open the Appointment Reminder message draft in its own window.

Explore

9. Save the message as a Word document with the filename **Appointment Reminder Unsent E-mail** in the **Tutorial.01\Cases** folder included with your Data Files. (*Hint:* Click File on the menu bar in the Message window, and then click Save As.)

10. Address the e-mail to your e-mail address, and then format the message by changing the word "tomorrow" to boldface and both instances of "Healthy Smiles Dentistry" to blue.

Explore

11. Add a flag to the message to mark it to remind you to follow up. Click the Message Flag button on the message toolbar, make sure that "Follow up" appears in the Flag to list box and that "None" appears in the Due by list box, and then click the OK button. Check the spelling, and then send the message.

12. Download your messages, and then use Help to find out more about flags, the process of marking a flag as completed, and changing the color of flags.

Explore

13. Use what you learned to mark the flagged Appointment Reminder message as completed. (*Hint:* Click the flag next to the message in the message list to change it to a check mark.) If you don't see the message flag, the flagged message may not retain its flag information when sent over the Internet via your ISP.

Explore

14. Reply to the Referral message with the text "Thank you for your referral. I'll be seeing Timmy next week and will update you then." Do not send the message. Close the message, saving the changes.

15. Display the Drafts folder, and then save the RE: Referral message in the **Tutorial.01\Cases** folder included with your Data Files as a Text Only file, using its subject as the filename.

16. Save each of the two messages in the Inbox that you received in this Case Problem in the **Tutorial.01\Cases** folder included with your Data Files as a Text Only file, using its subject as the filename.

17. Delete the messages you received, created, and sent in this Case Problem from the Inbox, Drafts, and Sent Items folders, delete the signature you created in this Case Problem, and then empty the Deleted Items folder.

Create

Create e-mail invitations for a graduation party by using and expanding on the skills you learned in this tutorial.

Explore

Explore

Explore

Explore

Case Problem 4

There are no Data Files needed for this Case Problem.

Party Planners   Jace Moran plans events ranging from company picnics to children's birthday parties to weddings. Right now, she is working on a graduation party. Jace is using Outlook to work on the budget and design the e-mail invitations.

1. Display the Inbox folder, verify that Word is set as the mail editor, and then change the default message format to HTML.

2. Create an e-mail using an Excel worksheet as the message body. Click Actions on the menu bar, point to New Mail Message Using, point to Microsoft Office, and then click Microsoft Excel Worksheet.

3. Address the e-mail to your e-mail address and use "Graduation Party" as the subject. In column A, enter a list of at least three foods for the party. In column B, enter the probable cost for the food. Total the cost column by clicking the blank cell below the last cost, clicking the AutoSum button on the Excel Standard toolbar, and then pressing the Enter key to finish the formula.

4. Click the Send this Sheet button on the message toolbar to send the e-mail message. Close Excel without saving the workbook.

5. Use stationery of your choice to create the party invitation message. Address the invitation to your e-mail address, and type "Celebrate" as the subject. Type the message body using the text "You're Invited..."; "Day:"; "Time:"; and "Place:" on separate lines, entering the appropriate day, time, and place.

6. Format the message attractively, using Word formatting features. Try changing the font, color, size, alignment, and so forth of existing text. Check the spelling, and then send the message.

7. Download your messages, if necessary, and then read the Graduation Party message to see the food costs.

8. Reply to the Graduation Party message, approving the budget. Check the spelling, and then send the message.

9. Download your message, and then read any unread messages.

10. Print the Celebrate and RE: Graduation Party messages.

11. Save the Celebrate message as an HTML file with the filename **Celebrate HTML** in the **Tutorial.01\Cases** folder included with your Data Files. (*Hint:* If the message did not retain HTML formatting, then continue with Step 12.)

12. Save the Celebrate message as a Text Only file with the filename **Celebrate Text** in the **Tutorial.01\Cases** folder included with your Data Files.

13. Open the saved Celebrate files by double-clicking each file from Windows Explorer. Compare the differences between the Celebrate HTML file and the Celebrate Text file.

14. Delete the messages you received and created in this Case Problem from the Inbox and Sent Items folders, and then empty the Deleted Items folder.

Quick Check Answers

Session 1.1

1. An item is a basic element that holds information in Outlook, such as an e-mail message. A folder is where these items are stored in Outlook.
2. A profile is a group of settings that specify how Outlook is set up for a user.
3. E-mail is the electronic transfer of messages between computers. It is inexpensive for communicating with others, whether nearby or far away. You can send and read messages at your convenience.
4. theexpresslane.com
5. Use plain text when you want to ensure that all recipients can read your message and to reduce the size of your outgoing message.
6. A mail editor is a tool you use to create e-mail messages.
7. Three of the following: reread your messages; be concise; use standard capitalization; check spelling and grammar; avoid sarcasm; don't send confidential information.
8. Sent Items folder

Session 1.2

1. The Inbox stores e-mail messages you have received. The Outbox stores e-mail messages you have written but not yet sent.
2. The message list displays a list of the e-mail messages you have received; the Reading Pane displays the contents of the message selected in the message list.
3. Reply responds only to the sender of the e-mail message; Reply to All responds to the sender and any other recipients of the e-mail message.
4. False. You must enter the recipient's e-mail address in the To text box.
5. A signature is text that can be automatically added to every e-mail message you send.
6. You can format the message text or use stationery.
7. Any two of the following: The message size may make the e-mail take longer to send and receive. Some e-mail recipients cannot receive attachments or have a size limit for incoming messages. Attachments may contain viruses. Outlook blocks attachment files of a certain format.
8. False. You can save the file to view later or you can open it directly from Outlook.

Objectives

Session 2.1
- Enter and edit contact information
- Assign categories to contacts
- Create a distribution list
- Use different folder views
- Print contact information
- Send and receive contact information

Session 2.2
- Send an e-mail message to a contact
- Write a letter and schedule an appointment with a contact
- Link activities to a contact
- Flag contacts for follow-up
- Filter and sort a contact list
- Merge a form letter with contacts
- Delete contacts and other Outlook items

Managing Contacts

Communicating with Members of a Company

Case

LinkUp

LinkUp is a car sharing company located in Philadelphia, Pennsylvania. Felicia Rogert founded the company in 2000. For urban dwellers who drive fewer than 10,000 miles per year, car sharing is becoming an increasingly popular alternative to owning a car. LinkUp's cars are located throughout the city's neighborhoods, close to members' homes and workplaces. LinkUp currently has about 1,000 members who prefer to share a fleet of 60 vehicles, rather than spend thousands of dollars on personal automobiles and all the associated expenses. These numbers are growing dramatically each month. Members pay for only the hours and miles they drive. LinkUp charges a $120 annual fee as well as nominal fees for the actual hours and miles driven, $2.50 and $0.50, respectively. Insurance, gasoline, and maintenance are included in the rates. Members reserve a car by phone or online for immediate or future use. At their reserved time, members use their access keys to unlock the closest available car, usually within five blocks of their location, and drive away. They return the car to the same location and lock it. LinkUp bills their credit card every month for actual usage.

LinkUp uses Outlook to keep track of its members and service providers, such as garages, cleaning companies, insurance providers, and so forth. Once all the identifying contact information is compiled in the Contacts folder, the information is available throughout Outlook. For example, LinkUp can send e-mail messages to specific contacts, write letters to them, assign tasks to them, and even schedule meetings or appointments with them.

In this tutorial, you will compile and organize LinkUp's contact list. Then you will send an e-mail message and write a letter to individual members. Finally, you will create a personalized form letter to send to LinkUp's members informing them of the latest cars being added to the company's fleet.

Student Data Files

▼**Tutorial.02**

▽ **Tutorial folder**

    LinkUp Letter.doc

▽ **Review folder**

    Frieda Cohn.vcf
    Vendor Letter.doc

▽ **Cases folder**

    Natalie.doc

Session 2.1

Creating Contacts

Most of our lives, both business and personal, involve interacting with people—writing letters, calling on the phone, or sending e-mail messages. As a result, many people have a variety of postal addresses, telephone numbers, and e-mail addresses. With so much contact information available for each person, a paper address book can become bulky and inconvenient. In fact, a paper address book can become downright messy as people change addresses, are assigned new area codes, or sign up for additional e-mail addresses. In addition, paper address books often do not provide much space to jot down personal details such as birthdays or children's names.

You can save as much or as little information about people as you like in Outlook. No matter what particulars you want to record about friends, family, coworkers, and business associates, the Contacts folder provides the place to do so. Each person or organization is called a **contact**. You can store business-related information about each contact, including job titles, phone numbers, postal and e-mail addresses, and assistants' names, as well as more personal information, such as notes, birthdays, anniversaries, and children's names.

The Contacts folder is included as part of a larger and more comprehensive **Address Book**, the collection of all address books or lists that you use to store names, e-mail addresses, fax numbers, and distribution lists. For example, if you work for a company, you have access to your personal contacts stored on your computer as well as possibly access to a company address book that contains all employee contact information stored on the company network. The Contacts folder is sometimes referenced as the Outlook Address Book, such as in the Address Book dialog box.

In today's connected world, most people have a lot of contact information. Consider Felicia's contact information. She has different mailing addresses for home and work. She has phone numbers for her home, main office, direct line, cell phone, pager, home fax, business fax, and assistant. She also has several e-mail addresses for personal and business use. A written record of all this information would require a full page in a paper address book; Outlook stores up to three addresses, nineteen phone numbers, three e-mail addresses, one Web page URL, one instant messaging address, plus related information in one place called a **contact card**.

When you create a contact, you open a blank contact card, and then enter all necessary information. Information you enter about a contact is actually individual units of data, called **fields**. For example, a complete contact name is actually comprised of several fields, as shown in Figure 2-1.

| Figure 2-1 | Complete name split into fields |

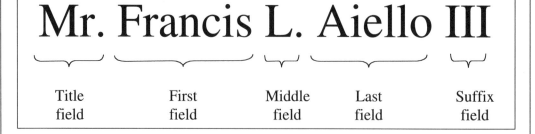

The field's name or label identifies the information stored in that field. Fields enable you to sort, group, or look up contacts by any part of the name. Without fields, you could not find a specific contact quickly or alphabetize your contact list by last name. Outlook uses fields to organize data in all its folders. You have already worked with fields such as To, From, and Subject in the Inbox folder to create e-mail messages.

Creating a Contact

Reference Window

- Click the New button on the Standard toolbar in the Contacts folder (*or* click the New button list arrow, and then click Contact).
- Enter the contact's name, job title, company, phone numbers, mailing address, e-mail addresses, and Web site (click the down arrow to select other address, number, or e-mail options) on the General tab.
- Click the Categories button and assign categories as needed.
- Click the Details tab and enter other business or personal data as needed.
- Click the Save and New button on the Standard toolbar to create another contact (*or* click the Save and Close button if this is the last contact you want to enter at this time).
- If the Duplicate Contact Detected dialog box opens, select whether to add this as a new contact anyway or merge this contact with an existing contact, and then click the OK button.
  or
- Drag an e-mail message, contact card attachment, or vCard attachment to the Contacts folder in the Navigation Pane, enter data, and then save the contact card as usual.

LinkUp stores information about its members and service providers in the Contacts folder. Felicia asks you to create new contact cards for several members.

To create a contact:

1. Click the **Contacts** button in the Navigation Pane. The Contacts folder is displayed. Notice that the New button on the Standard toolbar reflects the most likely item you'll want to create from this folder—a contact. See Figure 2-2.

Contacts main window Figure 2-2

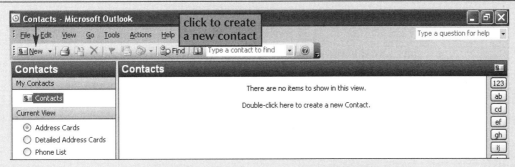

2. Click the **New** button on the Standard toolbar. A new Untitled Contact window opens, displaying text boxes in which you enter contact information.

3. Maximize the Contact window, if necessary. See Figure 2-3.

Figure 2-3 **Contact window**

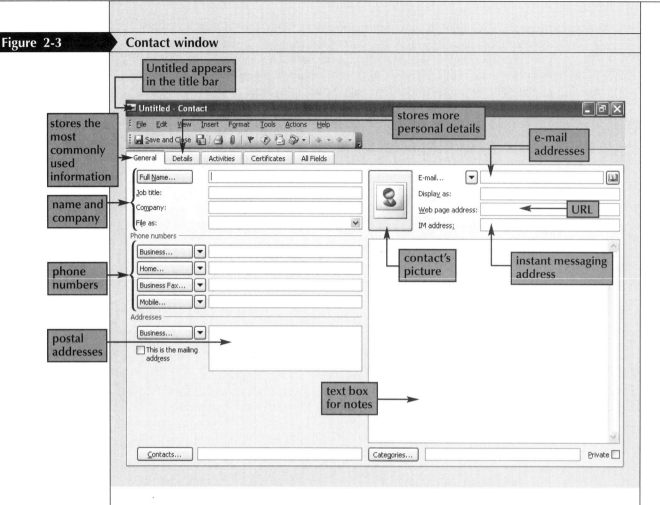

Contact information is entered on two tabs in the Contact window. The General tab stores the most pertinent information about a contact, including the contact's name, job title and company, phone numbers, and addresses. The Details tab contains less frequently needed personal and business information.

You can create contacts for people or organizations. If a contact is a person, then you type his or her name in the Full Name text box; the Job title and Company text boxes are optional for people. If the contact is an organization, you type a name in the Company text box, and leave the Full Name and Job title text boxes empty.

The File as list box shows how your contacts are ordered in the Contacts main window. If you enter a name and a company for a contact, Outlook suggests a variety of ways to display that contact in the contact list. It is best to use the same File as option for all your contacts so that the contact list is organized consistently. By default, Outlook alphabetizes contacts by last name.

You'll begin by entering a contact's name, job title, and organization.

To enter a contact's name and company:

1. Type **Mr. Francis L. Aiello III** in the Full Name text box, and then press the **Enter** key. The insertion point moves to the Job title text box and the contact name appears last name first in the File as list box. The title bar of the Contact window now contains the contact's name instead of "Untitled."

2. Click the **Full Name** button to open the Check Full Name dialog box. Although you entered the contact name in one text box, Outlook stores each part of the name as a separate field. See Figure 2-4.

Check Full Name dialog box ◀ Figure 2-4

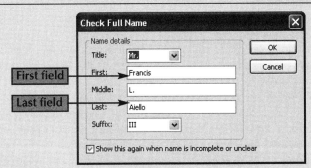

If Outlook cannot distinguish parts of a name, the Check Full Name dialog box will open automatically so that you can correct the fields. You can also open the dialog box to confirm that Outlook recognized the name properly.

3. Click the **Cancel** button to close the Check Full Name dialog box without making any changes.

4. Click in the **Job title** text box, type **Project Manager**, and then press the **Tab** key. The insertion point moves to the Company text box.

5. Type **Levinson Systems** in the Company text box, and then press the **Tab** key.

You want all contacts filed last name, first name, but you'll look at the other options.

6. Click the **File as** list arrow to view the five filing options. See Figure 2-5.

Contact card with name and job information ◀ Figure 2-5

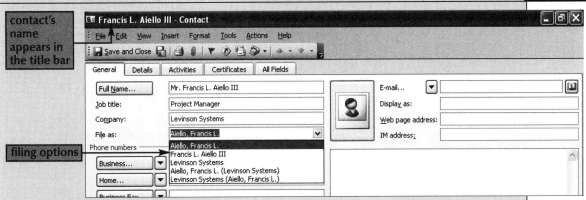

If two contacts had the same name, you might file these contacts as last name, first name (company name) to distinguish them.

7. Click **Aiello, Francis L.** to verify the selection and close the list box.

Next, you'll enter the contact's phone numbers. You can enter as many as 19 phone numbers per contact. No matter how you enter phone numbers—with or without spaces, hyphens, or parentheses—Outlook formats them consistently in the form (215) 555-3492. If you leave out the area code, Outlook inserts your local area code. Enter international phone numbers with the three-digit country code, such as 021. You can also include additional text after a number, such as "x385" for the contact's extension.

Outlook can automatically dial the phone numbers for your contacts if you have a modem installed on your computer. If you use Outlook to dial your calls, it dials all the numbers until it reaches a letter, in this case "x." Otherwise, Outlook dials the additional numbers, although most telephone systems ignore any extra dialed numbers.

The contact card displays four phone numbers at once—the Business, Home, Business Fax, and Mobile phone fields by default. You can enter phone numbers in any or all of the four displayed phone fields as needed, leaving the phone fields blank if appropriate. You can also change the field labels to access any of the other 15 phone fields or change the order that phone numbers appear on the card. It is possible to display any of the phone fields two, three, or even four times on a contact card. Be aware that you are looking at the multiple displays of the same stored field. Any changes you make to the number in one field will appear in all displays.

Next, you'll enter Francis's business, pager, and home phone numbers.

To enter a contact's phone numbers:

1. Click in the **Business** text box in the Phone numbers area, and then type **215 555 9753**.

2. Press the **Tab** key. Outlook formats the phone number with parentheses around the area code and a hyphen after the prefix, even though you did not type them. It underlines the number when it recognizes it as a valid phone number.

   Trouble? If the Location Information dialog box opens, enter the appropriate information about your location, and then click the OK button. If the Phone and Modem dialog box opens, verify the information and then click the OK button.

3. Click the **down arrow** button ▾ next to Home. The check mark next to Business indicates that there is a number entered for that field. See Figure 2-6.

Available phone number fields ◄ **Figure 2-6**

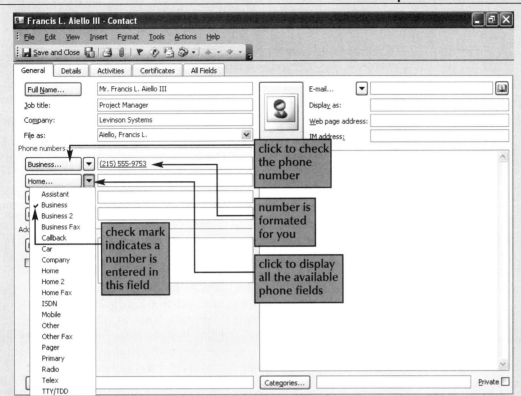

You can select which number you want to enter and display in this text box. In this case, you'll enter Francis's pager phone number.

▶ **4.** Click **Pager** to change the field label, type **215 555 9752**, and then press the **Tab** key.

▶ **5.** Change the Business Fax field label to **Home**, type **215 555 6441** as the Home phone number, and then press the **Enter** key.

You need to enter the extension for Francis's business line. You can do that by editing the existing number.

▶ **6.** Click in the **Business** text box to the right of the phone number, press the **space-bar**, type **x384**, and then press the **Enter** key.

If Outlook is unsure how to distinguish parts of a number, it may open the Check Phone Number dialog box. You can open this dialog box for any number to confirm that Outlook recognized the number properly.

▶ **7.** Click the **Business** button. The Check Phone Number dialog box opens so you can verify the number. This dialog box is similar in function and appearance to the Check Full Name dialog box. See Figure 2-7.

Figure 2-7 Check Phone Number dialog box

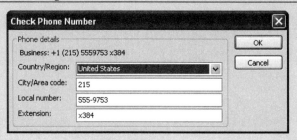

8. Click the **Cancel** button to close the dialog box.

You can enter as many as three postal addresses for each contact: Business, Home, and Other. Outlook assumes that you want to send printed correspondence to whichever address you enter first, although you can change this at any time. Only one address can be designated as the mailing address. By default, Outlook is set for you to enter a business address first. If you want another type of address to be the mailing address, as with most of LinkUp's members, you can set the mailing address to home or other.

You enter addresses by typing in the Address text box and pressing the Enter key between lines so that the address follows the standard postal addressing. Outlook organizes the address into its appropriate fields, such as Home Address Street, Home Address City, and Home Address State. If an address is complex, you might want to click the Address button to open the Check Address dialog box and enter the address parts in the appropriate fields.

You'll enter Francis's home address and specify that it is the mailing address.

To enter a contact's home mailing address:

1. Click the **down arrow** button ⏷ next to Business in the Addresses area, and then click **Home**. The insertion point is in the Address text box, ready for you to enter the home address.

2. Type **12 Haymarket Blvd.**, and then press the **Enter** key. The insertion point moves to a new line.

3. Type **Philadelphia, PA 19107**.

You'll verify that Outlook recorded the address in the correct fields, although you don't usually need to do so for a simple address.

4. Click the **Home** button in the Addresses area. The Check Address dialog box opens. See Figure 2-8.

Check Address dialog box ◄ Figure 2-8

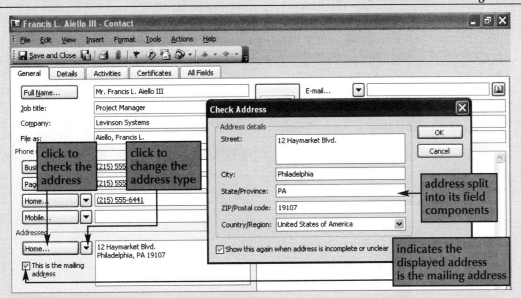

Trouble? If the Check Address dialog box is obscuring the address you typed, drag it by its title bar to another location on the screen.

5. Click the **Cancel** button to close the dialog box.

The address is entered and the This is the mailing address check box is checked. Outlook assumes that the first address you enter for a contact is the mailing address. You could uncheck this check box, enter a business or other address, and then check this option to specify one of those as the mailing address.

If you enter an address as the wrong address type, you can use the Office Clipboard to move the address to the correct text box. Select the address in the address text box, press the Ctrl+X keys to cut the address to the Clipboard, switch to the Business, Home, or Other address text box as needed, click in the address text box, and then press the Ctrl+V keys to paste the address.

Today, many people have a variety of e-mail addresses for business and personal use. Outlook accepts three e-mail addresses for each contact, which are labeled E-mail, E-mail 2, and E-mail 3. You should enter the primary address you plan to use in the E-mail field, so you don't need to think about which address to select. The Display as text box shows how the email address will appear in the To text box of e-mail messages. The default is to show the contact's full name followed by the e-mail address in parentheses. You can change this, if you prefer, by typing a new display name.

In most cases, each contact has a unique e-mail address to which you can send e-mail messages. For this tutorial, you will use your own e-mail address.

To enter a contact's e-mail address:

1. Click in the **E-mail** text box, and then type your e-mail address.

2. Press the **Tab** key. Outlook underlines the address when it recognizes it as a valid e-mail address. Usually, Outlook would enter the contact's name in the Display as text box, but because your e-mail address is already associated with the name you entered when you set up your e-mail account, that user name appears in the Display as text box. You'll change this.

3. Select the text in the **Display as** text box, and then type **Francis Aiello**. See Figure 2-9.

Figure 2-9   Completed General tab in Contact window

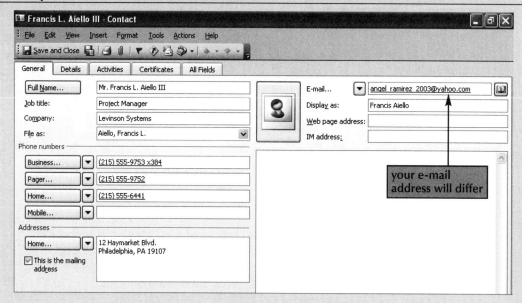

In addition to general contact information, most people have other information that is helpful to record. The Details tab provides a place to enter this additional information. You can record business details such as the contact's department, office, and profession as well as the names of the contact's manager and assistant. You can also record personal details, such as a contact's nickname, spouse's name, birthday, or anniversary.

When you enter a birthday or an anniversary date, Outlook requires that you include a year. If you enter only a month and day, Outlook adds the current year to the date. You might use 1900 (rather than the current year) when you don't know the year to ensure that you don't inadvertently assume an incorrect age or anniversary year. Once you save the contact, Outlook adds a recurring event (an occurrence that repeats at regular intervals) to your calendar for those dates.

You'll enter a couple of these details for Francis.

To enter information on the Details tab and close a contact:

1. Click the **Details** tab. Notice the different types of information you can enter. See Figure 2-10.

Details tab in Contact window ◄ Figure 2-10

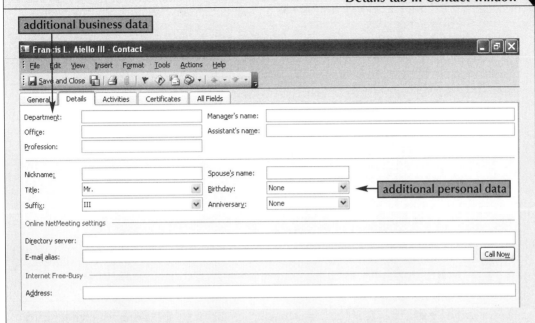

You'll enter Francis's nickname and birthday.

2. Click in the **Nickname** text box, and then type **Frank**.

You can enter a birthday or anniversary by typing a date or selecting a day from a calendar.

3. Select the text in the Birthday text box, type **8/20/1969**, and then press the **Tab** key.

A dialog box opens, indicating that the item must be saved.

4. Click the **OK** button to save the date information.

You have entered all the contact information for Francis, so you can save and close the Contact window.

5. Click the **Save and Close** button on the Standard toolbar. The contact card appears in the Contacts main window. See Figure 2-11.

Contacts main window with contact card ◄ Figure 2-11

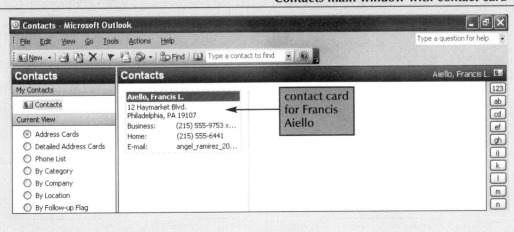

Trouble? If the Duplicate Contact Detected dialog box opens, then Outlook detected an existing contact with the same name or e-mail address as the contact you are entering. Click the Add this as a new contact anyway option button, and then click the OK button.

Trouble? If the contact card on your screen does not look like the one shown in Figure 2-11, click the Address Cards option button in the Current View pane in the Navigation Pane.

Francis's contact card appears in the Contacts main window, and his birthday is added to the Calendar. Next, you'll enter additional contacts for Felicia.

To enter additional contacts:

1. Click the **New** button on the Standard toolbar to open a new contact card.

2. Enter the following contact: name **Jill E. White**, home phone **215-555-1224**, home fax **215-555-4331**, address type **Home**, home mailing address **19 Hillcrest Way, Philadelphia, PA 19107**, your e-mail address, Display as **Jill White**, and spouse **Karl**.

   When you need to enter multiple contacts, you can save and close one contact card and open a new contact card in the same step.

3. Click the **Save and New** button 🖼 on the Standard toolbar.

   The Duplicate Contact Detected dialog box opens because Outlook found an existing contact with the same e-mail address as the contact you're entering.

4. Click the **Add this as a new contact anyway** option button, and then click the **OK** button. Jill's contact information is saved and Outlook opens a new contact card.

5. Enter the following contact: name **Michael Lang**, home phone **215-555-0785**, address type **Home**, home mailing address **2938 Catherine Street, Philadelphia, PA 19102**, and nickname **Mike**.

6. Click the **Save and New** button 🖼 on the Standard toolbar to save Mike's contact information and open a new contact card.

7. Enter the following contact: name **Felicia Rogert**, job title **President**, company **LinkUp**, business phone **215-555-9797**, business fax **215-555-9701**, pager **215-555-2157**, address type **Business**, business mailing address **2932 12th Street, Philadelphia, PA 19102**, and Web page address **www.linkupcarsharing.com**.

8. Click the **Save and New** button 🖼 on the Standard toolbar to save Felicia's contact information and open a new contact card.

As your contact list grows, you may inadvertently try to reenter an existing contact or you may encounter two or more contacts with the same name. Outlook helps prevent the former and informs you of the latter by checking new names against those already in your contact list. If Outlook detects that another contact already has the same name or e-mail address as the current contact, it opens the Duplicate Contact Detected dialog box, as you have already seen, so you can decide whether to add the contact anyway or combine it with an existing contact.

The next contact you'll enter, a vendor for LinkUp, has the same name as a LinkUp customer.

To enter a contact with a duplicate name:

1. Enter the following business contact: name **Michael Lang**, job title **Mechanic**, company **Aldrich Garage**, business phone **215-555-8715**, mobile phone **215-555-2145**, address type **Business**, business mailing address **78 Carpenter Street**, **Philadelphia, PA 19109**, and nickname **Mike**.

2. Click the **Save and Close** button on the Standard toolbar. The Duplicate Contact Detected dialog box opens. See Figure 2-12.

Duplicate Contact Detected dialog box   **Figure 2-12**

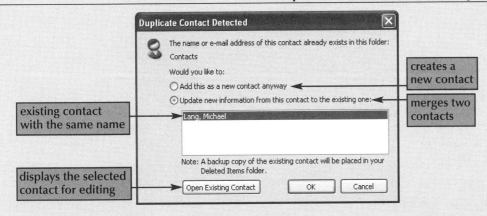

You'll change the File as name to help distinguish the two Michael Langs.

3. Click the **Cancel** button in the dialog box to return to the contact.

   Trouble? If the original Michael Lang contact card opens for editing, you clicked the Open Existing Contact button. You want to return to the new Michael Lang contact card instead. Click the Close button in the contact card title bar to close the Contact window for the original Michael Lang, and then continue with Step 4.

4. Click the **File as** list arrow on the General tab, and then click **Lang, Michael (Aldrich Garage)**. Now each Michael Lang will appear differently in the contact list so you can distinguish the two.

5. Click the **Save and Close** button on the Standard toolbar. The Duplicate Contact Detected dialog box reopens.

6. Click the **Add this as a new contact anyway** option button, and then click the **OK** button. The Contacts main window displays each of the five contacts you entered. See Figure 2-13.

Figure 2-13 ▶ **Contacts main window with contacts**

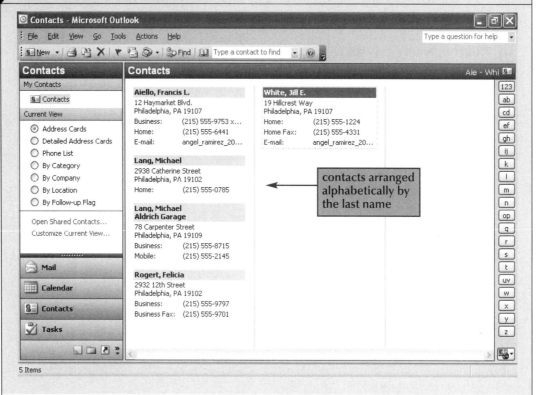

The contacts you entered are arranged in alphabetical order by last name.

Assigning Categories to Contacts

One way to classify your contacts (as well as all other Outlook items) is to assign each one to a category. A **category** is a keyword or phrase that you assign to an item to help organize and later locate and group related items, regardless of whether they are stored in the same folder. You can assign items to 20 general categories from the Master Category List, such as Business or Personal, or to more specific categories that you add to the master list, such as Employees, Members, project titles, or client names. You can assign as many categories as you like to an item. Using categories appropriately is the key to staying organized in Outlook.

Assigning Categories

By assigning categories consistently to contacts and other items, you can easily find all related items. LinkUp assigns each member contact to the category of "Key Customer" to distinguish them from other contacts. You'll assign the Key Customer category from the built-in Master Category List to Francis's contact card because Francis is a member of LinkUp.

Assigning a Category

- Right-click the item, and then click Categories (*or* double-click the item to open it, and then click the Categories button *or* click the item, click Edit on the menu bar, and then click Categories).
- Click one or more categories in the Available categories list in the Categories dialog box.
- To add a new category, click the Master Category List button, type the category name in the New category text box, click the Add button, and then click the OK button (*or* type the category name in the top text box of the Categories dialog box, and then press the Enter key or click the Add to List button).
- Click the OK button.
- If necessary, save and close the item.

You'll assign the Key Customer category to Francis's contact card.

To assign a category to a contact:

► **1.** Double-click the **Aiello, Francis L.** contact card in the Contacts main window to open its Contact window.

► **2.** Click the **Categories** button at the bottom of the Contact window. The Categories dialog box opens, showing all the categories available in the Master Category List.

► **3.** Click the **Key Customer** check box to assign that category to the contact. See Figure 2-14. The top text box shows all the categories assigned to the selected item.

Categories dialog box | Figure 2-14

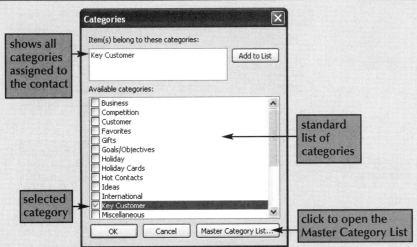

Trouble? If you see additional categories, then your Master Category List includes some custom categories. Continue with Step 4.

► **4.** Click the **OK** button. The category appears in the Categories text box at the bottom of the Contact window.

Although the category you just added to the task is accurate, it may be too general to help you organize your items effectively.

Adding Categories to the Master Category List

The categories that come with Outlook are fairly broad and not specific to any industry. As a result, you will often want to add more precise categories that reflect your work or business. For example, you might create categories for each client or project that you work with, each type of business contact, or each department in your organization.

Felicia wants to assign each contact to the category of "Members," "Vendors," or "Employees." You need to add the three categories to the master list. You'll assign the Members category to the open contact card because Francis is a member of LinkUp. Then you'll delete the Key Customer category from Francis's contact card as it is no longer used.

To add a custom category to the Master Category List:

▶ **1.** Click the **Categories** button in the Contact window. The Categories dialog box opens.

▶ **2.** Click the **Master Category List** button. The Master Category List dialog box that opens shows the list of available categories.

Because "Members" is not on the default list, you'll create it now. Be aware that categories are case sensitive, which means that Outlook sees "Members," "members," and "MEMBERS" as different categories.

▶ **3.** Type **Members** in the New category text box, and then click the **Add** button to enter this category in the list. See Figure 2-15.

Figure 2-15	Master Category List dialog box

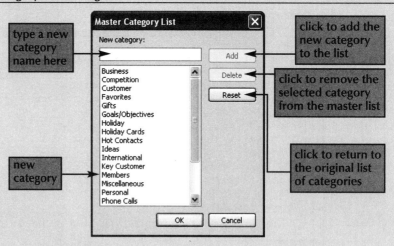

▶ **4.** Add the **Vendors** and **Employees** categories to the Master Category List.

▶ **5.** Click the **OK** button to return to the Categories dialog box.

You can assign one or more categories to any Outlook item. You can then use the Find command to locate all items associated with a specific category. You can add categories to an item from the Categories dialog box, the item's window, or a shortcut menu. You can remove a category from an item in these same locations.

To add and remove categories:

1. Click the **Members** check box in the Available categories list. The top text box shows the selected categories separated by a comma.

2. Click the **OK** button. The Categories dialog box closes and the Categories text box at the bottom of the Contact window lists the categories assigned to this contact.

   Although you could leave both categories, the Members category is much more appropriate. You'll delete the Key Customer category from the contact.

3. Drag to select **Key Customer,** the comma, and the following space in the Categories text box. See Figure 2-16.

Categories assigned to a contact — Figure 2-16

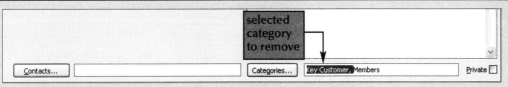

4. Press the **Delete** key. The Key Customer category is removed from the contact, but remains in the Master Category List.

5. Save and close the contact card.

Next, you'll assign categories to the other contacts that you created. Rather than open the Contact window each time, you'll use a shortcut menu to open the Categories dialog box.

To assign categories to contacts:

1. Right-click the **White, Jill E.** contact card, and then click **Categories** on the shortcut menu. The Categories dialog box opens.

2. Click the **Members** check box in the Available categories list, and then click the **OK** button.

3. Use the shortcut menu to assign **Lang, Michael** to the **Members** category, **Lang, Michael, (Aldrich Garage)** to the **Vendors** category, and **Rogert, Felicia** to the **Employees** category.

Creating a Distribution List

Sometimes you'll find that you repeatedly send one message—such as a weekly progress report or company update—to the same group of people. Rather than manually selecting the names one by one from the Contacts folder, you can create a distribution list. A **distribution list** is a contact card that stores a related group of contacts to whom you frequently send the same messages, such as all contacts in the Members category. A distribution list saves time and ensures that you don't inadvertently leave out someone. You can create multiple distribution lists to meet your needs, and contacts can be included in more than one distribution list.

Reference Window

Creating a Distribution List

- Click Actions on the menu bar, and then click New Distribution List.
- Click in the Name text box, and then type a name for the distribution list.
- Click the Select Members button near the top of the Distribution List window.
- Click the Show names from the list arrow, and then click Contacts.
- Double-click the names you want to add to the distribution list, and then click the OK button.
- Click the Categories button to assign a category, if you want.
- Click the Save and Close button on the Standard toolbar.

You'll create a distribution list that includes all of LinkUp's members.

To create a distribution list:

1. Click **Actions** on the menu bar, and then click **New Distribution List**. The Distribution List window opens.

2. Type **LinkUp Members** in the Name text box. This is the name for the distribution list that will appear in the contact list.

3. Click the **Select Members** button below the Name text box. The Select Members dialog box opens.

4. If necessary, click the **Show Names from the** list arrow, and then click **Contacts**. A contact appears in the left list box once for each e-mail address and fax number in your Contacts folder. See Figure 2-17.

| Figure 2-17 | Select Members dialog box |

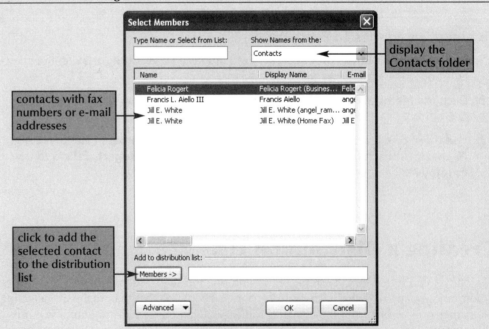

You'll add two members to the distribution list.

▶ **5.** Double-click **Francis L. Aiello III** to add the contact to the Add to distribution list text box. Double-clicking the name is the same as clicking the name and then clicking the Members button. Francis is now a member of the distribution list.

▶ **6.** Double-click the first **Jill E. White** (the one with the e-mail address listed, not the fax number) to add the contact to the Add to distribution list text box, and then click the **OK** button.

You'll assign the Members category to the LinkUp Members distribution list so that you can easily locate it.

▶ **7.** Click the **Categories** button, click the **Members** check box in the Categories dialog box, and then click the **OK** button. See Figure 2-18.

Completed Distribution List window ◀ **Figure 2-18**

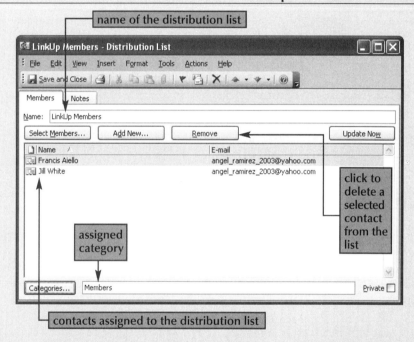

name of the distribution list

assigned category

click to delete a selected contact from the list

contacts assigned to the distribution list

▶ **8.** Click the **Save and Close** button on the Standard toolbar in the Distribution List window. The list appears as a contact in the Contacts main window with the group name displayed, as shown in Figure 2-19.

Figure 2-19 ▶ **Contacts main window with a distribution list**

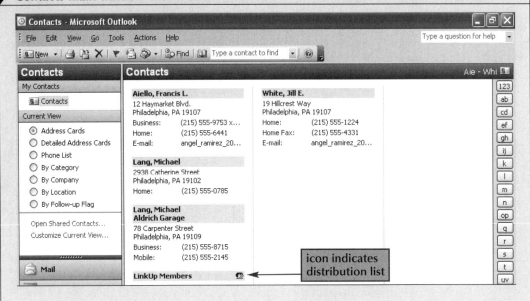

You can use the LinkUp Members distribution list to address e-mail messages just as you would use any one-person contact.

Working in Different Contact Views

There are a variety of ways to look at the information in the Contacts folder. **Views** specify how information in a folder is organized and which details are visible. For example, Address Cards view displays names and mailing addresses in blocks. Phone List view displays details about your contacts, such as name, job title, and telephone numbers, in columns. Each Outlook folder has a set of standard views from which you can choose.

To change the contact view:

▶ 1. Click the **Contacts** button in the Navigation Pane, if necessary. The My Contacts pane appears at the top of the Navigation Pane with the Contacts folder listed. The Current View pane appears below the My Contacts pane, and it lists all the available standard views for the Contacts folder. The default is Address Cards, which displays each contact's name, mailing address, up to four phone numbers, and the contact's e-mail address.

▶ 2. Click the **Detailed Address Cards** option button in the Current View pane. Your contacts appear in alphabetical order by last name as specified in the File as text box, and much of the information you entered is visible. See Figure 2-20.

Detailed Address Cards view Figure 2-20

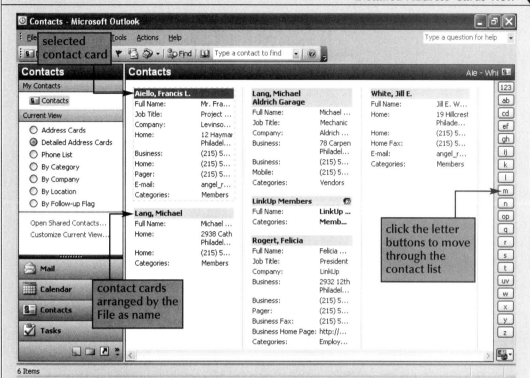

When you have many contacts, you can click a letter button on the right side of the screen to display contacts filed under that letter, and then scroll to find the specific contact you want.

3. Click the **Phone List** option button in the Current View pane. Contacts' names, companies, phone numbers, and other information appear in table columns.

4. Click the **By Company** option button in the Current View pane. Contacts appear grouped by the company names you entered earlier.

5. If necessary, click the **plus sign** button ⊞ for each category to display the names in each group.

6. Click the **By Category** option button in the Current View pane. The contacts you created earlier are grouped in three categories: Employees, Members, and Vendors.

7. If necessary, click the **plus sign** button ⊞ for each group to display the names it includes. See Figure 2-21.

Figure 2-21 **Contacts grouped by category**

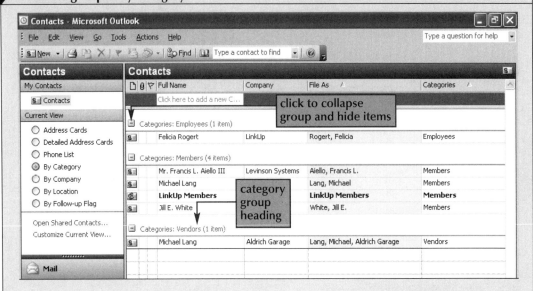

The Address Cards and Detailed Address Cards views are **card views**—the contacts are listed in blocks of information. All of the other views in the Contacts folder are **table views**—the contacts are listed in the form of a table. Table views are useful when you want to sort or group the contacts.

You can change the way you view your contacts at any time, depending on the task you need to accomplish.

Editing Contacts

Any aspect of a contact's information may change over time. A person or company may move to a new street address or be assigned a new area code. A person may change jobs. You may discover that you entered information incorrectly. Rather than deleting the card with the wrong information and starting over, you can update the existing contact card as needed by double-clicking the contact to open the Contact window and then editing the information. You can also make changes directly in the Contacts main window from the Address Cards or Detailed Address Cards view or any view that shows the field you want to edit.

Felicia tells you Jill White has moved to 27 Hamilton Street. You'll make this correction directly in the main window from Detailed Address Cards view.

To edit a contact card:

1. Click the **Detailed Address Cards** option button in the Current View pane.

2. Click the **w** button along the right side of the main window, and, if necessary, use the scroll bars to display the White, Jill E. contact card.

3. Click to the left of the street address in Jill's contact card to display the insertion point.

4. Drag to select **19 Hillcrest Way**. The entire street address is selected. See Figure 2-22.

Editing a contact's information ◄ Figure 2-22

▶ **5.** Type **27 Hamilton Street** to revise the address.

▶ **6.** Click anywhere outside Jill's contact card. Outlook saves the changes.

Just this one simple change demonstrates an advantage of Outlook over a paper system. No matter how minor or comprehensive the changes you need to make, your contact list remains neat and legible.

Printing a Contact List

Although most of the time you'll work with your contacts within Outlook, sometimes a printed list is helpful, such as when you need to hand out group members' contact information at a meeting. Outlook provides a variety of printing styles for your contacts; the available options differ depending on whether a card or table view is selected. The card views can be printed as successive blocks of information, in memo format on separate pages, or as a phone list with select information. The table views enable you to print only the actual list format you see. In either case, the printout can include all your contacts or only selected contacts. It is a good idea to preview prior to printing.

You'll preview and then print your entire contact list.

To preview and print your contact list:

▶ **1.** Click the **Print** button 🖨 on the Standard toolbar. The Print dialog box opens.

▶ **2.** Click **Card Style** in the Print style area, if it is not already selected.

▶ **3.** Click the **All items** option button in the Print range area, if it is not already selected, to indicate that you want to print the six contact cards (including the distribution list) you created earlier. See Figure 2-23.

Figure 2-23 ▶ **Print dialog box**

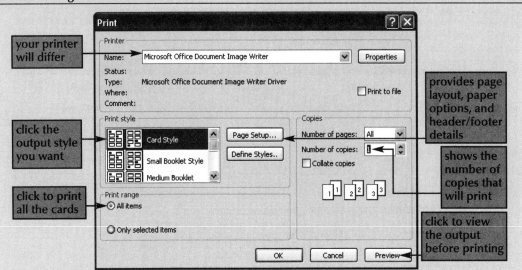

Trouble? If your contact list has more than six contacts, your printout will include all the contacts in the main window. If you want to print only the six contacts from this tutorial, click the Cancel button, press and hold the Ctrl key, click each of the six cards you want to print, release the Ctrl key, click the Print button, and then click the Only selected items option button. Then continue with Step 4.

4. Click the **Page Setup** button. The Page Setup: Card Style dialog box opens. You can change the layout and look of the printout from here.

5. In the Options area, click the **Blank forms at end** list arrow, and then click **None**. This ensures that you do not print any extra forms for jotting down information about new contacts.

6. Click the **OK** button to return to the Print dialog box.

7. Click the **Preview** button to view the page in Print Preview. See Figure 2-24.

Contact list in Print Preview | Figure 2-24

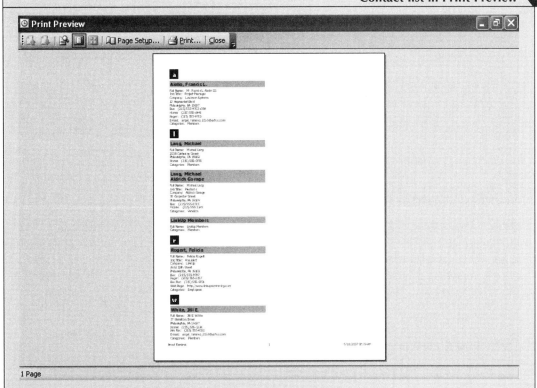

1 Page

▶ **8.** Click the **Print** button on the Print Preview toolbar.

▶ **9.** Click the **OK** button to send the contact list to the printer.

The contact list prints without blank forms.

Sending Contact Information to Others

If you need to send any of your contacts to others, you can do so quickly by forwarding the contact information. Forwarding contacts to a colleague or friend allows you to pass along or enter the information without retyping or copying and pasting the information. When you forward contact information as an Outlook Contact window, it contains the same data contained in your Contacts folder. Alternatively, you can send contact information as a vCard. A **vCard** (or virtual business card) is a file with the file extension .vcf that contains all of the information on the contact card. The vCard files are compatible with other popular communication and information management programs. You can also use vCards to exchange contact information with handheld personal digital assistants (PDAs).

Sending Contact Information by E-Mail

- Select one or more contacts.
- Click Actions on the menu bar, and then click Forward to send a contact card (*or* click Forward as vCard to send a vCard).
- Type the recipient's name or e-mail address in the To box (*or* click the To button and select a name).
- If you selected multiple contacts, type a subject in the Subject box.
- Click in the Message window and type your message.
- Send the e-mail.

You'll send contact information from a contact card by e-mail.

Sending Contact Information by E-mail

If the recipient uses Outlook, you can send that person the entire contact card. The recipient can then quickly drag the contact into his or her own Contacts folder. You can send one or more contact cards by e-mail. To do this, press and hold the Ctrl key as you click contacts to select nonadjacent entries, or click the first contact and press and hold the Shift key as you click the last contact to select consecutive entries.

To forward contact information:

1. Click **Lang, Michael Aldrich Garage** in the Contacts main window to select that contact.

2. Click **Actions** on the menu bar, and then click **Forward**. A Message window opens with an icon for the selected contact in the Attach text box. The subject lists FW: for forward and the selected contact name—in this case, Michael Lang.

3. Type **Francis L. Aiello** in the To text box, and then press the **Tab** key. After a moment, the name is underlined, indicating that Outlook has found and verified the e-mail address for this contact.

   Trouble? If the name you typed in the To text box does not become underlined, click the To button to open the Select Names dialog box, click Francis L. Aiello III in the list, click the To button at the bottom of the dialog box, drag to select Francis Aiello in the To text box, press the Delete key to delete that entry, and then click the OK button.

4. Click in the message body, type **Michael is LinkUp's ace mechanic. I highly recommend him. His contact information is attached.**, press the **Enter** key twice, and then type your name.

5. If necessary, click the Message format list arrow on the Standard toolbar in the Message window, and then click **Plain Text**. See Figure 2-25.

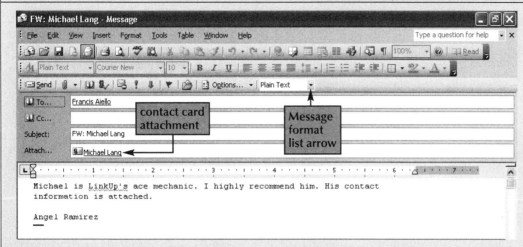

Trouble? If your e-mail message does not appear in a Word window, then you're using Outlook as your mail editor. The process of creating a message works similarly; continue with Step 6.

▶ **6.** Send the e-mail.

Receiving a Contact Card

Sometimes you'll be the recipient of forwarded contact information. You can add the contact information you receive by e-mail to your Contacts folder without retyping information.

You'll download your messages, and enter the contact information as a new contact.

To download and read your messages:

▶ **1.** Display the **Inbox** folder, and then download your e-mail messages, if necessary.

▶ **2.** Click the **FW: Michael Lang** message to view it in the Reading Pane, read the message, and then double-click the **Michael Lang** attachment icon in the Reading Pane to open the Contact window file.

▶ **3.** Review the contact information, and then click the **Close** button ☒ to close the Contact window.

Next, you'll create a new contact card for Michael Lang. You could have used the Save and Close button on the Standard toolbar in the Contact window when you had the card open. Because you have already closed the Contact window, you'll drag the contact card from the message to the Contacts folder.

To create a new contact card from an e-mailed contact card:

▶ **1.** Drag the **Michael Lang** attachment icon from the Reading Pane to over the **Contacts** button in the Navigation Pane until the My Contacts pane appears at the top of the Navigation Pane, and then continue to drag to **Contacts** in the My Contacts pane; do not release the mouse button. See Figure 2-26.

Figure 2-26 ▶ Dragging a contact card icon to Contacts folder

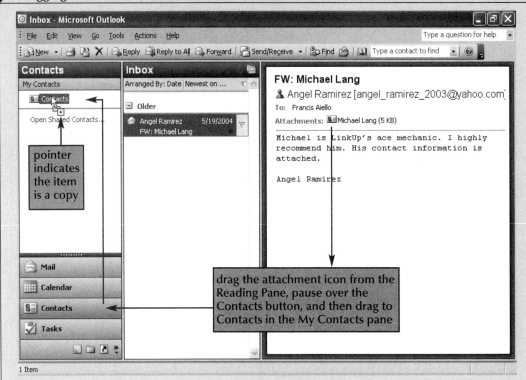

2. Release the mouse button.

   Because Michael Lang's information already appears in your contact list, the Duplicate Contact Detected dialog box opens. This time, you'll combine the two contacts.

3. Click the **Update new information from this contact to the existing one** option button, if necessary, click **Lang, Michael Aldrich Garage** in the list box, and then click the **Yes** button.

4. Display the **Contacts** folder.

So far, you have created, edited, and printed a contact list of some of LinkUp's members, vendors, and employees, and then exchanged a contact's information by e-mail. In Session 2.2, you will work with the contact list by communicating with specific contacts by e-mail and letter. Then you will send a form letter to only LinkUp members, informing them of the latest cars being added to the LinkUp fleet.

Review

Session 2.1 Quick Check

1. True or False: In Outlook, a contact is a person, but not an organization.
2. What is the purpose of the File as name?
3. What happens if you try to enter a contact with the same name or e-mail address as an existing contact?
4. Why should you assign categories to contacts?

5. Explain the purpose of views.
6. What is a distribution list?
7. Describe the process for selecting adjacent contacts.
8. How do you add the information from a contact card that was forwarded to you into your contact list?

Session 2.2

Working with Contacts

Once you have set up a contact list, there are many ways to work with it. You can access contacts from any folder and integrate them with other Outlook items. You can associate a contact with any Outlook item much as you would assign a category to the item. For example, you can link an appointment, a meeting, and a task to a contact by opening that item's window, clicking the Contacts button at the bottom of the window, and then selecting the contact. You can also connect one contact to another. This is helpful in keeping related contacts associated. In addition, a contact list enables you to more easily perform a variety of daily activities, including:

- Sending an e-mail to a contact
- Creating a printed letter addressed to a contact
- Scheduling an appointment or a meeting with a contact
- Assigning a task to a contact
- Dialing a contact's phone number from Outlook (as long as you have a modem installed on your computer and the computer is connected to a phone line)

These are probably the most common actions you'll perform. You can do any of these activities for a single contact or any of the first four activities for a distribution list. Because a distribution list does not have a phone number, you cannot call it.

Sending an E-mail to a Contact or Distribution List

Felicia asks you to send Francis an e-mail message reminding him to use the LinkUp credit card to pay for refilling a car with gas. You can quickly set up and send a message to anyone in the Contacts folder, as long as the contact has an e-mail address. You enter a subject and message, insert attachments, and specify a message format just as you would any other e-mail message.

To send an e-mail message to a contact:

1. If you took a break after the previous session, make sure the Contacts folder is displayed and the main window is set to Detailed Address Cards view.

2. Click **Aiello, Francis L.** in the Contacts main window to select that contact.

3. Click the **New Message to Contact** button 📧 on the Standard toolbar. A Message window opens addressed to Francis (your e-mail address appears in the To text box).

4. Change the message format to **Plain Text**, if necessary.

5. Create an e-mail with the subject **Paying for gas** and the message **Please use the LinkUp credit card you received with your membership package to purchase any gas you put into LinkUp automobiles. We cannot reimburse you for any gas charges billed to your personal credit card. Thank you.**

6. Press the **Enter** key twice and type your name. See Figure 2-27.

Figure 2-27	E-mail to a contact

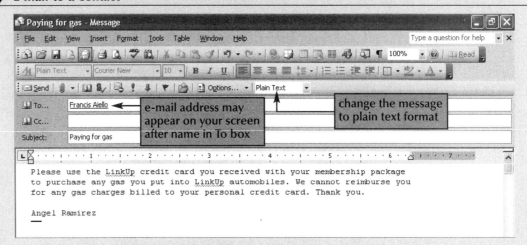

Trouble? If your e-mail message does not appear in a Word window, then you're using Outlook as your mail editor. The process of creating a message works similarly; continue with Step 7.

7. Send the e-mail.

Felicia asks you to send a message to all LinkUp members to inform them of the new billing cycle. Because you created the LinkUp Members distribution list, you can write and address the e-mail message without concern that you'll forget anyone. You send an e-mail message to a distribution list using the same steps as sending an e-mail message to a single contact, except you select the group name in the Contacts main window instead of an individual contact. Everyone on the list receives the same message.

Sending personal e-mails to groups of family and friends or sending commercial e-mails to people who request them are acceptable uses of distribution lists. Sending an unsolicited commercial e-mail, such as an advertisement, to a distribution list is an unacceptable use. For more information about unsolicited commercial e-mail, use your favorite search engine and search on the keywords "spam" or "unsolicited commercial e-mail" for a list of Web sites.

To send an e-mail message to a distribution list:

1. Click **LinkUp Members** in the Contacts main window to select the distribution list.

2. Click the **New Message to Contact** button 🖹 on the Standard toolbar. A Message window opens addressed to the LinkUp Members distribution list. If you click the plus sign button in the To text box, the distribution list group is expanded to show all the individual members; you cannot collapse the group into the distribution list.

3. Change the message format to **Plain Text**, if necessary.

4. Create an e-mail with the subject **Monthly billing** and the message **LinkUp will charge members' credit cards for their previous month's usage on the third business day of each month. The new billing date goes into effect next month. Thank you.**

5. Press the **Enter** key twice, and then type your name. See Figure 2-28.

Message to distribution list | Figure 2-28

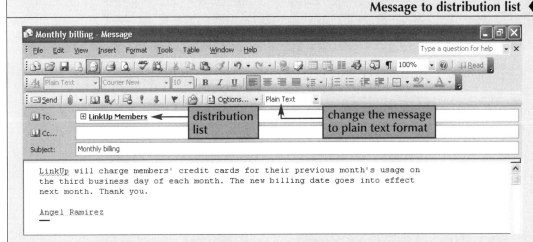

Trouble? If your e-mail message does not appear in a Word window, then you're using Outlook as your mail editor. The process of creating a message works similarly; continue with Step 6.

6. Send the e-mail.

7. Download your messages if necessary. You should have two new messages in your Inbox.

You can also write letters to an individual contact or a distribution list.

Writing a Letter to a Contact or Distribution List

Although e-mail is handy for sending quick messages, you may need to create a more formal printed letter that you can fax or mail to a contact. When you write a letter to a distribution list, every contact receives the same letter. Outlook uses the Word Letter Wizard to help you create the letter. The **Letter Wizard** is a tool that takes you step by step through the letter-writing process in Word. In the wizard, you select the look and format of the letter, verify the recipient's name and mailing address and your sender information, and then select a salutation and closing. The letter document then opens, ready for you to type the letter body.

Writing a Letter to a Contact

- Select one or more contacts.
- Click Actions on the menu bar, and then click New Letter to Contact.
- Select the appropriate page design and style, salutation and closing, and recipient and sender information in each step of the Word Letter Wizard. Click the Next button to move to the next step.
- Click the Finish button in the final Letter Wizard dialog box.
- Type the letter body, using Word's editing and formatting tools as desired.
- Click the Save button on the Standard toolbar to save the letter.

You'll write a letter to Jill White, welcoming her as a new LinkUp member.

To write a letter to a contact:

1. Click **White, Jill E.** to select that contact.

2. Click **Actions** on the menu bar, and then click **New Letter to Contact**. A blank document opens in Word and the Letter Wizard starts. See Figure 2-29.

Figure 2-29 | **Letter Wizard – Step 1 of 4 dialog box**

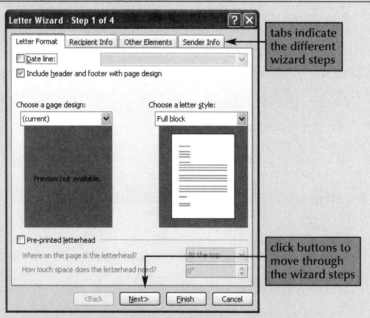

Trouble? If you do not have Word installed, a dialog box opens, indicating that you must install Word to use this feature. Click the OK button. You can read, but not perform, the rest of the steps in this section.

3. Click the **Choose a page design** list arrow, and then click **Contemporary Letter**.

4. Verify that **Full block** appears in the Choose a letter style list box, and then click the **Next** button.

The name and mailing address of the contact you selected in Outlook appears as the recipient information. You need to select only the letter salutation. Word provides several options in each category or you can enter your own.

5. Click the **Business** option button in the Salutation area. The standard business salutation "Dear Jill E. White:" appears in the list box.

The next step provides opportunities to enter other information, such as a reference line, subject line, or courtesy copy information, on the Other Elements tab. You don't need to enter any of this, so you'll skip right to the last step.

6. Click the **Sender Info** tab. You need to enter your name and address, and then specify the letter's closing.

7. Type your name in the Sender's name text box, if necessary, and then type your mailing address in the Return address text box, pressing the Enter key to place the street on its own line.

   Trouble? If the Return address box is dimmed, click the Omit check box to remove the check mark. You would leave the Omit option checked if you were using letterhead preprinted with a return mailing address.

8. Click the **Complimentary closing** list arrow, and then click **Sincerely yours,**.

9. Type **Membership Services** in the Job title text box, type **LinkUp** in the Company text box, and then press the **Tab** key. See Figure 2-30.

Letter Wizard – Step 4 of 4 dialog box | **Figure 2-30**

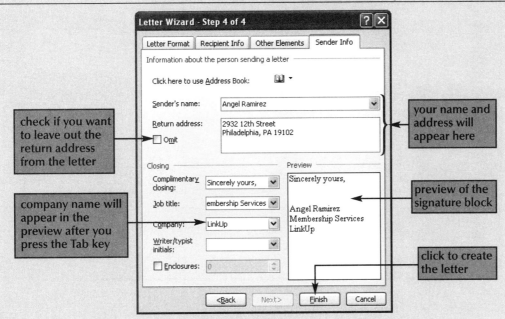

10. Click the **Finish** button. In a moment the letter opens, with placeholder text in the body selected so you can begin typing.

When you type the letter in Word, you have access to all of the word-processing and formatting tools in Word, including spelling and grammar checking.

To type the letter:

1. Type **Welcome to LinkUp! Our insurance company has approved your driving record at the standard rate. This means that your annual membership is $120, or just $10 per month. As a member, you'll have access to our entire fleet of cars. Just visit our reservation Web site to reserve a vehicle near you. Rental fees are calculated on an hourly rate of $2.50 and $0.50 per mile. Remember that these fees include insurance and gasoline. If the gas tank dips below the ¼ mark, please fill up the car and use your LinkUp credit card to pay. You will receive your LinkUp credit card in a separate mailing.**

2. Press the **Enter** key, and then type **If you have any questions, please do not hesitate to contact me. Thank you.** See Figure 2-31.

Figure 2-31 **Finished letter to contact**

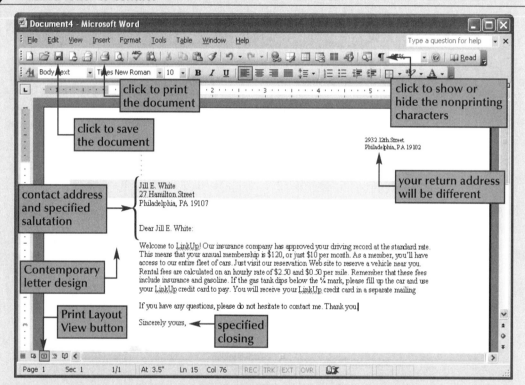

Trouble? If you do not see the shaded bar and graphic, then Word is displaying the letter in Normal view or Web Layout view. Click the Print Layout View button.

3. Click the **Save** button 🖫 on the Standard toolbar, and then save the letter as **Jill White Letter** in the **Tutorial.02\Tutorial** folder included with your Data Files.

4. Click the **Close** button ☒ on the Word title bar to close the letter and exit Word.

You can use any of the features and tools in Word to format and enhance your letter.

Scheduling Appointments, Meetings, or Tasks with a Contact

Contacts can help simplify the management of your calendar. Whenever you need to set aside time for someone in your contact list, you can quickly schedule an appointment or meeting by dragging that contact from the Contacts main window to the Calendar folder or by clicking New Meeting Request or New Appointment on the Actions menu. A blank Appointment window opens, with the contact name in the Contacts text box at the bottom of the window. You complete the window with the relevant information.

The process for assigning a task to a contact works similarly. Select the contact to whom you want to assign the task, and then click New Task for Contact on the Actions menu. You can also drag the contact to the Tasks folder. The task request opens, and you complete the window with the appropriate information.

You'll work with the Calendar and Tasks folders in Tutorial 3.

Linking Activities to Contacts

One way to track tasks, appointments, e-mail, notes, or documents related to a contact is to **link**, or connect, them to the contact. When you create an Outlook item, such as a task, you can link it to the related contact by entering the contact's name in the Contacts text box. You can also link any existing item to a contact. Then you can open the contact from any linked item just by clicking the contact's name in the Contacts text box. Many items are linked automatically to each other. For example, if you enter a birthday on a contact card, then that item is added to the Calendar and linked to that date in the Calendar.

Linking an Activity to a Contact	Reference Window

- Open the contact to which you want to link an item.
- Click Actions on the menu bar, point to Link, and then click Items.
- Click the folder that contains the items you want to link in the Look in list box, and then click one or more items in the Items list.
- Click the OK button.

When you entered Francis Aiello's birthday in his contact card, Outlook linked the recurring event to the contact.

To view an event linked to a contact:

1. Double-click the **Aiello, Francis L.** contact card in the Contacts main window to open it.
2. Click the **Activities** tab in the Contact window. See Figure 2-32.

Figure 2-32 ▶ **Activities for Francis L. Aiello III**

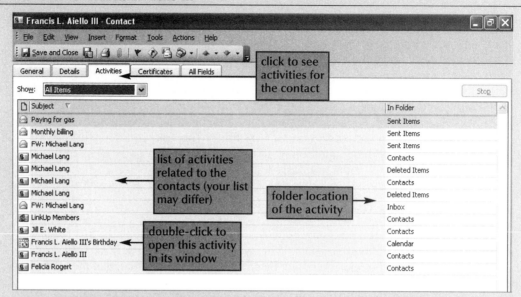

The list includes all items linked to Francis Aiello and his e-mail address (which is, in this case, your e-mail address).

3. Double-click **Francis L. Aiello III's Birthday** in the list. The Recurring Event window opens. See Figure 2-33.

Figure 2-33 ▶ **Event window for Francis L. Aiello III's Birthday**

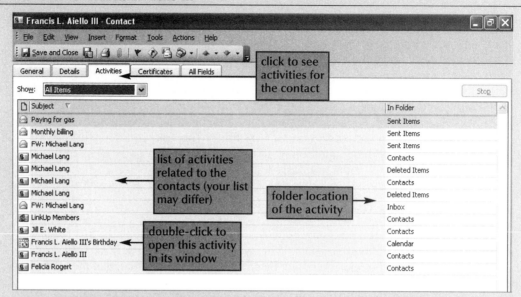

4. Click the **Close** button ⊠ on the title bar of the Recurring Event window to close it.

5. Click the **Close** button ⊠ on the title bar of the Contact window to close it.

Flagging a Contact for Follow-Up

At times, you need to remember to perform some activity related to a contact, such as calling that person to confirm a lunch appointment or verifying the status of a project. Rather than jotting yourself a reminder note, you can draw attention to the contact by flagging the contact for follow-up. The standard flags are Follow up, Call, Arrange Meeting, Send E-mail, and Send Letter. You can also choose a specific color for the flag. After you determine the action, you can set a reminder due date by which to complete the follow-up. You can select a due date from a calendar or enter a descriptive natural language date, such as "next Tuesday." If a due date passes without the flag being changed to Completed, then the contact becomes red as a visual reminder of the missed deadline.

Reference Window

Flagging a Contact for Follow-Up

- Select the contact with whom you want to follow up.
- Click the Follow Up button on the Standard toolbar.
- Click the Flag to list arrow, and then click a follow-up option.
- Enter or select a due date in the Due by text box, and then enter a time in the second Due by text box, if necessary.
- Click the OK button.
  or
- Switch to a table view, such as By Follow-up Flag.
- Click the flag icon or empty flag box to the left of the contact, click the flag status you want, and then press the Enter key.

You'll flag the contact cards for all contacts in the Members category to remind you to send a welcome letter to them.

To flag a contact for follow-up:

1. Select the **Aiello, Francis L.** contact card in the Contacts main window.

2. Click the **Follow Up** button ⬇ on the Standard toolbar. The Flag for Follow Up dialog box opens. See Figure 2-34.

Flag for Follow Up dialog box ◁ **Figure 2-34**

3. Click the **Flag to** list arrow, click **Send Letter**, and then press the **Tab** key.

▶ 4. Type **today** in the first Due by text box, and then press the **Tab** key. Outlook converts the text to today's date.

▶ 5. Type **5 pm** in the second Due by text box, and then click the **OK** button.

Trouble? If a dialog box opens indicating that the flag is past due, then the time is already later than 5 p.m. Click the Dismiss button in the Reminder dialog box, click the Follow Up button on the Standard toolbar, press the Tab key, type tomorrow in the Due by text box, and then click the OK button. Then, in Step 6, set the flag to be completed tomorrow by 5 p.m.

▶ 6. Set a Follow Up flag to send a letter to be completed today by 5 p.m. for the contacts **Lang, Michael** and **White, Jill E.**

The Address Cards view and the Detailed Address Cards view both display the follow-up reminder as the first line of the contact card. It also appears in the InfoBar of the open contact card.

You can change the view to display all the contacts flagged for follow-up in one group. This enables you to look at activities you need to complete. You can then plan your schedule by dragging flagged contacts to the Notes, Tasks, or Calendar folder to create notes, set up tasks, or schedule appointments to complete your follow-ups. You can also check off completed follow-up activities, clear flags that are no longer necessary, or add flags to other contacts.

Because you already sent the letter to Jill, you'll change the flag to complete.

To view contacts by flags and change flagged status:

▶ 1. Click the **By Follow-up Flag** option button in the Current View pane in the Navigation Pane. There are two groups, in this case, Followup Flag and Unflagged.

Trouble? If the items are sorted and not in labeled groups, click View on the menu bar, point to Arrange By, and then click Show in Groups.

▶ 2. Click the **flag** icon 🚩 to the left of Jill's contact. A list box opens with the option to add a Followup flag, a colored flag, or a Completed flag to the item or to mark the item as Unflagged. See Figure 2-35.

| Figure 2-35 | **Available flags in Contacts main window** |

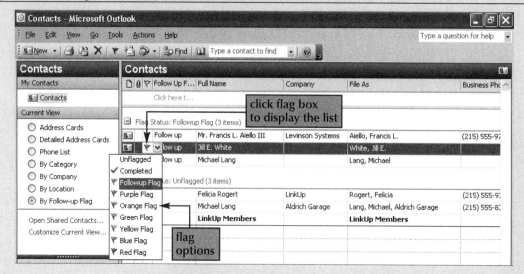

Trouble? If you do not see the items in each group, the groups are collapsed. Click the plus sign button ⊞ for each group to display the hidden contacts.

3. Click **Completed**, and then press the **Enter** key. Outlook changes that contact's flag status and moves it into the appropriate group.

   The contacts are organized into three possible groups: contacts that have outstanding flags (red flag icon), contacts that have completed flags (check mark icon), and contacts that have no flags (called unflagged or cleared). If you want to add a deadline or assign an activity other than follow-up, you must open the Flag for Follow Up dialog box for that contact.

4. Click the **Francis L. Aiello** contact to select it.

5. Click the **Follow Up** button ⚑ on the Standard toolbar, press the **Tab** key, type **yesterday** in the Due by text box, and then click the **OK** button. A Reminder dialog box opens, showing you all past due flags. See Figure 2-36.

Reminder dialog box ◀ Figure 2-36

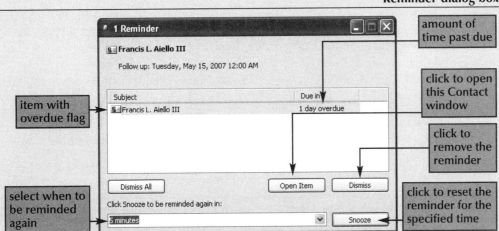

6. Click the **Snooze** list arrow, click **1 day**, and then click the **Snooze** button. The Reminder dialog box will reopen tomorrow if you have not yet marked the flag as completed.

7. Click another contact to deselect Francis's contact card. Francis's contact is now red, indicating it is past due. See Figure 2-37.

Contacts with flags ◀ Figure 2-37

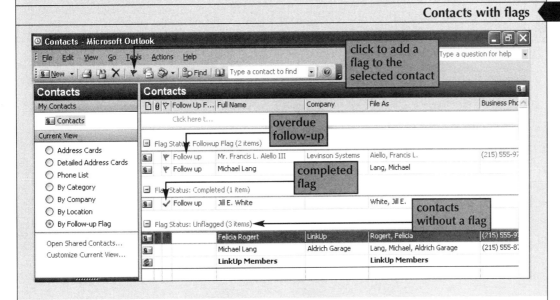

The flags provide one way to group your contacts. There are many other ways to organize them.

Organizing Contacts

The ability to organize and reorganize contacts quickly and cleanly is one of the most obvious advantages of Outlook over a paper address book. For example, you might arrange your contacts in groups by their assigned categories. You might display and hide certain contacts based on criteria that you set, such as contacts that reside in a certain city. You can choose the order you want contacts to appear in the main window, such as alphabetically by last name. For even greater contact management, you can combine any or all of these organization methods to create the exact presentation of your contacts that you want. This kind of flexibility is simply not available with paper address books.

Organizing Contacts by Category

The list of contacts you created earlier includes more than just members. Because each contact has been assigned a category, you can organize all the contacts by category by changing the view. You'll use the Current View pane to change the view.

To organize contacts by category:

1. Click the **By Category** option button in the Current View pane in the Navigation Pane. The contacts are organized into three categories—Employee, Members, and Vendors. See Figure 2-38.

Figure 2-38 ▶ Contacts organized by category

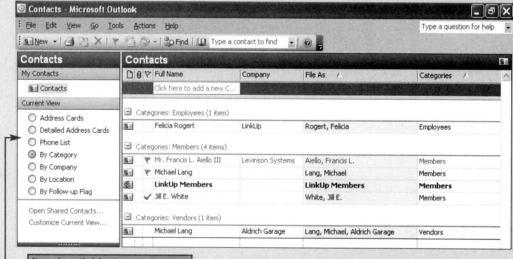

list of available Contacts views

Trouble? If you do not see the items in each category, the groups are collapsed. Click the plus sign button ➕ for each group to display the hidden contacts in each category.

Any contact that has more than one category assigned appears in multiple groups. For example, if you had left the Key Customer category in the Francis Aiello contact, there would have been a fourth category listed in the view and the contact would have appeared in two categories.

Arranging the contacts by category, follow-up flags, company, or other available views is helpful in separating the contacts into groups. However, sometimes you'll want to work with only a subset of your contacts (or other items) and temporarily hide the ones you don't need.

Filtering a View

Felicia wants to see the contact cards for all LinkUp members. You can display items in a folder that match certain criteria by setting a **filter**. In this case, you'll filter the contacts to display only the ones assigned to the Members category. The other contacts remain in the folder but are not visible until you remove the filter. A filter applies only to the current view. So if you set a filter in one view and then switch to another view, you'll see all the available contacts, not the set of filtered contacts, in the new view.

Filtering a View

- Click the Customize Current View link in the Current View pane in the Navigation Pane, and then click the Filter button in the Customize View dialog box (*or* right-click a blank area in the main window, and then click Filter).
- Set the filter options you want in the Filter dialog box (*or* click the Clear All button to remove an existing filter).
- Click the OK button in the Filter dialog box.
- Click the OK button in the Customize View dialog box, if necessary.

You'll filter the LinkUp contacts to display only those in the Members category.

To apply a filter:

1. Click the **Customize Current View** link in the Current View pane in the Navigation Pane. The Customize View dialog box opens.

2. Click the **Filter** button. The Filter dialog box opens, displaying criteria you can set to filter the contacts, such as by keyword or by e-mail address.

3. Click the **More Choices** tab, which provides additional filter options. See Figure 2-39.

Figure 2-39   **Filter dialog box**

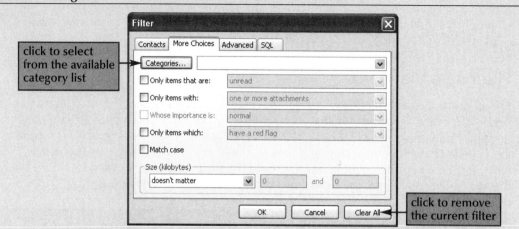

> **4.** Click the **Categories** button to open the Categories dialog box, click the **Members** check box in the Available categories list, and then click the **OK** button. You could have typed the category into the text box, but using the dialog box ensures that the spelling and capitalization are accurate.

> **5.** Click the **OK** button to return to the Customize View dialog box. The filter settings are listed in the Customize View dialog box. See Figure 2-40.

Figure 2-40   **Customize View dialog box**

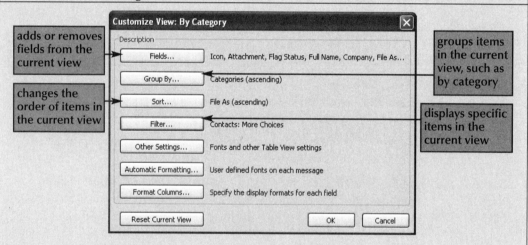

> **6.** Click the **OK** button to return to the main window. See Figure 2-41.

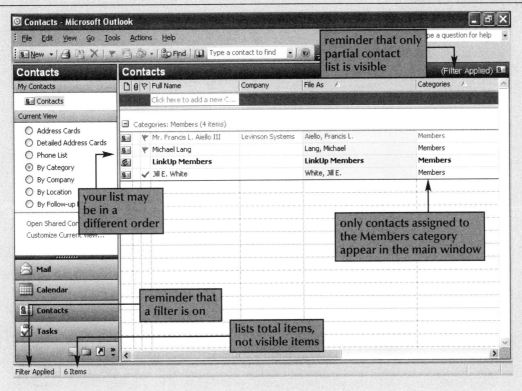

Filtered contact list — Figure 2-41

Only the four contacts that match your filter appear in the folder. As a reminder, the words "Filter Applied" appear in the status bar and the folder banner until you remove the filter from the view.

Sorting Contacts by Field

As you work with a filtered list of contacts, you might want to further organize them by changing their display order. Although Outlook often sorts contacts alphabetically by the File As field, you can re-sort contacts at any time. If you're using a table view, such as By Category, the quickest way to sort information is by clicking the appropriate column header. The arrow icons on the headers indicate the sort order. **Ascending order** arranges items alphabetically (A to Z), chronologically (earliest to latest), or numerically (lowest to highest). **Descending order** reverses the ascending sort order—Z to A, latest to earliest, or highest to lowest. If you're in a card view, then you'll need to use the Sort dialog box.

The Sort dialog box enables you to select up to four fields by which to sort. Each subsequent sort field is applied to the subset of the sort. For example, if you sort contacts by company and then by name, Outlook first arranges the contacts by company and then arranges the contacts by name within each company. You can also specify the order of each sort: ascending or descending.

Sorting by Fields

- Display the main window in the view you want to sort.
- Click the Customize Current View link in the Current View pane in the Navigation Pane, and then click the Sort button in the Customize View dialog box (*or* right-click the main window, and then click Sort).
- Click the Select available fields from list arrow, and then click a subset of fields.
- Click the Sort items by list arrow, click a field name, and then click the Ascending or Descending option button.
- If necessary, change the available fields option, click the top Then by list arrow, click a field name, and then click the Ascending or Descending option button. Repeat for the bottom Then by list arrow.
- Click the OK button in the Sort dialog box.
- Click the OK button in the Customize View dialog box, if necessary.

Felicia wants to organize the filtered contacts first by their ZIP code and then by their File As name.

To sort contacts using the Sort dialog box:

1. Click the **Customize Current View** link in the Current View pane in the Navigation Pane. The Customize View dialog box opens.

2. Click the **Sort** button. The Sort dialog box opens.

   Because there is such a variety of fields available by which to sort contacts, you can select a subset of fields to more easily find the field you want.

3. Click the **Select available fields from** list arrow, and then click **Address fields**.

4. Click the **Sort items by** list arrow, press **Z** to quickly move down the list, click **ZIP/Postal Code**, and then click the **Descending** option button.

5. Click the **Select available fields from** list arrow, click **Name fields**, click the active **Then by** list arrow, and then click **File As**. Your Sort dialog box should match Figure 2-42.

Figure 2-42

Sort dialog box

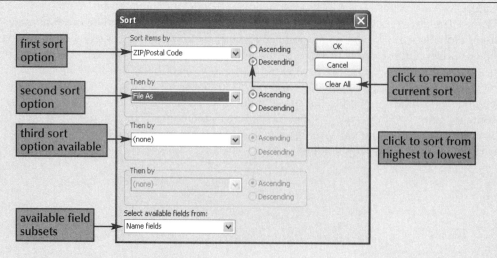

> **6.** Click the **OK** button. Because you selected a field that is not visible in the current view, Outlook gives you the option of customizing the view by adding the ZIP/ Postal Code field.

> **7.** Click the **No** button. The Group By, Filter, and Sort settings in the Customize View dialog box show how the contacts will be organized: ZIP/Postal Code (descending), File As (ascending).

> **8.** Click the **OK** button. Only the four contacts assigned to the Members category appear in the folder, in descending order by ZIP code (even though you can't see the ZIP/Postal Code field), and then alphabetical order by the File As name.

Felicia asks you to send a letter to all LinkUp members, informing them of the latest automobiles being added to the fleet. Because you want to send the letter to only the members, you can use the filtered view. The sort order you selected will enable you to more easily match the printed letters to their prepared envelopes. You'll create the letter with Word.

Creating a Word Mail Merge from Outlook

One of the most common activities businesses perform is to create one message and then send it to a large group of people by mail, fax, or e-mail. The trick to making people read these messages is to include a bit of personal information in each. If you send the message to your contacts or a distribution list, each person would receive the same message without any unique information. If you want to personalize each copy, you need to perform a mail merge.

Understanding Mail Merge

Mail merge is the process of combining a document file with a data file. A **document file** is the file that contains the standard text, such as the body of a letter in a Word document (called a main document in Word). A **data file** is a list of variable information, such as recipient names and addresses in an Outlook contact list (called a **data source** in Word). To specify what information to include in the document file from the data file, you insert **merge fields**, special codes that identify the variable information that should appear in that location. The letter you will create for Felicia will combine a standard message in a Word document with variable name and address information from your contact list.

| **Merging Outlook and a Word Document**

- Sort and filter the contacts you want to use.
- Click Tools on the menu bar, and then click Mail Merge.
- Click the All contacts in current view option button, and then click the All contact fields option button.
- Browse for an existing document file or create a new one.
- Click the Document type list arrow, and then click the document option you want.
- Click the Merge to list arrow, and then click the output option you want.
- Click the OK button in the Mail Merge Contacts dialog box.
- Type the standard text as needed in the Word document, using Word's editing and formatting features.
- Use the buttons on the Mail Merge toolbar to insert the appropriate merge fields at the location of the insertion point in the Word document.
- Click the Save button on the Standard toolbar to save the document file.
- If necessary, click the View Merged Data button on the Mail Merge toolbar to preview the final letters.
- Click the Merge to New Document button on the Mail Merge toolbar (*or* click the Merge to Printer button *or* click the Merge to E-mail button and then click the OK button).
- Click the Save button to save the merged documents.

You'll start to create the letter to LinkUp members by specifying the mail merge document file, data file, document type, and output option.

Creating the Form Letter

When you start the mail merge process from Outlook, you determine whether to include every contact field available in Outlook or only those visible in the current view. You also choose which contacts to include in the merge—all contacts in the current view, selected contacts in the current view, or a filtered contact list. For the LinkUp letter, you'll use the filtered contact list as the data file so that you include only members, not vendors or LinkUp employees.

After you indicate which contacts to use for the data file, then you specify whether you want to create a new document for the mail merge or use an existing one. In this case, Felicia already created the letter.

Next, you select the type of document you want to create and the final output. The main document types—form letters, mailing labels, envelopes, and catalog—and the output options—new document, printer, and e-mail—are the same as those available in Word. Each document type creates a different format: the Form letters document type combines standard text with merge fields to create correspondence; the Mailing labels document type accesses Word templates for standard adhesive labels sold by Avery and other companies; the Envelopes document type lets you select from standard mailing envelope sizes; and the Catalog document type provides a way to create lists of certain data, such as a list of names and fax numbers. The output options for all four types provide the option of creating a file, a hard copy, or a message.

To create a mail merge form letter:

▶ 1. Click **Tools** on the menu bar, and then click **Mail Merge**. The Mail Merge Contacts dialog box opens. See Figure 2-43.

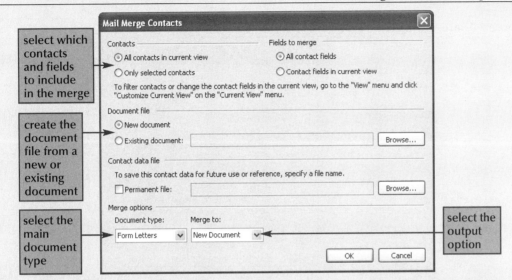

The labels on the figure read:
- select which contacts and fields to include in the merge
- create the document file from a new or existing document
- select the main document type
- select the output option

Trouble? If a dialog box opens, indicating that you must install Word to use this feature, then you do not have Word installed. Click the OK button in the dialog box. You can read but not perform the rest of the steps in this section.

The data file for this mail merge is the filtered contact list with access to all the available fields for each contact.

▶ 2. Click the **All contacts in current view** option button if it is not already selected, and then click the **All contact fields** option button if it is not already selected.

For this mail merge, you'll edit the letter that Felicia started rather than creating a new letter.

▶ 3. Click the **Existing document** option button, and then click the **Browse** button.

▶ 4. Double-click the **LinkUp Letter** document located in the **Tutorial.02\Tutorial** folder included with your Data Files. Outlook opens and verifies the document file.

You want a form letter that you will save to a file.

▶ 5. Verify that **Form Letters** is in the Document type list box in the Merge options area, and then verify that **New Document** is in the Merge to list box.

▶ 6. Click the **OK** button. Because a distribution list cannot be used in a merge, a dialog box opens, indicating that the LinkUp Members distribution list will not be included.

▶ 7. Click the **OK** button in the dialog box. Outlook exports the contacts and Word opens so you can finish the form letter.

Once the document file opens in Word, you can enter the appropriate merge fields where you want to insert variable information. The current date should appear on the letter below the WordArt logo for LinkUp. The Mail Merge toolbar in Word provides all the tools you need to finish the form letter. As you insert merge fields, you also need to type any punctuation and spaces that should appear between fields.

To insert merge fields in a form letter:

▶ **1.** Click in the second blank line below the date, and then click the **Insert Address Block** button 📄 on the Mail Merge toolbar. The Insert Address Block dialog box opens so you can select the format and contents of the inside address. See Figure 2-44.

Figure 2-44 ▶ Insert Address Block dialog box

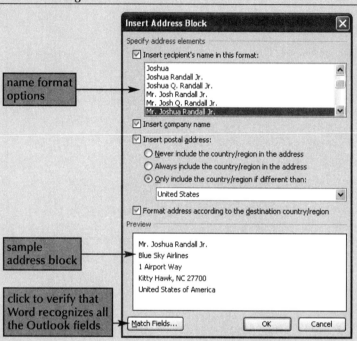

name format options

sample address block

click to verify that Word recognizes all the Outlook fields

▶ **2.** Verify that the dialog box selections match those shown in Figure 2-44, and then click the **Match Fields** button. The Match Fields dialog box opens so you can verify that Word recognizes the appropriate Outlook fields from which to obtain the address data. See Figure 2-45.

Figure 2-45 ▶ Match Fields dialog box

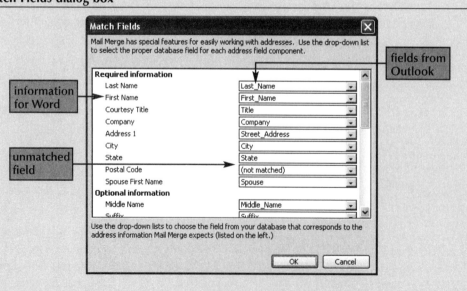

fields from Outlook

information for Word

unmatched field

Trouble? If ZIPPostal_Code appears in the Postal Code list box, then the Word field is already matched to the Outlook field. Continue with Step 4.

The Postal Code field is not matched, so you need to select the appropriate Outlook field in order to include that data. You'll select a field for this component

▶ **3.** Click the **Postal Code** list arrow in the Required information area to display a list of all the available Outlook fields, scroll to the end of the list, and then click **ZIPPostal_Code**.

▶ **4.** Click the **OK** button to close the Match Fields dialog box, and then click the **OK** button to close the Insert Address Block dialog box.

Next, you'll insert a field for the salutation.

▶ **5.** Select **Dear**, and then click the **Insert Greeting Line** button 📄 on the Mail Merge toolbar. The Greeting Line dialog box opens so you can select the format for the salutation. See Figure 2-46.

Greeting Line dialog box ◀ Figure 2-46

▶ **6.** Verify that the dialog box selections match those shown in Figure 2-46, click the **OK** button, and then press the **Enter** key. Figure 2-47 shows the letter with the inserted merge fields.

Figure 2-47 | Document file with merge fields

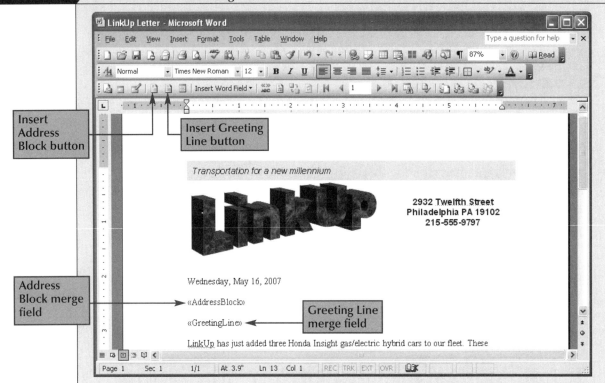

> **Trouble?** If you see characters between words or paragraph markers, the non-printing characters are not hidden. Displaying these characters is a matter of preference and will not affect your work. If you want to hide them, click the Show/Hide button ¶ on the Standard toolbar in the Word program window.

7. Press and hold the **Ctrl** key, press the **End** key, and then release both keys to quickly move the insertion point to the end of the letter.

8. Press the **Up arrow** key to position the insertion point on the blank line above Membership Services, and then type your name.

9. Click **File** on the menu bar, click **Save As** to open the Save As dialog box, and then save the document file as **New Cars Document File** in the **Tutorial.02\Tutorial** folder included with your Data Files.

10. Press and hold the **Ctrl** key, press the **Home** key, and then release both keys to quickly move the insertion point to the beginning of the letter.

With the data file specified and the document file saved, you're ready to perform the merge.

Merging the Letter and Contacts

You can merge the letter with all of your contacts or with a filtered set of contacts. Before you merge the document file and the data file, you should preview how the letters will look. It is a good idea to view the merged data and document to ensure that all the contact information appears in the letters as you expected. If you have an extremely large data file, you may want to spot check the letters rather than view each one.

Although you already specified the merge option as new document in Outlook, you have a chance to change this option when you actually merge the letter and contacts. With buttons on the Word Mail Merge toolbar, you can select to merge to a new document, to the printer, or to e-mail. You want to leave the merge option as new document.

To merge the letter and the contacts:

1. Click the **View Merged Data** button 🔳 on the Mail Merge toolbar. The merge fields are replaced by actual data. See Figure 2-48.

Preview of the letter merged with data ◀ **Figure 2-48**

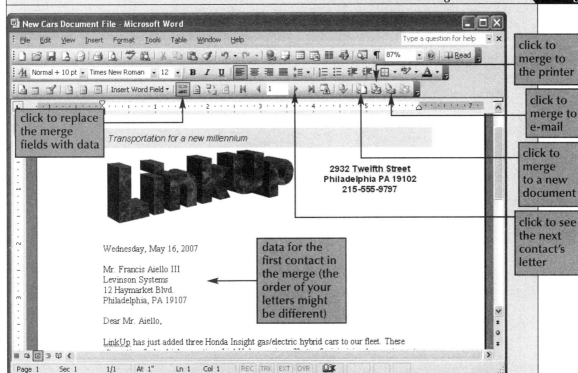

Trouble? If you see a different contact name in the inside address, your letter order might be different.

2. Read the letter to verify the data, and then click the **Next Record** button ▶ on the Mail Merge toolbar to move to the second letter.

3. Read the second letter to verify the data, click the **Next Record** button ▶ on the Mail Merge toolbar, and then read the third letter.

4. Click the **View Merged Data** button 🔳 on the Mail Merge toolbar when you have reviewed the third letter. The merge fields again appear.

   Because everything looks okay, you'll perform the merge.

5. Click the **Merge to New Document** button 🔳 on the Mail Merge toolbar. The Merge to New Document dialog box opens so you can verify the settings.

6. Click the **All** option button, if necessary, and then click the **OK** button.

A new file opens with the merged document and contact information. Each letter appears on its own page, so this document has three pages. You'll save the letters, and then you'll preview and print them.

7. Click the **Save** button 🔲 on the Standard toolbar and then save the merged document as **New Cars Letters** in the **Tutorial.02\Tutorial** folder included with your Data Files.

8. Click the **Print Preview** button 🔍 on the Standard toolbar to view the letters before printing them. See Figure 2-49.

Figure 2-49 ▶ **Merged letters in Print Preview**

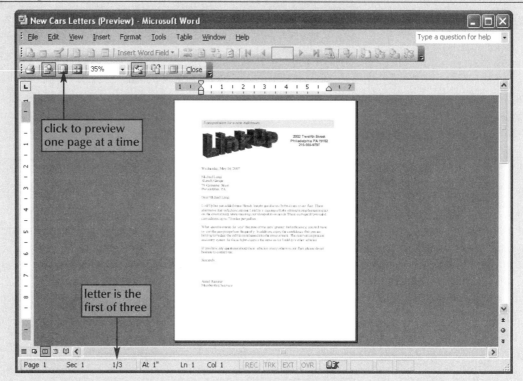

click to preview one page at a time

letter is the first of three

Trouble? If you see more than one letter, Print Preview is set to display multiple pages of a document. Click the One Page button on the Print Preview toolbar.

9. Scroll through all the letters, and then click the **Print** button 🖨 on the Print Preview toolbar to print all the letters.

10. Click the **Close** button on the Print Preview toolbar, and then click the **Close** button ⊠ on the Word title bar for each document to exit Word, saving changes to the **New Cars Document File** document.

As you can see, writing a letter to one contact or many is a fairly simple task.

Removing Customizations and Deleting Items

Once you're done with a particular organization or modified view, it is a good practice to return that view to its default settings. This ensures that you see all the available items each time. Also, you should remove any contacts that are outdated and that you no longer need. This keeps your contact list current and relevant.

Removing a Filter and Sort

Now that you've created the letters for the contacts in the Members category, you can remove the filter to redisplay all the contacts and reset the default sort for the view.

To remove a filter and a sort:

▶ 1. Click the **Customize Current View** link in the Current View pane in the Navigation Pane. The Customize View dialog box opens.

▶ 2. Click the **Filter** button to open the Filter dialog box, click the **Clear All** button, and then click the **OK** button. The filter is set to Off.

▶ 3. Click the **Sort** button to open the Sort dialog box, click the **Clear All** button, and then click the **OK** button. The sort is set to None.

▶ 4. Click the **OK** button. Outlook returns the view to its default sort and filter settings.

▶ 5. Click the **Address Cards** option button in the Current View pane in the Navigation Pane to return to the default Contacts view.

Before finishing, you'll delete any items you have created and stored in Outlook.

Deleting Categories from the Master Category List

You'll return the Master Category List to its default by removing the categories you added. When you delete a category, it is removed from the Master Category List, but it still appears assigned in the existing items, although it is not available to add to new items. You could also reset the list, which removes all the custom categories that have been added to the Master Category List.

You'll remove the Employees, Members, and Vendors categories from the Master Category List.

To delete categories:

▶ 1. Click **Edit** on the menu bar, and then click **Categories**. The Categories dialog box opens.

▶ 2. Click the **Master Category List** button. The Master Category List dialog box opens.

You can remove categories by selecting them in the Master Category List dialog box, and then clicking the Delete button. You could also click the Reset button, which returns the master category list to its original contents.

▶ 3. Click **Employees** in the list, and then click the **Delete** button to remove the category.

▶ 4. Click **Members** in the list, press and hold the **Ctrl** key, click **Vendors** in the list, release the **Ctrl** key, and then click the **Delete** button. The two categories are removed from the Master Category List.

▶ 5. Click the **OK** button in the Master Category List dialog box.

▶ 6. Click the **OK** button in the Categories dialog box.

Deleting Contacts and Other Outlook Items

Before you finish up, you'll remove any contacts, calendar items, and e-mail messages you created while working in Outlook. Remember to use the Ctrl key or the Shift key to select multiple items.

To delete contacts and e-mails:

1. Select the six contact cards you created in this tutorial, including the distribution list, and then press the **Delete** key. The contacts move to the Deleted Items folder.

2. Display the **Inbox** folder, select the three messages you received, and then press the **Delete** key to move the messages to the Deleted Items folder.

3. Display the **Sent Items** folder, and then delete the three messages you sent.

4. Display the **Calendar** folder, click **View** on the menu bar, point to **Arrange By**, point to **Current View**, and then click **Events**. The Calendar main window shows any scheduled events.

5. Click the **Francis L. Aiello III's Birthday** event, and then press the **Delete** key to move the event to the Deleted Items folder.

6. Click **View** on the menu bar, point to **Arrange By**, point to **Current View**, and then click **Day/Week/Month** to switch back to the Calendar view that shows the current date.

7. Click the **Folder List** button in the Navigation Pane, right-click the **Deleted Items** folder, click **Empty "Deleted Items" Folder** on the shortcut menu, and then click the **Yes** button to confirm the permanent deletion.

You have created, edited, and organized LinkUp contacts, as well as communicated with the contacts by sending individual e-mails and letters and personalized form letters. Felicia appreciates your help in keeping LinkUp members and vendors current and informed.

Review

Session 2.2 Quick Check

1. List three common activities you can perform with contacts.
2. What is the Letter Wizard?
3. What does a red flag icon next to a contact name indicate?
4. Describe what happens when you a filter a view.
5. Explain the difference between ascending order and descending order in a sort.
6. What happens when you send a letter to a distribution list versus when you create a mail merge letter?
7. Explain the difference between a document file and a data file in a mail merge.
8. Define merge fields.

Review

Tutorial Summary

In this tutorial, you created and edited contacts. You displayed the contacts in different views, printed your contact list, and grouped contacts into a distribution list to receive the same e-mail. You forwarded and received contact information by e-mail. You also learned different ways to work with a contact list. You communicated with a contact via e-mail and a printed letter. You organized the contacts by categories, filtered the contacts to view only LinkUp members, and changed the sort order of the filtered list. You then merged the filtered contact list and a letter Felicia wrote to create personalized form letters. Finally, you removed the filter and sort, reset the Master Category List, and deleted contacts and other items you created.

Key Terms

Address Book	data source	link
ascending order	descending order	mail merge
card view	distribution list	merge field
category	document file	table view
contact	field	vCard
contact card	filter	view
data file	Letter Wizard	

Practice

Practice the skills you learned in the tutorial using the same case scenario.

Review Assignments

Data Files needed for the Review Assignments: Frieda Cohn.vcf, Vendor Letter.doc

Felicia Rogert, founder and president of LinkUp, asks you to compile a contact list of the vendors the Philadelphia-based car sharing company uses. After creating the contacts, you'll write a letter to Felicia informing her of your status in locating a new mechanic. Then, you'll create a form letter to all the current vendors, asking them for referrals.

1. Display the Contacts folder, and then click the New button on the Standard toolbar to open a Contact window.
2. Enter the following contact: name "Joe Runningbear"; job title "Mechanic"; company name "Ace Engine Care"; business phone "215-555-8700 x12"; business fax "215-555-8763"; business mailing address "17 University Ave., Philadelphia PA 19287"; Assistant's name "Charley Boyd"; click the Save and New button.
3. Enter the following contact: name "Ann Nocella"; job title "Agent"; company name "A Plus Insurance"; business phone "215-555-3100 x645"; business fax "215-555-3101"; business mailing address "2949 Broad St., Philadelphia PA 19157"; Manager's name "Eva Lorenson"; click the Save and New button.
4. Enter the following contact: name "Walt Camden"; company name "Shiny Cars Detailing"; business phone "215-555-6741"; business mailing address "841 Carpenter St., Philadelphia PA 19157"; click the Save and New button.
5. Enter the following contact: name "Marya Little"; job title "Agent"; company name "Best Tires"; business phone "215-555-4150"; business fax "215-555-4157"; business mailing address "Callow Hill Blvd., Philadelphia PA 19107"; click the Save and New button.
6. Enter the following contact: name "Michael Lang"; job title "Mechanic"; company name "Aldrich Garage"; business phone "215-555-8715"; business fax "215-555-2145"; business mailing address "78 Carpenter St., Philadelphia PA 19109"; nickname "Mike"; click the Save and New button.

7. Enter the following contact: name "Felicia Rogert"; job title "President"; company name "LinkUp"; business phone "215-555-9797"; business fax "215-555-9701"; pager "215-555-2157"; business mailing address "2932 12th St., Philadelphia PA 19102"; your e-mail address (fix the Display as text); click the Save and Close button.

8. Add the "Vendors" and "Employees" categories to the Master Category List. Assign the Vendors category to all the contacts you created.

9. View the contacts as Detailed Address Cards in the Contacts main window.

10. Edit Marya Little's contact card to add "215-555-6110" as her mobile phone number.

11. View the contacts By Category, and then change Felicia Rogert from the Vendors category to the Employees category.

12. Create a distribution list called "LinkUp Suppliers" that includes all suppliers with a fax number (there should be four). Assign the category "Vendors" to the distribution list.

13. Switch to Detailed Address Card view, and then print the entire contact list in Card Style without any blank forms.

14. Flag Felicia Rogert's contact card with a follow-up flag using the "Send E-mail" text and no due date.

15. Send a new e-mail message to Felicia Rogert with the subject "Frieda Cohn's contact" and no message; attach the vCard file **Frieda Cohn** located in the **Tutorial.02\Review** folder included with your Data Files. (*Hint:* Click the Insert File button on the message toolbar.)

16. Download the message, drag the vCard attachment icon to the Contacts folder, and then save and close the new contact card.

17. Change the flag for Felicia Rogert's contact card to Completed.

18. Write a new letter to Felicia Rogert, using the Letter Wizard in Outlook, with the Elegant Letter page design and a Modified block letter style. Include a date line in the format of August 24, 2007. Select the informal salutation "Dear Felicia," and make sure your name and address appear as the sender. Use "Best wishes" as the closing. The signature block should include your name and "LinkUp" as the company.

19. Type the following as the letter body: "I have been researching garages that service the new hybrid cars to add to our vendor pool. As you suggested, I will be sending a letter to our current vendors asking for referrals. I expect that we should find someone within the next few weeks."

20. Save the document as **Felicia Rogert Letter** in the **Tutorial.02\Review** folder included with your Data Files, and then close the letter and exit Word.

21. Filter the contact list to display only the Vendors category.

22. Sort the list in ascending order by Business Address Postal Code, selecting the available field from the Address fields, and then in descending order by File As selected from the Frequently-used fields. Do not add any fields to the current view.

23. Select all the contacts except the distribution list. (*Hint:* Press the Ctrl+A keys to select all the contacts, press and hold the Ctrl key, click the LinkUp Suppliers contact to deselect it, and then release the Ctrl key.)

24. Start the mail merge process. Set up the mail merge to use only selected contacts and all contact fields. Use the existing document **Vendor Letter** located in the **Tutorial.02\Review** folder included with your Data Files as the document file. Create form letters that merge to a new document.

25. Click in the second blank line below the date, insert the Address Block merge field, and then match any fields that do not match. Click after "Dear," press the spacebar, and then insert the Greeting Line merge field using "(none)" in the first text box in the Greeting Line dialog box, and then the first name followed by a colon. Type your name above "Vendor Services" at the end of the letter.

26. Use the Save As command on the File menu to save the document file as **Vendor Referral Document File** in the **Tutorial.02\Review** folder included with your Data Files.

27. Click the View Merged Data button on the Mail Merge toolbar to verify that the business address and name for each contact appears correctly.

28. Merge the letters to a new document, and then save the document as **Vendor Referral Letters** in the **Tutorial.02\Review** folder included with your Data Files.

29. Preview and print the only the first letter, and then close Word, saving changes as needed.

30. Remove the filter and sort from the current view, delete the Employees and Vendors categories from the Master Category List, delete the contacts you created for these Review Assignments, delete the messages in the Inbox and Sent Items folder that you sent and received in these Review Assignments, and then empty the Deleted Items folder.

Case Problem 1

Ulvang Corporation   The director of human resources at Ulvang Corporation manages all employee communication with Outlook. The director has asked you to enter additional employees as contacts in Outlook, and then send a letter to one employee informing him of an earned comp day and send an e-mail to another employee confirming her scheduled appointment. The director also asks you to prepare mailing labels for all the employees in preparation for mailing them the updated company employee manual.

1. Display the Contacts folder.

2. Double-click the Contacts main window to open a blank Contact window. (*Hint:* Double-click a blank part of the background (not a contact card) in the main window.)

3. Create the following contact: name "Cicely Tivo"; job title "Sales Rep"; company name "Ulvang Corporation"; business phone "203-555-9000 x12"; business fax "203-555-9701"; business mailing address "9 Main St., Norwalk CT 06851"; your e-mail address (fix the Display as text box); category "Staff" (create a new category); click File on the menu bar and then click Save to save the contact and leave it open.

4. Click Actions on the menu bar, and then click New Contact from Same Company. A new contact card opens with duplicate information except the name, title, e-mail, and categories fields.

Apply

Apply the skills you learned in the tutorial to facilitate employee communication by setting up and using contacts for a human resources department.

Explore

5. Enter "Jack Lipson" as the name, "Sales Rep" as the job title, change the phone extension to "x13," assign "Staff" as the category, and then save and both close contacts cards.

6. Create the following new contacts from the same company, saving and closing each contact card. (*Hint:* Click a contact card whose information you want to duplicate to select it, click Actions on the menu bar, and then click New Contact from Same Company.)

   - your name, Sales Rep, x38, Staff
   - Erin Gleason, Sales Rep, x45, Staff
   - Lyle Nobless, Sales Rep, x47, Staff
   - Parker Karlen, Sales Rep, x32, Staff
   - Ross Bookland, Customer Rep, x22, Staff
   - Pamela Treemont, Customer Rep, x17, Staff

7. Add a flag for follow-up with no due date to Cicely's contact card.

8. Use the Letter Wizard in Outlook to write a letter to Ross, informing him that the overtime he worked during the latest product launch entitles him to a comp day. Use the date line, page design and letter style, salutation, and closing of your choice. Use your information as the sender name and address.

9. Save the letter as **Ross Letter** in the **Tutorial.02\Cases** folder included with your Data Files, print the letter, and then exit Word.

10. Send an e-mail message to Cicely with the subject "Tuesday Appointment" and the message "Don't forget that you have an appointment next Tuesday at 10 am with Human Resources to arrange your maternity leave. If you need to reschedule, please let us know. Thank you." Press the Enter key twice, and then type your name.

11. Download the message, if necessary, and then change the flag on Cicely's contact card from follow-up to Completed.

12. Organize the contacts by category, and then filter the view to display only the sales reps. (*Hint:* On the Contacts tab, search for "Sales Rep" in the Frequently-used text fields.)

13. Create a mail merge using all contacts in current view and all contact fields. Create a new document, set the document type as Mailing Labels, and merge to a new document.

14. Click the OK button in the dialog box that opens, and then click the Setup button in the Mail Merge Helper dialog box.

15. Select Avery standard labels, Product number "5160 – Address," and then click the OK button in the Label Options dialog box.

16. Click the Main document Edit button, click the Mailing Label document, insert the Address Block merge field in the first label, verifying that the fields match, and then click the Propagate Labels button on the Mail Merge toolbar.

17. Merge the labels to a new document, save the labels document as **Ulvang Mailing Labels** in the **Tutorial.02\Cases** folder included with your Data Files, and then print and close the document.

18. Save the document file as **Ulvang Document File** in the **Tutorial.02\Cases** folder included with your Data Files, and then close the document and exit Word.

19. Remove the filter you set, switch to Detailed Address Cards view, and then sort the contacts in descending order by the File As name field.

20. Print the entire contact list in Card Style, removing the blank contact card forms, if necessary.
21. Remove the sort from the Contacts folder, delete the custom category from the Master Category List, delete the contacts you created in this Case Problem from the Contacts folder, delete the message you created in this Case Problem in the Inbox and Sent Items folders, and then empty the Deleted Items folder.

Case Problem 2

Data File needed for this Case Problem: Natalie.doc

Wilmington Bank   Wilmington Bank has many customers who reside at the same address and share a telephone number. Carey Lincoln, executive vice president, wants to create separate contact cards for each customer, but connect those that share a residence and phone. Carey asks you to enter several contacts and connect related ones.

1. Display the Folder List, click Contacts in the Folder List to display the Contacts main window, and then create the following contact: name "Natalie Thiboau"; home phone "302-555-1574"; mobile phone "302-555-7874"; home mailing address "92 Park Street, Wilmington DE 19885"; category "Bank Customer"; spouse "Pierre"; save and close the contact.
2. Copy the contact by holding down the Ctrl key while you drag the contact card from the Contacts main window to Contacts in the Folder List, and then release the mouse button.
3. Switch to Detailed Address Cards view, edit the name on one of the Natalie Thiboau contact cards to "Pierre Thiboau" from within the main window, and then click outside the contact card to save it.
4. Open the Pierre Thiboau contact card and change the spouse name to "Natalie."
5. Assign Pierre as a contact for Natalie's card. Open Natalie's card, click the Contacts button on the General tab, click Contacts in the Look in list box, click Pierre Thiboau in the Items list, click the OK button, and then save and close Natalie's contact card.
6. Open Pierre's contact card to verify that Outlook assigned Natalie as the contact for Pierre, and then close the contact card.
7. Copy Pierre's contact card using the Ctrl+drag method you used in Step 2; change the name to "Channing Thiboau" and delete the spouse name from the card; save and close the contact card.
8. Create the following contact: name "Ari Finley"; home phone "302-555-8214"; home mailing address "7 Innsbruck Avenue, Wilmington DE 19885"; category "Bank Customer"; save and close the contact.
9. Create the following contact: name "Orlando Parkes"; home phone "302-555-3659"; home mailing address "23 Great Way Blvd., Wilmington DE 19885"; category "Bank Customer"; save and close the contact.
10. Print the entire contact list in Card Style, removing the blank contact cards forms at the end, if necessary.
11. Save each contact card you created as a vCard file in the **Tutorial.02\Cases** folder included with your Data Files. (*Hint:* Select the contact, click File on the menu bar, click Save As, change the Save as type, use the contact name as the filename, and then click the Save button.)

Challenge

Extend the skills you learned in the tutorial to create contact cards for bank customers and link related customer contact cards.

Explore

Explore

Explore

12. Filter the contacts to display only the two contacts related to Natalie Thiboau. Click the Advanced tab in the Filter dialog box, click the Field button, point to Frequently-used fields, click Contacts, click the Condition list arrow, click is (exactly), type "Natalie Thiboau" in the Value text box, and then click the Add to List button. Click the OK button in each dialog box.

13. Create a mail merge using all contacts in the current view and all contact fields. Select the existing document **Natalie** in the **Tutorial.02\Cases** folder included with your Data Files, select Catalog as the document type, and merge to a new document.

14. On the blank line at the top of the document, insert the Full_Name merge field, press the Tab key, insert the Home_Phone merge field, and then press the Enter key. (*Hint:* Click the Insert Merge Field button on the Mail Merge toolbar.)

15. View the merged data, and then merge to a new document. Type your name on a blank line below the catalog in the merged document.

16. Save the merged document as **Natalie Contacts Merged** in the **Tutorial.02\Cases** folder included with your Data Files, print the Natalie Contacts Merged document, and then close it.

17. Save the data file as **Natalie Data File** in the **Tutorial.02\Cases** folder included with your Data Files, and then exit Word, saving changes as needed.

18. Remove the filter from the view, delete the custom category from the Master Category List, delete the contacts you created in this Case Problem, and then empty the Deleted Items folder.

Case Problem 3

There are no Data Files needed for this Case Problem.

Mobley Collection Agency   Mobley Collection Agency (MCA) is hired by other companies to track down and obtain immediate payments from delinquent accounts. MCA employees contact late payers and arrange a mutually agreeable payment schedule. MCA retains 25% of all monies it collects as the fee for the services rendered. Currently, MCA is entering contacts in Outlook for nonpaying companies.

1. Create the following contact: company "Wagley Group"; business phone "650-555-2600 x145"; business mailing address "3873 University Way, Palo Alto CA 94301"; category "Phone Calls"; save and close the contact.

2. Create the following contact: company "Xpert Systems"; business phone "916-555-8540 x11"; business mailing address "83 Kilander Place, Gold River CA 95670"; category "Phone Calls"; save and close the contact.

3. Create the following contact: company "Music Miracles"; business phone "415-555-6000 x35"; business mailing address "39 Blake Street, Suite 4, Mill Valley CA 94941"; category "Phone Calls"; save and close the contact.

4. Create the following contact: company "EZ Training Workshops"; business mailing address "9273 Ethelanne Street, Berkeley CA 94701"; category "Making Payment"; save and close the contact.

5. Create the following contact: company "Connections"; business mailing address "56 Lake Blvd., Mill Valley CA 94941"; category "Making Payment"; save and close the contact.

6. Create the following contact: company "Desktop Designs"; business mailing address "83 Delores Street, Suite 9374, San Francisco CA 94102"; category "Making Payment"; save and close the contact.

7. View the contacts by category, and then print all rows of the contact list in Table Style. (*Hint:* Make sure that each category group is expanded; if the contacts are not visible on-screen, only the group heading appears on the printout.)

8. Forward all of the contacts in the Phone Calls category to your e-mail address using the subject "Phone Calls" and the message "We need to contact all these companies by telephone to encourage them to pay their outstanding bills immediately." Press the Enter key twice, and then type your name.

Explore ▶ 9. Forward as vCards all of the contacts in the Making Payment category to your e-mail address using the subject "Waiting" and the message "We need to contact all these companies by mail to make sure they have sent payment for their outstanding bills." Press the Enter key twice, and then type your name. (*Hint:* After selecting all the contacts in the category, click Actions on the menu bar, then click Forward as vCard.)

10. Send and receive the messages as needed.

11. Flag for follow-up all the contacts in both the Phone Calls and the Making Payment categories.

Explore ▶ 12. Filter the contacts to display only those with follow-up flags. (*Hint:* Click the Advanced tab in the Filter dialog box, click the Field button, point to Frequently-used fields, click Follow Up Flag, click the Condition list arrow, click is not empty, click the Add to List button, and then click the OK button.) This advanced filter enables you to set specific criteria by which to select contacts; this time you'll set a single criterion.

13. Change the follow-up flags for Wagley Group and Desktop Designs to Completed. These contacts remain visible.

14. Clear the follow-up flag for Xpert Systems and Connections by changing the flag to Unflagged. These contacts disappear from the filter.

Explore ▶ 15. Revise the filter to display only flagged contacts, not contacts with cleared or completed flags. (*Hint:* On the Advanced tab in the Filter dialog box, click the Remove button to move the filter criterion you set earlier to the edit boxes. Click the Field button, point to Frequently-used fields, click Flag Status, verify that equals appears in the Condition list box, click the Value list arrow, click Followup Flag, click the Add to List button, and then click the OK button.)

Explore ▶ 16. Add a second criterion to the filter so that only flagged contacts in the Making Payment category appear. (*Hint:* Open the Filter dialog box, add the Making Payment category to the filter from the More Choices tab as usual, leaving the other criterion on the Advanced tab.) Only the EZ Training Workshops contact in the Making Payment category that is flagged for follow-up appears in the main window.

17. Remove the filter, switch to Address Cards view, delete the custom category you added to the Master Category List, delete the contacts and any other items you created in this Case Problem, and then empty the Deleted Items folder.

Create

Create a form letter to send to all members of a fan club.

Case Problem 4

There are no Data Files needed for this Case Problem.

Fan Club   You are president of the fan club for your favorite movie star or sports figure. The fan club usually meets in a member's home once a month. The week before each meeting, you remind members of the upcoming meeting's date, time, and location. You just learned that a meeting of all the clubs around the world is scheduled next November. Rather than wait for the next meeting, you decide to send a personal letter to all members inviting them to attend the world meeting. You'll use Outlook to compile a list of the club members and keep in touch with them.

1. Create a contact card for yourself. Enter as much information about yourself as possible on the General and Details tabs. Save and close the card.

Explore

2. Save your contact information as a Rich Text Format file with your name as the file name, in the **Tutorial.02\Cases** folder included with your Data Files. (*Hint:* Select the contact, click File on the menu bar, click Save As, change the Save as type, type your name as the filename, and then click the Save button.)

3. Create five more contacts, entering a name, mailing address, phone number, and your e-mail address for each contact. Add each as a new contact anyway.

Explore

4. Click Tools on the menu bar, click Organize to open the Organize pane, and then click the Using Categories link. You'll use the Organize pane to create a new category and then assign it to each contact.

Explore

5. Type "Fan Club Members" in the Create a new category called text box, and then click the Create button.

Explore

6. Select each of the contacts you created (except the one for you), click the Add contacts selected below to list arrow, click Fan Club Members, if necessary, and then click the Add button. Click the Close button on the Organize pane title bar to close the Organize pane.

7. Select all the contacts you created, and then print the contact list in Memo Style. Do *not* start each contact on its own page and do *not* print attached files with items.

8. Filter the contact list to display only contacts assigned to the Fan Club Members category, sorted in ascending order by the File As field.

9. Start a mail merge letter using all contacts in current view (the filtered contact list) and all contact fields. Create a new document as the document file. Use form letters as the document type and merge to a new document.

10. Create a letter to send the members of your local fan club, inviting them to the international meeting of all the fan clubs. Include the appropriate merge fields to personalize the letter. Also include a description of the international meeting as well as the dates and location. End the letter with your name.

11. Save the document file as **Fan Club Document File** in the **Tutorial.02\Cases** folder included with your Data Files.

12. Merge the letter and the contacts to a new document, and then save the form letters as **Fan Club Letters** in the **Tutorial.02\Cases** folder included with your Data Files.

13. Print the letters, and then exit Word, saving documents as needed.

14. Delete the custom category you added to the Master Category List, delete the contacts you created in this Case Problem, and then empty the Deleted Items folder.

Quick Check Answers

Session 2.1

1. False; a contact can be a person or an organization.
2. The File as name specifies how your contacts should be ordered in the Contacts main window.
3. Outlook opens the Duplicate Contact Detected dialog box, enabling you to add the contact anyway, combine the new contact with an existing contact, or open the existing contact to edit it.
4. Categories make it simple to locate, organize, and group similar types of contacts.
5. Views change the way information is displayed in the main window, such as arranged as contact cards or grouped by category.
6. A distribution list is one entry that stores a related group of contacts to whom you frequently send the same messages.
7. Click the first contact, press and hold the Shift key, and then click the last contact.
8. Drag the contact card attachment icon from the e-mail message to the Contacts folder in the Navigation Pane or the Folders List.

Session 2.2

1. Any three of the following: send an e-mail, write a letter, schedule an appointment or a meeting, assign a task
2. A tool that walks you through the letter-writing process in Word when you write a letter to a specific contact or distribution list.
3. A red flag indicates that the contact has been marked for follow-up on some activity.
4. The main window displays only those items in a folder that match certain criteria, such as contacts assigned to the Key Customer category.
5. Ascending order arranges items alphabetically (A to Z), chronologically (earliest to latest), or numerically (lowest to highest). Descending order reverses the sort ascending order—Z to A, latest to earliest, or highest to lowest.
6. A distribution list letter is the same for all contacts, whereas a mail merge letter can be personalized for each contact.
7. A document file contains the standard text and merge fields, such as a letter in Word; a data file is the list of variable information, such as an Outlook contact list.
8. Merge fields are special codes that identify the variable information that should appear in that location.

Objectives

Session 3.1
- Create, customize, organize, send, and print notes
- Create a task list with one-time and recurring tasks
- Organize tasks by categories and views
- Assign a task to someone else
- Respond to a task request

Session 3.2
- Schedule appointments and events in the Calendar
- Print a calendar
- Plan and schedule a meeting
- Respond to a meeting request
- Check off completed tasks
- Schedule an online meeting
- Save your calendar as a Web page
- Delete notes, tasks, categories, appointments, events, and meetings

Planning Tasks and Schedules

Arranging a Meeting to Create a Company Web Site

Case

Wertheimer Accounting

Wertheimer Accounting is an accounting firm in Austin, Texas, that provides tax preparation as well as bookkeeping, payroll, and financial consulting services to local businesses. Established in 1998 by Lisa Wertheimer, the firm has developed a reputation as being dependable, affordable, reliable, and dedicated to working with smaller businesses. Lisa and her four associates prepare their clients' business and individual income tax returns; record, analyze, and verify financial documents for their clients; and provide advice about the tax advantages and disadvantages of certain business decisions.

Lisa's firm uses accounting software packages to summarize transactions for financial records and organize data for financial analysis. These accounting packages greatly reduce the amount of tedious, manual work associated with data and record keeping. In addition, all members of the firm use Outlook to communicate with clients, create their task lists, coordinate their schedules, and plan meetings to ensure that clients' needs are met in a timely way.

Lisa wants to expand the firm's client list. She plans to create a company Web site as a way to communicate with current clients and to attract new clients. She wants the site to include background about the firm—its history, goals, services, and staff—as well as tax-related content, such as a monthly Tax Tips section, a Latest Laws section, important tax dates, and other useful information. She intends to have a staff meeting to discuss the content.

In this tutorial, you'll jot down notes about the Web site and other tasks, update and organize a to-do list, and delegate a task. Then you'll schedule time to complete tasks and make appointments in the Calendar. Finally, you'll plan a meeting to discuss the Web site, and save your calendar as a Web page.

Student Data Files

There are no student Data Files needed for this tutorial.

Taking Notes

Outlook comes with a never-ending electronic pad stored in the Notes folder. Rather than plaster your desk and monitor with colored squares of paper, you can easily jot down and organize your ideas, questions, and reminders on electronic **notes**. You can leave a note open on the screen as you work or you can close it, knowing that it will never get buried under a file or inadvertently tossed in the garbage. Like other Outlook items, notes are saved automatically.

Using the New Button

The New button on the Standard toolbar creates the most logical item for the open folder. For example, clicking the New button in the Inbox folder creates a new e-mail message, and clicking it in the Contacts folder creates a new contact. The button's icon and the ScreenTip remind you which item it will create. You can use the button's list arrow to select any new Outlook item, regardless of which folder is displayed. In this way, you can create a note when the idea hits or a new contact when you receive the information, such as during a phone call, without a lot of extra mouse clicks, no matter which folder you are working with at the time.

Before you create any notes, you'll use the New button to create a contact card for yourself without changing folders.

To create a contact card:

1. Click the **New** button list arrow on the Standard toolbar, and then click **Contact**. A Contact window opens.

2. Enter contact information about yourself, including your name and e-mail address.

3. Save and close the contact card.

   Trouble? If the Duplicate Contact Detected dialog box opens, you already have a contact with the same name or e-mail address. Merge the two contacts or add as a new contact anyway, as needed.

Creating and Editing Notes

Even though clicking the New button on the Standard toolbar while in the Notes folder creates a new note, you can create a note from any folder using the New button list arrow. You'll create several notes to remind you of the items for your calendar.

To create a note:

1. Click the **New** button list arrow on the Standard toolbar, and then click **Note**. A square, yellow note appears, labeled with the current date and time.

Trouble? If your note is not yellow or the date and time don't appear, then the Notes settings are different on your computer. Click the Close button ☒ in the upper-right corner of the note to close it. Click Tools on the menu bar, click Options, click the Preferences tab, and then click the Note Options button. If necessary, change the color to Yellow, the size to Medium, the font to 10 pt Comic Sans MS, and then click the OK button. Click the Other tab, click the Advanced Options button, click the When viewing Notes, show time and date check box in the Appearance options area to insert a check mark, and then click the OK button in each dialog box. Repeat Step 1.

▶ 2. Type **Web site ideas: tax preparation tips and little-known deductions** as the note text. As you type, text wraps within the note's width. If you enter a long note, the text would scroll vertically. See Figure 3-1.

Outlook note ◀ Figure 3-1

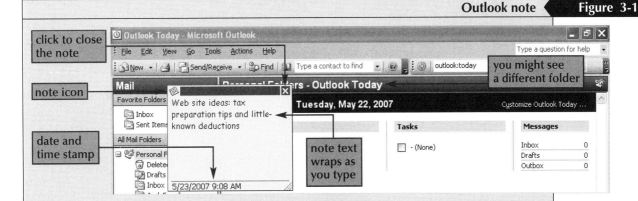

You can associate a note or any item with a contact. This enables you to find all items linked to a specific contact, no matter in which folder they are stored. You'll associate yourself as the contact for this note.

▶ 3. Click the **Note** icon 🖾 in the upper-left corner of the open note, and then click **Contacts**. The Contacts for Note dialog box opens.

▶ 4. Click the **Contacts** button in the Contacts for Note dialog box. The Select Contacts dialog box opens. See Figure 3-2.

Figure 3-2 ▶ Select Contacts dialog box

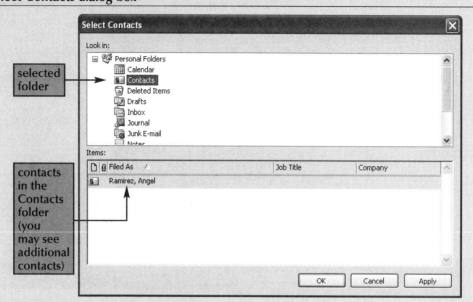

▶ **5.** Click your name in the Items list box, click the **OK** button, and then click the **Close** button to close the Contacts for Note dialog box. You are assigned as a contact for the note.

Notes remain open until you close them.

▶ **6.** Click the **Close** button ✕ in the upper-right corner of the note to close it.

The Notes main window displays an icon for each note you create along with the first few words of the note. It is helpful to type a few keywords in the first line of the note, such as "Web site ideas," so that you can know the note's content without having to open it.

To create additional notes:

▶ **1.** Click the **Notes** button 🔲 in the Navigation Pane to display the Notes folder. You can see the icon for the note you created in the Notes main window. See Figure 3-3.

Notes folder Figure 3-3

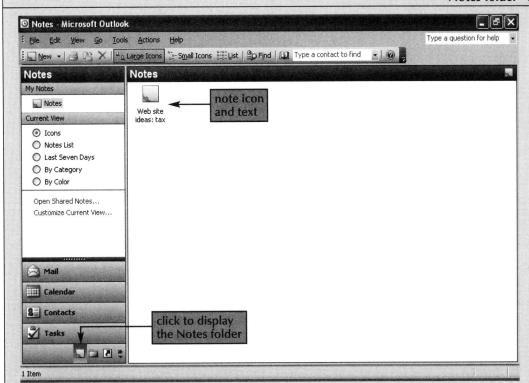

2. Click the **New** button on the Standard toolbar to create a new note.

3. Type **More Web site ideas: seasonal reminders for taxes; record-keeping hints; how to avoid audits; new tax rulings and laws** as the second note's text.

4. Assign yourself as the contact, and then close the note.

5. Create a third note with the text **Plan meeting about Web site**, do *not* assign a contact, and then close the note.

The Notes main window shows icons for the three notes you created.

Sometimes you might want to revise a note. You can edit the text in an open note, just as you can edit the text in any document.

To open and edit a note:

1. Double-click the **More Web site ideas** note to open it.

2. Double-click **taxes** to select the word, and then type **estimated payments**. The new text replaces the old.

3. Close the note.

Unlike with a paper pad and pen, when you edit the text in a note, the changes remain neat and legible. To make it easier to locate specific notes, you can assign categories to them.

Assigning Categories to Notes

You can classify your notes by assigning each one to a category, just as you did with contacts. Recall that a category is a keyword or phrase that you assign to an item to help organize and later locate and group related items, regardless of whether they are stored in the same folder. You can assign items to general categories from the Master Category List, such as Business and Personal, or to more specific categories that you add to the master list, such as Web Site and Payroll. You can assign as many categories as you like to an item.

Because you want to be able to organize your Outlook items related to the new Web site, you will create a category called "Web Site" and assign it to any notes, tasks, contacts, e-mail messages, and meetings related to creating and maintaining the company's Web site.

To assign a custom category to a note:

1. Right-click the **Plan meeting about Web site** note, and then click **Categories** on the shortcut menu. The Categories dialog box opens, showing all the available categories.

2. Click in the **Item(s) belong to these categories** list box, type **Web Site**, and then click the **Add to List** button. The category is added to the Master Category List.

3. Verify that the **Web Site** check box in the Available categories list contains a check mark.

4. Click the **OK** button. Like a contact, the category is not visible in the note.

5. Assign the **Web Site** category to the Web site ideas and More Web site ideas notes.

The three notes are assigned to the same category. You can add categories to an item from the Categories dialog box, the item's window, or a shortcut menu. You can remove a category from an item in these same locations.

Customizing the Look of Notes

You can customize your notes by changing their font, color, and size. Different colors are helpful for organizing your notes; for example, you can leave task notes as yellow and change informational notes to blue. Resizing notes enables you to display all the text in a large note or eliminate the excess space in a short note.

Reference Window | **Customizing a Note**

- Double-click the note to open it.
- Type new text and edit existing text as needed.
- Click the Note icon, point to Color, and then click the color you want (*or* right-click a closed note, point to Color on the shortcut menu, and then click a color).
- Drag any border of the note to resize the note.
- Click the Close button on the Note title bar to close the note.

You'll change the background color of the notes you created.

To change the color of notes:

▶ **1.** Right-click the **More Web site ideas** note, and then point to **Color** on the shortcut menu. The shortcut menu lists the five colors you can use for your notes—blue, green, pink, yellow, or white. See Figure 3-4.

Notes shortcut menu   Figure 3-4

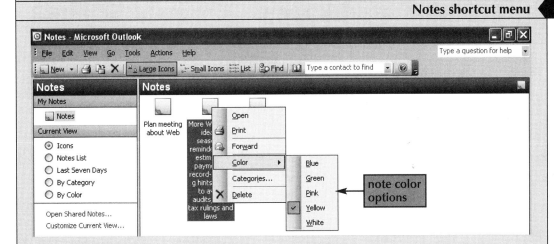

Because this is an informational note, you'll change it to blue.

▶ **2.** Click **Blue**, and then click outside the note to deselect it. The color of the note icon changes to blue.

▶ **3.** Right-click the **Web site ideas** note, point to **Color**, and then click **Blue**. The color of this note icon also changes to blue.

You can resize an open note by dragging from any border. The top and bottom edges change a note's height, whereas the left and right edges change a note's width. If you want to change both the height and width at once, you can drag the lower-right corner.

To resize a note:

▶ **1.** Double-click the **Plan meeting** note to open it.

▶ **2.** Point to the lower-right corner of the open note until the pointer changes to ↖↘.

▶ **3.** Drag the lower-right corner diagonally outward about two inches to expand the note height and width.

▶ **4.** Drag the lower-right corner diagonally inward so that the note text fits on one line and the bottom border is just below the word "Web site" to reduce the height and width, but do not release the mouse button. See Figure 3-5.

Figure 3-5 ▶ **Resized note**

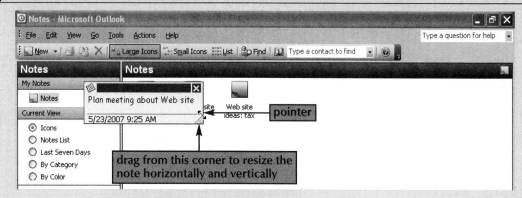

▶ **5.** Release the mouse button to resize the note.

▶ **6.** Close the note.

One advantage to keeping your notes in Outlook is that you can organize them in different ways to meet your needs.

Organizing Notes

From the Notes folder, you can organize the notes in a variety of views. One view shows all notes arranged by icons; the other views provide various list options. For example, you can view notes organized in a list by color or date. You can change views using the Current View pane in the Navigation Pane or the View menu.

To organize and view notes:

▶ **1.** Click the **By Color** option button in the Current View pane in the Navigation Pane. The existing notes become grouped by the note color—in this case, blue and yellow. The minus sign buttons ⊟ indicate that all items in the groups are visible. See Figure 3-6.

Notes grouped by color ◀ Figure 3-6

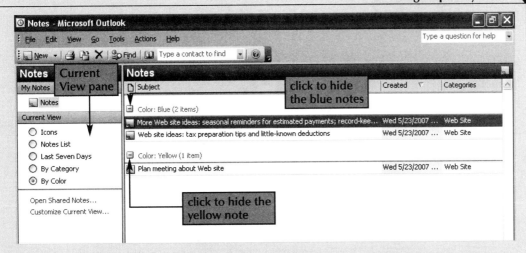

2. Click the **By Category** option button in the Current View pane in the Navigation Pane. The notes are grouped by assigned category—in this case, the Web Site category.

3. Click the **Icons** option button in the Current View pane in the Navigation Pane. The notes are arranged by icons.

There may be times when you'll want to pass notes to someone else.

Passing Notes to Others

One of the most convenient aspects of Outlook is the ability to integrate the various features. Some notes you'll want to pass to someone else. Rather than retyping your note in an e-mail message, you can include the note as the message body or an attachment.

The **AutoCreate** feature generates a new item when you drag an item from one folder to another. To create an e-mail with the note in the message body, drag the note to the Inbox in the Navigation Pane or Folder List. A new Message window opens and the note appears in the message body preceded by its date and time stamp, and the note's first line appears in the Subject line. You need only to address the e-mail and enter any additional text you want in the message body.

To create an e-mail and include the note as an attachment, right-click the note, and then click Forward. A Message window opens with the note included as an attachment and the Subject line completed. Again, you need only to address the e-mail and enter the text you want in the message body.

Printing Notes

Although one advantage of Outlook notes is that they don't clutter your desk with scraps of paper, sometimes you might want to print one or more notes. You can print all notes in the Notes folder using the Print command. When you print, you have the option of printing all the notes on one page or on separate pages. You can also print selected notes. Click one note to select it; to select two or more notes, press and hold the Ctrl key while you click the notes you want. These are the same selection techniques used in My Computer, Windows Explorer, and other Office programs.

You'll print the notes that refer to the Web site.

To print notes:

▶ 1. Click the **Web site ideas** note to select it, press and hold the **Ctrl** key, click the **More Web site ideas** note, and then release the **Ctrl** key. Both messages are selected.

▶ 2. Click the **Print** button on the Standard toolbar to open the Print dialog box. See Figure 3-7.

| Figure 3-7 | Print dialog box for notes |

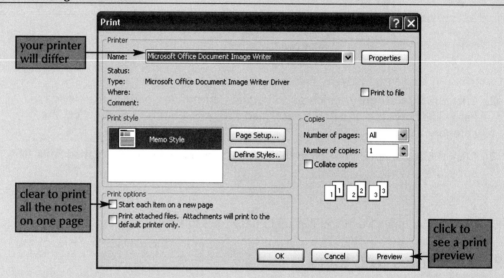

▶ 3. Click the **Start each item on a new page** check box to remove the check mark, if necessary. This way, both notes will print on the same page.

Trouble? If the Start each item on a new page check box is grayed out, then you cannot change this option. When you click the OK button in Step 4, each note will print on a separate page.

▶ 4. Verify that the correct printer appears in the Name text box, and then click the **OK** button.

The printout includes the text of both notes along with your name and the dates and times you created or edited them.

Notes are great as short-term reminders or storage, but you'll want to act on them promptly. Otherwise, your notes will collect into an unmanageable pile rather quickly. Some notes, such as the Plan meeting note, you'll want to move onto your task list.

Compiling a Task List

A to-do list is an effective way to remember all the tasks you need to accomplish. Outlook manages your to-do list through tasks. A **task** is any activity you need to complete. You can specify a start date and a due date to a task, assign a status and priority, and list what percentage of the task is complete. A task's priority is a subjective determination of the task's importance; assign a High, Normal, or Low priority as needed to help you sort your tasks. When you track a task, you follow its progress so you know how much you completed and when you completed it. A task can occur once, such as returning a phone call to plan a meeting, or it can occur repeatedly (called a **recurring task**), such as sending a monthly status report. Your tasks can simply list the things you need to complete, or you can include more details, such as a due date, a start date, status, priority, percentage complete, and other notes.

Creating Tasks

You can create a task from scratch or from an existing Outlook item. When you create a task from scratch, you must enter a subject—a short description of a task, such as "Organize Web site ideas." If you want to include more descriptive information, such as additional notes, a starting date, a due date, and a priority, you need to open the Task window.

To create a task from an existing item, you can use the AutoCreate feature. For example, dragging a note icon from the Notes main window to the Tasks folder creates a task. Outlook opens a new Task window and inserts relevant information from the original item into the appropriate fields, such as subject and date text boxes, and places the contents of the original item in the notes text box at the bottom of the Task window. You can enter additional information in the open window.

Reference Window

Creating a Task

- Click the New button list arrow, and then click Task (*or* drag an item to the Tasks folder).
- Enter a task subject; select the due date and priority, if necessary; and enter other task details you want to record.
- Click the Save and Close button on the Standard toolbar.
  or
- Display the Tasks folder, and select the view with the task details you want to record.
- Click in each text box and enter the appropriate information, such as a task subject or due date.

You'll use AutoCreate to set up a task by moving the yellow note from the Notes folder to the Tasks folder.

To create a task from a note:

1. Drag the yellow **Plan meeting** note to the Tasks button in the Navigation Pane. When you release the mouse button, a Task window with information from the note opens; the first line of the note is entered in the Subject text box.

2. Click the **Due date** list arrow. A calendar opens below the Due date field. Today's date is surrounded by a border and is shaded.

3. Click tomorrow's date to assign a deadline for the task.

4. Click the **Priority** list arrow, and then click **High** to change the task's urgency level.

You can assign a contact to a task in the same way as you assigned a contact to a note. This note did not have a contact assigned to it; if it had, the name would have appeared in the Contacts text box. You can assign a task to one or more contacts.

5. Click the **Contacts** button in the lower-left corner of the Task window, and then double-click your name in the Items list box. Figure 3-8 shows the completed Task window.

| Figure 3-8 | Completed Task window |

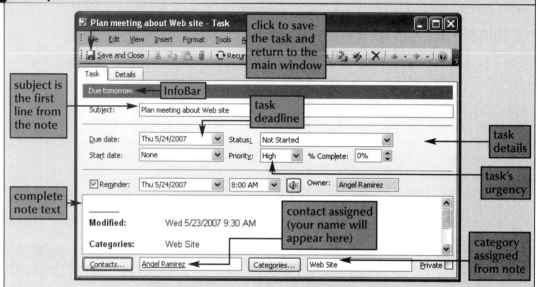

6. Click the **Save and Close** button on the Standard toolbar. The task is saved with the additional information.

You could keep both the note and the task, depending on your working style. However, because you no longer need the note you converted to a task, you'll delete it.

To delete a note:

1. Click the yellow **Plan meeting** note to select it, if it is not already selected.

2. Click the **Delete** button ☒ on the Standard toolbar. The note is moved to the Deleted Items folder, where it remains until you empty the folder.

Next, you'll display the Tasks folder to view the new task and create additional tasks. The Tasks folder displays all the tasks you created, and provides a task list to which you can add new tasks.

To create a one-time task from the Tasks folder:

1. Click the **Tasks** button in the Navigation Pane to display the Tasks folder.

   You want to switch to the view that shows a list of task subjects and due dates.

2. Click the **Simple List** option button in the Current View pane in the Navigation Pane, if necessary. See Figure 3-9.

Tasks in Simple List view | Figure 3-9

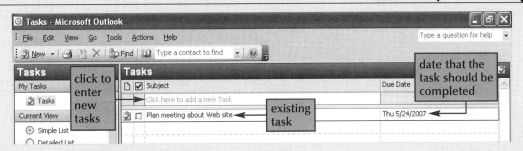

3. Click the **Click here to add a new Task** text box.

4. Type **Organize Web site ideas** as the subject of the task. You can now enter a due date.

5. Click the **Due Date** text box, click the **Due Date** list arrow to display the calendar, select the date for next Tuesday, and then press the **Enter** key.

   The task is saved and added to the list of tasks above the Plan meeting task.

The Simple List view in the Tasks folder shows only a few fields of information. The first column identifies the type of item by icon—in this case, a task. The second column identifies whether the task is complete; an unchecked check box indicates that the task is not complete and a check mark indicates that the task is complete. If you want to see additional information, you can switch to another view to display more fields. For example, when you switch from the Simple List view to the Detailed List view, you see each task's priority, status, percentage complete, and assigned categories.

A task can be updated from any view in the Tasks folder. To change a task's information, you can type data into the appropriate text box. For example, if you wanted to enter status information for a task, you would switch to Detailed List view, click that task's Status text box, and then select from the list of options that are displayed, which include Not Started, In Progress, Completed, Waiting on someone else, and Deferred. You could also enter any necessary data in the Task window, which contains all the fields. You open the Task window for any task by double-clicking its name in the task list.

Creating a Recurring Task

When a specific task must be repeated at some regular interval, you can set up a recurrence pattern for it rather than create a new task each time. You might set a recurring task for paying estimated taxes, compiling monthly reports, or planning quarterly staff meetings. You can set a recurrence pattern for an existing task or a new one. The recurrence pattern tells Outlook when the task is due.

Reference Window | **Creating a Recurring Task**

- Create a new one-time task or open an existing one-time task.
- Click the Recurrence button on the Standard toolbar in the Task window.
- Set the recurrence pattern and range in the Task Recurrence dialog box.
- Click the OK button in the Task Recurrence dialog box.
- Click the Save and Close button on the Standard toolbar in the Task window.

You want the Tax Tips section of the Web site updated on a regular basis. This is a recurring task. You'll create a new, recurring task that reminds you each time you need to write the update for the Tax Tips section. A reminder, when set, plays a sound and opens a Reminder window on the date and time you specified. From the window, you can choose to dismiss or snooze the alarm. You turn on the reminder for a task by checking the Reminder check box, and then selecting the appropriate date and time in the Reminder list boxes.

To create a recurring task:

1. Click the **New** button on the Standard toolbar to open a new Task window.

2. Type **Write Tax Tips for Web site** as the task subject.

3. Click the **Recurrence** button on the Standard toolbar in the Task window. The Task Recurrence dialog box opens.

You set the recurrence pattern and range. The recurrence pattern determines how you want a task to recur—the frequency with which the task should recur and whether the task should recur on a certain date or day in each time period or after a specified interval after the last occurrence. The range of recurrence determines when the recurrence starts and ends, if it has a specified end date.

You'll set the recurrence pattern to be monthly on the last Monday of every month.

To set the recurrence pattern:

1. Click the **Monthly** option button in the left column of the Recurrence pattern area.

   The right column of the Recurrence pattern area changes to reflect options for monthly recurrences. You fill in the options and click the list arrows to describe your recurrence pattern.

2. Click the middle option button to the left of the word **The** in the right column of the Recurrence pattern area.

3. Click the first list arrow in the line, click **last**, click the next list arrow, and then click **Monday**. The Recurrence pattern line should read "The last Monday of every 1 month(s)."

   Next, you'll set the range of recurrence to begin next Monday and end after six occurrences.

4. Click the **Start** list arrow to display a calendar, and then click the date for next Monday.

5. Click the **End after** option button, press the **Tab** key to select 10, and then type **6**. Your dialog box should match Figure 3-10.

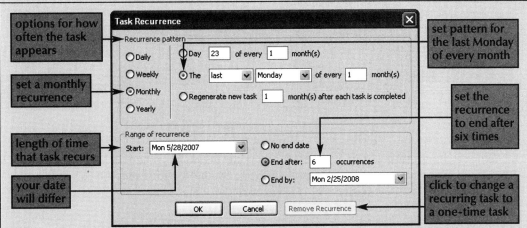

options for how often the task appears

set a monthly recurrence

length of time that task recurs

your date will differ

set pattern for the last Monday of every month

set the recurrence to end after six times

click to change a recurring task to a one-time task

The task will occur monthly on the last Monday of each month, beginning next Monday and continuing for the next six months.

6. Click the **OK** button to return to the Task window. The InfoBar indicates the due date of the first occurrence and the recurrence pattern. See Figure 3-11.

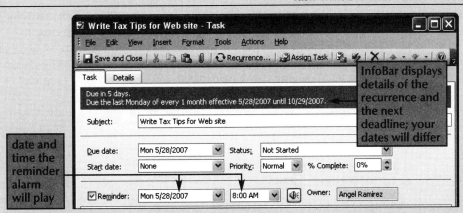

InfoBar displays details of the recurrence and the next deadline; your dates will differ

date and time the reminder alarm will play

7. Click the **Save and Close** button on the Standard toolbar in the Task window. The task appears on the task list with a recurrence icon 🔃 and the next due date. See Figure 3-12.

Figure 3-12 **One-time and recurring tasks**

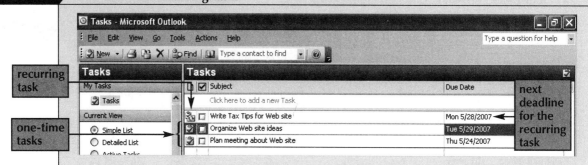

You can choose to skip any occurrence of a recurring task by opening the task, clicking Actions on the menu bar in the Task window, and then clicking Skip Occurrence. Outlook sets the due date to the next scheduled occurrence.

Organizing Tasks

A benefit of listing your tasks in Outlook is that you can arrange them in a variety of ways without rewriting the list. Just like you changed the color of different types of notes, you can distinguish tasks in a variety of ways—by categories, by due dates, or by subject.

Assigning Categories to Tasks

When you created a task from a note, the note's category was automatically assigned to the task. You can also add categories to an item from the Categories dialog box, the item's window, the folder's main window, or a shortcut menu. You can remove a category from an item in these same locations. When you make a change to an existing task, whether adding a category, changing due dates, specifying a percentage complete, or modifying a recurrence pattern, you are updating the task.

You'll assign the Ideas category from the default Master Category List to the Organize Web site ideas task.

To assign categories to a task:

1. Double-click the **Organize Web site ideas** task to open its Task window.

2. Click the **Categories** button at the bottom of the window. The Categories dialog box opens.

3. Click the **Ideas** check box and the **Web Site** check box to assign both categories to the task.

4. Click the **OK** button. The categories appear in the Category text box at the bottom of the Task window.

5. Save and close the task.

6. Right-click the **Plan meeting about Web site** task, and then click **Categories** on the shortcut menu. Even though you did not open the item, you can assign a category. The Web Site category is already assigned to this task, which was created from the note with the Web Site category.

Trouble? If Categories does not appear on the shortcut menu, you have selected the task for editing. Press the Esc key to close the shortcut menu, and then repeat Step 6 making sure you right-click a blue area of the selected task.

7. Verify that the **Web Site** check box contains a check mark in the Categories dialog box, and then click the **OK** button.

The two tasks are now both assigned to the Web Site category, and the Organize Web site ideas task is also assigned to the Ideas category.

Viewing Tasks by Category

The Tasks folder is in Simple List view, which does not show all details of the tasks. You should select the view that best meets your current need. If you want to group items by a particular heading, for example, the By Category view organizes tasks by category. In a table view, you can click a column header to sort the items, such as chronologically by due date. This is similar to the way columns work in Windows Explorer and other Microsoft applications.

To view tasks by categories:

1. Click the **Detailed List** option button in the Current View pane in the Navigation Pane. You can see additional details about your tasks, including the High priority icon ❗ next to the Plan meeting task and the categories assigned to the Organize Web site ideas and Plan meeting tasks.

2. Click the **By Category** option button in the Current View pane in the Navigation Pane. Each group lists the tasks included in those categories. The Organize Web site ideas task appears in both category groups to which it is assigned. See Figure 3-13.

   Trouble? If you don't see the tasks in each category, the category groups are probably collapsed. Click the plus sign button ⊞ next to each category to expand the group.

Tasks grouped by category | Figure 3-13

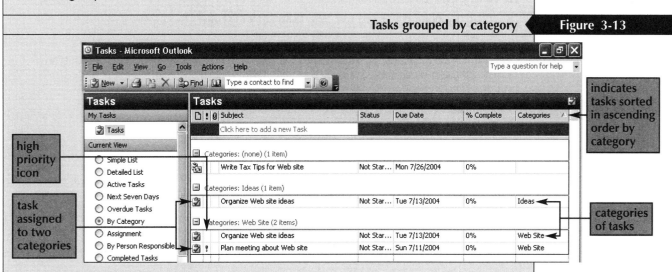

3. Click the **Subject** column header to sort the tasks alphabetically.

▶ **4.** Click the **Due Date** column header to sort the tasks by due date, and then click the column header again to reverse the order. The direction of the arrow in the column header indicates ascending or descending order.

▶ **5.** Right-click the **Subject** column header, point to **Arrange By** on the shortcut menu, and then click **Categories**. The tasks are again arranged in groups by their categories.

Another advantage to assigning one or more categories to an Outlook item is that you can use the Find command to locate all items associated with a specific category. You'll work with the Find feature in Tutorial 4.

Assigning a Task

So far, you own all of the tasks you created. As the **task owner**, you are responsible for the task. Only the task owner can change the task's information. Sometimes, however, you'll want to give someone else responsibility for a task. When you **assign** a task, you delegate it to someone else. For example, Lisa might assign a task to design the company Web site to Shoshona Gray, the newly hired webmaster. Each assigned task involves two people—one to send a **task request** (an e-mail message with details about the task to be assigned) and one to respond to the task request. The person who sends the task request transfers ownership of the task to the recipient once that person accepts the task. Although the original owner can keep an updated copy of the task in his or her task list and receive status reports (depending on the task options set in Outlook), only the current owner can change the task details. If the person declines the task request, the sender remains the task owner. Note that to process a task request, both the sender and receiver must be using Outlook for e-mail.

Before you send a task request, you'll verify the task options.

To verify the task options:

▶ **1.** Click **Tools** on the menu bar, and then click **Options**. The Options dialog box opens.

▶ **2.** If necessary, click the **Preferences** tab, and then click the **Task Options** button. The Task Options dialog box opens. See Figure 3-14.

Figure 3-14 | **Task Options dialog box**

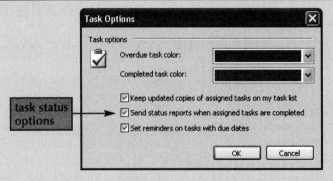

task status options

3. Verify that the three check boxes contain check marks.

4. Click the **OK** button in the Task Options dialog box, and then click the **OK** button in the Options dialog box.

Task requests are always sent in Rich Text Format (RTF), even if you have your mail format set to plain text or HTML.

Assigning a Task

Reference Window

- Create a new task or open an existing task.
- Click the Assign Task button on the Standard toolbar in the Task window.
- Check or uncheck the check boxes to determine whether you keep a copy of the task and receive a status report.
- Type the contact or distribution list name in the To text box (or click the To button and select a name or distribution list from the Contacts folder).
- Click the Send button on the Standard toolbar in the Task window, click the OK button to turn off the task reminder, and then send the message, if necessary.

You cannot assign a task to yourself. To complete the steps in this section and the Responding to a Task Request, Receiving a Response to a Task Request, and Updating a Task sections, you'll need to exchange e-mail addresses with a classmate who also is using Outlook to send and receive e-mail. If you don't have a classmate to work with, ask your instructor for an e-mail address you can use. Otherwise, you should read but not complete these sections.

To assign a task to another person:

1. Create a contact card for a classmate, including his or her name and e-mail address.

2. Click the **New** button on the Standard toolbar in the Tasks folder. A new Task window opens.

3. Type **Web site design** in the Subject text box.

4. Click the **Due date** list arrow to display a calendar, click the right scroll arrow twice to advance the months, and then click the same date number as today to select a due date two months from today.

5. Click the **Priority** list arrow, and then click **High**.

6. Click the **Categories** button, click the **Web Site** check box, and then click the **OK** button.

7. Click the **Assign Task** button on the Standard toolbar in the Task window. The Task window changes to include a To text box, in which you can specify the task recipient. See Figure 3-15.

Figure 3-15 | **Task window for assignment**

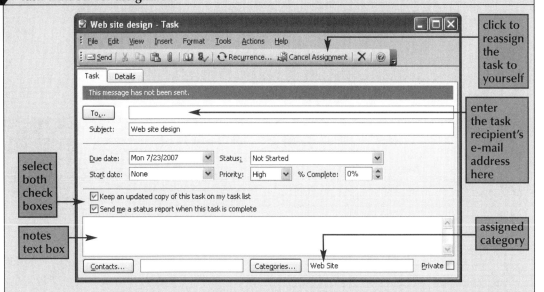

8. Make sure the **Keep an updated copy of this task on my task list** and **Send me a status report when this task is complete** check boxes are selected.

   The Keep an updated copy of this task on my task list check box creates a copy of the task in the original owner's task list. The original owner receives updates when the assigned owner changes the task. The Send me a status report when this task is complete check box specifies that the original owner receive a message indicating that the task is complete when the new owner finishes it.

   Now you need to send the task request.

To send the task assignment:

1. Type your classmate's name in the To text box, and then press the **Tab** key. After a moment, Outlook recognizes the name as a contact with an e-mail address in your Contacts folder, and replaces the recipient's name with his or her name and e-mail address. You can address the task to anyone in the Contacts folder, just as you would address an e-mail message.

2. Click the **Send** button on the Standard toolbar.

   A dialog box opens to remind you that the task reminder has been turned off because you are no longer the task owner.

3. Click the **OK** button to confirm that the task reminder is turned off. The task icon changes to ![icon] to indicate that it has been assigned.

4. If necessary, send the message.

   Before a task is assigned to another person, that person must receive and respond to the task request.

Responding to a Task Request

The task request appears as an e-mail message in the recipient's Inbox. The person who receives the task request can accept, reject, or reassign the task. Remember, to process a task request, both the sender and recipient must be using Outlook for e-mail. By accepting the task, the recipient becomes the new owner and the only person who can update the task. If the recipient declines the task, it returns to the original owner, who can then assign it to someone else or return the task to his or her own task list. When you accept or reject a task, you can also choose to include a message with your response. To assign a task to someone else, you must use the Assign Task button on the Standard toolbar in the Task window. Recipients who assign the task to someone else can no longer change the task, but they can keep it in their task list and receive status reports, giving them the same rights and control over the task as the original owner.

Only the current task owner can update a task. If the task was assigned to other people before the current task owner, every change that the owner makes to the task is copied automatically to the task in the previous owners' task lists if they kept a copy of the task. When the current owner completes the task, the previous owners receive a status report if they requested one.

The next set of steps requires that you have received a task request from your classmate. If you have not received a task request, you can read but not complete the next set of steps.

To accept a task request:

1. Display the **Inbox** folder, download your messages, if necessary, and then click the task request e-mail that your classmate sent you. An icon 📋 appears in the message header indicating that this message is a task request. The basic information about the task request appears in the Reading Pane, along with buttons to accept or reject the task assignment. See Figure 3-16.

Received task request ◄ **Figure 3-16**

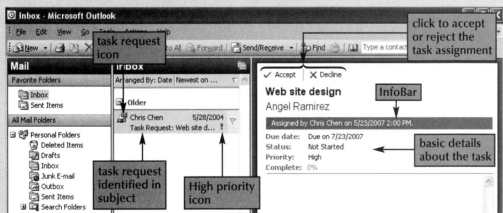

Trouble? If the task request message does not yet appear, wait a few minutes and then repeat Step 1.

Trouble? If you do not have Accept and Decline buttons on the Standard toolbar in the Task window, or if they are grayed out and unavailable, then the person who sent you the task needs to enable Rich Text Format for your contact card. Delete the task you received, then ask the person who sent you the task to open your contact card, right-click the e-mail address in the E-mail text box, and then click Outlook Properties. The E-mail Properties dialog box opens. Click the Internet format list arrow, click Send using Outlook Rich Text Format, and then click the OK button. Save and close the Contact window.

2. Open the task request message. The InfoBar shows the name of the person who assigned the task and the date on which the task was assigned. See Figure 3-17.

| Figure 3-17 | Task request message |

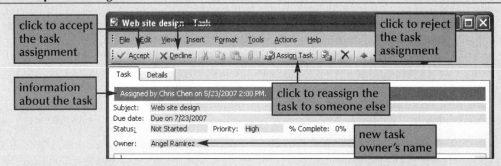

The Standard toolbar of the task request message has two additional buttons—the Accept button and the Decline button. You'll click the Accept button to take on the task. If you wanted to reject the request, you would click the Decline button.

3. Click the **Accept** button on the Standard toolbar to accept the request. The Accepting Task dialog box, shown in Figure 3-18, opens.

| Figure 3-18 | Accepting Task dialog box |

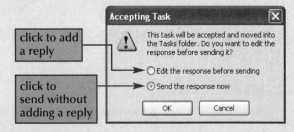

4. Click the **Edit the response before sending** option button, and then click the **OK** button.

5. Type **I'd be happy to complete this task.** in the Task window's notes text box. Your acceptance appears in the InfoBar. See Figure 3-19.

Accepted task request message ◄ Figure 3-19

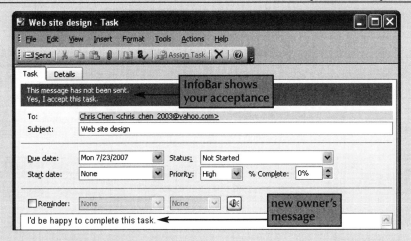

▶ **6.** Send the message.

Outlook sends your acceptance reply, adds the task to your Tasks folder, and makes you the owner of the task. As owner, you have full access to the task and can update information about that task.

Receiving a Response to a Task Request

When you receive a response to a task you assigned, it appears in your Inbox with your other e-mail messages. The task response message in the Inbox displays a message header, which indicates whether the recipient accepted or declined the task. To view any more detailed replies, you must open the message. If you opted to keep a copy of the task, the task remains in your task list and includes a reminder of the new task owner—the only person who can update or change the task. If you do not keep a copy, Outlook removes the task from your list.

You'll download the task request response from your classmate.

To receive a task request response:

▶ **1.** Display the **Inbox**, and then download the task request response message, if necessary.

▶ **2.** Click the **Task Accepted: Web site ...** message in the message list. The message icon has changed to 📝 and the subject is now prefaced with "Task Accepted" to indicate the acceptance of the task request. The InfoBar in the Reading Pane also indicates that the task is accepted and owned by another person. See Figure 3-20.

Figure 3-20 Received task request acceptance

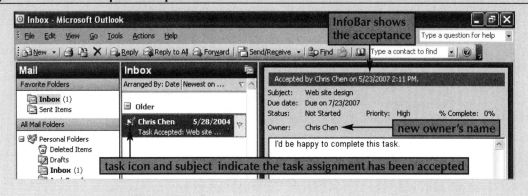

Next, you'll update the tasks you own and receive the update on the tasks you assigned to a classmate.

Updating a Task

When the task owner updates the task, everyone who is keeping a copy of the task receives a status report via e-mail and Outlook updates the task in each person's task list. When the task has been completed, Outlook sends a status report to any original owners who requested one. The current task owner can see the names of everyone who will receive updates and status reports in the Updated list box on the Details tab in the Task window.

You'll open the assigned task that you accepted and update the task status and details. The Details tab in the Task window provides space to indicate the date a task is finished, how much time the task is expected to take, how much time has already been spent, mileage, and billing information.

To update the assigned task you accepted:

1. Display the **Tasks** folder. The task you assigned to your classmate appears with the assigned task icon 📝 next to it, and the task you accepted from your classmate appears with the accepted task icon 📑 next to it. Both tasks are listed in the Web Site category group. (They might be in a different order than in the figure.) See Figure 3-21.

Tasks folder **Figure 3-21**

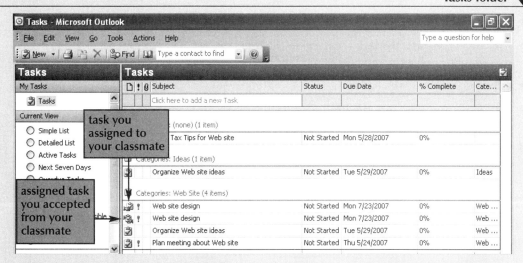

2. Double-click the **Web site design** task with the icon 🐫 to open the task that you accepted from your classmate in its own window. The InfoBar specifies that you have accepted this task.

3. Click the **Status** list arrow, and then click **In Progress**.

4. Click the **Details** tab.

5. Press the **Tab** key to select the value in the Total work text box, type **10**, and then press the **Tab** key to select the text in the Actual work text box. Outlook changes the total work to days based on the default setting of eight-hour days.

6. Type **2** in the Actual work text box, and then press the **Tab** key. See Figure 3-22.

Details tab of the Task window **Figure 3-22**

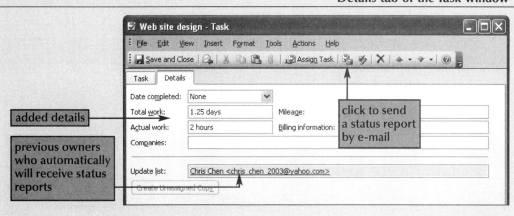

7. Save and close the task.

Because the original owner requested to receive status reports, Outlook sends an e-mail message to your classmate with information about the modified task. You could also choose to send a status report to any recipient from an open task by clicking the Send Status Report button on the Standard toolbar in the Task window. A Message window opens with the task subject in the Subject line and all the task details in the message body. You address the message as usual and add text to the message body as needed.

You should receive an e-mail message from your classmate about the modified task.

To review the status report message and view the updated assigned task:

▶ 1. Display the **Inbox**, and then download your messages, if necessary.

▶ 2. Click the **Task Update** message in the message list, and review the changes in the InfoBar in the Reading Pane.

▶ 3. Display the **Tasks** folder.

▶ 4. Open the **Web site design** task with the assigned task icon 📇 that you assigned to your classmate in its own window.

▶ 5. Review the changes in the Status text box and on the Details tab, and then close the Task window.

So far you have jotted down notes, and created and assigned tasks. To ensure that you complete all of your tasks in a timely manner, you can schedule time to work on them using your calendar. You'll do this in the next session.

Review	## Session 3.1 Quick Check

1. What are Notes?
2. From what view can you create a note?
3. Explain the difference between a task and a recurring task.
4. What happens when you drag a note to the Tasks folder?
5. True or False: An Outlook item can be assigned to only one category.
6. What is a task request?
7. How many people does it take to assign a task? Are there any special requirements for them?
8. Can the original owner update an assigned task?

Session 3.2

Scheduling the Calendar

The Calendar is a scheduling tool for planning and recording your upcoming appointments, events, and meetings. Each of these terms has a special meaning in Outlook. An **appointment** is an activity with a specific start and end time that you schedule in your calendar but that does not involve other people using Outlook or resources. For example, Shoshona might schedule an appointment in her calendar to block out time to design the company Web page, attend a class on HTML programming, or interview a prospective summer intern. An **event** is a one-time or annual activity that lasts 24 hours or more, such as a seminar, trade show, or vacation. An annual event occurs each year on a specific date, such as a holiday, birthday, or anniversary. A **meeting** is an appointment to which you invite people or for which you reserve resources, including conference rooms and projection equipment. Meetings can take place either face to face or online. You can send meeting requests only if all parties use Outlook for e-mail.

Viewing the Calendar

The Calendar main window can be arranged in a variety of views that resemble traditional planner books. The most familiar-looking view—Day/Week/Month—provides space for recording events, appointments, and meetings. You can select the time span shown in this view, depending on your needs and preferences. You can also display the **TaskPad**, a summary list of the tasks in the Tasks folder. There are additional table views, available on the View menu, that show lists of active appointments, recurring meetings, events, and so on.

You'll switch between the various Calendar views.

To navigate within the Calendar:

1. If you took a break after the previous session, make sure Outlook is running.

2. Display the **Calendar** folder.

3. If necessary, click **View** on the menu bar, point to **Arrange By**, point to **Current View**, and then click **Day/Week/Month**. The Standard toolbar contains a variety of buttons that change the way you view the Calendar—as a daily, weekly, or monthly planner.

4. If necessary, click the **Day** button on the Standard toolbar to display the Calendar as a daily planner. See Figure 3-23.

Calendar in Day view ◄ Figure 3-23

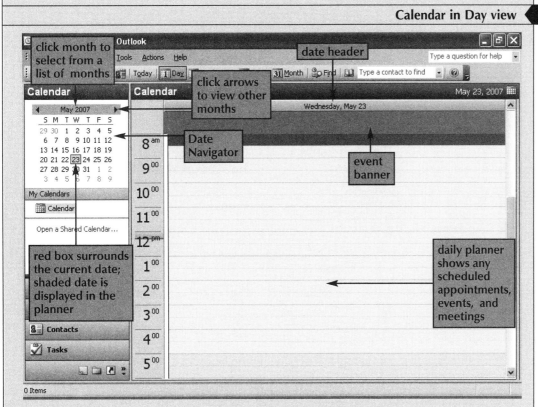

5. Click the **Week** button on the Standard toolbar to view seven days in the planner.

6. Click the **Work Week** button on the Standard toolbar to view five days in the planner.

7. Click the **Month** button on the Standard toolbar to view a one-month planner.

8. Click the **Day** button on the Standard toolbar to return to Day view.

Another way to move around your calendar is with the Date Navigator. The **Date Navigator** enables you to quickly display any month or date in the planner. A shaded box indicates which day or days appear in the planner. A box surrounds today's date. A date in boldface indicates that an event or appointment is scheduled on that day. You can click any date on the Date Navigator calendar to display its planner. If you want to see the planner for a day that isn't currently visible in the Date Navigator, you can use the arrows and month name to bring other calendars into view.

You'll display different days in the planner using the Date Navigator.

To move around the Calendar with the Date Navigator:

1. Click the date for next Monday on the Date Navigator. The planner changes to show that day's schedule.

2. Click the scroll arrow on the right of the current month's name in the Date Navigator to move to the next month's calendar.

3. Click the month name in the Date Navigator to display shortcuts to the three months before or after the month displayed; do not release the mouse button. See Figure 3-24.

Figure 3-24 ▶ **Date Navigator shortcuts**

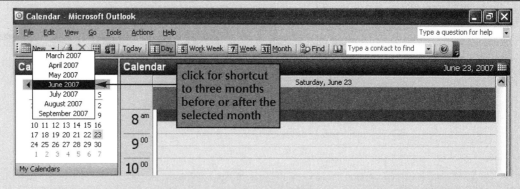

4. Click the next month in the shortcut list. The Date Navigator shifts calendars to display the month you selected.

5. Click the **Today** button on the Standard toolbar. The Calendar returns to the current day.

You can customize the Calendar by changing the fields visible on the screen or the font and size of the text. To do so, you would click View on the menu bar, point to Arrange By, point to Current View, and then click Customize Current View. The Customize View dialog box contains buttons that enable you to modify the view settings.

Scheduling Appointments

You can schedule and change appointments in your own calendar, and you can give others (who use Outlook) permission to do the same. Likewise, other people can give you permission to make and modify schedules in their calendars. To let people know about your availability, you can specify how time is blocked out for an appointment, as indicated in Figure 3-25.

Appointment availability codes   Figure 3-25

TIME SHOWN AS	BORDER COLOR	AVAILABILITY TO OTHERS
busy	solid blue	unavailable
free	clear	available
tentative	blue and white stripes	available
out of office	solid purple	unavailable

You can then color code each appointment, meeting, or event, using the Calendar Coloring button on the Standard toolbar. Each color denotes a different purpose, such as red for important, blue for business, green for personal, and so forth. So an important, tentative appointment would appear in your calendar as red with a striped blue border, and an important, busy appointment would appear as red with a solid blue border.

Although you can create an appointment using the New button on the Standard toolbar, you can also schedule an appointment by dragging a task from the Tasks folder to the Calendar folder or from the Calendar TaskPad to the planner.

Reference Window

Scheduling an Appointment

- Drag an item to the Calendar folder or planner (*or* click the New button list arrow, and then click Appointment).
- If necessary, enter an appointment subject, type or select a location, select start and end times, turn on or off the reminder, select how the time appears in your calendar, and assign categories and contacts.
- To create a recurring appointment, click the Recurrence button on the Standard toolbar in the Appointment window, set a recurrence pattern and duration in the Appointment Recurrence dialog box, and then click the OK button.
- Click the Save and Close button.
  or
- Drag to select the appointment duration on the Calendar planner, type the appointment subject, and then press the Enter key.
- To add more details or a recurrence pattern, double-click the appointment to open its window.

You'll drag a task to schedule an appointment for completing the "Plan meeting about Web site ideas" task.

To schedule an appointment from a task:

▶ 1. Click **View** on the menu bar, and then click **TaskPad**. The list of tasks from the Tasks folder appears in the lower-right corner of the Calendar main window and the Date Navigator moves to the upper-right corner of the Calendar main window. See Figure 3-26.

| Figure 3-26 | TaskPad displayed in the Calendar main window |

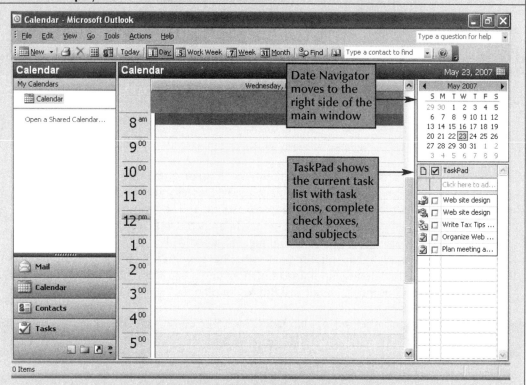

▶ 2. Drag the **Plan meeting about Web site** task from the TaskPad onto the planner. An Appointment window opens.

The task's subject and category are already assigned to the appointment. You could edit the subject or assign additional categories if needed. You can see the Due Date and Priority (High), Status, Percent Complete, Total and Actual work, Owner, Contacts, and Categories in the appointment's notes text box. All of this information is entered from the Task window.

▶ 3. If necessary, maximize the window.

▶ 4. Type **Conference Room** in the Location text box. This text box records the place where the appointment occurs. Outlook remembers all locations you enter, so next time you could choose this location from the list.

The appointment time is the same as the date and time you created the task, which is in the past, as indicated in the InfoBar. You'll schedule the appointment for the future.

▶ 5. Press the **Tab** key twice to move to the date Start time text box.

Next, you'll enter the block of time during which you plan to work on the task. You could type specific dates and times in the Start time and End time text boxes or select from the calendar that opens when you click the Start time and End time list arrows. However, we often think of dates and times in reference to where we are right now. The **AutoDate** feature converts natural-language date and time descriptions, such as "one week from today" and "noon," into the numerical format that represents the month, day, and year or time, respectively. You can also type abbreviations, such as "Wed" or "Feb," and holiday names with or without punctuation, such as "New Year's Day." To remove a date or time, just type "none" in the text box.

You'll enter the start and end times for the appointment.

To schedule the appointment's start and end times:

▶ **1.** Type **next Tuesday** in the date Start time text box, and then press the **Tab** key. The correct date for next Tuesday appears in the date Start time text box, the InfoBar disappears, and the insertion point is in the time Start time text box.

▶ **2.** Type **ten** in the time Start time text box, and then press the **Tab** key twice. The end time is already set to next Tuesday's date because the end time cannot precede the start time.

▶ **3.** Click the time **End time** list arrow, and then click **11:00 AM (1 hour)** to enter the time you think you'll be finished with the meeting plan.

The reminder is set by default when you schedule a new appointment (unless the default settings for Outlook were changed). Fifteen minutes before the scheduled appointment, a sound will play and a Reminder window opens to alert you to the upcoming appointment; you can then dismiss or snooze the alarm. You can turn off the reminder for a meeting by clearing the Reminder check box. Or, you can change the amount of time for the reminder by selecting a time from the list or typing a new time in the text box.

You'll set the reminder, and then save the appointment.

To set the reminder and finish the appointment:

▶ **1.** If necessary, click the **Reminder** check box to insert a check mark.

▶ **2.** Click the **Reminder** list arrow, and then click **5 minutes**.

The only other item you need to change for this appointment is how you show this time on your calendar. You can set the appointment time as unavailable (Out of Office or Busy) or available (Free or Tentative) to others. People who have access to your calendar then know when you are occupied.

▶ **3.** Click the **Show time as** list arrow, and then click **Tentative**. If anything urgent comes up, this block of time appears as available on your calendar.

▶ **4.** Click the **Label** list arrow, and then click **Needs Preparation**. See Figure 3-27.

Figure 3-27 Completed Appointment window

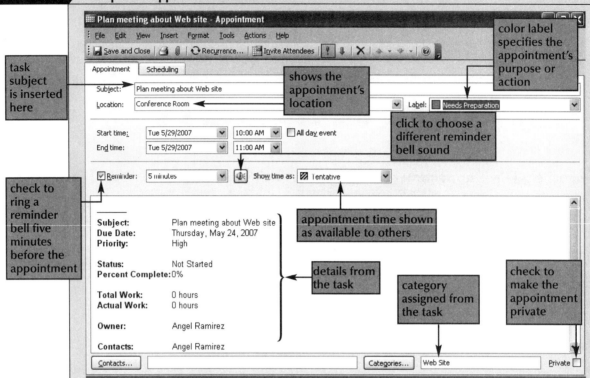

5. Click the **Save and Close** button on the Standard toolbar. Next Tuesday's date appears in bold in the Data Navigator to indicate that you have an appointment scheduled on that day.

6. Click next Tuesday's date in the Date Navigator. The Plan meeting appointment spans the one-hour block from 10 a.m. to 11 a.m. The appointment border is blue and white striped to remind you that the time is scheduled as Tentative, and the appointment block is a gold color to remind you that it Needs Preparation. A reminder bell icon 🔔 appears next to it to indicate that the reminder feature is on for this appointment.

You can also schedule appointments by selecting the date and time in the planner and then typing the appointment subject. Like tasks, you can add categories to your appointments to help you organize them. You'll schedule a second appointment for next Tuesday.

To schedule an appointment by selecting the date and time:

1. Click **2:00** in the planner to select the 2:00 to 2:30 block. The 2:00 to 2:30 block of time changes to dark blue to indicate that it is selected. To extend the appointment time, you could continue to drag down to select additional half-hour blocks.

2. Type **Create meeting agenda** as the appointment name. As you begin to type, a white text box opens in the time block. The solid blue border of the text box indicates that the appointment is shown as Busy in your calendar.

3. Press the **Enter** key. The second appointment is saved in your calendar.

4. Click the **Calendar Coloring** button 🖩 on the Standard toolbar, and then click **Important** to color code the appointment. See Figure 3-28.

Calendar with appointments   **Figure 3-28**

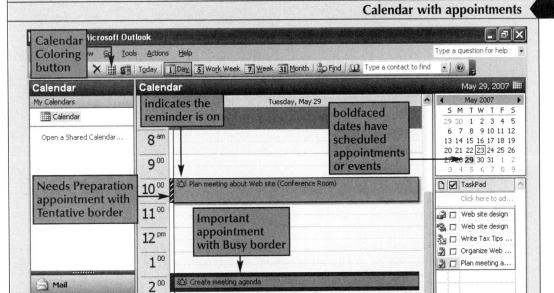

After looking at both appointments, you realize you need to create the meeting agenda before you plan the meeting. You could reschedule the appointment by opening its Appointment window and changing the times. A simpler method is to move the appointment by selecting it and then dragging it to a new location on the planner.

To reschedule an appointment by dragging:

1. Click the **Create meeting agenda** appointment to select it.

2. Point to the leftmost border of the appointment. A move pointer ✛ indicates that you can drag the appointment to a new location. See Figure 3-29.

Selected appointment   **Figure 3-29**

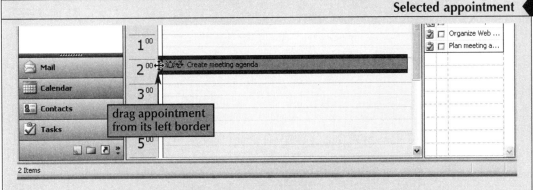

3. Drag the **Create meeting agenda** appointment up by its left border so that it occurs from 9:00 a.m. to 9:30 a.m.

Trouble? If you resized the time, making the appointment longer or shorter, then you dragged the top or bottom border rather than dragging the appointment block to a new time slot. Drag the top or bottom border until the appointment spans one half hour, and then repeat Steps 1 through 3, being careful to drag from the appointment's left border.

You'll change the Create meeting agenda appointment to last one hour.

4. Point to the bottom border of the **Create meeting agenda** appointment until the pointer changes to ↕, use the pointer to drag the bottom border down so that the appointment extends from 9:00 a.m. to 10:00 a.m., and then press the **Enter** key. The appointments occur one right after the other and each spans a one-hour block.

As you can see, with Outlook you can quickly reschedule any meeting as well as see a visual image of how the appointments are scheduled for your day.

Scheduling a Recurring Appointment

The plan is to schedule a meeting every week for the next month to discuss the Wertheimer Accounting Web site and you must create an agenda for each meeting. Rather than schedule the same appointment for each of the next three weeks, you will make this appointment recurring. A **recurring appointment** repeats on a regular basis, such as weekly or on the third Tuesday of the month. To schedule a new recurring appointment, you can click the Actions menu, click New Recurring Appointment, and then enter the recurrence information as well as the appointment information. If the appointment already exists, you can change it to a recurring appointment.

To schedule a recurring appointment:

1. Double-click the **Create meeting agenda** appointment to open its Appointment window.

2. Click the **Recurrence** button on the Standard toolbar. The Appointment Recurrence dialog box opens. See Figure 3-30.

Figure 3-30	Appointment Recurrence dialog box

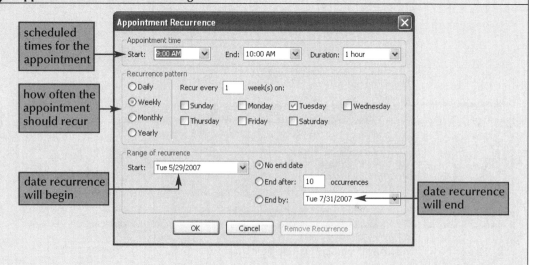

3. In the Recurrence pattern area, click the **Weekly** option button if it is not already selected, and make sure that this appointment is set to Recur every **1 week(s)** on **Tuesday**.

4. In the Range of recurrence area, make sure that the Start list box shows next Tuesday's date, click the **End by** option button, press the **Tab** key twice, and then type **one month** in the End by text box.

5. Click the **OK** button. The Appointment window changes to reflect the recurrence. The InfoBar displays a reminder that one occurrence of the appointment is adjacent to another appointment. The recurrence pattern is summarized below the Location text box. See Figure 3-31.

Recurring Appointment window ◄ **Figure 3-31**

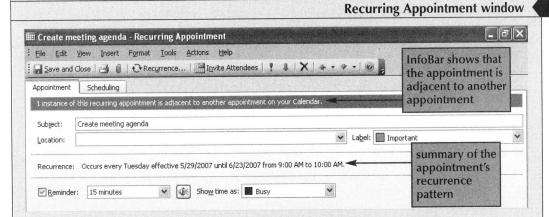

6. Use the **Categories** button to add the **Web Site** category to the appointment.

7. Click the **Save and Close** button on the Standard toolbar. The recurrence icon appears below the reminder bell icon in the appointment block in the planner.

Time is now blocked out each Tuesday for the next month to plan the meeting agenda, as indicated by the boldface dates in the Date Navigator.

Scheduling Events

Events are blocks of time that last from midnight to midnight. They can occur for one or more days, such as a one-day training seminar or a three-day health fair. Unlike appointments, events are always scheduled as free time in your calendar. To block out a specific time to attend an event, you must create an appointment. You schedule a one-day event and a multiday event in similar fashion. In Day/Week/Month view, you can quickly create an event by double-clicking the date heading of the day of the event.

Scheduling an Event

- Drag an item to the Calendar folder or planner (*or* click the New button list arrow, and then click Appointment).
- Click the All day event check box; if necessary, enter an appointment subject and category, type or select a location, select a start and end date, turn on or off the reminder, and select how the time appears in your calendar.
- To create a recurring event, click the Recurrence button on the Standard toolbar in the Appointment window, set a recurrence pattern and duration in the Appointment Recurrence dialog box, and then click the OK button.
- Click the Save and Close button.
  or
- Click the date heading on the Calendar planner for the first day of the event; if necessary, drag to select the date heading for additional days, type the event subject, and then press the Enter key.
- To add more details or a recurrence, double-click the event to open its window.

Wertheimer Accounting has planned a seminar for next week to review the latest changes to the tax code. You'll add this two-day event to your calendar.

To schedule an event:

1. Click the **Work Week** button on the Standard toolbar to display the five workdays for next week in the planner.

2. Click the date heading for next Wednesday. The box below the date changes to white, indicating that you can type in it.

   This action would create a one-day event. You want to create a two-day event.

3. Drag to select the date headings for Wednesday and Thursday. Both boxes are white when selected.

4. Type **Tax Code Seminar** as the event subject. See Figure 3-32.

Figure 3-32 | **Calendar in Work Week view**

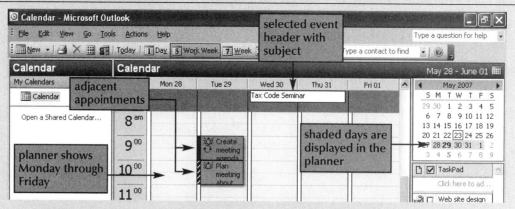

5. Press the **Enter** key. The default reminder is applied to the event; you can see the reminder bell icon. You want to turn the reminder off and add a location for the event.

6. Double-click the **reminder bell** icon in the Tax Code Seminar event heading. The Event window opens.

Trouble? If a new Event window opens, you probably clicked the date heading rather than the event heading. Close the Event window, position the pointer on the reminder bell icon, and then double-click.

Because the All day event check box is selected, the window does not provide options to set starting and ending times.

7. Click the **Location** list arrow, and then click **Conference Room**. Outlook remembered the room location you entered earlier.

8. Click the **Reminder** check box to remove the check mark and turn off the reminder.

9. Click the **Save and Close** button on the Standard toolbar. The reminder bell icon no longer appears on the event in the planner and Conference Room is indicated in parentheses in the event header.

Now that you've scheduled some appointments and an event, you'll print your calendar.

Printing a Calendar

A printed calendar is helpful when you need to leave your office and want to take your schedule along. Outlook provides a variety of printing styles you can choose for your calendar. You can print each day, each week, or each month on a separate page, or you can choose other memo or list styles. You'll print next week's calendar. Outlook changes the print specifications to match the Calendar view you are showing.

To print your calendar:

1. Click the **Print** button on the Standard toolbar. The Print dialog box opens. See Figure 3-33.

Calendar Print dialog box | Figure 3-33

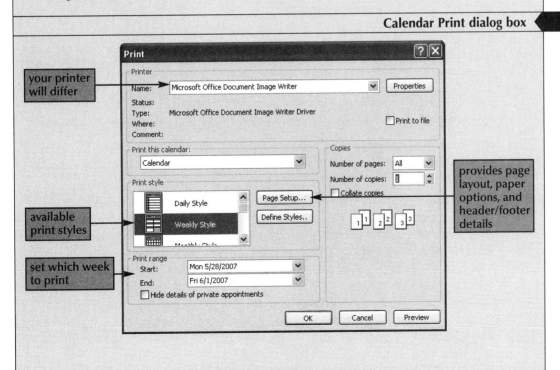

your printer will differ

available print styles

set which week to print

provides page layout, paper options, and header/footer details

2. Click **Weekly Style** in the Print style list, if it is not already selected.

3. Click the **Start** list arrow and then select next Monday's date, if necessary. Next Monday is the first day you want to print.

    You can also use AutoDate to set the start and end dates. Next Friday is the last day you want to print.

4. If necessary, press the **Tab** key, type **next Friday** in the End text box, and then press the **Tab** key.

    Outlook changes the date to display next Friday's date, the last day that you want to print.

5. Click the **Preview** button to see your calendar as it will print on paper. See Figure 3-34.

| Figure 3-34 | Calendar in Print Preview |

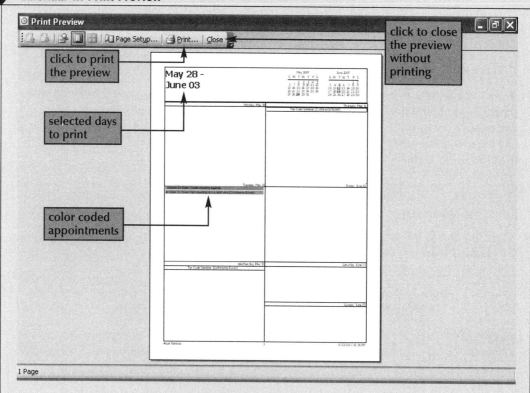

Although you chose Friday as the last day to print, when you choose Weekly Style, Outlook prints the week, starting with Monday and ending on Sunday, that contains the starting and ending dates you chose.

6. Click the **Print** button on the Print Preview toolbar, and then click the **OK** button in the Print dialog box. The dates you selected from your calendar print on a single page. If you have a color printer, you can see the color coding for the appointments on the printed page.

You are ready to schedule the meeting to discuss the Web site.

Planning a Meeting

Recall that a meeting differs from an appointment in that it includes other people and resources. A meeting can take place face to face or online (such as a NetMeeting). When planning a meeting, you specify the people who should attend and the resources to be reserved; you also pick a date and time for the meeting. All invitees must be using Outlook to take advantage of the features. Each invitee and resource receives an e-mail message with the meeting request. You receive e-mail replies when they respond to the request, enabling you to easily track who can attend and what resources are reserved.

Selecting Meeting Attendees and Resources

Meeting **attendees** are the people you invite to a meeting. You can select attendees from your Contacts folder or enter other names. Anyone who has an e-mail address will receive an e-mail meeting request. If you have access to their calendars, Outlook will display their free and busy times and you can find a meeting time that is most convenient to all invitees.

Meeting **resources** include conference rooms, audiovisual equipment, and other available company materials. Before you can reserve a resource, it must have its own mailbox on your server. The resource then becomes self-sufficient, accepting and rejecting meeting requests automatically. It accepts any invitation when it is available, and the meeting is automatically entered in the resource's calendar. The resource administrator can restrict the ability to schedule the resource. For example, if only managers are allowed to book certain conference rooms, permissions can be set so that requests from managers are accepted and requests from nonmanagers are declined. To schedule a resource, you must have adequate permissions to reserve the resource.

Sending a Meeting Request

Before sending meeting requests, you need to plan the details of your meeting. Consider whom you are inviting, what resources you need, when the meeting will occur, and where the meeting will take place. Once you know this information, you are ready to create the meeting. You can create meetings in several ways: (1) The New Meeting Request command enables you to specify the meeting details and attendees, and then check their schedules if they are on the same network. (2) The Plan a Meeting command enables you to select meeting attendees and resources, and then specify a meeting time and place or have Outlook find one for you. (3) The Invite Attendees command enables you to add people to an existing appointment or event, which changes the item to a meeting.

| **Planning a Meeting**

- Display the Calendar folder, click Actions on the menu bar, and then click Plan a Meeting.
- Click the Add Others button to open the Select Attendees and Resource dialog box.
- Click a contact to invite and click the Required, Optional, or Resources button for each invitee, and then click the OK button.
- Click the AutoPick button or enter a date and time for the meeting, and then click the Make Meeting button.
- Enter a subject, location, category, notes, and other details as needed.
- Click the Send button on the Standard toolbar in the Meeting window, click the Close button in the Plan a Meeting dialog box, and then, if necessary, send the messages.
  or
- Click the New button list arrow, and then click Meeting Request (*or* open an existing appointment and click the Invite Attendees button on the Standard toolbar in the Appointment window).
- Click the To button, click a contact to invite, click the Required, Optional, or Resources button for each invitee, and then click the OK button.
- Enter a subject, location, start and end times, category, notes, and other details as needed.
- Click the Send button on the Standard toolbar and then, if necessary, send the messages.

You'll schedule the meeting to discuss the company's Web site.

To complete the steps in this section and the steps in the Responding to a Meeting Request section, you'll need to work with a classmate. You can use the same classmate as you did in Session 3.1. If you don't have a classmate to work with, ask your instructor for an e-mail address and create a contact card using that name and e-mail address. Otherwise, you will not be able to complete all of the steps in these sections.

To schedule a meeting:

1. Click **Actions** on the menu bar, and then click **Plan a Meeting**. The Plan a Meeting dialog box opens. See Figure 3-35.

Figure 3-35 | **Plan a Meeting dialog box**

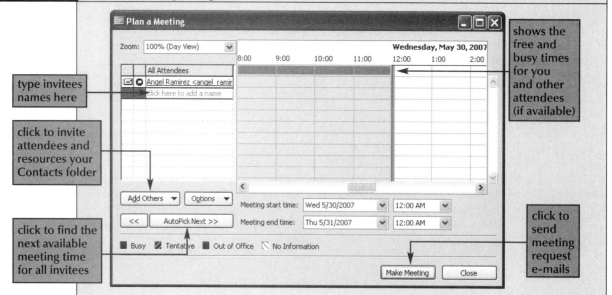

type invitees names here

click to invite attendees and resources your Contacts folder

click to find the next available meeting time for all invitees

shows the free and busy times for you and other attendees (if available)

click to send meeting request e-mails

2. Click the **Add Others** button, and then click **Add from Address Book**. The Select Attendees and Resources dialog box opens. See Figure 3-36.

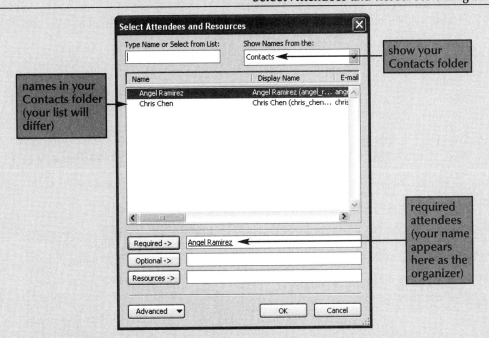

Trouble? If the Select Attendees and Resources dialog box doesn't display the names you entered in your Contacts folder, you need to display the Contacts folder. Click the Show Names from the list arrow, and then click Contacts.

Trouble? If a warning dialog box opens telling you that the address list could not be displayed because the Contacts folder associated with this address list could not be opened, click the OK button to close the dialog box, then, in the Select Attendees and Resources dialog box, click the Show Names from the list arrow, and then click Contacts.

3. Click your classmate's name in the Name list box, and then click the **Required** button.

Trouble? If you don't have a contact card for a classmate, you'll need to get one.

Required and Optional attendees appear in the To text box on the Appointment tab in the Meeting window, and Resources appear in the Location text box. You are listed in the Required list by default.

4. Click the **OK** button.

Each invitee appears in the All Attendees list in the Plan a Meeting dialog box. The icons to the left of their names indicate whether a meeting invitation by e-mail will be sent to them and lists their status (meeting organizer, required attendee, optional attendee, or resource). When you point to each icon, a ScreenTip appears to identify that icon. If you have access to their calendars, Outlook will display their free and busy times.

5. Use the horizontal scroll bar to scroll through the free/busy times.

Your schedule includes Tentative and Busy indications. If you had access to the invitee's calendar, Outlook would display that person's free and busy times. If you have access to others' schedules, the **AutoPick** feature is a great way to select the best time for all invitees because it automatically selects the next available free time for all invitees.

6. Click the **AutoPick Next** button. A vertical bar selects the next available free time for all invitees.

You can use the left scroll arrow button to find the first previous available free time for the meeting. You'll enter a convenient date and time.

7. Pressing the **Tab** key to move from field to field, set the Meeting start time for **next Wednesday** at **10 am** and the Meeting end time for **next Wednesday** at **1 pm**. See Figure 3-37.

Figure 3-37 | **Meeting time selected by AutoPick**

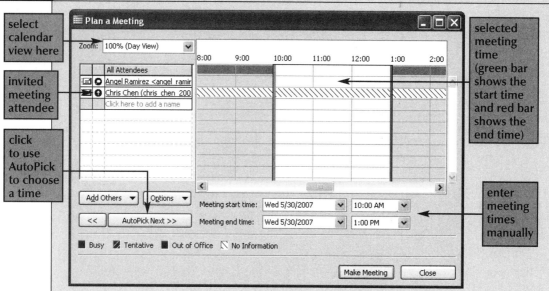

8. Click the **Make Meeting** button. The Meeting window opens with the invited attendee's name and e-mail address inserted in the To text box. See Figure 3-38.

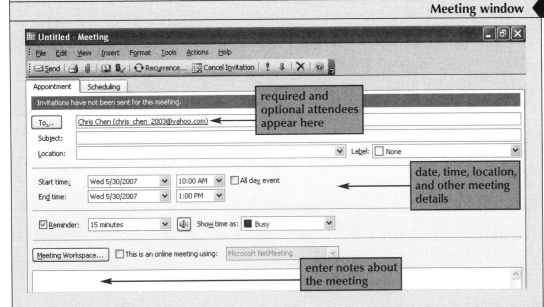

As with an appointment, you must specify the meeting subject, location, and so forth.

▶ **9.** Type **Company Web Site** as the subject.

▶ **10.** Select **Conference Room** as the location.

▶ **11.** Click the **Categories** button, select **Web Site** as the category, and then click the **OK** button.

Next, you'll insert the notes you created earlier into the meeting invitation.

Inserting Notes into a Meeting Request

You can insert any item into another as text, an attachment, or as a shortcut. For example, if you wanted to include an agenda, meeting minutes, or other information that invitees should review before the meeting, you could attach a file to your meeting request, just as you would attach a file to any other e-mail message. You'll insert the notes you created earlier with ideas for the Web site.

To insert notes text into a meeting request:

▶ **1.** Click **Insert** on the menu bar, and then click **Item**. The Insert Item dialog box opens.

▶ **2.** Click **Notes** in the Look in list box, click the **Text only** option button, and then press and hold the **Ctrl** key as you click each blue note to select it. See Figure 3-39.

Figure 3-39 **Insert Item dialog box**

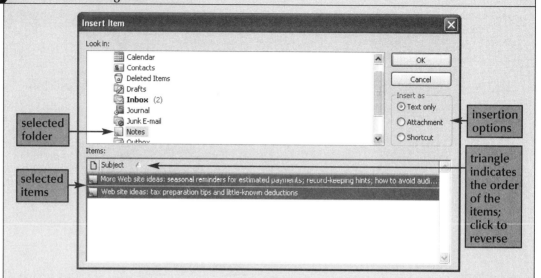

3. Click the **OK** button.

The notes' text, dates, contacts, and categories appear in the notes text box of the meeting request. Next, you finish scheduling the meeting by sending the meeting request and closing the Plan a Meeting dialog box.

To finish scheduling the meeting:

1. Click the **Send** button on the Standard toolbar to send the meeting request. You can see the time for which the meeting is scheduled is listed as busy for all attendees in the Plan a Meeting dialog box.

   Trouble? If you did not select a classmate's name as an attendee when you scheduled the meeting, then a message appears telling you that there are no recipient names in the To box and asking if you want to save and close the meeting instead. Click the No button, type your name in the To text box, and then repeat Step 1.

2. Click the **Close** button in the Plan a Meeting dialog box. The scheduled meeting appears in your calendar. The location is indicated in parenthesis. The meeting icon 🕮 distinguishes this entry from an appointment.

The meeting request is sent to the invitees you selected.

Responding to a Meeting Request

As a meeting invitee, you receive and respond to a meeting request in a similar way to how you receive and respond to a task request. When you receive a meeting request in your Inbox, the e-mail message displays a meeting request icon 🖃. You have four options for responding to a meeting request. You indicate whether you can definitely, possibly, or cannot attend the meeting by clicking the Accept, Tentative, or Decline button, or you can suggest a new meeting time by clicking the Propose New Time button. If you prefer, you can first check your schedule by clicking the Calendar button. When you send a reply, you have the option of adding comments to the return message. Once you reply, Outlook updates your calendar accordingly.

To respond to a meeting request:

1. Display the **Inbox**, and then download your messages, if necessary.

Trouble? If the message does not appear, wait a few minutes and then repeat Step 1. If the message still does not appear, confirm that your classmate sent the message request to you.

2. Select the meeting request message in the message list. Buttons appear at the top of the Reading Pane, enabling you to respond quickly. See Figure 3-40.

Meeting request in the Reading Pane | **Figure 3-40**

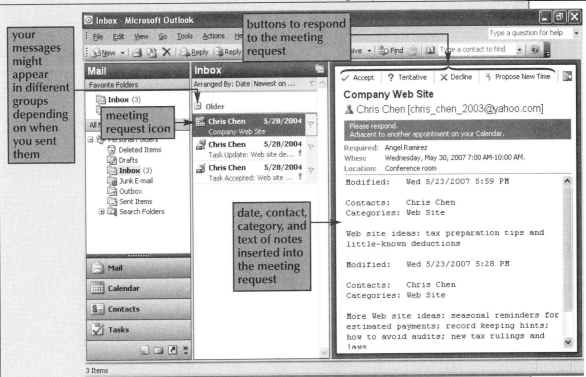

3. Click the **Propose New Time** button at the top of the Reading Pane.

Trouble? If you did not exchange meeting requests with a classmate and sent the meeting request to yourself, a dialog box opens, telling you that you do not need to respond to the meeting because you are the meeting organizer. Click the OK button, and then read, but do not complete, Steps 4 through 7.

4. Click the time **Meeting start time** list arrow and then click **10:30 AM**. See Figure 3-41.

Figure 3-41 | Propose New Time dialog box

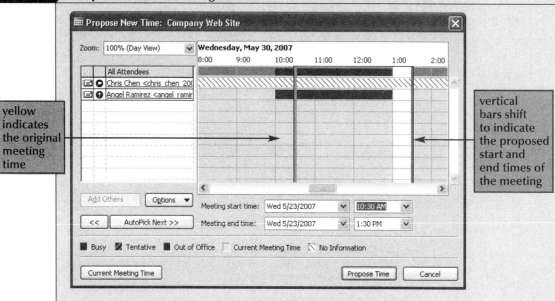

yellow indicates the original meeting time

vertical bars shift to indicate the proposed start and end times of the meeting

5. Click the **Propose Time** button. A Message window opens.

6. Type **I have a conflict with another appointment. Could we start at 10:30 instead?** in the notes text box. See Figure 3-42.

Figure 3-42 | Propose New Time message

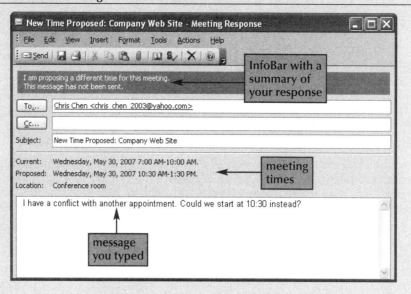

InfoBar with a summary of your response

meeting times

message you typed

7. Send the message.

Reviewing and Changing Meeting Details

As the meeting organizer receives replies, Outlook compiles the responses. You can see a summary of responses and view attendees availability from the Meeting window. The Appointment tab in the Meeting window summarizes the responses you received, for example, "2 attendees accepted, 0 tentatively accepted, 0 declined." The Attendee Availability tab lists the people who are invited and, depending on the option you choose, their free/busy times or their attendance status. Invited participants also can see these details about all the other participants.

To review attendee availability:

1. Download your messages, if necessary, to receive the meeting request response from your classmate, and then click it to view it in the Reading Pane, if necessary.

   Trouble? If you did not select a classmate's name as an attendee when you scheduled the meeting, then you will not receive a meeting request response.

2. Display the **Calendar** folder, and then double-click the **Company Web Site** meeting that you organized to open it. The meeting you organized has a solid blue border.

   Trouble? If the InfoBar indicates that you proposed a new time for the meeting and if the first line below the InfoBar indicates that your classmate is the organizer, then you opened the meeting that your classmate organized. Click the Close button ⊠ on the Meeting window title bar, and then repeat Step 2.

3. Review the InfoBar on the Appointment tab, which shows the current tally of responses.

4. Click the **Scheduling** tab in the Meeting window. This tab is similar to the Make Meeting dialog box.

5. Click the **Tracking** tab in the Meeting window. You see the current status of the invited attendees. See Figure 3-43.

Tracking tab in the Meeting window ◄ **Figure 3-43**

After you review the attendees' status, you may need to make changes to the meeting. You can update a meeting request by adding or removing meeting attendees and resources.

To add or remove attendees:

▶ 1. Click **Actions** on the menu bar, and then click **Add or Remove Attendees**. The Select Attendees and Resources dialog box opens.

You can add attendees or resources by selecting them, and then clicking the Required, Optional, and Resources buttons. You can remove an attendee or resource by clicking its name in the Required, Optional, or Resources box, and then pressing the Delete key.

You don't need to make any changes, so you'll close the dialog box without updating the meeting.

▶ 2. Click the **Cancel** button.

▶ 3. Save and close the Meeting window.

Trouble? If you did not select a classmate's name as an attendee when you scheduled the meeting, a dialog box opens, telling you that you have changed the meeting and asking if you want to send the updated meeting to the attendees. Click the No button.

Scheduling meetings with others can be done more efficiently if you have access to the other participants' calendars and they have access to yours. The meeting organizer can quickly see when participants have free time, and invite them to a meeting during that time. You can share your Calendar folder or individual calendar items with other people.

Some calendar items will include details you won't want others to see, such as notes about a doctor's appointment or discussions about budget cuts. In these cases, you can mark appointments as private by clicking the Private check box in the Appointment window. People who have access to your calendar will see that you have an appointment, but they won't be able to see any information about that appointment.

If you're using Outlook with Exchange Server, sharing calendar information is automatic. If you're not using Outlook with Exchange Server or want to share your calendar with people who don't have an Exchange account, you can use the Internet, an intranet, or a network folder. You set the number of months of your calendar you want to publish (up to 36 months) and how often you want to update your published calendar (up to every 60 minutes) in the Free/Busy Options dialog box. If you use a server location to publish your free/busy information on a server, anyone who knows the location can access your free/busy times. When you plan a meeting, you can view the times when people are free or busy in a meeting request, in an open Meeting window on the Scheduling tab, or from an Internet or Intranet location where the times are published.

Checking Off Completed Tasks

One of the most satisfying aspects of a task list is crossing off completed items. You can do this from either the Tasks folder or the Calendar TaskPad. Because you have finished a task on your task list—planning a meeting—you can mark it as completed.

To check off a completed task:

▶ 1. If necessary, display the **Calendar** folder.

2. Click the check box in the completed column for the "Plan meeting about Web site" task in the TaskPad. A check mark appears in the box, and the task is crossed out. See Figure 3-44.

Calendar with appointments and meetings | Figure 3-44

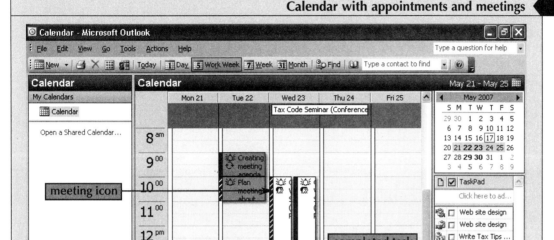

If you check off a task inadvertently, just click it again to return to the task in progress.

Scheduling an Online Meeting

Business trips are becoming an expense of the past. It is no longer necessary to gather colleagues from around the country or world in one room to discuss an ongoing project, project financial status for the upcoming quarter, or plan a presentation. Nowadays, people can be scattered around the world and still collaborate effectively. For example, Lisa and Shoshona no longer have to meet in the same room to discuss their latest Web site design as long as they have access to the Internet and a program such as Microsoft NetMeeting. **NetMeeting**, a program that comes with Windows 2000 and XP, enables two or more participants to communicate over the Internet or an intranet. In addition to the speech interaction of a telephone conference call, NetMeeting participants can also communicate by typing messages to each other, and share files and applications. With the proper equipment, they can even use real-time video. This is useful for providing technical support, conducting training sessions, and offering distance learning classes. NetMeeting is best for small group meetings.

The amount of extra equipment you need depends on how you plan to use NetMeeting. You can use NetMeeting without video or audio. If you want to use the sound capabilities of NetMeeting, you will need a microphone, a sound card, and speakers, headphones, or a headset, which are commonly included with basic computer systems. You don't need any extra equipment to view another participant's video; if you want to send video, you will need a camera that interfaces with your computer (such as an inexpensive Web or PC camera). Such collaboration allows two or more people to work on one document at the same time, or see each other and converse even if the people are in different locations.

All attendees must be running NetMeeting to participate in the online meeting. One way to ensure that the participants are available and running NetMeeting is to schedule a NetMeeting. You can schedule a NetMeeting in much the same way as you schedule a regular meeting. After opening a Meeting window, you schedule the meeting as usual, and then specify that the meeting is an online meeting. The window expands so that you can specify the directory service, select whether you want to send all participants a reminder notice and start the meeting automatically, and select a document to collaborate on. A **directory server** or **Internet Locator Server (ILS)** is a server that lists individuals who are available for a NetMeeting. If you don't have access to a private ILS, you can find Web sites that have listings of public ILSs. Search the Web for "netmeeting servers" to find links to these Web sites. NetMeeting has a Directories main window, which displays a list of people who are connected to the selected directory server.

You must be using NetMeeting 3.0 or later to schedule a NetMeeting with Outlook 2003.

Reference Window

Scheduling a NetMeeting

- Create a meeting request and fill out the meeting information.
- Click the This is an online meeting using check box to insert a check mark.
- Click the This is an online meeting using the list arrow, click Microsoft NetMeeting, verify the directory server, and then select a document, if necessary.
- Send the meeting request.
- Click Start Meeting on the reminder message to begin the NetMeeting.

In addition to NetMeeting, two other types of online meetings are available—Windows Media Services and Microsoft Exchange Conferencing. Which type of meeting you'll set up depends on the number of people involved and the purpose and content of the meeting. NetMeeting is best for one-to-one or small group meetings. **Windows Media Services**, part of Windows Server 2003, is a streaming media server that hosting companies can use to deliver the same audio and video content to many people over the Internet. Users need a player, such as the Windows Media Player, to view or listen to the event. **Microsoft Exchange Conferencing** is used to enable people in many locations to interact with one another in real time using audio and video content. There are additional add-in programs for Outlook, such as **Microsoft Live Meeting**, which you can use to conduct virtual meetings.

You'll use NetMeeting to schedule a meeting with Lisa to discuss the Web site budget.

To schedule a NetMeeting:

1. Click the **New** button list arrow on the Standard toolbar, and then click **Meeting Request**. A new Meeting window opens.

2. Click the **To** button to open the Select Attendees and Resources dialog box.

3. Verify that **Contacts** is selected in the Show Names from the list box, double-click your classmate's name to add that person to the list of required attendees, and then click the **OK** button.

4. Type **Web site budget** in the Subject text box. This meeting description will appear as the NetMeeting conference name.

▶ **5.** Enter a Start time of **next Friday 8:00 AM**, and then enter an End time of **next Friday** at **9:30 AM**. You could also use the Scheduling tab to view the other participant's schedule and select a meeting time.

▶ **6.** Click the **This is an online meeting using** check box to insert a check mark. The window expands to show additional options, as shown in Figure 3-45.

Meeting window for NetMeeting ◀ **Figure 3-45**

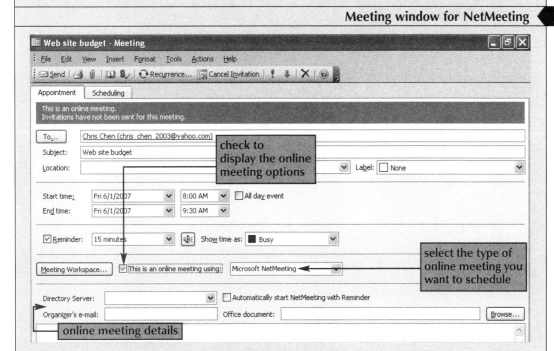

▶ **7.** Verify that **Microsoft NetMeeting** appears in the This is an online meeting using list box.

▶ **8.** Type **ils.dcbiz.crosslink.net** in the Directory Server list box, and then type your e-mail address in the Organizer's e-mail text box.

▶ **9.** Click the **Automatically start NetMeeting with Reminder** check box to insert a check mark.

▶ **10.** If your e-mail address does not appear automatically in the Organizer's e-mail text box, type it there now.

Participants will receive a reminder notice before the meeting by the amount of time specified in the Reminder text box, and NetMeeting will start automatically.

▶ **11.** Send the meeting invitation, and then verify that the Web site budget appears on your calendar. See Figure 3-46.

Figure 3-46 **Calendar with scheduled online meeting**

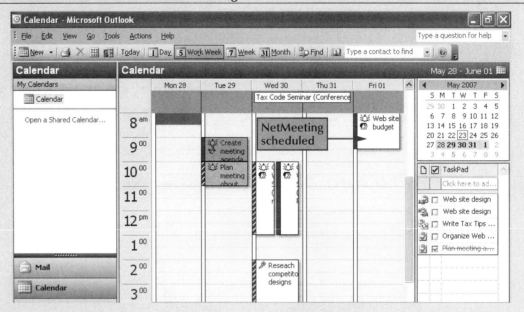

12. Download your messages, if necessary, then read the meeting invitation from your classmate.

Recipients must reply to the NetMeeting invitation just as they would a regular meeting invitation. Before the meeting, scheduled attendees will receive a message with a reminder that the meeting will begin shortly.

When you want to join a NetMeeting as a participant, you can click the Join Meeting button on the meeting request or the Reminder message. You can also right-click the meeting item on your calendar, and then click the Join Meeting option. The meeting organizer will see Start Meeting rather than Join Meeting.

All participants in the current call are listed in the NetMeeting Current Call main window along with information about their audio, video, and file- and application-sharing capabilities.

Depending on their capabilities, participants can collaborate in a variety of ways. Net-Meeting participants can see what other meeting participants are doing, exchange text messages with Chat, draw with others on an electronic Whiteboard, share applications and documents, or transfer files.

Saving a Calendar as a Web Page

You can save a calendar as a Web page and then share it with others. For example, Lisa might post a calendar with important client dates as a page on the company intranet, or she might include a calendar of tax form and payment due dates on the company's Web site. Client dates and other information would appear on the calendar as appointments. When you save a calendar as a Web page, you specify the start and end dates that should display, and you indicate whether to include appointment details from the Appointment window text box.

Other people can view the Web page calendar, as long as they know its URL; for example, Lisa's company could use the URL http://www.wertheimeraccounting.com/calendar/duedates.html to indicate the location of its calendar of due dates for filing tax forms and submitting payments on its Web site.

Saving a Calendar as a Web Page

- Display the calendar, click File on the menu bar, and then click Save as Web Page.
- Enter the dates to include on the Web page in the Start date and End date list boxes.
- Clear or select the Include appointment details check box and the Open saved web page in browser check box.
- Type your name in the Calendar title text box, and then browse for or enter the path and filename for the save location.
- Click the Save button.

You'll save next week's calendar as a Web page to see how this process works.

To save a calendar as a Web page:

1. Switch to the **Calender** folder, if necessary, click **File** on the menu bar, and then click **Save as Web Page**. The Save as Web Page dialog box opens. See Figure 3-47.

Save as Web Page dialog box　　Figure 3-47

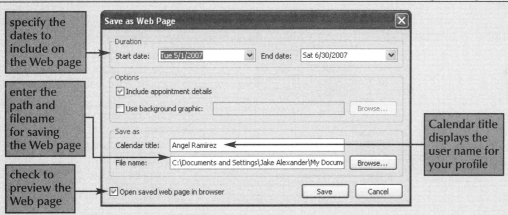

2. Type **next Monday** in the Start date list box.

3. Press the **Tab** key to move to the End date list box, and then type **next Friday**. The Web page Calendar will appear in month format, but only the appointments scheduled between the dates you specified will be included.

4. Verify that the **Include appointment details** check box contains a check mark. This option saves the details contained in the notes text box on your calendar item, such as details about appointment or meeting times.

5. Type your name in the Calendar title text box if it is not already there.

   This information becomes the name of the calendar Web page. If you do not enter a title, the user name for your profile becomes the title.

6. Click the **Browse** button, locate the **Tutorial.03\Tutorial** folder included with your Data Files, type **Calendar** in the File name text box, and then click the **Select** button.

7. Verify that the **Open saved web page in browser** check box contains a check mark. After Outlook saves your calendar as a Web page, the Web page calendar will open in your browser so that you can preview it.

8. Click the **Save** button. After a few moments, the saved Web page calendar opens in your default browser. If necessary, scroll down to see the dates with scheduled appointments, events, and meetings. If the dates span between two months, you'll need to click the Next Month button ▶ next to the current month's name to display the next month's calendar and see the rest of the scheduled appointments. See Figure 3-48.

Figure 3-48	**Web page calendar previewed in a browser**

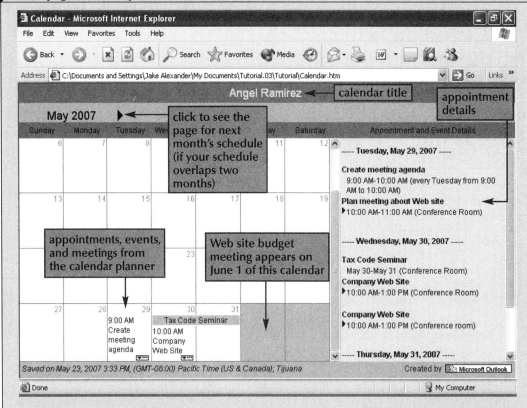

The Web page will display in both Internet Explorer and Netscape Navigator but with some minor differences.

9. Close the browser window.

Before you finish for the day, you'll delete any Outlook items you created.

Deleting Outlook Items

You can delete any Outlook items you are finished with and don't want to store. For example, most notes are used as reminders or temporary storage. After you act on them, these notes have no value except to create electronic clutter and use up storage. Other items, such as your calendar appointments, events, and meetings, you might want to archive (store in a compressed storage file) for later reference. This time, you'll delete all the e-mail messages, notes, tasks, categories, appointments, events, and meetings you created.

You'll start by removing the Web Site category you added to the Master Category List. When you remove a category, it still appears in the existing items, although it is not available to add to new items.

To delete a category:

▶ **1.** Click **Edit** on the menu bar, and then click **Categories**. The Categories dialog box opens.

Trouble? If the Categories command is not available, display the Contacts folder, and then repeat Step 1.

▶ **2.** Click the **Master Category List** button. The Master Category List dialog box opens.

▶ **3.** Click **Web Site** in the list, and then click the **Delete** button to remove the category.

▶ **4.** Click the **OK** button in the Master Category List dialog box, and then click the **OK** button in the Categories dialog box.

Next, you'll remove the Calendar items you created. Remember that you can use the Ctrl key to select multiple items to delete at one time. When you delete a recurring appointment, you are given the option of deleting one occurrence or all occurrences. When you delete a meeting request, you are given the option of sending a cancellation message to the attendees.

To delete Calendar items:

▶ **1.** Press and hold the **Ctrl** key, and then click each appointment, event, and meeting in your calendar that you created in this tutorial (look at the Date Navigator and use the dates in bold as a guide). Six items are selected.

▶ **2.** Click the **Delete** button ⊠ on the Standard toolbar. All one-time items are removed and a dialog box opens. The dialog box differs depending on the order in which you selected the items to be deleted, as described below:

- For each recurring appointment you delete, a dialog box will open asking whether you want to delete one or all occurrences of the recurring appointment.

- For each meeting that you delete and that you organized, a dialog box will open asking whether you want to delete the meeting and send a notice to the attendees that the meeting has been cancelled or if you want to delete the meeting without sending a cancellation.

- For each meeting that you delete that was organized by someone else, a dialog box will open asking whether you want to delete the meeting and send a response to the meeting organizer or if you want to delete the meeting without sending a response.

Read Steps 3-5 before continuing. The exact order that the dialog boxes appear depends on the order in which you selected the appointments you are deleting. You may need to perform Step 5 before you perform Step 3.

3. For the recurring appointment, click the **Delete the series** option button in the dialog box that asks whether you want to delete one or all occurrences of the recurring appointment, and then click the **OK** button. All occurrences of the appointment are moved to the Deleted Items folder.

4. For the meetings that you organized, click the **Delete without sending cancellation** option button, and then click the **OK** button. The meetings are removed without Outlook sending cancellation notices to the attendees.

5. For the meetings to which you were invited, click the **Delete without sending response** option button, and then click the **OK** button. The meetings are removed without Outlook sending a response to the meeting organizer.

When you are finished, the calendar will be cleared of all appointments, meetings, and events.

Trouble? If all of the appointments and events were not deleted, select them again and repeat Steps 2 through 5, as necessary.

Next, you'll delete all the tasks you created from the TaskPad. Like a recurring appointment, you can choose to delete one or all occurrences of a recurring task. If you delete an assigned task, you have the option of declining the task, marking the task complete, or just deleting the task.

To delete tasks from the TaskPad :

1. Press and hold the **Ctrl** key, click the **Web site design** task in the TaskPad, click each of the other tasks you created in this tutorial, and then release the **Ctrl** key.

2. Press the **Delete** key. A dialog box opens, asking whether you want to decline and delete, mark complete and delete, or just delete the assigned Web site design task.

3. Click the **Delete** option button in the dialog box, and then click the **OK** button. A second dialog box opens, asking whether you want to delete one or all occurrences of the recurring task, Write Tax Tips for Web site.

4. Click the **Delete all** option button in the dialog box, and then click the **OK** button. The selected tasks disappear from the TaskPad. Your calendar should have no items left on it that you created in this tutorial.

   Trouble? If your calendar still has items that you created in this tutorial, select each item and then press the Delete key to remove them.

5. Click **View** on the menu bar, and then click **TaskPad**. The TaskPad returns to its default hidden state and the Date Navigator moves back to the left of the planner.

Finally, you'll delete the messages, notes, and contacts you created in this tutorial.

To delete e-mails and notes:

▶ **1.** Delete any messages from the **Inbox** and **Sent Items** folders that you created or received in this tutorial, including task requests, task responses, and meeting invitations.

▶ **2.** Display the **Notes** folder, and then delete both blue notes you created in this tutorial.

▶ **3.** Display the **Contacts** folder, and then delete any contact cards you created in this tutorial.

All the items you deleted are moved to the Deleted Items folder. The Deleted Items folder acts like the Windows Recycle Bin—items remain in the folder until you empty the folder. This way, you can selectively restore items you may not have wanted to delete, unless you've already emptied the folder.

To work with the Deleted Items folder:

▶ **1.** Display the **Folder List**, and then click the **Deleted Items** folder.

The Deleted Items main window shows all the items you deleted from the other folders. You can change the views of the Deleted Items main window just like the other folders' main windows.

▶ **2.** Drag the **Organize Web site ideas** task from the Deleted Items main window to Tasks in the Folder List. The task moves back to the Tasks folder.

▶ **3.** Display the **Tasks** folder. The item is restored to its original location.

▶ **4.** Drag the task from the **Tasks** folder to **Deleted Items** in the Folder List. Once again, the item is moved.

All the items remain in the Deleted Items folder until you empty it. Once you empty this folder, the items can no longer be retrieved.

▶ **5.** Right-click **Deleted Items** in the Folder List, and then click **Empty "Deleted Items" Folder** on the shortcut menu.

▶ **6.** Click the **Yes** button to confirm that you want to permanently delete these items. The folder text should indicate that there are no items to show in this view.

Lisa is looking forward to the meeting you planned to talk about the content and design of the new company Web site. Outlook makes it simple and convenient to plan schedules and coordinate meetings.

Session 3.2 Quick Check

Review

1. Explain the difference between an appointment, an event, and a meeting.

2. What is the TaskPad?

3. What happens if you drag a task from the Tasks folder to the Calendar folder?

4. Explain the purpose of AutoDate and how it works.

5. What is a meeting request?

6. How does AutoPick work?

7. Describe what happens when you delete a recurring appointment from Outlook.

8. True or False: Once you move an item into the Deleted Items folder, you cannot retrieve it.

Review

Tutorial Summary

In this tutorial, you worked with the Notes, Tasks, and Calendar folders. You jotted down organized, customized and printed notes. You created a to-do list with one-time and recurring tasks, and then you organized your tasks by adding categories and changing the view of the Tasks folder. You assigned a task to someone else and responded to a task request sent to you. Next, you used the Calendar to set up and view your schedule. You scheduled appointments and events, and printed your calendar. You planned a meeting and sent e-mail invitations to invitees, and you responded to the meeting request that you received. You scheduled an online meeting. Finally, you saved your calendar as a Web page.

Key Terms

appointment	event	recurring task
assign	Internet Locator Server (ILS)	resource
attendee	meeting	task
AutoCreate	Microsoft Exchange Confer-	task owner
AutoDate	encing	task request
AutoPick	Microsoft Live Meeting	TaskPad
Calendar	NetMeeting	Windows Media Services
Date Navigator	note	
directory server	recurring appointment	

Practice

Practice the skills you learned in the tutorial using the same case scenario.

Review Assignments

There are no Data Files needed for the Review Assignments.

Assad Fahid handles the payroll for Wertheimer Accounting's clients. He asks you to work with him to help prepare his task list and schedule for the next few months. He needs to prepare the payroll for two clients—Beau Foods, an independent corner grocery store, and Photos & More, a film developer and framing company. He also asks you to set up a meeting with a potential client—Best Cleaners, a small dry-cleaning company that uses environmentally safe dry-cleaning methods. You'll create a schedule for the coming days and plan a meeting with Assad and Chris Newson of Best Cleaners.

To complete all of the Review Assignments, you will need to work with a classmate who also is using Outlook. If you do not have a classmate to work with, you will need to skip the steps in which you are asked to send messages or respond to a message you receive.

1. Create a contact card for yourself using your name and e-mail address.

2. Create a green note with the text "Plan meeting with Best Cleaners," assign yourself as the contact, and then close the note.

3. Create a pink note with the text "Prepare payroll for Beau Foods," assign yourself as the contact, and then close the note.

4. Create a new category called Payroll, and then assign the Payroll category to the green note.

5. Create a task from the green note with a due date of tomorrow, and then delete the green note.

6. Create a new green note with the text "Talk about advantages of outsourcing payroll; mention reliability and accuracy of our firm; and offer Beau Foods as reference"; and then close the note.

7. Assign the Payroll category to the pink and green notes.

8. Create a pink note with the text "Purchase more laser checks," assign the Payroll category to the note, create a new category called Supplies, assign that to the note, and then close the note.

9. View the notes by color, and then print the notes in memo style. Do not start each note on a new page.

10. Create a task with the subject "Prepare Photos & More payroll" and a due date of next Friday. Assign the task to the Payroll category.

11. Create a recurring task from the Prepare payroll for Beau Foods pink note with a monthly recurrence pattern that occurs the first Friday of every month and ends after three occurrences.

12. Create a contact card for a classmate using the classmate's name and e-mail address, and then assign the recurring task to your classmate. (*Hint:* You may need to enable the Outlook Rich Text Format for the recipient.)

13. Decline the task assignment you receive from your classmate; do not edit the response before sending.

14. View the tasks by category.

15. Schedule an appointment for the Prepare Photos & More payroll task for next Tuesday morning between 10 AM and 10:15 AM. Do not enter a location. Change the label to "Important." Turn off the reminder.

16. Drag the Prepare payroll for Beau Foods note to the Calendar folder in the Navigation Pane to schedule an appointment for next Thursday between 1:30 PM and 2:30 PM. Change the label to "Needs Preparation."

17. Create a two-day event with the subject "Health Fair" to begin next Wednesday. Turn off the reminder.

18. Create a recurring appointment to attend the event on both days between 10 AM and 1 PM. Show the time as Tentative.

19. Change the time for the Prepare payroll for Beau Foods appointment to between 2 PM and 2:30 PM by dragging the appointment start time in the planner.

20. Preview and print your calendar for next week in Weekly Style.

21. Schedule a two-hour meeting for next Tuesday starting at 1 PM with your classmate as a required attendee, the subject "Best Cleaners payroll," and the location "Assad's Office." Show the time in your calendar as Busy and label as Must Attend. Insert the green note as text only in the text area of the meeting request, and then send the meeting request.

22. Reply to the meeting request by proposing a new time. Select a starting time of 12:30 PM. Include the message "Let me know if this time works."

23. Check off the Plan meeting with Best Cleaners task as completed.

24. Schedule a one-hour NetMeeting with a classmate on the subject "Outsourcing Payroll." Send the meeting request.

25. Accept the Outsourcing Payroll meeting request you receive from your classmate.

26. Save your calendar for next week as a Web page. Use the filename **Schedule** and save it to the **Tutorial.03\Review** folder included with your Data Files. View the calendar in your default browser, and then close the browser.

27. Delete all of the categories (Payroll, Supplies), notes, tasks, contact cards, messages, and calendar items that you created or received in these assignments (delete the meetings without sending a cancellation or responses), and then empty the Deleted Items folder.

Case Problem 1

There are no Data Files needed for this Case Problem.

Balloon Creations   Wendy and Matthew Connors, as Balloon Creations, entertain at private parties and corporate events by fashioning animals and other objects out of balloons. They are hired to practice their craft at birthday parties, fundraisers, grand openings, and other special events. In addition, they offer classes where they teach others how to create objects from balloons. They use Outlook to organize their schedule.

1. Create a contact card for a classmate using the person's name and e-mail address. (If you don't have a classmate to work with, you can read but not complete all the steps in this Case Problem.)

2. Create a pink note with the text "Buy supplies" on one line, press the Enter key twice to double space, and then type "balloons, markers, helium" on another line. Add your classmate as a contact for the note. Assign the Suppliers category to the note, and then close it.

3. Create a yellow note with the text "Meet Randy for lunch on Tuesday," assign the Personal category, and then close the note.

4. Open the pink note, edit the text to "colored balloons, black markers, refill helium tank," and then close the note.

5. Create a task from the pink note with a due date of next Wednesday, no reminder, and a High priority.

6. Create a task with the subject "Confirm Thursday's party with Helen Pine," a due date of next Tuesday, and no reminder.

7. Assign the Confirm Thursday's party with Helen Pine task to your classmate.

8. Decline the task request you receive from your classmate.

9. Create an appointment from the yellow note by dragging the note from the Notes main window to the Calendar button in the Navigation Pane. Set the appointment at Bob's Diner for next Tuesday between 11:30 AM to 1 PM. Set a reminder for one hour before the appointment. Show the time as Out of Office and add the Personal label.

10. Create an appointment from the Confirm Thursday's party task for Monday at 3 PM to 3:30 PM. Set a reminder for 10 minutes before the appointment. Show the time as Free.

11. Create appointments for the following with no locations, using the default appointment reminder, and show the time as Busy:

Day	Time	Subject
Monday	Noon to 3 PM	Advanced Animals Class
Tuesday	1:30 PM to 4:30 PM	Jeremy Gottleib's 5th Birthday Party
Thursday	11:30 AM to 3:30 PM	Helen Pine Sweet 16
Friday	1 PM to 6 PM	Public Radio Benefit Party
Saturday and Sunday	10 AM to 3 PM	Firefighter Carnival

12. Change the Advanced Animals Class to a recurring appointment that recurs every two weeks on Monday for the next month.

Explore

13. Change the Firefighter Carnival on both days to all-day events. Show the time as Busy and turn off the reminder. (*Hint:* Open the Appointment window, and then click the All day event check box to insert a check mark. If you set an appointment for the two days using a recurrence pattern, remove the recurrence first.)

14. Send a meeting request to a classmate on the subject "Carnival Plans," scheduling a one-hour meeting for next Monday at 9 AM. Propose a new time of 9:30 AM when you receive the meeting request from your classmate.

15. Schedule a two-hour NetMeeting with a classmate on the subject "Sweet 16 Details" for next Tuesday at 10 AM. Accept the meeting request when you receive it from your classmate.

16. Preview your calendar in Daily Style, and then print it.

17. Delete all the notes, tasks, messages, appointments, and events you created in this Case Problem, and then empty the Deleted Items folder.

Apply

Apply what you learned in the tutorial to organize a rental schedule for a music studio.

Case Problem 2

There are no Data Files needed for this Case Problem.

Velez Studio Bruce Velez runs a music studio with the latest recording, mixing, and editing equipment. Musicians rent the studio by the half hour to record their music. Bruce uses Outlook to track the tasks he needs to complete to keep the studio running and to organize the studio rental schedule.

1. Create a white note with the text "Check speaker connections," and then close it.

2. Create a yellow note with the text "Buy new microphone," assign the Suppliers category to the note, and then close it.

3. Create a task from the microphone note, assigning it to the category "Equipment" that you add to the Master Category List. Do not assign a due date or priority.

4. Create a task with the subject "Calibrate equipment" that recurs daily every weekday starting next Monday and ending after five occurrences. Set the priority to Low and the reminder for 9 AM. Save and close the task.

5. View the tasks by category, and then expand each category group to display the tasks, if necessary.

6. Change the Calibrate equipment task priority to High. (*Hint:* Click the Priority text box, and then click High.)

7. Change the status of the Buy new microphone task to In Progress and mark it as 25% complete.

Explore

8. Send a status report to yourself for the Buy new microphone task. Click the Send Status Report button on the Standard toolbar of the Buy new microphone Task window (use the ScreenTips to identify this button), type your e-mail address in the To text box, and then send and receive the message.

9. Print all rows of the task list in Table Style.

10. Display the Calendar folder and then set the view to Work Week.

11. Create an appointment for Leslie Gorman (Subject) in the Studio for next Monday between 10 AM and 1 PM and no reminder. Type "Need to hook up harp to recording equipment" in the notes text box. Add the Important label to the appointment. Assign the appointment to the Key Customer category. Save and close the appointment.

Explore

12. Copy the appointment to Wednesday starting at 1 PM. Click the Monday appointment to select it, press and hold the Ctrl key, drag the appointment to Wednesday between 1 PM and 4 PM, and then release the Ctrl key.

13. Create appointments for Wes Carpenter (Subject) in the Studio for next Tuesday between 11:30 AM and 4:30 PM and for next Thursday between 1 PM and 5 PM. Turn off the reminders.

14. Create appointments for Rick Anders (Subject) in the Studio for next Wednesday and next Thursday between 9 AM and noon. Turn off the reminders.

15. Create an event for next Thursday with the subject "Local Battle of the Bands" and turn off the reminder. Select the event and then use the Calendar Coloring button to add the Must Attend label to event.

16. Create a task from the event with the subject "Distribute studio brochure at battle of the bands". (*Hint:* Drag the event from the Calendar to the TaskPad or to the Tasks folder in the Navigation Pane. Modify the subject in the Task window.)

17. Print your calendar for the next work week in Calendar Details Style.

18. Delete all the notes, tasks, e-mails, appointments, events, and the category (Equipment) you created in this Case Problem, and then empty the Deleted Items folder.

Case Problem 3

Challenge

Extend what you learned in the tutorial to organize staff and movie schedules for a video store chain.

There are no Data Files needed for this Case Problem.

Movie Madness Movie Madness is a video store chain that rents videos and DVDs of current and classic movies to walk-in customers and shows films in its stores. The stores are open 24 hours a day, 7 days a week, so that customers can rent videos or watch a movie no matter what the day or time. Renna Lisant, manager of Movie Madness, organizes the staff and movie schedules using the Outlook Calendar, saves the calendar as a Web page, and then posts the schedule on the company intranet. This week, the stores are showing their customers' favorite 100 movies, based on customers' rental history.

1. Create a contact card for yourself using your name and e-mail address.

2. Create a yellow note with the text "Prepare list of top 100 movies"; press the Enter key twice to double space; and type "Create this list from the customer database. Find out which 100 movies were rented most frequently in the last 24 months." Close the note.

Explore

3. Create an e-mail message from the note by dragging the note from the Notes main window to the Inbox icon in the Folder List. (*Hint:* Click the Notes icon in the Navigation Pane, and then click the Folder List icon in the Navigation Pane.) Address the e-mail to yourself. The subject is the first line of the note. Send the message, and then download it, if necessary.

Explore

4. Create a task from the e-mail by dragging the e-mail message from the Inbox main window to the Tasks icon in the Folder List. Set a due date of this Friday, set the priority to High, and turn off the reminder.

Explore

5. Assign the task to yourself. Send the task request. Click the OK button in the dialog box to acknowledge that you cannot assign a task to yourself. Click the Cancel Assignment button, and then save and close the task window.

Explore

6. Copy the yellow note onto the desktop so that it is visible even when Outlook is closed or minimized. You can drag the note to the desktop or you can select the yellow note, press the Ctrl+C keys to copy the note to the Clipboard, minimize Outlook to display the desktop, click a blank area of the desktop, and then press the Ctrl+V keys to paste the note. You can open, close, and print the note just as you would from within Outlook.

Explore

7. Verify that the note now exists in both the Notes folder and on the desktop. Maximize the Outlook window, and verify that the original note still exists in Outlook. Minimize the Outlook window, and then double-click the note on the desktop to open it. Close the note, click it to select it (if necessary), press the Delete key to move the item to the Recycle Bin, and then click the Yes button, if necessary, to confirm the deletion. Now maximize the Outlook window, and verify that the original note still appears in the Notes folder.

Explore

8. Create a second task with the subject "Set up next week's staff schedule" and a due date of four hours from now. (*Hint*: Type "four hours from now" in the Due date text box.) Assign the task to the new category called "Schedule." Save and close the task.

9. Change the Calendar to Work Week view.

10. Schedule the staff for next Monday through Friday by creating a new appointment for each shift. Each shift lasts eight hours and recurs every two days. End each recurrence next Friday. Turn off the reminder. One staff member works each shift. Enter the staff member's name as the appointment's subject; do not enter a location. Show the time as Free. The staff includes you, Lydia Jiminez, Frank Zapata, Chris Soto, Corrie Beppu, and Maurice Singleton. (*Hint:* You will have three appointments for Monday and three appointments for Tuesday. The Monday appointments will recur on Wednesday and Friday; the Tuesday appointment will recur on Thursday.)

11. Use the Calendar Coloring button to add the Must Attend label to four of the appointments you just created. (*Hint:* The coloring is applied to the entire series.)

12. Check off the Set up next week's staff schedule task as completed.

13. Create an event for each day next week with a different movie title of your choice for the subject; these are the movies that will be shown that day. Turn off the reminders.

14. Create a contact card for a classmate using that person's name and e-mail address. If you don't have a classmate to work with, you can read but not complete all the steps in this Case Problem. (*Hint:* Change the e-mail properties to Outlook Rich Text Format, if necessary.)

Explore

15. Plan a meeting for next Tuesday from 10 AM to 11 AM in the Conference Room with your classmate and the entire staff of Movie Madness, except the staff member whom you assigned to work that shift; use "Staff Meeting" as the subject. (*Hint:* Open the Plan a Meeting dialog box. Type the names of staff members listed in exercise 10 in the All Attendees list by clicking the Click here to add name text box and typing a name.) Click the envelope icon next to each name except your classmate and yourself, and click Don't send meeting to this attendee. Click the Make Meeting button, enter the subject and location, click the Send button on the Standard toolbar, and then click the Yes button to save and close the meeting.

16. Accept the meeting request you receive from your classmate and send the response now.

Explore

17. Preview next week's calendar in the Tri-fold Style, and then print it. Select the print style in the Print dialog box, click the Preview button in the Print dialog box, and then click the Print button on the Print Preview toolbar.)

18. Save next week's calendar as a Web page with the filename **MovieSchedule** to the **Tutorial.03\Cases** folder included with your Data Files. View the Web page in your browser, and then close the browser.

19. Delete all the contacts, notes, tasks, appointments, events, meetings (sending a cancellation notice for the meeting you organized and without sending a response for the meeting you accepted), and category (Schedule) that you created in this Case Problem, and then empty the Deleted Items folder.

Create

Create notes, tasks, and a schedule to plan a fundraiser for a nonprofit organization by using and expanding on the skills you learned in this tutorial.

Case Problem 4

There are no Data Files needed for this Case Problem.

Family Services   Family Services is a nonprofit organization that provides aid to needy families. They provide clothing, household goods (such as dishes, vacuum cleaners, and furniture), and money to pay for rent, food, and necessary items that the organization cannot get donated. Ada Cox, the director of Family Services, is planning the annual fundraiser to encourage community members to donate goods and money. Ada asks you to jot down ideas for the fundraiser's theme, create a task list, and then schedule time to complete those tasks. The fundraiser will take place three weeks from this Friday.

1. Create at least three notes with ideas for the fundraiser, and then close them. For example, one note might suggest possible themes; another might include a reminder to send directions to party guests.

2. Color code the notes, using at least two colors.

3. Add a new category called "Fundraiser" to the Master Category List.

4. Assign the Fundraiser category to the three notes.

5. Print all the Fundraiser notes.

6. Create a task list of at least four activities that Ada must complete before the fundraiser. For example, she might need to finalize the number of guests and provide that information to a caterer.

7. Assign all tasks to the Fundraiser category.

8. Schedule appointments to complete each task during the week before the party.

Explore

9. Create a new task request to yourself with the subject "Create raffle drawing," a due date of the Monday before the party, and assigned to the Fundraiser category. (*Hint:* Click the New button list arrow, and then click Task Request to open a Task Request window without first creating a task.)

Explore

10. Click the Cancel Assignment button on the Task Request Standard toolbar to change the task assignment to a regular task.

11. In the notes text box, type "To raise additional money during the fundraiser, arrange a raffle drawing. Ask local businesses to donate an item or service ranging in value from $10 to $150. We'll sell tickets for the drawing and give away the donations as prizes."

Explore

12. Send a status report to a classmate for the Create raffle drawing task. Click the Send Status Report button on the Standard toolbar of the Create raffle drawing Task window (use the ScreenTips to identify the correct button), type your classmate's e-mail address in the To text box, and then send the message. Download the message your classmate sends to you. (If you don't have a classmate to work with, you can read but not complete all the steps in this Case Problem.)

13. Plan a final meeting with a classmate and Ada with the subject "Finalize plans" for the Thursday before the fundraiser between 3 PM and 4 PM, and assign it to the Fundraiser category.

Explore

14. Don't send a meeting request to Ada. (*Hint:* Click the e-mail icon to the left of Ada's name, and then click Don't send meeting to this attendee.)

15. Insert any appropriate notes as text only into the notes text box of the Meeting window.

Explore

16. Insert the Create raffle drawing task as an attachment into the notes text box of the Meeting window.

17. Send the meeting request, and then click the Yes button to save and close the meeting.

18. Decline the meeting request you receive.

19. Preview and print your calendar for the week of the party, using the Weekly Style.

20. Save your calendar as a Web page, using the filename **FundraiserCalendar** in the **Tutorial.03\Cases** folder included with your Data Files. Preview the Web page, and then close the browser window.

Explore

21. Find all Outlook items that are assigned to the Fundraiser category check box. (*Hint:* Click Tools on the menu bar, point to Find, and then click Advanced Find to open the Advanced Find window. Select Any type of Outlook item in the Look for list. Click the More Choices tab, click the Categories button, click the Fundraiser check box, and then click the OK button. Click the Find Now button.)

Explore

22. Select all the items and then press the Delete key. Click the Yes button to confirm that you want to delete all the items. (*Hint:* To select all the items, click the first item, press and hold the Shift key, click the last item, and then release the Shift key.) Delete the meeting without sending a cancellation.

23. Click the Close button in the title bar of the Advanced Find window to close the window, delete the category that you created in this Case Problem, delete the messages that you sent and received in this Case Problem, and then empty the Deleted Items folder.

Review

Quick Check Answers

Session 3.1

1. A never-ending electronic notepad in Outlook to jot down ideas, reminders, and other thoughts
2. You can create a note from any view using the New button list arrow on the Standard toolbar.
3. A task is a one-time item on your to-do list that you want to perform. A recurring task occurs repeatedly.
4. The AutoCreate feature converts the note to a task.
5. False
6. A task request is an e-mail message with details about the task to be assigned.

7. You need two people to assign a task—one to send the task request and one to respond to the task request. Both must be using Outlook to send and receive e-mail.

8. No, only the current owner can update a task.

Session 3.2

1. An appointment is an activity that does not involve other people or resources. An event is an activity that lasts one or more full days. A meeting is an appointment with other people or resources.

2. The TaskPad is a summary list of the Tasks folder that appears in the Day/Week/Month view of the Calendar.

3. Outlook schedules an appointment using the task's subject, notes, and categories.

4. AutoDate converts natural-language date and time descriptions—such as "one week from today" and "noon"—into the numerical format that represents the month, day, and year or time, respectively.

5. A meeting request is an e-mail message which each invited attendee and resource receives and responds to.

6. If you have access to others' calendars, AutoPick selects the next available free time for all invited people and resources.

7. You have the option of moving one or all occurrences of the appointment to the Deleted Items folder.

8. False; you can retrieve any item from the Deleted Items folder until you empty it.

Objectives

Session 4.1
- Attach message flags
- Add voting buttons, delivery receipts, delivery dates, and categories to messages
- Create subfolders and file messages
- Create rules with the Rules Wizard to organize the Inbox
- Use conditional formatting to organize items

Session 4.2
- Find, sort, group, and filter messages
- Archive messages
- Set up the Junk E-mail Filter

Managing Your Inbox

Organizing E-Mail Messages to Arrange a Cleaning Crew

Case

Speedy Cleaning Company

Nadya Rutskoi manages Speedy Cleaning Company, which has provided pre- and post-party cleanup services for individuals in the Washington, D.C. area since 1992. Whether clients are having an intimate wedding, a lavish New Year's Eve party, or a formal business-related gathering, the Speedy Cleaning team makes their homes spotless. Before and after an event, Nadya sends a cleanup crew with enough people to thoroughly clean the house in four hours. A two-person crew can efficiently clean a smaller home, whereas a dozen or more people might be required for larger homes. The crew arrives with its own cleaning supplies and equipment, and each crew member has an assigned task, such as vacuuming, dusting, polishing, window washing, and so forth.

Rather than hiring full-time employees, Speedy Cleaning relies on independent contractors who can accept or decline any offered job. This enables Speedy Cleaning to accommodate clients who plan events well in advance and also those who decide to throw last-minute events. Nadya uses Outlook to communicate with clients and contractors, schedule cleanup times, and arrange cleaning crews.

In this tutorial, you will help Nadya prepare for an upcoming birthday party hosted by the Gormanns. You will send and receive messages with flags, voting buttons, and other tracking and delivery options. You will create subfolders in the Inbox so you can file messages both manually and with rules you create. Then you will use automatic formatting to color messages and meetings based on specific conditions. Next, you will find, sort, group, and filter messages. Finally, you will archive messages, and then set up the Junk E-mail Filter to detect spam messages.

Student Data Files

There are no student Data Files needed for this tutorial.

Session 4.1

Flagging Messages

Some messages you send require a specific response or action from the recipients. Although the subject should be informative and the message can provide any explicit instructions, often a more obvious reminder would better draw attention to your request. A **Quick Flag** is a colored flag icon that appears in the message list. The flag also includes text that appears in an InfoBar in the Reading Pane or the Message window. You can choose from preset flag text or create your own, such as "Need Cleaning Crew."

Flags can also include a deadline. You can select a specific due date or enter descriptive words, such as "tomorrow," that Outlook converts to the correct date. When a recipient receives and stores a flagged message in the Inbox, Outlook displays a reminder at the appropriate time. Reminders are activated only from flagged messages in the Inbox. If the recipient moves the message to another folder, no reminders appear.

After you send a flagged message, your copy of the message in the Sent Items folder retains the flag (along with a reference to it in the InfoBar). You can add a flag to a message in this folder the same way as you would a new message. Be aware that you will not be reminded on the specified date.

You'll create an e-mail message, and then add a Need Cleaning Crew flag with a due date for one week from today to the message.

To create a message flag:

1. Click **Tools** on the menu bar, click **Options**, and then click the **Mail Format** tab. You need to change the default message format to HTML.

2. Click the **Compose in this message format** list arrow, click **HTML**, and then click the **OK** button.

3. Create a new e-mail message addressed to your e-mail address with the subject **Schedule Cleaning Crew** and the message **Please set up a five-person cleaning crew for the Gormann event two weeks from today.**, press the **Enter** key twice to double space, and then type your name.

4. Click the **Message Flag** button ⮟ on the Standard toolbar. The Flag for Follow Up dialog box opens.

5. Click the **Flag to** list arrow to display the preset flag options. Although you may often find it appropriate to select from these, in this case you'll type your own.

6. Click in the **Flag to** text box and type **Need Cleaning Crew**. See Figure 4-1.

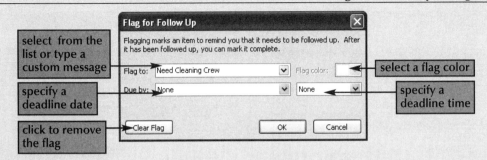

You want to add a due date to this flag for one week from today at 5 p.m.

7. Click the left **Due by** list arrow, click the date for one week from today, click the right **Due by** list arrow, and then click **5:00 PM**.

8. Click the **OK** button. The Flag for Follow Up dialog box closes and you return to the Message window. The InfoBar shows the flag message. See Figure 4-2.

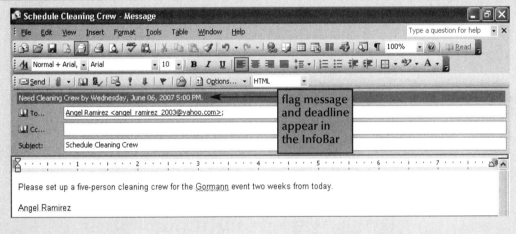

9. Send the message.

When the recipient receives the message, the message displays a red flag in the message list in the Inbox. The recipient could choose to put the request on the task list, create a reminder note, or schedule an appointment to respond to the message flag by dragging the message to the Tasks, Notes, or Calendar folder. Once the flag request is complete, the recipient can mark the flag completed. This can be done in the Inbox or in the Flag for Follow Up dialog box.

To respond to a flagged message:

1. Display the **Inbox**, and then download your messages, if necessary. The flag icon appears next to the Schedule Cleaning Crew message header. You cannot see the flag text in the message list, but it is visible in the InfoBar in the Reading Pane. See Figure 4-3.

Figure 4-3 | **Received message with a flag**

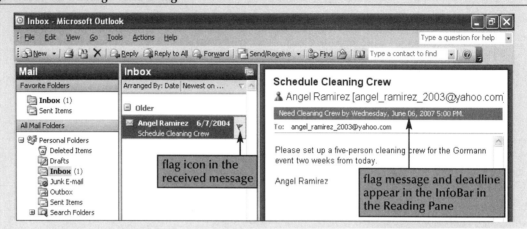

Trouble? If the flag does not appear with your received message, try opening the message in a message window. If the flag still does not appear, then your ISP may not support message flags. You will not see the flag text in Step 1 or Step 3.

2. Click the **Schedule Cleaning Crew** message to select it, click the **Reply** button on the Standard toolbar, and then reply with the message **I'll send out an e-mail right away.**

3. Send the message. The InfoBar in the original e-mail changed to include information about the reply and related messages. See Figure 4-4.

Figure 4-4 | **Replying to an e-mail with a Quick Flag**

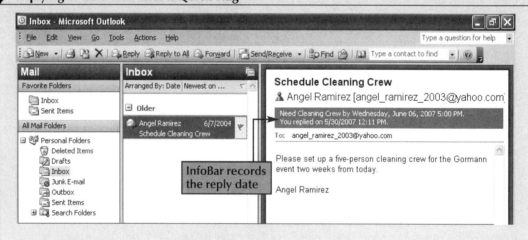

Next, you will send an e-mail message to locate team members, so you'll mark the flag complete. You could do that with the Follow Up button in the open Message window or with the flag icon directly in the Inbox. You'll change the flag status from the Inbox because the message is closed.

To change the status of a message flag:

1. Right-click the **flag** icon 🚩 for the Schedule Cleaning Crew message. The shortcut menu has commands for selecting a flag color, marking the flag as complete, adding a reminder to the flag, or clearing the flag. See Figure 4-5.

Changing the status of a flag ◄ Figure 4-5

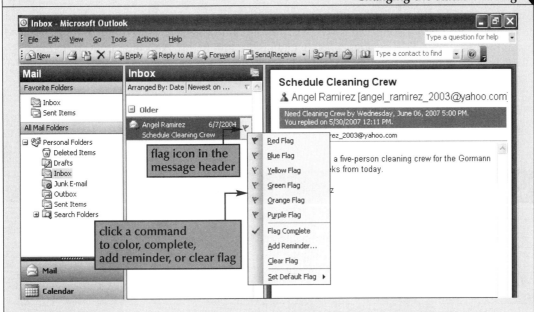

Trouble? If you don't see the flag icon, the Inbox may not be in a view that displays this information. Click View on the menu bar, point to Arrange By, point to Current View, click Messages, and then repeat Step 1.

▶ 2. Click **Flag Complete** on the shortcut menu. The flag icon changes to a check mark and the completion date is added to the text in the InfoBar. See Figure 4-6.

Updated message flag ◄ Figure 4-6

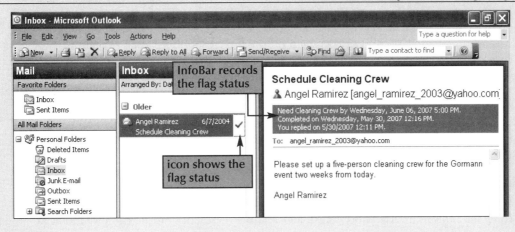

You can also add flags to messages you receive to help organize them and make certain messages stand out. Right-click the flag icon in the message list, and then click the flag color on the shortcut menu that you want to add to the message. You can also add a reminder to the flag with text and a deadline. Right-click the flag icon in the message list, and then click Add Reminder on the shortcut menu to open the Flag for Follow Up dialog box.

Next, you'll send an e-mail message to ask for information about a cleaning crew member's availability.

Setting Message Options

Outlook sets up new messages based on the default options specified in the Options dialog box. These options include setting the priority and privacy of a message, adding voting buttons, requesting receipts, and specifying the initial and expiration delivery dates. You can override these options for specific messages using the Options button in the Message window.

The available message options may differ, depending on whether you are using Outlook with Exchange Server, Microsoft Mail, or another MAPI-compliant e-mail system. If you are using an Internet mail server, check with the administrator to determine which capabilities (if any) it provides.

Reference Window | **Setting Message Options**

- Create a new e-mail message.
- Click the Options button on the Standard toolbar in the Message window.
- Select appropriate options, such as voting buttons, receipts, delivery and expiration dates, and categories, and then click the Close button.
- Send the message.

You will use voting buttons, delivery receipts, and an expiration date in the message you'll create to determine a crew member's availability.

Specifying Votes and Message Delivery

When you want people to respond to a multiple-choice question, you can ask the recipients of a message to cast a vote. **Voting buttons** provide a limited set of possible options from which recipients can choose one answer. Outlook has three standard sets of voting buttons: Approve or Reject; Yes or No; and Yes or No or Maybe. These work well for a variety of purposes, such as evaluating a proposal or responding to an invitation. In other cases, you may need to customize the voting buttons. For example, you may need to have people select a meeting day, choose a lunch entree, or pick a team leader. In these cases, you can create custom voting buttons to elicit the information you need. You can include as many buttons as you like in a set of voting buttons.

You create custom voting buttons by typing the button names, separated by semicolons (but no spaces), in the Message Options dialog box, for example: Monday;Wednesday;Friday or Pizza;Fish and Chips or Lars;Caryl;Mac;Sophie.

Each message can contain only one set of voting buttons, whether you use a standard set or create a custom set. The voting buttons do not appear in the Message window until after the message is sent. Outlook also adds an InfoBar with the text, "Please respond using the buttons above." Both the sender and the recipient must be using Outlook to use voting buttons.

You'll create a message in which consultants can specify their availability by clicking a Yes, No, or Maybe voting button.

To create a message with voting buttons:

1. Create a new e-mail message addressed to your e-mail address with the subject **Available for pre-party cleaning?** and the message **The Gormann birthday party is two weeks from today and will require pre-party cleaning from 6 a.m. to 10 a.m. Please click a voting button to indicate whether you are available.**, press the **Enter** key twice, and then type your name.

2. Click the **Options** button on the Standard toolbar. The Message Options dialog box opens.

   Although you could define your own buttons, this time you will use a default set.

3. Click the **Use voting buttons** list arrow, and then click **Yes;No;Maybe**. See Figure 4-7.

Message Options dialog box ◄ Figure 4-7

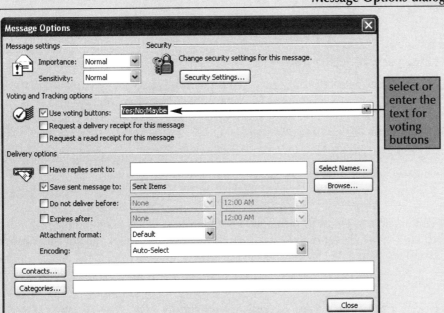

You could send the message as is. However, because this message is time sensitive, you want to know when the message is received and opened.

Tracking Message Delivery

Like phone messages and letters, you cannot be sure that someone has received your e-mail message unless they reply. However, confirming receipt of every incoming e-mail and then later crafting a more complete reply can be time-consuming for the recipient. Instead, you can have Outlook notify you when the recipient receives the message, when the recipient opens the message, or both. You set delivery and read receipts in the Message Options dialog box.

To request message delivery receipts:

1. Click the **Request a delivery receipt for this message** check box to insert a check mark. You will receive a message when the recipient receives the message.

▶ **2.** Click the **Request a read receipt for this message** check box to insert a check mark. You will receive a message when the recipient opens the message (although you have no guarantee that the recipient has actually read the message unless he or she replies).

With Outlook, you can determine when a message is delivered or deleted. When you delay the delivery time, Outlook stores the message in your Outbox and then delivers it on the specified delivery date. You can also set an expiration date and time for a message. The message is deleted if the recipient hasn't opened it by the date and time you specified.

Because a response from the cleaning employee becomes irrelevant after next Monday, the day you finalize the cleanup crew, you decide to have the message expire next Monday at 9 a.m. Because this message is time sensitive, you want to deliver it immediately.

To set delivery time limits:

▶ **1.** Click the **Expires after** check box, press the **Tab** key to select the date in the left Expires after list box, type **next Mon**, and then press the **Tab** key. The time in the right Expires after list box is selected, and Outlook inserts the correct date for next Monday in the left Expires after text box.

▶ **2.** Type **9 a.m.** in the right Expires after text box, and then press the **Tab** key. Outlook expands the time to show 9:00 AM.

You can assign categories to messages from the Message Options dialog box. You have access to the Master Category List, and you can create and assign categories as needed. You'll assign the Schedule category to the message.

To assign a category to an e-mail message:

▶ **1.** Click the **Categories** button. The Categories dialog box opens.

▶ **2.** Type **Schedule** in the Item(s) belong to these categories text box, click the **Add to List** button to add the category to the Master Category List and insert a check mark, and then click the **OK** button. Although your dates will differ, your Message Options dialog box should look similar to Figure 4-8.

◀ **Figure 4-8**

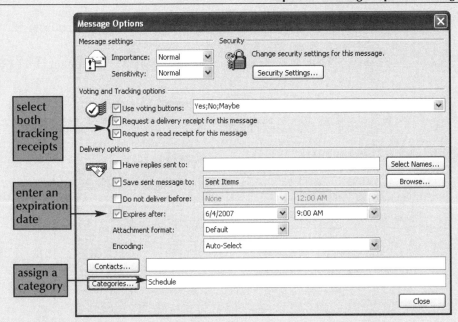

3. Click the **Close** button in the Message Options dialog box.

4. Send the message.

The message you just sent did not mention the location of the party. This information could be helpful to some potential crew members.

Recalling or Resending Messages

Given the speed with which you can send e-mail messages, sometimes you may wish you could bring back or modify part of a message, such as when you type an incorrect time or date for a proposed meeting or wish to include additional details, such as the Gormann party location. With Outlook, you can attempt to recall or resend the message. A **recall** removes unread copies of the message from the recipient's Inbox or replaces the unread message with a corrected one. You can recall a message only if both the sender and recipient have Outlook running, and the message remains unopened in the recipient's Inbox. This is common sense, as removing a message that the recipient has already read or removed from his or her Inbox would be confusing for the recipient who has already seen the message. You must have requested a read receipt when sending the message in order for Outlook to determine whether it was read; otherwise, Outlook cannot recall the message.

If the message cannot be recalled, you might want to simply send a corrected version. To do so, click Resend This Message on the Actions menu. A Message window opens with the original message and recipients. You can modify it as needed and then send the revised message to the recipients as usual. Because the original message may still be unread in the recipient's Inbox or may have been read, you might want to add a message flag to draw attention to this newer version.

You will attempt to recall the message you just sent and add information about the party location.

To recall a message:

▶ **1.** Display the **Sent Items** folder.

Trouble? If a dialog box opens, informing you that the sender has requested a read receipt, click the Yes button to send the read receipt response.

▶ **2.** Double-click the **Available for pre-party cleaning?** message to open its Message window.

▶ **3.** Click **Actions** on the menu bar, and then click **Recall This Message**. The Recall This Message dialog box opens. See Figure 4-9.

Figure 4-9 ▶ **Recall This Message dialog box**

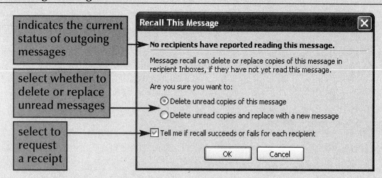

Nadya suggests that you send the directions to the Gormann house only to those who respond that they can work the party, so you don't need to recall the message.

▶ **4.** Click the **Cancel** button, and then close the Message window.

▶ **5.** Display the **Inbox**.

If you request a message recall, you will receive messages in your Inbox informing you of the success or failure of the recall.

Casting a Vote

Messages with voting buttons and tracking options arrive the same way as any other message—in your Inbox. The voting options are available in both the Reading Pane and the open Message window. One way to ensure that recipients respond using the voting buttons is to include that instruction in the message body, as you did with the Available for pre-party cleaning? message.

From the Reading Pane, the recipient can click the InfoBar and then click the vote in the menu that opens. From the open Message window, the recipient can click the appropriate voting button above the InfoBar. The selection is added to the subject line and the recipient has the option of adding a note to the reply e-mail. After the reply is sent, the InfoBar in the original message changes to reflect the recipient's vote as well as the date and time it was made.

You'll respond to the Available for pre-party cleaning? message using the voting buttons.

To cast a vote using the voting buttons:

► **1.** If necessary, download your messages.

► **2.** Double-click the **Available for pre-party cleaning?** message to open its Message window. A dialog box opens, informing you that the sender has requested a read receipt. You can choose whether to send the receipt. See Figure 4-10.

Read receipt message | Figure 4-10

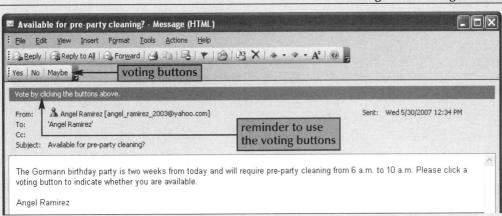

Trouble? If you responded to the read receipt message in the previous set of steps, or if the read receipt dialog box does not appear, continue with Step 4.

► **3.** Click the **Yes** button. The Available for pre-party cleaning? message opens. The voting buttons appear above the InfoBar. See Figure 4-11.

Message with voting buttons | Figure 4-11

Trouble? If you do not have Yes, No, and Maybe voting buttons just above the message window, or if they are grayed out and unavailable, then you need to enable Rich Text Format for your own contact card. Delete the message you received, then open your contact card, right-click the e-mail address in the E-mail text box, and then click Outlook Properties to open the E-mail Properties dialog box. Click the Internet format list arrow, click Send using Outlook Rich Text Format, and then click the OK button. Save and close the Contact window, if necessary. Go back to page 207 and repeat the steps from that point. If, after doing this, you still don't see the voting buttons or InfoBar, you are probably not using Outlook with Exchange Server, Microsoft Mail, or another MAPI-compliant e-mail client. Click the Reply button on the Standard toolbar, and then continue with Step 6.

► **4.** Click the **No** voting button. A dialog box opens, confirming your response and giving you the option to add a message to your reply e-mail. The first option returns your vote to the sender. The second option opens a reply Message window so you can type a response. Either option adds the text of the voting button you selected to the subject line. See Figure 4-12.

Figure 4-12 | Message dialog box after using voting buttons

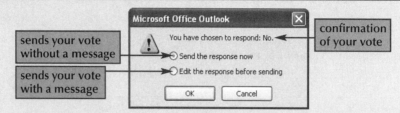

5. Click the **Edit the response before sending** option button, and then click the **OK** button. A reply Message window opens, in which you can type a response.

6. Type **I will be on vacation for that week.** in the message area.

7. Send the message. The InfoBar in the original message reflects your vote and the date and time of your response.

8. Close the **Available for pre-party cleaning?** message.

The benefit of using voting buttons rather than having recipients type their replies is that Outlook can tally the votes for you.

Tracking Votes and Message Delivery

When you receive replies, each e-mail shows the recipient's vote as well as any message that was added. You can open, view, and save those messages the same way as any other messages.

To receive voting replies:

1. Download your messages, if necessary. New messages appear in your Inbox. One message is a read receipt and another contains the vote reply. See Figure 4-13.

Figure 4-13 | Received read receipt and voting reply

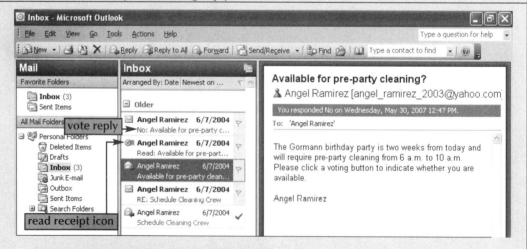

Trouble? If you don't see the read receipt, you are probably not using Outlook with Exchange Server or a mail server that offers this capability. Skip to Step 3. If your voting reply looks different from the one shown in Figure 4-13, then you were not able to use the voting buttons in the preceding set of steps. Skip Steps 2 through 3 and continue with the next section, "Organizing Your Inbox."

2. Click the **Read: Available for pre-party cleaning?** message to display it in the Reading Pane and see the date the recipient opened the message. See Figure 4-14.

Read receipt message | Figure 4-14

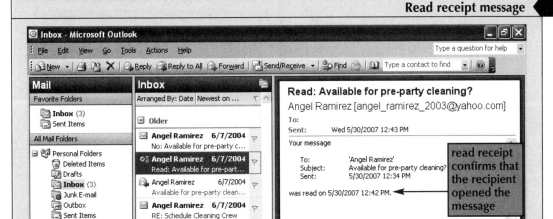

3. Click the **No: Available for pre-party cleaning?** message in the message list. You can see the vote response in both the InfoBar in the Reading Pane and the subject.

A copy of the original message you sent with the voting buttons is stored in the Sent Items folder. This e-mail not only records your outgoing message, it also tracks the recipients' votes as well as delivery and read dates. Once you receive replies, a special icon marks the message in the Sent Items folder. When you open the message, it contains two tabs—the Message tab shows your original message; the Tracking tab lists all the recipients' names and votes as well as the dates of the delivery and read receipts, if requested.

To track votes and message delivery:

1. Display the **Sent Items** folder. The icon next to the Available for pre-party cleaning? message indicates that the vote tally will be collected in this e-mail. See Figure 4-15.

Figure 4-15 ▶ Sent Items folder with tracked item

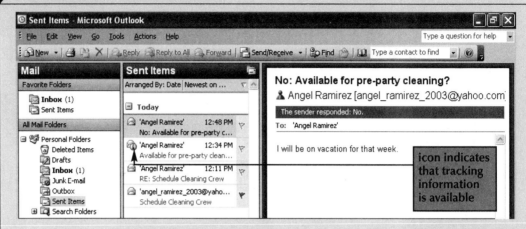

2. Open the **Available for pre-party cleaning?** message. You want to review the information on the Tracking tab.

3. Click the **Tracking** tab in the Message window. See Figure 4-16.

Figure 4-16 ▶ Tracking tab for read receipts and votes

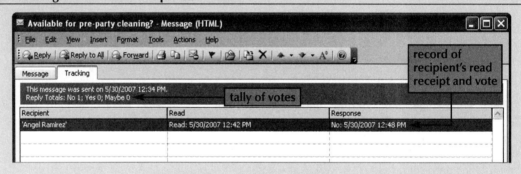

You can see the date and time the message was delivered and read as well as what votes were cast. The InfoBar tallies the votes for the entire group of recipients.

4. Close the Message window, and then display the **Inbox**.

As you work, items will begin to pile up, especially in the Inbox. To work effectively and efficiently, you'll need to "clean house" periodically by moving items from one folder to another.

Organizing Your Inbox

As you can readily see, messages can collect quickly in your Inbox. Even if you respond to each message as it arrives, all the original messages remain in your Inbox. Some messages you'll want to delete. Others you'll want to file and store, just as you would file and store paper memos in a file cabinet. In fact, the Folder List acts like an electronic file cabinet. After you create an organizational system, you create and label a series of folders, and subfolders within folders, in which to store items. For example, Nadya might create folders in which to store messages for Speedy Cleaning and for each client within the Inbox folder.

You'll use the Folder List to switch between folders and organize your messages. Moving messages between the main window and the Folder List works in much the same way as Windows Explorer to manage your files.

Creating Personal Folders

You can create personal folders at the same level as the default folders, such as Inbox, Outbox, and Sent Items, or you can create subfolders within any folder. Where you choose to place folders is a matter of personal preference. Some people prefer to group folders they create within the default folder of the same type (such as creating a mail folder within the Inbox); others prefer to keep any folders they create within the Personal Folders at the same level as the default folders. For now, you'll create two subfolders in the Inbox folder, named Speedy Cleaning and Gormann. Once you create a subfolder, either the plus sign button or the minus sign button precedes the main folder. Which button appears depends on whether the subfolders are displayed (minus sign button) or hidden (plus sign button).

When you create a folder, you supply a name, select the type of Outlook items you want to store in it, and choose its location. Each folder can store only one type of item—appointment, contact, journal, mail, note, or task. You'll create folders to store mail messages.

To create subfolders:

▶ **1.** Display the **Folder List**. The Folder List shows the full folder structure, including any subfolders or other personal folders you created.

▶ **2.** Click the **New** button list arrow on the Standard toolbar, and then click **Folder**. The Create New Folder dialog box opens.

In this dialog box, you'll name the folder, select the type of items the folder will contain, and choose the folder's location.

▶ **3.** Type **Speedy Cleaning** in the Name text box.

▶ **4.** Click the **Folder contains** list arrow, view the options, and then click **Mail and Post Items**. You can also create subfolders to store appointments, contacts, journal entries, notes, and tasks.

▶ **5.** Click **Inbox** in the Select where to place the folder list as the location for your new folder. See Figure 4-17.

Figure 4-17 Create New Folder dialog box

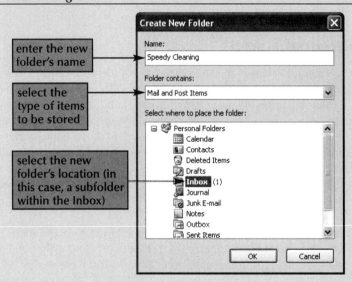

enter the new folder's name

select the type of items to be stored

select the new folder's location (in this case, a subfolder within the Inbox)

> **6.** Click the **OK** button. The new folder appears in the Folder List indented below the Inbox.
>
> **Trouble?** If you cannot see the subfolder, the Inbox is probably collapsed. Click the plus sign button ⊞ to display the subfolder.

> **7.** Repeat Steps 2 through 6 to create a subfolder named **Gormann** that contains **Mail and Post Items** in the **Inbox**. The Folder List shows the two new subfolders for Mail and Post Items in the Inbox folder. See Figure 4-18.

Figure 4-18 Subfolders added to the Inbox

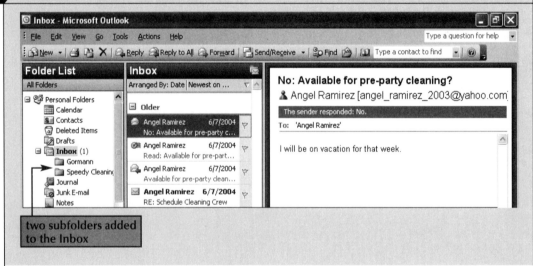

two subfolders added to the Inbox

Now you can file any messages related to Speedy Cleaning Company in its folder and any messages relating to the specific client in its own folder.

Filing Messages

The ability to move items from one folder to another helps you to keep your tasks, appointments, notes, and messages organized. The simplest way to file an item is to drag it from one folder to another. When you drag an item into a folder that stores that type of item, the item is moved. When you drag an item to a folder that stores another type of item, a new window opens for that folder's item so you can enter additional information to complete that item. For example, dragging a message from the Inbox to another mail folder moves the message, but dragging a message from the Inbox to the Calendar folder opens a new Appointment window and copies the message body into the notes text box. You can then enter the times, add a location, or set a reminder as needed to complete the appointment.

Moving Items Between Folders

Reference Window

- Display the Folder List, and expand folders to display the folders between which you want to move items.
- In the Folder List, click the folder with the items you want to move.
- Drag the item from the main window to the destination folder in the Folder List.
  or
- Display the main window with the item you want to move.
- Select the item or items you want to move.
- Click the Move to Folder button on the Standard toolbar, and then click the destination folder you want (*or* click Edit on the menu bar, click Move to Folder, select the destination folder in the Move Items dialog box, and then click the OK button).

You'll file the messages you sent and received for Speedy Cleaning in its folder.

To file messages:

1. If necessary, click the **plus sign** button ⊞ next to the Inbox in the Folder List to display the Gormann and Speedy Cleaning subfolders.

2. Select the **Schedule cleaning crew** message in the message list in the Inbox pane. This is the first message you will move.

3. Drag the **Schedule cleaning crew** message to the **Speedy Cleaning** subfolder in the Folder List. The message moves from the Inbox into the subfolder.

You want to move all messages related to Speedy Cleaning Company into the subfolder. You could continue to move each message individually, but it is faster to move all of them at once. Remember that the Ctrl key enables you to select nonadjacent messages, whereas the Shift key enables you to select a range of adjacent messages.

To file multiple messages:

1. Click the **Re: Schedule cleaning crew** message. This is the first message you want to file.

2. Press and hold the **Ctrl** key while you click the three **Available for pre-party cleaning?** messages that you want to move, and then release the **Ctrl** key.

Trouble? If you have only two Available for pre-party cleaning? messages, the read receipt didn't arrive. Just select the two messages.

▶ 3. Drag the selected messages from the Inbox into the **Speedy Cleaning** subfolder.

▶ 4. Click the **Speedy Cleaning** subfolder to view the moved messages. See Figure 4-19.

Figure 4-19 ▶ **Messages filed from the Inbox**

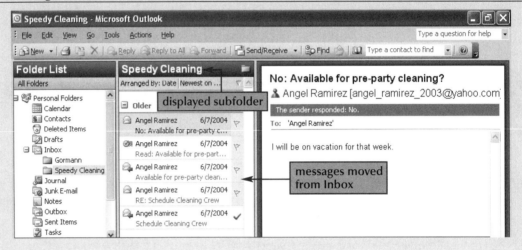

You can also have Outlook file messages for you.

Creating Rules with the Rules Wizard

Rather than manually filing all your messages, you can create rules that specify how Outlook should process and organize them. For example, you can use rules to:

- Move messages to a folder based on their subject.
- Flag messages about a particular topic.
- Assign categories to sent or received messages based on their content.
- Forward messages to a person or distribution list.
- Delete messages from a specific sender.
- Delay message delivery by a specified amount of time.
- Reply automatically to certain messages using a message you've created.

Each **rule** includes three parts: the *conditions* that determine whether a message is to be acted on, the *actions* that should be applied to qualifying messages, and any *exceptions* that remove a message from the qualifying group. For example, a rule might state that all messages you receive from Nadya (condition) are moved to the Speedy Cleaning folder (action) except for ones marked as High importance (exception). Outlook can apply rules to incoming, outgoing, or stored messages.

You create rules with the **Rules Wizard**, a feature that guides you step by step through the rule-writing process. As you build a rule, you continue to refine the sentence that describes the conditions, actions, and exceptions.

If you are using Outlook with Exchange Server, you must be online to use the Rules Wizard.

Creating a Rule with the Rules Wizard

- Click Tools on the menu bar, and then click Rules and Alerts.
- Click the New Rule button.
- Select a rule, and then click the Next button.
- Select conditions and click any link to set values as needed, and then click the Next button.
- Select exceptions (if necessary), click any link to set values as needed, and then click the Next button.
- Click the Finish button.
- Click the OK button.

You want to create a rule to move all messages related to the Gormann birthday party to the Gormann folder. You'll select the condition, define the actions, and then add the exceptions.

To start the Rules Wizard:

1. Click **Tools** on the menu bar, and then click **Rules and Alerts**. The Rules and Alerts dialog box that opens lists any existing rules.

2. Click the **New Rule** button at the top of the dialog box. The Rules Wizard dialog box opens, displaying a list of the most common rules. See Figure 4-20.

Rules Wizard dialog box

Figure 4-20

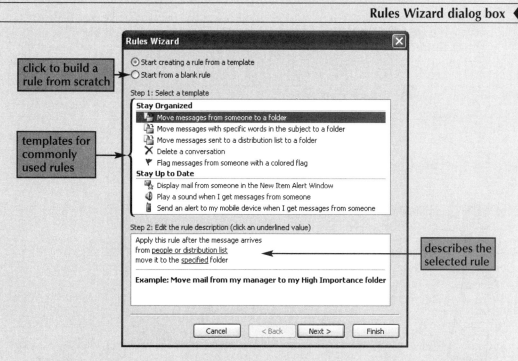

Trouble? If a dialog box opens warning you that mail sent and received using HTTP mail accounts cannot be filtered using the Rules Wizard, click the OK button.

Outlook provides templates for a variety of commonly used rules, which already include conditions and actions that you clarify by entering the appropriate words, senders, categories, folders, and so forth, depending on the rule itself. If you prefer, you can start with a blank rule—Check messages when they arrive or Check messages after sending—which provides access to a variety of conditions and actions that you can use to create the exact situation you want. You select the conditions and actions you want in the dialog boxes that follow.

You'll select a rule template that already includes a similar condition and action—Move messages with specific words in the subject to a folder. All you need to do is select the exact condition you want, and then enter the appropriate values for the condition and the action. You could do this by clicking the hyperlinks or by moving through the dialog boxes. You'll use the dialog box method this time, so you can see the other conditions and actions that are available.

To select a rule template and specify a condition:

1. Click **Move messages with specific words in the subject to a folder** in the Step 1 list box. The Step 2 list box displays the sentence with the condition and action for the selected rule.

2. Click the **Next** button to set the conditions for the selected rule. You need to change the condition for the rule you selected.

3. Click the **with specific words in the subject** check box to remove the check mark, and then scroll down and click the **with specific words in the subject or body** check box to insert a check mark to modify the conditions for the selected rule. The specific words link, which is colored and underlined, indicates that you need to enter the words or values that will trigger the action (displayed below the condition). See Figure 4-21.

| **Figure 4-21** | **Conditions added to the selected rule** |

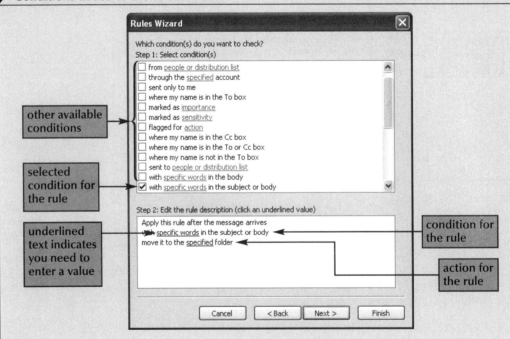

You could add and remove conditions to further clarify the rule. When you specify multiple conditions, all the conditions must be met for the action to occur. Outlook compares the message to the conditions in the order they appear in the list. If a condition in the list is met, Outlook continues to the next condition in the list. Once a condition is not met, the action will not occur.

4. Click the **specific words** link in the Step 2 list box. The Search Text dialog box opens.

You enter which keywords or phrases will trigger Outlook to move an incoming message when they appear in the subject line or message body. Outlook will search for the exact word or phrase you type, so spelling, capitalization, and spaces count.

5. Type **Gormann** in the Specify words or phrases to search for in the subject or body text box, and then click the **Add** button. The word appears in the Search list box surrounded by quotation marks. See Figure 4-22.

Search Text dialog box　◀　Figure 4-22

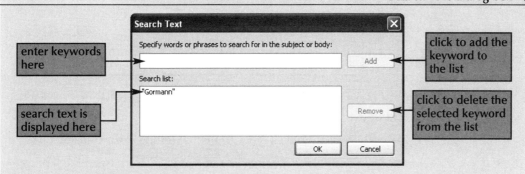

6. Click the **OK** button. The word Gormann remains underlined, so you can edit the value at any time by clicking the link.

Next, you determine the action that will occur when the rule's condition is met. The rule you selected already displays the appropriate action, but you need to enter a value. You'll advance to the next Rules Wizard dialog box so you can see the available actions.

To set the rule's action and exception:

1. Click the **Next** button in the Rules Wizard dialog box. The Rules Wizard dialog box displays a list of available actions.

2. Click the **specified** link in the Step 2 list box. The Rules and Alerts dialog box opens so you can select the appropriate folder or create a new one.

3. Click the **plus sign** button ⊞ next to Personal Folders, if necessary, click the **plus sign** button ⊞ next to Inbox, if necessary, click the **Gormann** folder, and then click the **OK** button. The Step 2 list box shows the rule you created. See Figure 4-23.

Figure 4-23	Rule with a condition and an action

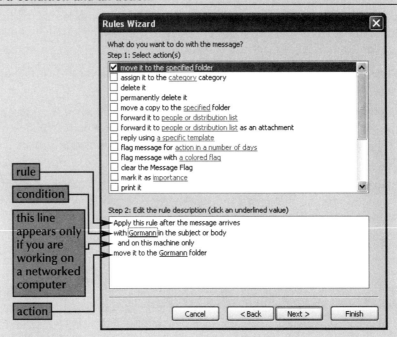

4. Click the **Next** button to advance to the Rules Wizard dialog box that lists available exceptions to add to the rule.

Because you have no exceptions, you'll move to the next Rules Wizard dialog box.

5. Click the **Next** button. The Rules Wizard dialog box has options for naming, applying, and turning on the rule.

Naming a rule enables you to turn the rule on or off and reuse it as needed. Use short, descriptive names for rules so that you can identify them in the dialog box. You can also select whether you want to apply the rule to messages that already appear in the folder selected in the Folder List and whether you want to turn on this rule.

To name and save the rule:

1. Type **Gormann Party** in the Step 1 text box.

2. Verify that a check mark appears only in the **Turn on this rule** check box. See Figure 4-24.

Saving the rule with a name  Figure 4-24

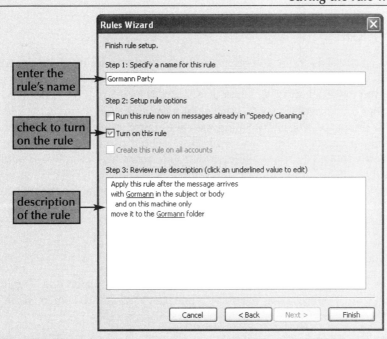

enter the rule's name

check to turn on the rule

description of the rule

▶ **3.** Click the **Finish** button to save the rule and return to the original Rules and Alerts dialog box. See Figure 4-25.

Rules and Alerts dialog box Figure 4-25

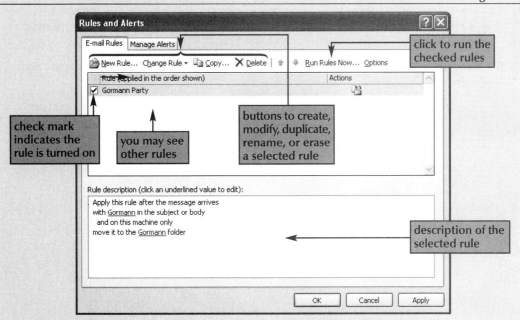

click to run the checked rules

check mark indicates the rule is turned on

you may see other rules

buttons to create, modify, duplicate, rename, or erase a selected rule

description of the selected rule

Trouble? If a dialog box opens and displays the message "This rule is a client-only rule, and will process only if Outlook is running," then you are set up to run Outlook with Exchange. This message appears because Outlook has determined that the rule requires access to your computer to run. Click the OK button. Outlook saves the rule and adds "(client only)" after the name of the rule in the Rules Wizard dialog box to remind you that your computer must be logged onto Exchange for the rule to be run.

The Rules Wizard dialog box enables you to manage existing rules as well as to create new ones.

Managing Rules

You can turn on or off the rules you create and change the order in which the rules are applied. Rules are turned on when a check mark appears in the check box that precedes their names. You can click the check box as needed to turn a rule on or off. For example, if the Gormanns were regular clients, you might turn off the Gormann Party rule after the event to make the processing of incoming messages faster, but not delete the rule. If you have more than one rule, the rules are applied sequentially in the order they are listed. You can click the Move Up or Move Down button to rearrange the rules. In addition, you can run rules at any time.

You decide to run the Gormann Party rule now to quickly organize the messages in the Inbox and its subfolders.

To run a rule:

1. Click the **Run Rules Now** button in the Rules and Alerts dialog box. The Run Rules Now dialog box opens. Here you select the rules you want to run, in which folders to run the rules, and what messages should be affected.

2. Click the **Gormann Party** check box in the Select rules to run list box to insert a check mark.

3. Click the **Browse** button next to the Run in Folder text box, and then double-click **Inbox**.

4. Click the **Include subfolders** check box to insert a check mark. You include the subfolders to be sure that all messages are checked for the rule, not just the main folders.

5. If necessary, click the **Apply rules to** list arrow, and then click **All Messages**. See Figure 4-26.

Figure 4-26 ▶ **Run Rules Now dialog box**

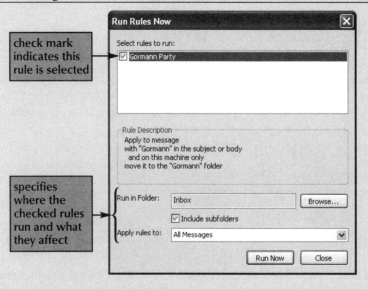

check mark indicates this rule is selected

specifies where the checked rules run and what they affect

▶ **6.** Click the **Run Now** button. All the messages with Gormann in the subject or body are moved to the Gormann folder.

▶ **7.** Click the **Close** button in the Run Rules Now dialog box.

▶ **8.** Click the **OK** button in the Rules and Alerts dialog box to close it.

Rules can help keep your Inbox organized with a minimum of effort from you.

To verify that the rule moved the messages:

▶ **1.** Display the **Speedy Cleaning** folder, if necessary. Two messages remain in the folder; neither message contains the search text "Gormann."

Trouble? If you have only one message remaining in the folder, then you never received the read receipt e-mail. Continue with Step 2.

▶ **2.** Display the **Gormann** folder. The three messages the Rules Wizard moved all contain the search text "Gormann" in the subject or body of the message.

▶ **3.** Display the **Inbox**.

Next, you'll send a message that doesn't meet the rule's criteria to see how the rule works with incoming messages. You'll assign the message a High importance level.

To send a nonrule message:

▶ **1.** Create a new e-mail message addressed to your e-mail address with the subject **Client Referrals** and the text **Our clients seem very happy with our cleaning crews. I've received four inquiries this week from potential customers who were referred by current clients.**, press the **Enter** key twice to double space, and then type your name.

▶ **2.** Click the **Importance: High** button [!] on the Standard toolbar to change the message's importance to High.

▶ **3.** Send the message, and then download the message, if necessary.

▶ **4.** Verify that the message remains in the Inbox.

Another helpful feature of the Rules Wizard is the ability to import and export rules. When you export rules, you save them to a file, creating a backup file that you can retrieve later or import to another computer. When you import rules, you retrieve the rules file.

You'll export your rule to a backup file.

To export a rule:

▶ **1.** Click **Tools** on the menu bar, and then click **Rules and Alerts** to open the Rules and Alerts dialog box.

▶ **2.** Click the **Options** button at the top of the dialog box. The Options dialog box opens, enabling you to import or export the list of rules. If you are using Exchange, this dialog box also contains buttons to update the list of rules on the Exchange server.

▶ **3.** Click the **Export Rules** button in the Options dialog box. The Save Exported Rules as dialog box opens, which functions like the Save As dialog box.

▶ **4.** Save the rules file as **Gormann Party Rule** in the **Tutorial.04\Tutorial** folder included with your Data Files.

▶ **5.** Click the **Save** button in the Save Exported Rules as dialog box.

▶ **6.** Click the **OK** button in the Options dialog box.

▶ **7.** Click the **OK** button in the Rules and Alerts dialog box to close it.

Now that the rule is saved on a disk, you can share the rule with other Outlook users.

Applying Conditional Formatting

Another way to organize your Inbox is to highlight messages from particular senders by creating a rule to format certain messages you receive. Formatting options include the font, font style, font size, effects, and color. For example, by default, Outlook applies boldface to unread messages in your Inbox. You can choose to add other formatting to messages you receive based on specific conditions. For example, Nadya could color all messages she receives from employees as green and all messages from vendors as maroon, or she could color all messages with a High importance as red, a Normal importance as blue, and a Low importance as yellow. This is called **conditional formatting** or automatic formatting.

You can apply conditional formatting to items in any folder. Some folders already have specific automatic formatting rules for items, such as the Inbox. You can create other automatic formatting rules to meet your needs. When you add an automatic formatting rule to a folder, you name the rule, select the font formatting you want to apply, and then set the conditions under which the formatting is applied. You choose the conditions by setting a filter, which Outlook uses only when reviewing items to see whether they fit the rule. The filter does not hide any item.

Reference Window | **Applying Conditional Formatting to Items**

- Display the folder whose items you want to conditionally format.
- Click View on the menu bar, point to Arrange By, and then click Custom (*or* right-click the main window, and then click Customize Current View *or* click the Customize Current View link in the Current View pane in the Navigation Pane).
- Click the Automatic Formatting button in the Customize View dialog box.
- Click the Add button in the Automatic Formatting dialog box.
- Type a rule name in the Name text box.
- Click the Font button, select the formatting you want, and then click the OK button.
- Click the Condition button, select the appropriate options in the Filter dialog box, and then click the OK button.
- Click the OK button in the Automatic Formatting dialog box, and then click the OK button in the Customize View dialog box.

You'll use blue and boldface to highlight all messages you receive with a High importance level to try out the conditional formatting feature.

To apply conditional formatting:

▶ 1. Click **View** on the menu bar, point to **Arrange By**, and then click **Custom**. The Customize View dialog box opens.

▶ 2. Click the **Automatic Formatting** button. The Automatic Formatting dialog box opens, showing a list of rules for conditional formatting in the Inbox. See Figure 4-27.

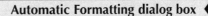 Automatic Formatting dialog box Figure 4-27

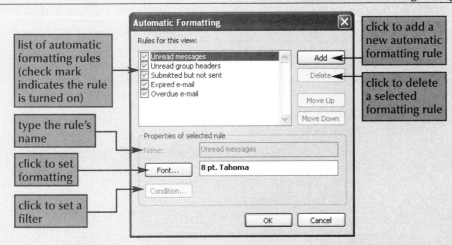

▶ 3. Click the **Add** button to create a new, untitled rule, and then type **High Importance E-mail** in the Name text box to name the automatic formatting rule.

▶ 4. Click the **Font** button. The Font dialog box opens so you can select the formatting you want to apply. In this case, you want to change the font color to blue and bold.

▶ 5. Click the **Color** list arrow, click **Blue** in the Color list, and then click **Bold** in the Font style list box.

▶ 6. Click the **OK** button to close the Font dialog box. The Font text box displays a sample of the formatting you selected.

▶ 7. Click the **Condition** button. The Filter dialog box opens, so you can set up a filter to determine which messages will be colored. See Figure 4-28.

| Figure 4-28 | Messages tab in the Filter dialog box |

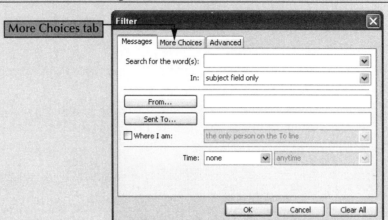

8. Click the **More Choices** tab in the Filter dialog box, click the **Whose importance is** check box to insert a check mark, click the list arrow next to this option, and then click **high**. See Figure 4-29.

| Figure 4-29 | More Choices tab in the Filter dialog box |

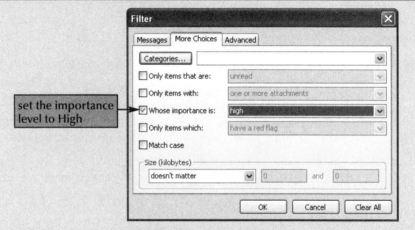

9. Click the **OK** button to close the Filter dialog box, click the **OK** button to close the Automatic Formatting dialog box, and then click the **OK** button to close the Customize View dialog box.

You'll test the rule you just created. If you have other messages in your Inbox that meet the criteria, the formatting is also applied to those messages.

To test the conditional formatting rule:

1. Send an e-mail message to your e-mail address with the subject **High importance**, the message **This e-mail should be blue.**, and a **High** importance level.

2. Send a second e-mail message to your e-mail address with the subject **Low importance**, the message **This e-mail should not be blue.**, and a **Low** importance level.

3. Download your messages. The two test messages appear in your Inbox. The High importance message is colored blue and boldface, as is the Client Referrals message that was already in your Inbox. The Low importance message is in the default black. See Figure 4-30.

Inbox with conditionally formatted messages ◄ **Figure 4-30**

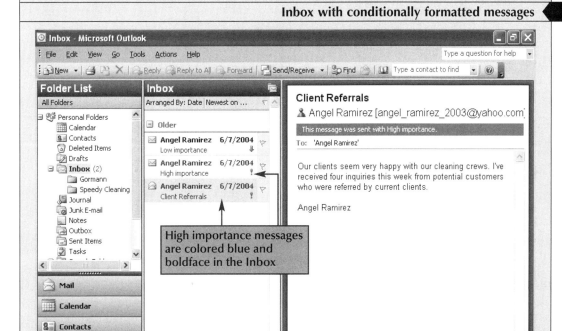

Trouble? If you do not have importance level icons attached to your message, then you need to enable Rich Text Format for your own contact card. Delete the messages you received, then open your contact card, right-click the e-mail address in the E-mail text box, and then click Outlook Properties to open the E-mail Properties dialog box. Click the Internet format list arrow, click Send using Outlook Rich Text Format, and then click the OK button. Save and close the Contact window, if necessary. Repeat Steps 1 through 3.

Conditional formatting is helpful in identifying specific messages in your Inbox at a glance. You can follow the same process to apply conditional formatting to items in other folders. For example, you could format with a particular color all appointments or meetings that are scheduled for a particular time, scheduled with a particular contact, or assigned to a certain category. When you create conditional formatting for other folders, the options in the Filter dialog box reflect the items for those folders.

You have started to arrange a cleaning crew for an upcoming event by sending and replying to e-mails with flags and voting options. You have also set up a rule to move specific messages into an appropriate folder. In the next session, you will find and organize messages in various ways so you can easily locate and arrange the messages. Then you will archive messages and set up the Junk E-mail Filter.

Session 4.1 Quick Check

1. What is a Quick Flag?
2. Explain the purpose of voting buttons.
3. Why would you request message delivery and read receipts?
4. True or False: You can create folders at the same level as the default folders or within any folder.
5. List two ways to file messages.
6. Describe the three parts of a rule.
7. What is one reason you might export rules?
8. How is conditional formatting helpful?

Session 4.2

Rearranging Messages

After you place your messages in a variety of folders, you can further arrange them. Finding, sorting, grouping, and filtering provide different ways to organize your messages within a folder.

Finding Messages

As your folder structure becomes more complex and the number of stored messages increases, it might become difficult to locate a message you filed. Rather than taking the time to manually search through multiple folders, you can have Outlook find the desired message. The Find command searches for text listed in the To, Cc, or Subject text box of the messages currently displayed. For example, you can search for all the cleaning crew messages in the Gormann folder. For searches of more than one criterion or multiple folders and subfolders, you must use the Advanced Find feature.

Reference Window | **Finding Messages**

- Display the folder you want to search.
- Click the Find button on the Standard toolbar (*or* click Tools on the menu bar, point to Find, and then click Find) to open the Find bar.
- Type the search text in the Look for text box on the Find bar.
- Click the Options button on the Find bar, and then click Search All Text in Each Message, if necessary, to search the subject and body of the message.
- Click the Find Now button.
  or
- Click the Options button on the Find bar, and then click Advanced Find (*or* click Tools on the menu bar, point to Find, and then click Advanced Find).
- Select the location in which you want to look.
- Specify the search criteria on the Messages, More Choices, and Advanced tabs in the Advanced Find dialog box.
- Click the Find Now button.

You'll use the Find feature with the messages you filed in the Gormann Party folder.

To find all messages related to cleaning crew:

1. If you took a break after the last session, make sure Outlook is running and the Folder List is displayed.

2. Display the **Gormann** subfolder.

3. Click the **Find** button on the Standard toolbar. The Find bar opens above the main window, indicating that it will find items in the open folder, in this case, the Gormann folder.

   Trouble? If the Find bar is not above the main window, you probably closed it when you clicked the Find button. Repeat Step 3.

4. Type **cleaning crew** in the Look for text box on the Find bar. This is the phrase for which you want to search. You'll leave the Search In text box set to Gormann, though you could change it to search all the Mail folders, mail you sent, mail you received, or another folder.

5. Click the **Options** button on the Find bar, and make sure a check mark appears next to **Search All Text in Each Message**. Outlook will search for the text in the To, Cc, and Subject boxes as well as the message body. If you clear the check mark, the search is faster but not as thorough.

6. Press the **Esc** key to close the menu, and then click the **Find Now** button on the Find bar. After a moment, the only two messages in the Gormann folder that contain the text "cleaning crew" appear in the main window, although the status bar shows that there are actually more items in the folder. See Figure 4-31.

Search results with the Find bar | Figure 4-31

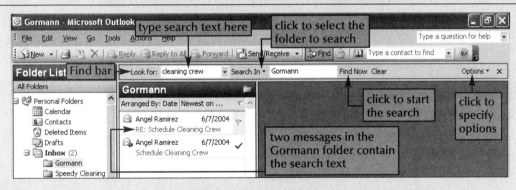

7. Click the **Clear** button on the Find bar to redisplay all the messages in the current folder. You could also close the Find bar to redisplay all messages in that folder.

As you can see, simple searches quickly locate information within a folder based on simple text criteria. However, when you want or need to do a more complex search, you will need to open the Advanced Find window. Depending on what type of item (file, message, note, and so forth) you are looking for, the options that you can specify as search criteria in the three tabs change. For example, with message items you can search for a variety of criteria. From the Messages tab you can specify keywords, specific sender and recipient names, and dates. The More Choices tab for messages provides search access based on assigned categories, status, priority, attachments, and size. The Advanced tab for any type of item enables you to create a custom criterion by specifying the field and results you want to locate, such as Flag Status equals Completed. If you want to narrow the search results to very specific items, you can specify that items match several criteria.

You'll search for any messages in all folders that include the text "Gormann" and the text "cleaning crew" in the subject or message body.

To conduct an advanced find:

1. Click the **Options** button on the Find bar, and then click **Advanced Find**. The Advanced Find window opens. See Figure 4-32.

Figure 4-32 Advanced Find window

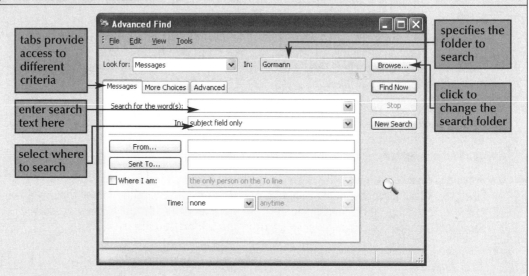

The search is set to look for messages in the Gormann folder. However, you want to look for messages in the Personal Folders, which will search all the folders.

2. Click the **Browse** button to open the Select Folder(s) dialog box, click the **Personal Folders** check box to insert a check mark, click the **Gormann** check box to remove the check mark, click the **Search subfolders** check box to insert a check mark, if necessary, and then click the **OK** button.

3. Type **Gormann;cleaning crew** in the Search for the word(s) text box. The semicolon separates search criteria. Outlook will search for this text only in the subject line of the e-mail.

4. Click the **More Choices** tab. You'll set the importance level on this tab.

5. Click the **Whose importance is normal** check box to insert a check mark. This specifies that Outlook should find only messages that have a Normal importance.

   The search text you specified on the Messages tab may appear in both the subject and the message body. You will return to that tab and change the criterion.

6. Click the **Messages** tab, click the **In** list arrow, and then click **subject field and message body**. This specifies that Outlook should look for the search text in two places.

7. Click the **Find Now** button. Outlook searches in all folders for all messages that match your criteria and displays the search results in a pane at the bottom of the window. See Figure 4-33.

Advanced Find window with search results ◀ Figure 4-33

search text

search location

search results

six messages contain the specified search text

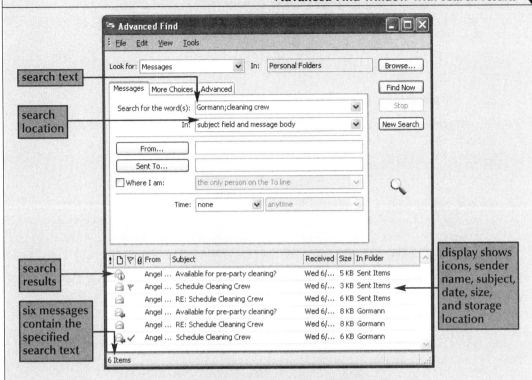

display shows icons, sender name, subject, date, size, and storage location

Trouble? Sometimes only the three messages in the Sent Items folder are found as a result of this search. Continue with the next set of steps.

You will perform the same search but change the importance level to High to see how altering even one criterion can change the find results.

To perform a second advanced find:

1. Click the **More Choices** tab.

2. Click the **Whose importance is** list arrow, and then click **high**.

3. Click the **Find Now** button. Outlook searches in all folders for all messages that match your criteria and displays the search results in the pane at the bottom of the window. This time only one message in the Inbox and one message in the Sent Items folder match your criteria.

4. In the Advanced Find window, double-click the **Client Referrals** message that is in the Inbox folder to open that message.

5. Read the message, and then close the Message window.

If you don't find the message or messages you were expecting, check your search criteria to be sure they are not too restrictive and that you have spelled any search text correctly.

You can move, delete, or respond to messages directly from the Advanced Find window. You'll move the Client Referrals message from the Inbox into the Speedy Cleaning folder.

To move a message from the Advanced Find window:

1. From the Advanced Find window, right-click the **Client Referrals** message that is in the Inbox, and then click **Move to Folder** on the shortcut menu. The Move Items dialog box opens and provides access to all the folders and subfolders in Outlook.

2. Expand the **Inbox**, if necessary, and then click the **Speedy Cleaning** folder to select it.

3. Click the **OK** button. The message moves from one folder to another.

4. Verify that the Client Referrals message has moved to the Speedy Cleaning folder by looking at the In Folder column at the bottom of the Advanced Find window.

5. Click the **Close** button ☒ on the title bar of the Advanced Find window to close it, and then click the **Find** button on the Standard toolbar to close the Find bar.

6. Display the **Speedy Cleaning** folder, and then confirm that the Client Referrals message was moved there. Notice that the conditional formatting is no longer applied to the message now that it is no longer in the Inbox. You'll add a Quick Flag to the message to help make the message stand out.

7. Right-click the **flag** icon for the Client Referrals message, and then click **Purple Flag** on the shortcut menu.

The Find and Advanced Find features work similarly for all Outlook folders and items. Another way to find specific messages is with Search Folders.

Using Search Folders

Search Folders are folders that display any e-mail messages that match specific search criteria. Any messages that meet a Search Folder's criteria are displayed in that Search Folder but remain stored in their current Outlook folders. Outlook has several preset Search Folders. For example, the For Follow Up Search Folder displays any flagged messages you have stored, the Large Mail Search Folder displays any messages larger than 100 KB, and the Unread Mail Search Folder displays all messages that have an unread icon. A message can appear in more than one Search Folder. For example, a flagged message that is 200 KB and still marked as unread will be displayed in at least three Search Folders: For Follow Up, Large Mail, and Unread Mail. You can use the existing Search Folders, customize them to better fit your needs, or create your own Search Folders.

If you delete a Search Folder, the messages that were displayed in that folder are not deleted because they are actually stored in other Outlook folders. However, if you delete an individual message from a Search Folder, the message is also deleted from its storage folder.

You'll use Search Folders to look for flagged messages and unread messages.

To view the For Follow Up Search Folder:

1. Click the **plus sign** button ⊞ next to Search Folders in the All Folders pane in the Navigation Pane, if necessary. The For Follow Up folder appears in the Search Folders list.

   Trouble? If a minus sign button ⊟ appears next to Search Folders instead of the plus sign button, the list is already expanded. Skip to Step 2.

2. Click **For Follow Up** in the All Mail Folders pane. One flagged message appears in the main window under the group heading "Purple Flag." See Figure 4-34. If you had more than one message flagged and used different flag colors, the messages would appear organized in different groups.

For Follow Up Search Folder

Figure 4-34

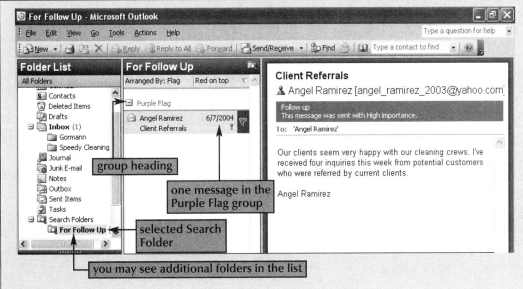

You'll use the New Search Folder dialog box to open the Unread Mail Search Folder.

To view the Unread Mail Search Folder:

1. Make sure the Search Folders list is still expanded, if necessary, and then verify that the Unread Mail folder does not appear as a subfolder in the Search Folders.

   Trouble? If you already have an Unread Mail folder in your Folder List, read but do not complete the rest of these steps.

2. Right-click **Search Folders** in the All Folders pane in the Folder List, and then click **New Search Folder**. The New Search Folder dialog box opens. See Figure 4-35.

| Figure 4-35 | New Search Folder dialog box |

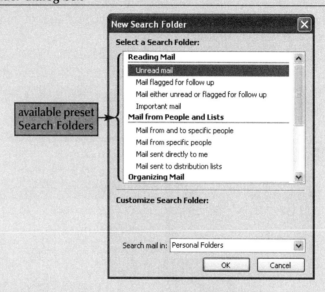

available preset
Search Folders

3. Review the available Search Folders, click **Unread mail** in the Select a Search Folder list box, and then click the **OK** button. The contents of the Unread Mail Search Folder appear in the main window. Any messages you haven't yet read are listed. See Figure 4-36.

| Figure 4-36 | Unread Mail Search Folder |

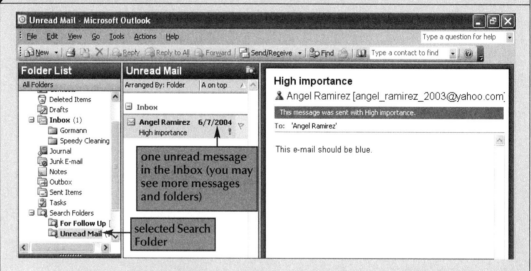

one unread message
in the Inbox (you may
see more messages
and folders)

selected Search
Folder

Trouble? If you see fewer or more messages, you may have inadvertently changed a message icon from unread to read when moving it between folders or you may have received messages unrelated to this tutorial. Continue with the tutorial.

4. Read each of the messages in this folder so that they are no longer flagged in boldface as unread.

Another way to manage files is to change a folder's arrangement or view.

Switching Arrangements and Views

There are a variety of ways to look at items in a folder. You are already familiar with views, which specify how items in a folder are organized and which details are visible. Each Outlook folder has a set of standard views from which you can choose. **Arrangements** are a predefined organization of how items in a view are displayed. Views and arrangements enable you to see the same items within a folder in different ways. For example, Messages view displays a table view of your messages, which you can sort. The Message Timeline arrangement displays messages sorted by date, which enables you to quickly see all your messages organized by specific date. A bar above a message indicates the amount of time that the message was open.

You'll look at the messages in the Gormann folder in different views and arrangements.

To switch views and arrangements:

1. Display the **Gormann** folder. The folder contents are arranged in the default Messages view arranged by date. All the messages appear in the Gormann folder arranged according to the date they were received.

2. Click **View** on the menu bar, point to **Arrange By** to display the list of available arrangements, and then point to **Current View** to display the list of available views.

3. Click **Message Timeline**. The messages in the Gormann folder appear along a timeline on the date they were sent. See Figure 4-37.

Message Timeline view ◄ | Figure 4-37

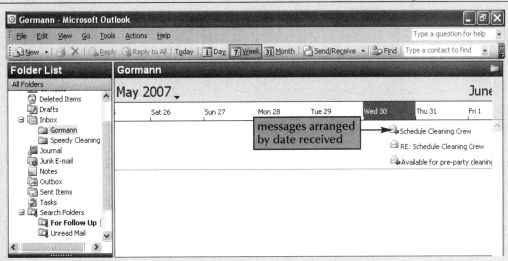

4. Drag the horizontal scroll bar to scroll the timeline from the current date back to the previous month, and then scroll back to the current date. Because there are no other messages in the folder, the other dates are empty.

5. Click **View** on the menu bar, point to **Arrange By**, point to **Current View**, and then click **Messages**. The folder returns to the default view.

6. Click **View** on the menu bar, point to **Arrange By**, and then click **Conversation**. All the messages appear in the main window arranged according to their subjects. The most recent message for each subject is displayed. See Figure 4-38.

Figure 4-38 Conversation arrangement

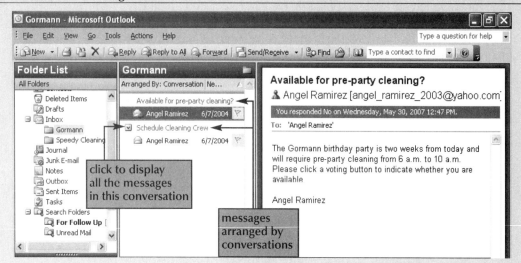

The other arrangements display the e-mail messages in different ways.

▶ **7.** Click **View** on the menu bar, point to **Arrange By**, and then click **Date**. The folder returns to its default arrangement.

Sorting Messages

Recall that sorting is a way to arrange items in a specific order—either ascending or descending. Ascending order arranges messages alphabetically from A to Z, chronologically from earliest to latest, or numerically from lowest to highest. Descending order arranges messages alphabetically from Z to A, chronologically from latest to earliest, or numerically from highest to lowest.

By default, all messages are sorted in descending order by the date and time they were received. You can, however, change the field by which messages are sorted; for example, you might sort e-mail messages alphabetically by sender. You make this change quickly by selecting a different view or arrangement. Alternatively, you can sort messages by multiple fields; for example, you might sort e-mail messages alphabetically by sender and then by subject. You can sort by as many as four fields at one time. You use the Sort dialog box to perform this type of multilevel sort.

The simplest way to change the sort order of a single field is to click a column heading in the main window. Each time you click the heading, the column alternates between ascending order (indicated by an up triangle) and descending order (indicated by a down triangle). If the arrangement and view shows more than one field, you can press and hold the Shift key as you click other column headings to add additional sort criteria to the view. If you click a column heading without pressing the Shift key, you replace the previous sort criterion.

You'll sort your messages by the date received field.

To sort messages in the Gormann folder by the date received:

▶ **1.** Click the **Newest on top** column heading (this may appear as Newest on. . . on your screen). The sort order reverses to ascending by date, as indicated by the up arrow icon in the column heading, and the column heading changes to Oldest on top.

Trouble? If a shortcut menu opens, you clicked the Arrange By column heading. Press the Esc key to close the shortcut menu, and then repeat Step 1, being careful to click the Newest on top column header.

The view remains in this sort order until you change it.

▶ **2.** Click the **Oldest on top** column heading. The arrow icon again points down to reorder the messages in descending order by the received date.

If you want to sort your messages by fields that are not visible in the main window, you'll need to open the Sort dialog box. You can sort messages in any view except Message Timeline view.

You could further customize a view by removing some of the existing column headings and adding others.

Grouping Folder Items

Grouping is a way to separate related folder items. Certain views are set up to arrange items in commonly used groups, such as By Sender or By Conversation Topic. When you switch to these views, each sender or subject becomes a different group. A plus sign button indicates that a group contains the number of messages indicated; you click the plus sign button to expand the grouping to display the messages. A minus sign button indicates that the grouping is expanded; you click the minus sign button to hide the messages in that group. If an item is assigned to more than one group, it appears in both groups, although there is still only one copy of the item in the folder.

Grouping Items	Reference Window

- Click View on the menu bar, point to Arrange By, and then click a grouping view, such as Conversation.
  or
- Click View on the menu bar, point to Arrange By, and then click Custom (*or* click the Customize Current View link in the Current View pane in the Navigation Pane).
- Click the Group By button in the Customize View dialog box.
- Click the Group items by list arrow, and then click a field to group by. Select a sort order as needed.
- Click the first Then by list arrow, click a field, and then select a sort order as needed.
- Select a third and fourth grouping, if necessary.
- Click the OK button in the Group By dialog box.
- Click the OK button in the Customize View dialog box.

You arranged the messages in the Gormann folder in a variety of groups when you changed the arrangement and view of the folder, such as to Conversation.

If the preset group views are not enough, you can create your own groupings using as many as four fields. When you create multilevel groups, items are grouped within groups; for example, you can group messages by sender and then group messages by subject within each sender group. You open the Group By dialog box to create custom groupings.

To create custom groups:

1. Click **View** on the menu bar, point to **Arrange By**, and then click **Custom**. The Customize View dialog box opens.

2. Click the **Group By** button. The Group By dialog box opens. See Figure 4-39.

Figure 4-39	Group By dialog box

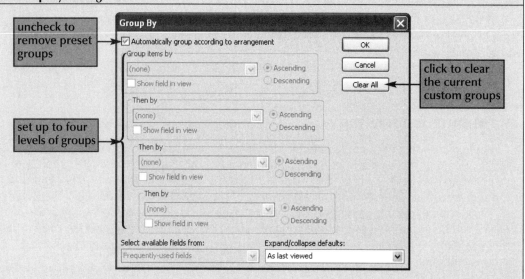

3. Click the **Automatically group according to arrangement** check box to remove the check mark. The Group items by list becomes available so you can set the top-level grouping.

4. Click the list arrow, and then click **From**. The first Then by list becomes available so you can set the second-level grouping.

5. Click the first **Then by** list arrow, and then click **Subject**. The second Then by list becomes available so you can set a third-level grouping. You'll use a two-level grouping this time.

6. Click the **OK** button in the Group By dialog box, and then click the **OK** button in the Customize View dialog box. The messages are grouped first by sender and then within each sender group by subject. Graphically, you can see how the groups are nested within each other. See Figure 4-40.

Messages grouped by sender and then by subject | Figure 4-40

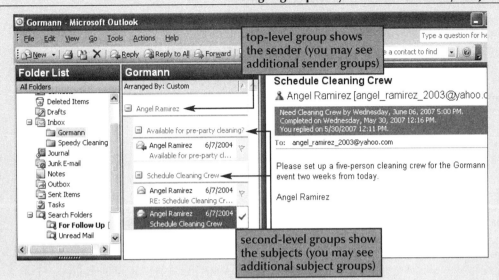

7. Click **View** on the menu bar, point to **Arrange By**, click **Custom**, and then click the **Group By** button.

8. Click the **Clear All** button to remove the custom grouping you set up, and then click the **Automatically group according to arrangement** check box to insert a check mark. This returns the arrangement to its defaults.

9. Click the **OK** button in the Group By dialog box, and then click the **OK** button in the Customize View dialog box.

The helpfulness of grouping becomes even more apparent when you accumulate a large number of messages (or items in other folders). Another technique that helps to organize items is to filter the view.

Filtering a Message View

You can filter which messages appear in a view using the same process you used to filter a contact list. Recall that a filter displays only those items in a folder that match certain criteria. Items that do not match the criteria are hidden from view, although they are still in the folder. Filtering does not move or remove items. For example, you could filter your messages to display only the ones from Nadya. Messages from other people would remain in the folder but hidden until you remove the filter.

To apply a filter, you display the appropriate folder, click View on the menu bar, point to Arrange By, and then click Custom to open the Customize View dialog box. Click the Filter button. The Filter dialog box in which you specify the criteria for the filter opens. You may want to click the Clear All button so that no preexisting criteria influence the new filter criteria. Enter the filter options you want in the Filter dialog box, such as the word for which to search or the sender's name. Review your options to verify accuracy (including spelling), and then click the OK button in the Filter dialog box. The Customize View dialog box recaps your filter options. Review the settings, and then click the OK button to close the Customize View dialog box. Only the messages that match your filter will then appear in the folder. As a reminder, the words "Filter Applied" appear in the status bar and folder banner until you remove the filter from the folder. To remove the filter, open the Filter dialog box again and then click the Clear All button.

Archiving Messages

Eventually, even the messages in your subfolders can become too excessive to manage easily. More often than not, you don't need immediate access to the older messages. Rather than reviewing your filed messages and moving older ones to a storage file, you can archive them. The **Archive** feature lets you manually transfer messages or other items stored in a folder to a Personal Folders file when the items have reached the age you specify. A **Personal Folders file** is a special storage file with a .pst extension that contains folders, messages, forms, and files; it can be viewed only in Outlook. Outlook calculates the age of an e-mail message from the date the message was sent or received, whichever is later. You can also have Outlook perform this process automatically with the **AutoArchive** feature, which moves or deletes messages or other items that have reached the age you specify each time you start Outlook. AutoArchive can also empty the Deleted Items folder.

When you create an archive, your existing folder structure from Outlook is re-created in the archive file and all the messages are moved from Outlook into the archive file. If you want to archive only a subfolder, the entire folder structure is still re-created in the archive file; however, only the messages from the selected subfolder are moved into the archive file. For example, if you archive the Gormann folder, the archive file will include both the Inbox and the Gormann subfolder, but only the message in the Gormann subfolder will be moved. Any messages in the Inbox folder remain in the Outlook Inbox. All folders remain in place within Outlook after archiving—even ones from which all the messages have been archived.

Archiving Messages Automatically

When you turn on AutoArchive, you have several options. AutoArchive runs only when you start Outlook; you can select whether a prompt appears before the archive process begins. You can select how often AutoArchive runs; the default for messages is every 14 days. You can set the name and location of the archive file and you can determine whether expired e-mail messages are deleted from Outlook and the Deleted Items folder after the archiving.

Reference Window	**Setting Up AutoArchive**

- Click Tools on the menu bar, click Options, and then click the Other tab in the Options dialog box.
- Click the AutoArchive button.
- Click the Run AutoArchive every 14 days check box to insert a check mark, if necessary, and then specify the frequency you want.
- Select whether you want to receive a message prompt before the AutoArchive and whether expired e-mail messages are deleted.
- Verify the archive file location.
- Click the OK button.

You'll set up AutoArchive to run every 14 days, and then verify the other options and archive file location.

To set up AutoArchive:

1. Click **Tools** on the menu bar, and then click **Options**. The Options dialog box opens.

2. Click the **Other** tab, and then click the **AutoArchive** button. The AutoArchive dialog box opens.

3. Note whether the **Run AutoArchive every 14 days** check box is checked, click the **Run AutoArchive every 14 days** check box to insert a check mark, if necessary, verify that **14** appears in the text box, and then verify that the settings in your dialog box match those in Figure 4-41.

AutoArchive dialog box | Figure 4-41

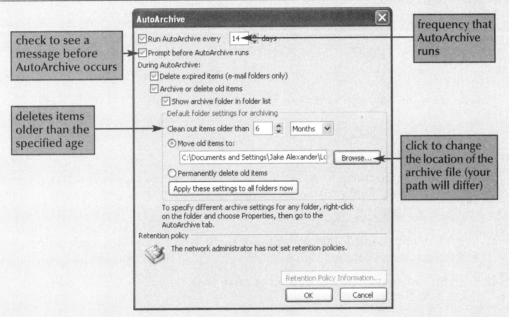

check to see a message before AutoArchive occurs

frequency that AutoArchive runs

deletes items older than the specified age

click to change the location of the archive file (your path will differ)

4. Click the **OK** button in the AutoArchive dialog box, and then click the **OK** button in the Options dialog box.

Outlook will automatically archive all the Outlook folders and subfolders (except Contacts folders) every 14 days. The items that are moved into the archive file are those that have expired or reached a specified age. Each folder has a default expiration period for its items, as listed in Figure 4-42.

Figure 4-42 ⟩ Default expiration periods for Outlook items

FOLDER	EXPIRATION PERIOD	CALCULATION METHOD
Calendar	6 months	Date started or last modified
Contacts	None	Not archived
Deleted Items	2 months	Date moved into folder
Drafts	6 months	Date created or last modified
Inbox	6 months	Date received or last modified
Journal	6 months	Date entered or last modified
Notes	6 months	Date created or last modified
Outbox	3 months	Date created or last modified
Sent Items	2 months	Date sent
Tasks	6 months	Date completed or last modified; uncompleted tasks are not archived

You'll review the AutoArchive options for the Gormann folder.

To review a folder's AutoArchive properties:

▶ **1.** Right-click the **Gormann** folder in the Folder List, and then click **Properties**. The Properties dialog box for that folder opens.

▶ **2.** Click the **AutoArchive** tab.

▶ **3.** Click the **Archive this folder using these settings** option button, if necessary, and then leave the default Clean out items older than time period at 3 Months.

▶ **4.** Click the **Move old items to default archive folder** option button, if necessary. See Figure 4-43.

Figure 4-43 ⟩ Gormann Properties dialog box

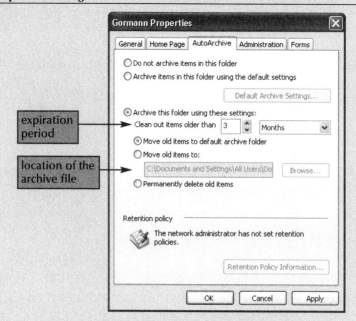

5. Click the **OK** button.

Because the messages in the Gormann folder are all recent and the AutoArchive will occur every two weeks, these messages will remain in Outlook for almost six months. Rather than wait, you can archive the folder manually.

Archiving Mail Messages Manually

You can archive a folder at any time, such as when you finish a project or event. If you have set up AutoArchive, you can use those settings for the manual archive. If you have not set up AutoArchive, you can specify which folders to archive, the age of items to archive, whether to include items excluded from AutoArchive, and the name and location of the archive file.

To manually archive a folder:

1. Click **File** on the menu bar, and then click **Archive**. The Archive dialog box opens. See Figure 4-44.

Archive dialog box | Figure 4-44

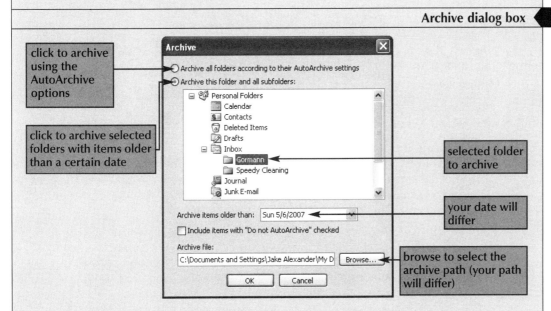

2. If necessary, click the **Archive this folder and all subfolders** option button.

3. If necessary, click the **plus sign** button ⊞ next to Inbox to display the subfolders, and then click the **Gormann** folder.

4. Type **tomorrow** in the Archive items older than text box, and then press the **Tab** key. Outlook will move any files dated with today's date or earlier to the archive file.

5. Click the **Browse** button. The Open Personal Folders dialog box opens.

6. Change the Save in location to the **Tutorial.04\Tutorial** folder included with your Data Files, type **Gormann Archive** as the filename, and then click the **OK** button.

7. Click the **OK** button in the Archive dialog box. A dialog box opens, informing you that the date you entered is in the future and could cause all items in the folder to be archived.

8. Click the **Yes** button to confirm that you want to archive all the items in the folder. All of the messages in the Gormann folder are moved into the archive file you specified. The empty Gormann folder remains in the folder structure. The Archive Folders file you just created remains open in the Folder List.

9. Click the **plus sign** button 🛨 next to Archive Folders in the Folder List to expand it, click the **plus sign** button 🛨 next to Inbox in the Archive Folders list to expand it, and then click the **Gormann** folder. The archived items are visible in the main window.

Once the archive file is created, you can add additional folders and items to that archive file by dragging folders and items from the main window into the open Archive Folders file in the Folder List. Note that you cannot move the default folders, such as the Inbox or Sent Items folders, into the Archive Folders file, but you can copy those folders into the Archive Folders file by pressing the Ctrl key as you drag.

To add folders to an archive:

1. Drag the **Speedy Cleaning** folder from the Inbox in the Personal Folders list to the Inbox in the Archive Folders list. The Speedy Cleaning folder moves to the Archive Folders file.

2. Drag the **Low importance** and **High importance** messages from the Inbox main window to the Inbox in the Archive Folders list. The two messages move from the Inbox into the Archive Folders file.

3. Press and hold the **Ctrl** key, drag the **Sent Items** folder messages from the Personal Folders list to the Archive Folders list, and then release the **Ctrl** key. The Sent Items folder is copied into the Archive Folders file. The original folder and all its items remain in the Personal Folders list.

   Trouble? If a dialog box opens, saying that you cannot move the item, you tried to move rather than copy the Sent Items folder. Click the OK button to close the dialog box, and then repeat Step 3, being careful to hold down the Ctrl key as you drag the Sent Items folder into the Archive Folders list.

Archiving folder contents enables you to retrieve the items later, if necessary.

Retrieving Items from an Archive Folders File

Archived folders let you keep the contents of your folders manageable and current while providing the security of knowing older information is available if you need access to the information. You won't need the archives unless you want access to a stored item. You can access items in your archive files several ways: you can open the file using the Open command on the File menu and then drag the items you need to a current folder; you can add the archive file to your profile; or you can restore all the items in the archive file by using the Import and Export command on the File menu.

For now, you're done with the archive file, so you'll close it.

To close an archive file:

▶ 1. Right-click **Archive Folders** in the Folder List, and then click **Close "Archive Folders"** on the shortcut menu. The archive file closes, and is stored in the folder you specified.

Using Mailbox Cleanup

The Mailbox Cleanup command, available on the Tools menu, provides an overview of your Outlook folders. When you click it, the Mailbox Cleanup dialog box opens. From here, you can: view the size of the various folders in Outlook; quickly search for items older than a specified number of days or larger than a specified size; run the AutoArchive command; view the contents and size of the items in the Deleted Items folder or empty it; and, if you are using Microsoft Exchange, view or delete the contents of your Conflicts folder.

Detecting Spam

The reliance on e-mail for both business and personal communication continues to increase. Most people have at least one e-mail address, and a growing number of people have multiple e-mail addresses. This pervasive use of e-mail has a downside—unsolicited messages, better known as junk e-mail or **spam**. Businesses, both large and small, use e-mail as an inexpensive and quick way to get a message to many people. The messages may be to entice you to purchase a service or product, or even to join a business. Although some of these unsolicited messages are legitimate and wanted, a majority of unsolicited e-mails are unwanted and may have pornographic or fraudulent content. These unsolicited and unwanted messages can quickly overwhelm your Inbox, much as junk mail clutters your postal mailbox. (For more information about spam, search for Web sites about "spam" or "unsolicited commercial e-mail.")

Outlook uses a two-pronged approach, collectively called the **Junk E-mail Filter**, to help cope with this barrage of unsolicited e-mail. The two parts of the Junk E-mail Filter are: (1) Junk E-mail Lists, and (2) technology that evaluates the content of each message you receive to determine its probability of being spam.

When you receive an e-mail message, Outlook checks the sender's e-mail address and domain name against the Junk E-mail Lists, which are collections of e-mail addresses and domain names whose messages you always or never consider spam. If the e-mail address appears on the Blocked Senders List—senders you always consider spammers—the message is moved into the Junk E-mail folder. If the e-mail address appears on the Safe Senders List or the Safe Recipients List, the message is moved into the Inbox. The Safe Senders List contains the individual senders you never consider spammers; this list includes all contacts in your Contacts folder and Global Address Book. The Safe Recipients List is a list of domain names and e-mail addresses for any mailing lists, distribution lists, or other subscription lists to which you belong and never want to consider spammers. E-mail messages from the Blocked Senders List are always treated as junk e-mail. E-mail messages from the Safe Senders and Safe Recipients lists are never treated as junk e-mail. If an e-mail address appears on both the Blocked Senders List and either the Safe Senders List or the Safe Recipients List, the message will not be marked as junk to prevent inadvertently deleting a message you want to see.

If the sender's e-mail address or domain name does not appear on any of the Junk E-mail Lists, the message is then evaluated by the Junk E-mail Filter. The filter uses a machine learning technology to evaluate the characteristics of the message, determine the probability that each characteristic is associated with spam, and then generate an overall rating for the message. Based on the setting in the Outlook Junk E-mail Options dialog box, the message is classified as spam or good e-mail based on the rating. Suspected spam is moved to the Junk E-mail folder, whereas a good e-mail is moved into the Inbox. You can adjust the setting in the Outlook Junk E-mail Options dialog box to determine the level of protection you want.

This multifaceted approach to unsolicited messages—technological analysis of e-mail combined with blocked and safe lists—is more effective at controlling junk mail than relying on a single method.

The Junk E-mail Filter can be used with an Exchange Server e-mail account in Cached Exchange Mode, an Exchange Server account that delivers to a Personal Folders file, HTTP e-mail accounts (such as Hotmail), POP3 e-mail accounts, and IMAP accounts. The Junk E-mail Filter is not available if you are using an Exchange Server e-mail account, working online, and using a version earlier than Exchange Server 2003 or if you are using a MAPI-compliant e-mail account.

Reference Window | **Setting the Junk E-Mail Filter**

- Display a Mail folder, click Actions on the menu bar, point to Junk E-mail, and then click Junk E-mail Options (*or* click Tools on the menu bar, click Options, and then click the Junk E-mail button on the Preferences tab).
- Select the level of junk e-mail protection you want.
- Click the Permanently delete suspected junk e-mail instead of moving it to the Junk E-mail folder check box if you want to delete suspected spam without the opportunity to look at it.
- Click the Blocked Senders tab, click the Add button, enter an e-mail address or domain name, and then click the OK button; repeat for each name you want to add (*or* right-click a junk e-mail, point to Junk E-mail, and then click Add Sender to Blocked Senders List).
- Click the Safe Senders tab, click the Add button, enter an e-mail address or domain name, and then click the OK button; repeat for each name you want to add (*or* right-click an e-mail, point to Junk E-mail, and then click Add Sender to Safe Senders List or Add Senders' Domain (@example.com) to Safe Senders List).
- Click the Safe Recipients tab, click the Add button, enter an e-mail address or domain name, and then click the OK button; repeat for each name you want to add (*or* right-click an e-mail, point to Junk E-mail, and then click Add Recipient to Safe Recipients List).
- Click the OK button.

Setting the Protection Level for the Junk E-Mail Filter

You can choose what level of filtering you want Outlook to perform. The Junk E-mail Options provide four levels of protection.

- **No Automatic Filtering.** Moves only e-mail from senders on the Blocked Senders List to the Junk E-mail folder. You'll likely see a large number of junk e-mails in your Inbox.
- **Low.** Moves only e-mail with a very high probability of being spam to the Junk E-mail folder. You'll likely see a large number of junk e-mails in your Inbox.
- **High.** Moves most e-mail with a probability of being spam to the Junk E-mail folder, along with some legitimate e-mail. You'll see few junk e-mails in your Inbox, but you'll need to check the Junk E-mail folder for messages that were sent there incorrectly.

- **Safe Lists Only.** Moves all e-mails to the Junk E-mail folder except messages from those senders on your Safe Senders List or Safe Recipients List. You'll see no junk e-mails in your Inbox, but you'll need to check the Junk E-mail folder regularly for messages from senders not on the safe lists that you want.

You cannot change the protection level if you are using an Exchange Server e-mail account and working online.

If you find that Outlook is consistently moving only junk e-mail into the Junk E-mail folder, then you can choose to have Outlook permanently delete those messages instead of sending them to the Junk E-mail folder. Be aware that these messages are not moved into the Deleted Items folder; they are permanently deleted without giving you the opportunity to review them to check for messages you want that inadvertently ended up marked as junk e-mail.

You'll view the protection level of the Junk E-mail Filter.

To view the protection level of the Junk E-mail Filter:

1. Display the **Inbox**.

2. Click **Actions** on the menu bar, point to **Junk E-mail**, and then click **Junk E-mail Options**. The Junk E-mail Options dialog box opens with the Options tab displayed. See Figure 4-45.

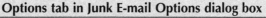
Options tab in Junk E-mail Options dialog box | Figure 4-45

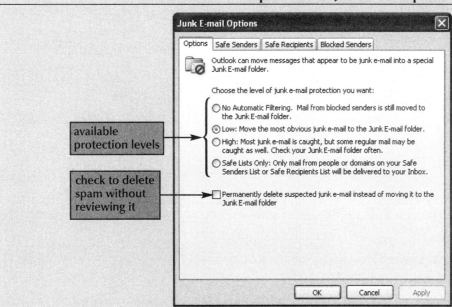

3. Review the available protection levels. You won't make any changes to the protection level of the Junk E-mail Filter on your computer.

Once you've set the protection level you want, you can build the Junk E-mail Lists.

Adding Names to the Junk E-Mail Lists

You can add any e-mail address or domain name to the three Junk E-Mail Lists. The process is as simple as entering the e-mail address and domain names you want to completely block or unblock. You can do this from the Junk E-mail Options dialog box or from a shortcut menu by right-clicking an e-mail message from the sender you want to mark as safe or blocked, pointing to Junk E-mail, and then clicking the appropriate command. To save time, Outlook considers all your contacts as safe senders, though you can turn off this default setting.

To add names to the Junk E-mail Lists:

▶ 1. Click the **Safe Senders** tab in the Junk E-mail Options dialog box. See Figure 4-46.

Figure 4-46   **Safe Senders tab in Junk E-mail Options dialog box**

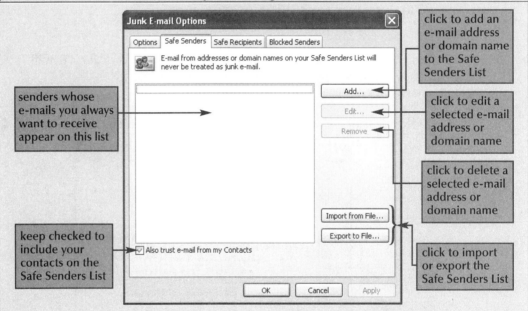

▶ 2. Click the **Add** button. The Add address or domain dialog box opens. You enter someone's full e-mail address or the domain name that you want to add to the list.

You won't add any contacts to the Safe Senders List.

▶ 3. Click the **Cancel** button in the Add address or domain dialog box. You return to the Junk E-mail Options dialog box.

The process for adding names to the Safe Recipients and Blocked Recipients lists is the same as for adding names to the Safe Senders List.

▶ 4. Click the **Safe Recipients** tab in the Junk E-mail Options dialog box. You would add the e-mail address and domain names for any subscription lists you belong to here. You won't add any names to this list, but you will add your e-mail address to the Blocked Senders List to see how the filter works.

▶ 5. Click the **Blocked Senders** tab in the Junk E-mail Options dialog box, and then click the **Add** button. The Add address or domain dialog box opens.

6. Type your e-mail address in the text box, and then click the **OK** button in the Add address or domain dialog box. You return to the Junk E-mail Options dialog box, and your e-mail address appears in the Blocked Senders List.

7. Click the **OK** button in the Junk E-mail Options dialog box. Now, any e-mail messages you receive from your e-mail address will be moved into the Junk E-mail folder.

You'll send yourself an e-mail message to test that the Blocked Senders List works.

To test the Blocked Senders List:

1. Create an e-mail message addressed to your e-mail address with **Blocked Sender Test** as the subject and **This message should move into the Junk E-mail folder.** as the message.

2. Send the message, and then download your messages. The number next to the Junk E-mail folder shows one message is in the folder.

   Trouble? If a dialog box opens telling you that a message has been moved to the Junk E-mail folder, click the Close button.

   Trouble? If the Junk E-mail folder indicates that you received more than one junk e-mail, you probably received messages unrelated to this tutorial. Right-click each message that is not junk e-mail, point to Junk E-mail, and then click Add Sender to Safe Senders List, Add Senders' Domain (@example.com) to Safe Senders List, or Add Recipient to Safe Recipients List to ensure that messages from these recipients are not added to the Blocked Senders List.

   Trouble? If the message did not move into the Junk E-mail folder, your contact information is probably included in your Contacts folder. Delete the message you just sent to yourself. Click Actions on the menu bar, point to Junk E-mail, click Junk E-mail Options, click the Safe Senders tab, click the Also trust e-mail from my Contacts check box to remove the check mark, and then click the OK button. Repeat Steps 1 and 2.

Occasionally, you should review messages in the Junk E-mail folder to make sure that messages you don't consider to be spam are not being moved there.

Marking E-Mail Messages as Not Junk

Because the Junk E-mail Filter is not perfect, messages that are not spam may well be moved to the Junk E-mail folder. You should review the messages Outlook places in the Junk E-mail folder to ensure that only true junk e-mail is in the folder and that no e-mail messages that you want to receive in your Inbox have been sent there by mistake. How often you review the messages in the Junk E-mail folder depends on the protection setting you selected, how many e-mail messages you tend to receive in a day, and the number of "good" e-mails that you find in the Junk E-mail folder. You can quickly move any messages in the Junk E-mail folder that you don't consider spam back into your Inbox. When you mark a message in the Junk E-mail folder as not junk, Outlook prompts you to add the sender to the Safe Senders List or Safe Recipients List.

If you're using an Exchange Server e-mail account and working online, you must be using Exchange Server 2003 or later.

You'll display the Junk E-mail folder to see the test message that you sent, and then you'll mark the message as not junk.

To mark a message as not junk:

▶ **1.** Display the **Junk E-mail** folder, if necessary. The Blocked Sender Test message appears in the message list. See Figure 4-47.

Figure 4-47	Junk E-mail folder

▶ **2.** Click the **Blocked Sender Test** message, and then click the **Not Junk** button on the Standard toolbar. The Mark as Not Junk dialog box opens, asking whether you always want to trust e-mail from that sender. See Figure 4-48.

Figure 4-48	Mark as Not Junk dialog box

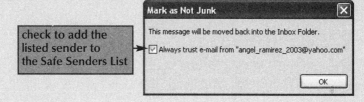

If you leave the check box checked, then the sender's e-mail will be added to the Safe Senders List or the Safe Recipients List. In this case, you'll uncheck the option, and leave your e-mail on the Blocked Senders List.

▶ **3.** Click the **Always trust e-mail from** check box to remove the check mark.

▶ **4.** Click the **OK** button. The Blocked Sender Test message is moved to the Inbox.

▶ **5.** Display the **Inbox** and confirm that the Blocked Sender Test message was moved.

Next, you'll edit the Blocked Senders List to remove your e-mail address from the list.

Editing the Junk E-Mail Lists

You can make changes to the Junk E-mail Lists at any time. You can edit a domain name or e-mail address included on any of the lists, or you can delete a domain name or e-mail address from any of the lists. You can make these changes directly in the Junk E-mail Options dialog box. Just select the name you want to edit or delete, and then click the Edit button to reopen the Edit address or domain dialog box and make the changes you need or click the Remove button to delete the name from the list.

To remove a name from the Junk E-mail Lists:

▶ 1. Click **Actions** on the menu bar, point to **Junk E-mail**, click **Junk E-mail Options**, and then click the **Blocked Senders** tab in the Junk E-mail Options dialog box.

▶ 2. Click your e-mail address in the list box on the Blocked Senders tab, and then click the **Remove** button. Your e-mail address is removed from the list.

▶ 3. Click the **Safe Senders** tab, and then click the **Also trust e-mail from my Contacts** check box to insert a check mark, if necessary.

▶ 4. Click the **OK** button in the Junk E-mail Options dialog box. Now, any e-mail messages you receive from yourself will appear in the Inbox as usual.

You'll send yourself another e-mail message to test that removing your e-mail from the Blocked Senders List works.

To test the edited Blocked Senders List:

▶ 1. Create an e-mail message address to your e-mail address with **Unblocked Sender Test** as the subject and **This message should appear in the Inbox.** as the message.

▶ 2. Send the message, and then download your messages. The message should appear in the Inbox.

▶ 3. Verify that the Unblocked Sender Test message appears in the Inbox.

Trouble? If the Unblocked Sender Test message is moved into the Junk E-mail folder, you'll need to add your e-mail address to the Safe Senders List. Right-click the message, point to Junk E-mail, and then click Add Sender to Safe Senders List to ensure that new messages from yourself are not moved to the Junk E-mail folder.

As with your Contacts folder, you'll want to review the Junk E-mail Lists periodically to ensure that the lists are current and accurate.

Deleting Rules, Formatting, Folders, and Items

Before you end your Outlook session, you should delete the Gormann Party rule, the automatic formatting, and the folders and category you created in this tutorial. You'll also delete the messages you sent and received in this tutorial.

To delete rules:

▶ 1. Click **Tools** on the menu bar, and then click **Rules and Alerts** to open the Rules and Alerts dialog box.

▶ 2. Click **Gormann Party** in the Rules (applied in the order shown) list, and then click the **Delete** button on the toolbar at the top of the dialog box.

▶ 3. Click the **Yes** button to confirm the deletion.

4. Click the **OK** button to close the Rules and Alerts dialog box.

5. Click **View** on the menu bar, point to **Arrange By**, click **Custom**, and then click the **Automatic Formatting** button in the Customize View dialog box. The Automatic Formatting dialog box opens.

6. Click the **High Importance E-mail** rule to select it, and then click the **Delete** button.

7. Click the **OK** button to close the Automatic Formatting dialog box, and then click the **OK** button to close the Customize View dialog box.

Next, you'll turn off AutoArchive.

To turn off AutoArchive:

1. Click **Tools** on the menu bar, click **Options**, and then click the **Other** tab in the Options dialog box.

2. Click the **AutoArchive** button. The AutoArchive dialog box opens.

3. Recall the state of the **Run AutoArchive every 14 days** check box when you first opened this dialog box in this tutorial, and then click the **Run AutoArchive every 14 days** check box to remove the check mark if you checked it during the tutorial.

4. Click the **OK** button in the AutoArchive dialog box, and then click the **OK** button in the Options dialog box.

You'll remove the custom category and any remaining folders or messages you created in this tutorial.

To delete the category, folder, and messages:

1. Right-click any e-mail message header in the main window, click **Categories** on the shortcut menu, click the **Master Categories List** button, delete the **Schedule** category from the Master Category List, and then click the **OK** button twice to close the dialog boxes.

2. Select the **Gormann** subfolder in the Folder List, press the **Delete** key, and then click the **Yes** button to confirm the deletion.

3. Select the **Unread Mail** folder in the Folder List, press the **Delete** key, and then click the **Yes** button to confirm the deletion of the folder but not the items it displayed.

4. Delete the **Blocked Sender Test** and **Unblocked Sender Test** messages you sent and received in this tutorial from the Sent Items and Inbox folders.

5. Delete any other messages you sent in this tutorial from the Sent Items folder.

6. Empty the **Deleted Items** folder.

Nadya is confident that the Gormanns will have a spotless house for their upcoming party. Your work ensures that the cleaning crews will be fully staffed and arrive on time at the correct address.

Review

Session 4.2 Quick Check

1. Discuss the difference between Find and Advanced Find.
2. Describe the simplest process for sorting messages by two criteria.
3. What is the purpose of grouping items?
4. What is the purpose of archiving?
5. Explain the difference between Archive and AutoArchive.
6. Define spam.
7. How does Outlook detect spam?
8. True or False: You cannot remove an e-mail address or domain name from the Junk E-mail Lists once you have added it.

Review

Tutorial Summary

In this tutorial, you sent and received messages with flags, voting buttons, delivery receipts, and specific delivery dates. You created subfolders in the Inbox in which you filed messages both manually and by using rules. You used the conditional formatting feature to color messages to help organize them. Then you found, sorted, and grouped messages to organize them in various ways. You archived the messages in your Inbox and Sent Items folder. Finally, you worked with the Junk E-mail Filter.

Key Terms

archive	Junk E-mail Filter	Rules Wizard
arrangement	Quick Flag	Search Folders
AutoArchive	Personal Folders file	spam
conditional formatting	recall	voting button
grouping	rule	

Practice

Practice the skills you learned in the tutorial using the same case scenario.

Review Assignments

There are no Data Files needed for the Review Assignments.

Nadya Rutskoi is planning to attend a conference for professional cleaners about cleaning methods with the smallest environmental impact. The conference is next month and she needs to arrange her travel plans. In addition, she wants to plan a lunch meeting for all the independent contractors who work for Speedy Cleaning Company to introduce the new methods to them.

1. Create a new e-mail message addressed to your e-mail address with the subject "Eco-cleaning Conference" and the message "The conference takes place in Montreal on the 4th through the 8th of next month. Please arrange air travel and hotel for the conference." Press the Enter key twice, and then type your name.

2. Add a Quick Flag with the text "Make travel arrangements" and a due date of next Friday. Send the message.

3. Download the message, reply with the text "Liz has your plane tickets and hotel room all set up.", change the message importance to "High," and then send the message.

4. Create a new message to your e-mail address with the subject "Lunch Meeting" and the message "Nadya Rutskoi, President of Speedy Cleaning Company, invites you to a lunch meeting to learn about the latest cleaning methods that maximize spotlessness and minimize environmental degradation. Please use the voting buttons to RSVP. Thank you." Press the Enter key twice, and then type your name.

5. Add a High importance to the message.

6. Add the Yes, No, Maybe voting buttons to the message.

7. Set up the message options to request a read receipt, assign the Business category to the message, and then send the message.

8. Download your messages, open the Lunch Meeting message, send a read receipt if asked, and then reply by clicking the No voting button. Do not add a reply message, and then close the Message window. (If you don't see the voting buttons, reply to the message, and then type No in the message body.) Send the message.

9. Download your messages, and then read the read receipt and the Lunch Meeting reply you sent.

10. Open the original Lunch Meeting message in the Sent Items folder, display the Tracking tab, review the responses you received, and then close the Message window.

11. Create a subfolder named "Nadya" that contains Mail and Post Items placed in the Inbox.

12. Create a subfolder named "Conference" that contains Mail and Post Items placed in the Nadya folder.

13. File all the messages you created in these Review Assignments from the Inbox to the Nadya folder.

14. Create a rule that moves all the messages related to the conference to the Conference folder. Name the rule "Conference."

15. Run the Conference rule, and then verify that the proper messages were moved into the Conference folder.

16. Export the rule to the **Tutorial.04\Review** folder included with your Data Files, using the filename **Conference Rule**.

17. Create an automatic formatting rule named "My e-mail" to color all e-mail messages you receive from your e-mail address as purple. Confirm that the messages you sent to yourself in these Review Assignments change color. (*Hint*: You'll need to set this rule in the Inbox, Nadya, and Conference folders.)

18. Use the Advanced Find feature and then find all the messages with the word "environmental" or "conference" in the subject or message body. Make sure you search all the folders in the Inbox.

19. Click the In Folder column heading to sort the messages you found by folder, press and hold the Shift key, and then click the Subject column heading to sort the messages by Subject within each folder.

20. Click the More Choices tab, add the criterion Whose importance is high, and run the Find command again.

21. Move the message you found to the Conference folder, close the Advanced Find window, and then close the Find bar.

22. Group the messages in the Nadya folder using the Conversation arrangement.

23. Archive the Nadya folder as **Nadya Archive** in the **Tutorial.04\Review** folder included with your Data Files. Both the Nadya folder and the Conference folder are saved in the archive file. Close the archive.

24. Add your e-mail address to the Blocked Senders List in the Junk E-mail Options dialog box.

25. Create a new message to your e-mail with the subject "Blocked Sender" and the text "This message will go to the Junk E-mail folder." Send the message.

26. Download the message, and confirm that the message goes to the Junk E-mail folder.

27. Mark the Blocked Sender message as not junk, and then delete your name from the Blocked Senders List.

28. Delete the rule, the subfolders, the automatic formatting rule, and the sent and received messages created in these Review Assignments, and then empty the Deleted Items folder.

Case Problem 1

There are no Data Files needed for this Case Problem.

Emergency Training Group   Carroll Jameson started the Emergency Training Group to provide CPR, Heimlich, and basic first aid skills training. Individuals can join a group class or organizations can arrange training sessions for their members or employees. Once a year, Carroll sends out an e-mail asking attendees to rate the training session his company provided.

1. Create a new e-mail message addressed to your e-mail address with the subject "Customer Feedback" and the message "It's time for our annual customer survey. Please send an e-mail message to our customers to determine their level of satisfaction with our training session." Press the Enter key twice, and then type your name.

2. Add a flag to the message with the preset text "Do not Forward" and no due date. Send the message.

3. Create a conditional formatting rule named "Status e-mail" that formats messages in the Inbox with the Status category in navy.

4. Download the message, and then reply with the text "What do you think of the following question: Please rate your level of satisfaction with the Emergency Training Group session you attended in the last 12 months, using the voting buttons." Send the message.

5. Download the message, and then reply with the text "Use that question and include five levels on the voting buttons—completely satisfied, very satisfied, satisfied, somewhat dissatisfied, completely dissatisfied." Send the message, and then download it.

6. Create a new message to your e-mail address with the subject "Satisfaction Survey" and the message "Emergency Training Group is always striving to ensure that you are ready for any situation you encounter. Please rate your level of satisfaction with the session you attended in the last 12 months, using the voting buttons. Thank you." Press the Enter key twice, and then type your name.

7. Add custom voting buttons by typing "Completely Satisfied;Very Satisfied;Satisfied;Somewhat Dissatisfied;Completely Dissatisfied" in the Use voting buttons text box. Do not type a space after each semi-colon.

8. Request a read receipt and a delivery receipt for this message, and then assign the Status category. Send the message.

Apply

Apply what you learned in the tutorial to get customer feedback on emergency training sessions.

Explore

9. Download the message, verify that it appears in navy in the Inbox, send a read receipt if requested, and then reply by selecting the Somewhat Dissatisfied voting button and adding the message "Please contact me to discuss the situation further." Double space and then type your name. Send the message.

10. Download the message and the read receipt, and then reply with the text "We would like to know why you are not satisfied and what we can do to improve the situation. Carroll Jameson will contact you tomorrow." Send the message.

11. Open the original Satisfaction Survey message in the Sent Items folder, display the Tracking tab, review the tally, and then close the message.

12. Display the Folder List, if necessary, create a subfolder named "Carroll Jameson" that contains Mail and Post Items placed in the Inbox, and then create a second subfolder in the Inbox named "Customers."

13. Download your messages, if necessary, and then file all the messages related to the customer feedback survey in the Customers folder.

14. Create a rule that moves all messages that contain the name "Carroll Jameson" into the Carroll Jameson folder. Name the rule "Carroll." Run the Carroll rule.

15. Export the rule to the **Tutorial.04\Cases** folder included with your Data Files, using the filename **Carroll Rule**.

16. Create an automatic formatting rule named "Carroll Folder" that formats all messages in the Carroll Jameson folder with the color red.

17. Archive all the messages in the Carroll Jameson folder as **Carroll Jameson Archive** in the **Tutorial.04\Cases** folder included with your Data Files. Close the archive.

18. Delete the rule, conditional formatting rule, messages, and subfolders you created in this Case Problem, and then empty the Deleted Items folder.

Case Problem 2

Challenge

Extend what you learned in the tutorial to use rules to organize messages for a real estate agent.

There are no Data Files needed for this Case Problem.

Getaway Havens   Finding affordable vacation house rentals can be difficult for people living far from their intended destination. Getaway Havens, founded by Mindy Sterne in 1987, presents prospective vacationers with a list of prescreened rental properties throughout the United States. Properties are rated on their location, cleanliness, and prices. Mindy relies on Outlook to communicate with clients and organize messages because vacationers and property owners reside throughout the world.

1. Create a new e-mail message addressed to your e-mail address with the subject "Prepare for the rush" and the message "We're heading into the high season. Get ready for an increase in customer inquiries." Press the Enter key twice to double space, and then type your name. Change the message importance to High. Send the message.

Explore

2. Create a rule named "Important Messages" that notifies you with an alert with the message "Open this message immediately. It's very important." when messages arrive marked as High importance. Create the rule by starting from a blank rule; check messages when they arrive; set the condition "marked as importance" and change "importance" to High; select the action "display a specific message in the New Item Alert window" and change "a specific message" to the custom message above.

Explore

3. Create another Check messages when they arrive rule, with the condition "contact" or "call" in the subject or body, the action flag message for Follow up by 1 day, and the name "Follow Up." (*Hint:* Start from a blank rule, select the appropriate conditions and actions in the Rules Wizard dialog box, and then edit the values to match those in this step.)

4. Export the Important Messages and Follow Up rules to the **Tutorial.04\Cases** folder included with your Data Files, using the filename **Getaway Rules**.

5. Delete the Important Messages and Follow Up rules.

6. Display the Folder List, if necessary, and then create a subfolder named "Follow Up" that contains Mail and Post Items placed in the Personal Folders at the same level as the Contacts and Inbox folders.

7. Move the Follow Up folder to within the Inbox folder by dragging it to the Inbox.

Explore

8. Import the Getaway Rules file. Click the Options button in the Rules and Alerts dialog box, click the Import Rules button in the Options dialog box, select **Getaway Rules** (which you saved in the **Tutorial.04\Cases** folder included with your Data Files), click the Open button in the Import Rules from dialog box, and then click the OK button in the Options dialog box.

Explore

9. Modify the Important Messages rule by adding a second action to move a copy of the message to the Follow Up folder. (*Hint:* Select the message in the Rules Wizard dialog box, click the Change Rule button, click Edit Rule Settings, and then click the Next button until the What do you want to do with the message list appears. Select the appropriate action, enter the value, and then click the Finish button.)

10. Export the modified rule again with the name **Important Messages Modified** in the **Tutorial.04\Cases** folder included with your Data Files.

11. Create a new e-mail message addressed to your e-mail address with the subject "Looking for information" and the message "Please contact me with information about your rental rates for 3-bedroom houses on Martha's Vineyard in September." Double space and then type your name. Send the message.

12. Create a new message to your e-mail address with the subject "Rate increases" and the message "Note that rates will be increasing 20% for all vacation rentals between May 31 and August 31. Please be sure to include the appropriate rates in any quotes you send out. Thank you." Double space and type your name. Change the priority to High. Send the message.

13. Download your messages. Select each message in the New Item Alerts dialog box, and then click the Open Item button. Read each message, and then close it.

14. Click the Close button in the New Item Alerts dialog box, and then verify that the Rate increases and Prepare for the rush messages appear in the Follow Up folder as well as in the Inbox.

Explore

15. Open the Inbox folder in its own window by right-clicking the folder, and then clicking Open in New Window.

16. Clear the message flag on the Looking for information message in the Inbox folder.

17. Create a new subfolder called "Getaway" that contains Mail and Post Items placed within the Inbox. Move all messages you created for this Case Problem from the Inbox into it, and then drag the Follow Up folder so it is a subfolder in the Getaway folder.

18. Group the messages in the Getaway folder by Importance by changing the folder's arrangement.

Explore

19. Make a copy of the Getaway subfolder in the Inbox. Click the Getaway subfolder to select it, press and hold the Ctrl key while you drag the folder to the Inbox, and then release the mouse button and the Ctrl key. The copied folder appears with the name Getaway1.

Explore

20. Rename the Getaway1 subfolder. Right-click the Getaway1 subfolder, click Rename "Getaway1," type "Important Getaway" as the new folder name, and then press the Enter key.

21. Filter the messages in the Important Getaway folder to show only those messages whose importance is High. (*Hint*: Right-click in the Message window, click Filter on the shortcut menu, click the More Choices tab in the Filter dialog box, and then set the filter criterion.)

22. Archive the Getaway folder as **Getaway Archive** in the **Tutorial.04\Cases** folder included with your Data Files. Archive the Important Getaway folder as **Important Getaway Archive** in the **Tutorial.04\Cases** folder. The filter remains intact in the archived folder. Close the archives.

23. Close the Inbox window, delete the rules, messages, and subfolders you created in the Case Problem, and then empty the Deleted Items folder.

Challenge

Challenge yourself by using custom voting buttons to track responses for a polling company.

Case Problem 3

There are no Data Files needed for this Case Problem.

Viewpoint Polls Viewpoint Polls is hired by various organizations to take the pulse of the United States about various issues, such as gun control, civil rights, and prison reform. Right now, they are trying to determine for which political party people would vote in an upcoming election. Viewpoint Polls has begun to elicit responses by e-mail.

1. Create a new e-mail message addressed to your e-mail address with the subject "Political Party Preference" and the message "Viewpoint Polls is taking an independent survey to determine the current popularity of political parties. Please select the party you most affiliate with. Thank you for your time." Double space and then type your name.

Explore

2. Add custom voting buttons for each of the following: Democrat, Green, Independent, Reform, Republican, Socialist, Other, and Undecided. (*Hint:* Type each button name separated by semicolons but no spaces in the Use voting buttons text box.) Send the message.

Explore

3. Download the message, and then reply by clicking the InfoBar in the Reading Pane, and then clicking the party affiliation of your choice. Send the reply without adding a message.

4. Download the message, open the original Political Party Preference message in the Sent Items folder, and then review the vote tally on the Tracking tab.

5. Create a subfolder named "Viewpoint" that contains Mail and Post Items placed in the Inbox.

Explore

6. Create a rule that moves messages from your e-mail address into the Viewpoint folder. Run the rule on the current contents of the Inbox.

7. Create a new message to your e-mail address with the subject "Survey results" and the message "Please create a report with all the survey results received to date as of next Friday. Thank you." Double space and then type your name.

8. Add a flag to the message with the text "Create survey report" and a due date of next Friday at 5 p.m. Send the message.

9. Download the message, and then reply with the text "So far we haven't received very many replies. We should have a better response rate by next Friday." Send the message. (*Hint:* The message should be in the Viewpoint folder.)

10. Download the message, and then reply with the text "Let me know by next Wednesday if we have a response rate of less than 65%." Send the message, and then download it.

Explore ▶ 11. Open the Viewpoint subfolder in its own window by right-clicking the folder, and then clicking Open in New Window on the shortcut menu.

12. Change the arrangement to group by subject all the messages moved by the rule you created.

Explore ▶ 13. Move all the messages in the Survey results group to a new subfolder named "Survey Report" within the Viewpoint folder using the Move to Folder button on the Standard toolbar. (*Hint:* Select all the messages in the group, click the Move to Folder button on the Standard toolbar, click Move to Folder, click the New button in the Move Items dialog box, create the Survey Report subfolder, select the Viewpoint subfolder, and then click the OK button in both dialog boxes.)

14. Find all the messages in Outlook with the words "survey report" or "response rate" in the subject or message body and whose importance is Normal. (*Hint:* Click the Browse button, and then click Personal Folders.)

Explore ▶ 15. Save the search as **Viewpoint Search** in the **Tutorial.04\Cases** folder included with your Data Files. (*Hint:* Click File on the menu bar in the Advanced Find window, click Save Search, change the save in location and filename, and then click the OK button.)

16. Close the Advanced Find window, and then close the Viewpoint folder window.

17. Archive the **Viewpoint** folder and all its subfolders as **Viewpoint Archive** in the **Tutorial.04\Cases** folder included with your Data Files. Copy the Sent Items folder into the archive, and then close the archive.

18. Delete the rule, messages, and subfolders you created in this Case Problem, and then empty the Deleted Items folder.

Create

Use voting buttons, subfolders, and rules to determine the favorite movie actors of three classmates.

Case Problem 4

There are no Data Files needed for this Case Problem.

Favorite Movie Actors Discussions of favorite movie actors (male or female) are common among groups of friends. Find out who is the favorite actor among three classmates. You will need the e-mail addresses for three classmates; if you do not have three classmates' e-mail addresses, use your own e-mail address.

1. Create a subfolder called "Favorite Actors" that contains Mail and Post Items placed in the Inbox.

2. Create a rule named "Actor" that moves all incoming messages that contain the word "actor" into the Favorite Actors subfolder.

3. Export the Actor rule to the **Tutorial.04\Cases** folder included with your Data Files, using the filename **Actor Rule**.

4. Create a new message to three classmates' e-mail addresses (or one message to your e-mail address) with the subject "Favorite actor" and text that asks them to participate in your survey. Include your name.

5. Add a message flag that asks recipients to reply to your message today. Send the message(s).

6. Download your messages. Respond to each flagged message you receive, letting the senders know you will participate in their surveys.

7. Change each message flag to Completed.

8. Create a new message to the same three classmates (or one message to your e-mail address) with the subject "Vote for an actor" and a message that thanks the recipients for participating, and asks them to vote for one of the actors listed in the voting buttons. Add voting buttons for the names of five of your favorite male and/or female actors. Send the message(s).

9. Download your message(s), and then reply to each Vote for an actor message by voting for your favorite actor and adding a message that indicates your favorite movie with that actor. Send the messages.

10. Download your messages, and display the Favorite Actors subfolder. Review the vote tally.

11. Use the Group By dialog box to group the messages by sender name (the From field), and then by subject. If necessary, expand the groups.

12. Select all the messages by pressing the Ctrl+A keys, and then print all rows of the message list in Table Style. (*Hint:* Click File on the menu bar, and then click Print.)

13. Change the grouping order to subject, and then sender name, and then print all the messages in the expanded groups in Table Style.

14. Sort the grouped messages in descending order by subject and then in ascending order by sender.

15. Archive the Favorite Actors folder as **Actors Archive** in the **Tutorial.04\Cases** folder included with your Data Files. Close the Archive Folders.

Explore
16. Open the archive file you created. Click File on the menu bar, point to Open, and then click Outlook Data File. The Outlook Data File dialog box opens. Change the Look in location to the **Tutorial.04\Cases** folder included with your Data Files, and then double-click the **Actors Archive** file to open it.

Explore
17. Copy the Sent Items folder to the Actors Archive file. Press and hold the Ctrl key as you drag the Sent Items folder to the Archive Folders. Release the Ctrl key. The folder and messages are duplicated in the archive file.

18. Close the archive file, delete the rule, messages, and subfolder you created in this Case Problem, and then empty the Deleted Items folder.

Review

Quick Check Answers

Session 4.1

1. A Quick Flag is an icon in the message list as well as an InfoBar with text and an optional due date.

2. Voting buttons provide a preset list of answers from which recipients select one; vote responses are tracked on the sender's copy of the sent message, providing a current tally.

3. A delivery receipt confirms that your message arrived in the recipient's Inbox; a read receipt confirms that the message was opened (but not necessarily read).

4. True

5. You can file messages manually by dragging messages from the Inbox to the appropriate subfolder or automatically by setting up rules.

6. Conditions specify which messages to act on; actions define what should happen to the qualified messages; exceptions remove messages from the qualifying group.

7. To create a backup file that you can retrieve later or import to another computer

8. Conditional formatting is helpful in identifying specific messages in a folder at a glance.

Session 4.2

1. Find locates messages based on one criterion in a folder; Advanced Find locates messages based on multiple criteria in any folder.
2. Click the column heading that is the first sort criterion, press and hold the Shift key, click the column heading that is the second sort criterion, and then release the Shift key.
3. Grouping separates related folder items, such as by subject or sender.
4. Archiving removes older messages to a storage file that you can later access.
5. Archive is the manual transfer of messages; AutoArchive is an automated process that occurs each time you start Outlook.
6. Spam is junk e-mail, or unsolicited and unwanted messages.
7. Outlook uses a two-pronged approach, collectively called the Junk E-mail Filter, to help cope with spam. The two parts of the Junk E-mail Filter are: (1) Junk E-mail Lists, and (2) technology that evaluates the content of each message you receive to determine its probability of being spam.
8. False. You can make changes to the Junk E-mail Lists at any time.

Objectives

Session 5.1
- Record activities in the Journal
- View and edit journal entries
- Send Office files via e-mail
- Send and receive faxes

Session 5.2
- Import and export files
- Save items as another file format
- Communicate with instant messages
- View Web pages and set up a folder home page
- Print journal entries

Integrating Outlook with Other Programs and the Internet

Using the Journal, Importing and Exporting Files, and Sending Instant Messages

Case

Ace Realty

Ace Realty was founded eight years ago to provide an alternative, independent realtor to the residents of Omaha, Nebraska. Ace Realty provides professional real estate advice for buying and selling residential properties. The Ace team strives to help clients buy or sell their homes in the least amount of time, for the best price, and with the least stress. The Ace philosophy is to put the clients' best interests first. As a result, most clients are repeat customers or referred by satisfied customers.

The Ace team consists of Khris Reilly, Ty Mumford, Cassandra Esquivez, and Raymond Chee. They all use Outlook to arrange their schedules, organize their tasks, and compile contact lists of buyers, sellers, lenders, and others. In addition, they rely heavily on the integration abilities of Outlook to exchange information with each other and with their clients. They frequently create e-mail messages from Office documents. They also import data from other programs into Outlook, and export their Outlook data into other file formats. As they work, they use the Journal to track their activities. You'll work with Cassandra as she helps Arlo and Nancy Kirnen find a home that meets their needs and expectations for a price they can afford.

Student Data Files

▼Tutorial.05

  ▽ Tutorial folder   ▽ Review folder   ▽ Cases folder

       Homebuyers.mdb   Description.doc   Frame.txt

       Mortgage.xls   Homesellers.xls   Seminar.doc

                                                     Seminar Tasks.pst

In this tutorial, you will turn on the Journal, and then track your activities both manually and automatically. You'll use Office documents to create and send e-mail messages, and you'll create Office documents from Outlook. You'll learn how to send and receive faxes with Outlook. Then you'll import data created in other Office programs into Outlook, and export Outlook data into file formats that programs other than Outlook can use. You'll communicate with instant messages, view Web pages from Outlook, and set up a folder home page. Finally, you'll print the journal entries that were created.

Session 5.1

Recording Activities in the Journal

As you work, it is sometimes helpful to be able to look back at a timeline of your activities. You may want to find exactly when you wrote a certain letter. Or, you may want to recall exactly how you spent a particular workday. Many people write down details of their day in a paper appointment book. In Outlook, you record this information in the Journal. The Journal is a diary that records the date, time, and duration of your actions with Outlook items, Office files, and other activities. The Journal can record activities automatically or you can manually record them yourself.

Cassandra at Ace Realty uses the Journal to keep records of her daily activities, including e-mail messages she sends and receives, telephone calls she makes, and Office files she works on.

To view the Journal:

1. Click the **Folder List** button 🗀 in the Navigation Pane, and then click **Journal** in the Folder List. The Journal opens in the main window. See Figure 5-1.

Journal main window 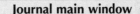 Figure 5-1

Trouble? If a dialog box opens, saying that the Journal can automatically track Office documents and e-mail associated with a contact, then the Journal is not set to automatically track activities. Click the No button to close the dialog box and leave the Journal turned off.

Trouble? If the Journal is set to display a different view than the one shown in the figure, click the Week button on the Standard toolbar.

Before you work with the Journal, you'll add a task to the Tasks folder and enter the Kirnens as a contact in a subfolder named Ace that you'll create in the Contacts folder.

To enter a task and a contact:

1. Create a new task with the subject **Prepare mortgage worksheet** and the due date of **next Tuesday**.

2. Create a new contact for **Arlo Kirnen**, home phone number **402-555-1574**, home fax **402-555-6789**, address type **Home**, home mailing address **17 Dodge Road, Omaha, NE 98182**, your e-mail address (fix the Display as name), and spouse's name **Nancy**.

You'll set up the Journal to record entries for any e-mails related to the Kirnens.

Recording Journal Entries Automatically

The Journal will record the date and time of each action for the Outlook items and the Office files you specify. You can set up the Journal to record the following Outlook items: e-mail messages; meeting requests, responses, and cancellations; and task requests and responses. Although you can check one item, multiple items, or all the items, the Journal will record the selected items for only the contacts you specify.

Be aware that when you add entries to your contact list, you must manually select those contacts if you want to record items to or from them in the Journal. You can also have the Journal record files you create, open, close, and save in Access, Excel, Power-Point, and Word, as long as those programs are installed on your computer. Outlook creates a shortcut to each Office file in the Journal, even if Outlook isn't running.

Reference Window	**Recording Journal Entries Automatically**

- Click Tools on the menu bar, and then click Options.
- Click the Preferences tab, and then click the Journal Options button.
- Click the desired items' check boxes in the Automatically record these items list box.
- Click the desired contacts' check boxes in the For these contacts list box.
- Click the desired programs' check boxes in the Also record files from list box.
- Click the OK button in the Journal Options dialog box.
- Click the OK button in the Options dialog box.

Cassandra asks you to set up the Journal to record e-mail messages and Office files related to the Kirnens. If you have other Office-compatible applications installed on your computer, you can also have the Journal record any activities with those files.

To set up the Journal to record entries automatically:

1. Click **Tools** on the menu bar, and then click **Options**. The Options dialog box opens.

2. Click the **Preferences** tab, if necessary, and then click the **Journal Options** button. The Journal Options dialog box opens. See Figure 5-2.

Journal Options dialog box | Figure 5-2

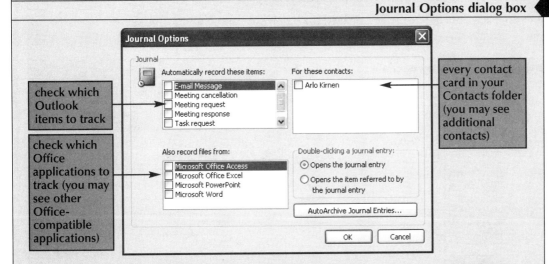

3. Click the **E-mail Message** check box in the Automatically record these items list box.

4. Click the **Arlo Kirnen** check box in the For these contacts list box.

5. Click the **Microsoft Office Access**, **Microsoft Office Excel**, **Microsoft Power-Point**, and **Microsoft Word** check boxes in the Also record files from list box. All the Office applications and Office-compatible applications installed on your system appear in the dialog box.

   Trouble? If you don't see the Access, Excel, PowerPoint, or Word check boxes, then Office is not installed on your computer. If the Office programs are not installed on your computer, you will not be able to complete certain activities in this tutorial. Continue with Step 6.

6. Click the **OK** button in the Journal Options dialog box.

7. Click the **OK** button in the Options dialog box.

Although no outward change is visible in Outlook, the Journal will track any e-mail messages you send to or receive from Arlo as well as any Office documents you work on.

Adding Journal Entries Manually

If you don't have the Journal set up to record entries automatically, you can enter them manually. You can also manually create entries for items, files, and actions that the Journal does not record automatically. These include Outlook items such as appointments, notes, and incoming phone calls as well as those items that you didn't check in the Journal Options dialog box; documents for non-Office programs, or Office programs not installed on your computer; and activities you have already completed, printed documents you receive, or actions such as conversations or items you purchase.

When you start a new journal entry, you must enter certain information: the date, the time, and the duration. If the duration is not significant, then leave the default 0 minutes entry.

To record a journal entry manually:

▶ **1.** Click **Journal** in the Folder List, and then click the **New** button on the Standard toolbar. A new Journal Entry window opens. See Figure 5-3.

Figure 5-3　　　　**Blank Journal Entry window**

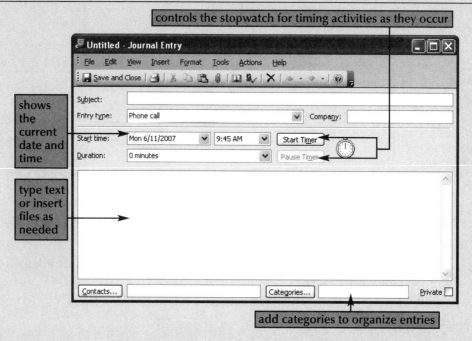

▶ **2.** Type **Mortgage Worksheet for the Kirnens** in the Subject text box.

▶ **3.** Click the **Entry type** list arrow, and then click **Conversation**.

▶ **4.** Click the **Duration** list arrow, and then click **10 minutes**.

▶ **5.** Type **Raymond talked with Arlo Kirnen. Arlo and Nancy are sending in their list of debts for the mortgage worksheet today.** in the notes text box at the bottom of the dialog box.

▶ **6.** Type **Raymond Chee** in the Contacts text box.

　　If Raymond had been in your contacts list, you could have clicked the Contacts button and then selected him from the list. You'll use this method to also assign Arlo as a contact to this entry.

▶ **7.** Click the **Contacts** button to open the Select Contacts dialog box, click **Kirnen, Arlo** in the Items list, and then click the **OK** button. See Figure 5-4.

Completed Journal Entry window | Figure 5-4

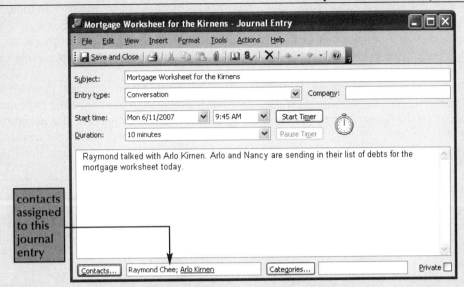

contacts assigned to this journal entry

8. Click the **Save and Close** button on the Standard toolbar in the Journal Entry window to close the Journal Entry window.

   The entry appears in the Journal main window in the By Type view.

9. Click the **Day** button on the Standard toolbar, click the **plus sign** button ⊞ next to Entry Type: Conversation, if necessary, and then scroll to the right, if necessary, until you see the journal entry on the timeline. See Figure 5-5. The current day is highlighted in blue in the timeline.

Journal with a Conversation entry | Figure 5-5

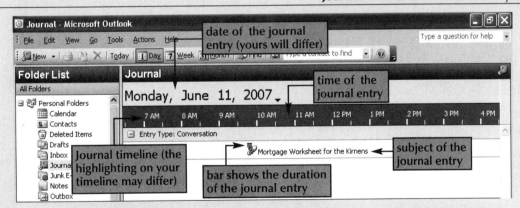

date of the journal entry (yours will differ)

time of the journal entry

Journal timeline (the highlighting on your timeline may differ)

subject of the journal entry

bar shows the duration of the journal entry

Trouble? If the Journal on your screen looks different from the one in the figure, you need to change the view. Click View on the menu bar, point to Arrange By, point to Current View, click By Type, and then repeat Step 9.

10. Click the **Week** button on the Standard toolbar. The main window shows days instead of hours along the timeline, and the current day is again highlighted.

You can use Outlook to chronicle things you do, such as a conversation, as well as significant events, such as the date a new real estate agent started working at Ace. You can also record existing items in the Journal.

Recording Existing Items in the Journal

Even if you've worked on or completed a task, held a meeting, or sent an e-mail message that was not recorded in the Journal, you can still create a journal entry. When you create an entry that references an existing item, Outlook adds a shortcut to the item in the Journal Entry window. If you double-click the shortcut icon in the Journal, the item's window opens so you can review or modify details.

The quickest way to create a journal entry from an existing item is to drag the item to the Journal folder. The AutoCreate feature then starts a new journal entry using the information from the dragged item. You can modify the information as needed. If you **right-drag** (drag an item using the right mouse button rather than the left), a shortcut menu opens with several options, as described in Figure 5-6.

Figure 5-6	Journal shortcut menu options

Shortcut Menu Option	Resulting Action
Copy Here as Journal Entry with Shortcut	Starts a new journal entry with a shortcut to the item in the notes text box.
Copy Here as Journal Entry with Attachment	Starts a new journal entry with a copy of the item attached (represented by an icon) in the notes text box.
Move Here as Journal Entry with Attachment	Starts a new journal entry with the item moved into the notes text box; the item is removed from its original folder.

Earlier, you added a task and entered the Kirnens in the contact list. These activities were not entered in the Journal, so you'll manually record them now. You'll mark down the time you've already spent working on the Prepare mortgage worksheet task you set up earlier.

To add an existing task to the Journal:

1. Click **Tasks** in the Folder List to display the Tasks folder and leave the All Folders pane visible.

2. Right-drag the **Prepare mortgage worksheet** task to the **Journal** folder in the Folder List, and then click **Copy Here as Journal Entry with Shortcut** on the shortcut menu. The task's Journal Entry window opens with a shortcut to the task inserted in the notes text box. You could double-click this shortcut to open the Task window. See Figure 5-7.

Journal entry with a shortcut to a task Figure 5-7

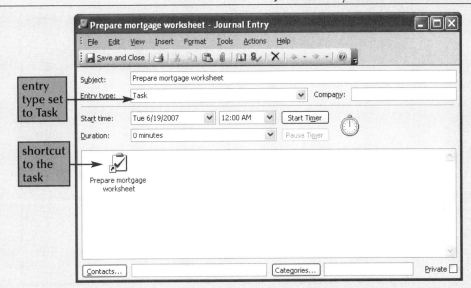

3. Change the Start time to **11:30 AM** and the duration to **1 hour**.

4. Click the **Save and Close** button on the Standard toolbar. The Journal Entry window closes and the entry is recorded in the Journal.

The ability to enter an item you completed is important if you decide to track an activity after you have already invested time and effort in it. Being able to record how long you worked on various tasks or spent at appointments is helpful if you need to track your total time on a project for reporting or billing purposes. You can also record when you entered a contact in Outlook, as a reminder of the initial association.

You'll add Arlo Kirnen's contact card to the Journal as an attachment. This way, you can print his contact card with the journal entry at a later time.

To add an existing contact to the Journal:

1. Click **Contacts** in the Folder List to display the contents of the Contacts folder and leave the Folder List visible.

2. Right-drag the **Arlo Kirnen** contact to the **Journal** folder, and then click **Copy Here as Journal Entry with Attachment** on the shortcut menu. The Journal Entry window for Arlo Kirnen opens with a copy of the contact item inserted as an attachment in the notes text box. See Figure 5-8.

Figure 5-8 ▶ **Journal entry with an attachment**

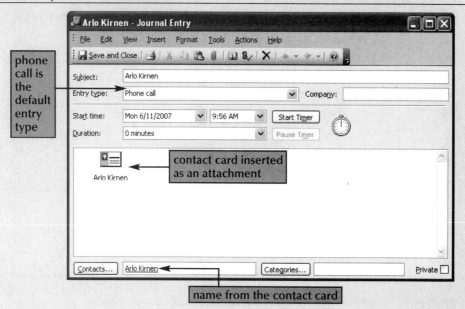

phone call is the default entry type

contact card inserted as an attachment

name from the contact card

▶ **3.** Click the **Save and Close** button on the Standard toolbar in the Journal Entry window. The Journal Entry window closes and the entry is recorded in the Journal.

In addition to recording existing items in the Journal, you can also record files.

Adding Existing Documents to the Journal

You can add journal entries for any file or document you have created in Office or Office-compatible programs. Why would you want to do this? First, it enables you to organize and track all files and items related to a specific project or task. Second, it enables you to find and open the files from Outlook, where they can be associated with a specific subject, contact, or time frame rather than searching for them with Windows Explorer or My Computer. You choose whether to include a copy of the file in the entry or insert an icon or a text shortcut that you can click to open the original file.

You'll create a journal entry for the mortgage worksheet that you're developing.

To create a journal entry for an existing file:

▶ **1.** Click the **New** button list arrow on the Standard toolbar and then click **Journal Entry**. A new Journal Entry window opens.

▶ **2.** Type **Mortgage worksheet** in the Subject text box, click the **Entry type** list arrow, and then click **Microsoft Office Excel**. As you can see, many types of entries are available in the list.

▶ **3.** Click in the notes text box, type **Mortgage worksheet with categories and formulas**, and then press the **Enter** key.

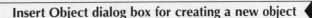

4. Click **Insert** on the menu bar in the Journal Entry window, and then click **Object**. The Insert Object dialog box opens. See Figure 5-9.

Insert Object dialog box for creating a new object ◄ Figure 5-9

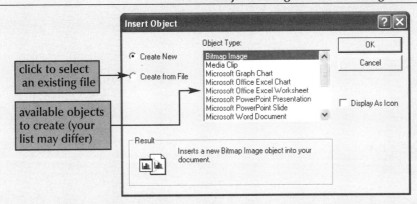

5. Click the **Create from File** option button.

6. Click the **Browse** button below the Create from File text box, and then double-click **Mortgage** in the **Tutorial.05\Tutorial** folder included with your Data Files. The path to the file appears in the File text box.

7. Click the **Display As Icon** check box to insert a check mark, and verify that the Link check box is unchecked. Text or an icon with text appears below the Display As Icon check box. This is what will appear in the notes text box in the Journal Entry window. See Figure 5-10.

Insert Object dialog box for inserting a file ◄ Figure 5-10

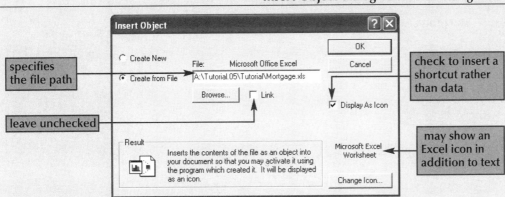

8. Click the **OK** button. A shortcut to the file appears as an icon with text or only as text identifying the file type in the notes text box of the Journal Entry window. See Figure 5-11.

Figure 5-11 Journal entry with a shortcut to a file

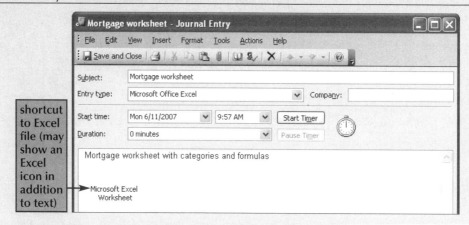

You can open the Excel file simply by double-clicking this shortcut icon or descriptive text in the Journal Entry window.

9. Double-click the **Microsoft Excel Worksheet** shortcut in the Journal Entry window. The workbook opens in Excel. See Figure 5-12.

Figure 5-12 Mortgage worksheet opened in Excel

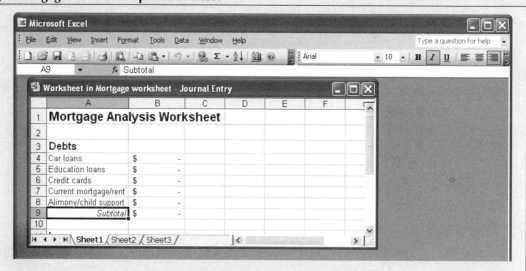

Trouble? If you see more of the worksheet than shown in Figure 5-12, Excel or the worksheet is probably maximized on your screen. The content of the worksheet is the same. Continue with Step 10.

Trouble? If the worksheet opens in the Journal Entry window, click it once to select the entire object, press the Delete key, repeat Steps 4 through 8, right-click (instead of double-click) the shortcut in Step 9, click Open on the shortcut menu, and then continue with Step 10. If the worksheet still won't open in its own window, double-click the worksheet object to open an editable worksheet within the Journal Entry window. (Note that the toolbars and menu bar in the Journal Entry window change to include Excel commands.) Skip Step 10 and continue with Step 11.

10. Click the **Close** button ☒ on the Excel title bar. The Excel window closes.

11. Click the **Save and Close** button on the Standard toolbar in the Journal Entry window. The Journal Entry window closes and the entry is recorded in the Journal.

Next, you'll review the journal entries you have created.

Viewing Journal Entries

When you switch to the Journal folder, you see a timeline with all your entries grouped by type of item, such as task, conversation, and Microsoft Excel. You can display or hide all the entries in a particular group as needed by clicking the plus sign or minus sign button. After you've had the Journal on for a while, you may find it difficult to find a specific entry by scrolling. Instead, you can jump to a particular date or expand or collapse the timeline to display entries for a day, a week, or a month. You can also change the view to group entries by contact or category or as a table without any groups.

To view journal entries:

1. Display the **Journal** folder. The Journal appears in the By Type view for the current week with today's date highlighted and four entry types. See Figure 5-13.

Journal in By Type view ◄ Figure 5-13

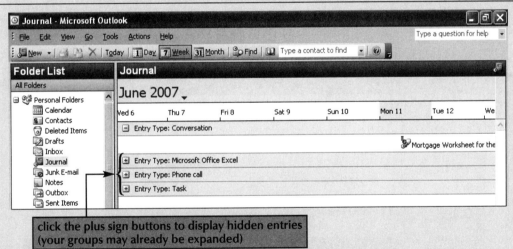

click the plus sign buttons to display hidden entries
(your groups may already be expanded)

2. If necessary, click the **plus sign** button ⊞ for each group. The exact location of your journal entries on the timeline will differ, depending on how quickly you performed the steps in the tutorial. See Figure 5-14.

Figure 5-14

Journal with entry type groups expanded

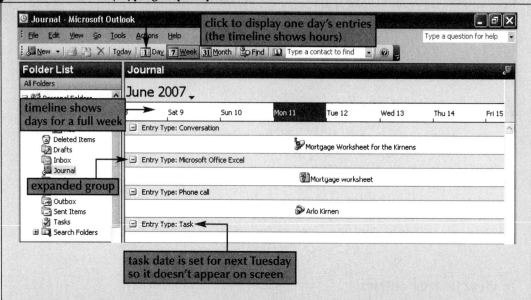

3. Click the **Day** button on the Standard toolbar, click the **Today** button on the Standard toolbar, and then scroll, if necessary, to see the entries for today. The main window displays a timeline of the day's recorded activities. See Figure 5-15.

Figure 5-15

Journal entries in Day view

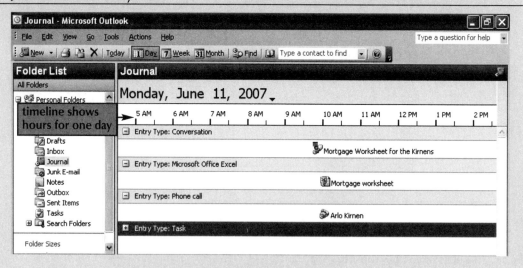

You can move to other dates in the timeline by scrolling or using a calendar.

4. Click the date under the folder banner in the main window. A calendar opens, as shown in Figure 5-16.

Calendar for moving around the Journal

Figure 5-16

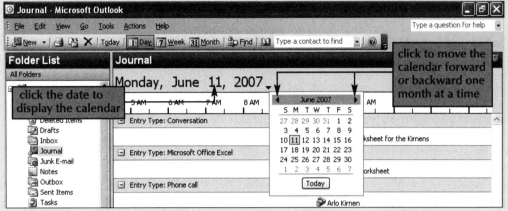

5. Click the date for next Tuesday. The Journal immediately moves to that date; you should see the task you created for that day.

   Trouble? If you don't see the task you created, the task is probably scheduled for a time not visible in the main window. Scroll the view to an earlier or later time, as needed, until you see the task.

6. Click the **Today** button on the Standard toolbar. The Journal returns to the current day.

   All Outlook folders have a timeline view that functions similarly to the Journal timeline view.

7. Click **View** on the menu bar, point to **Arrange By**, point to **Current View**, and then click **Entry List**. See Figure 5-17.

Journal in Entry List view

Figure 5-17

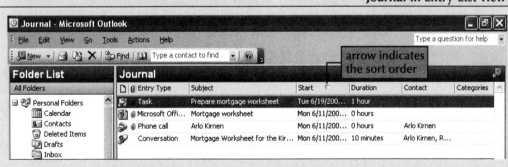

The entries are arranged in a table view without any groupings. The sort order is currently in descending order by Start date. You can sort, group, and filter the Journal according to your needs.

8. Click the **Subject** column heading to sort the entries by that field. The arrow in the Subject column heading points up, which indicates ascending order.

   Trouble? If the arrow in the Subject column heading points down, indicating descending order, click the Subject column heading again to reverse the sort order to ascending.

9. Click the **Start** column heading to sort the entries by date in descending order.

Recall that you can press the Shift key as you press column headings to sort by more than one column. You'll leave the Journal on as you continue to work in Outlook.

Creating E-Mail with Office Applications

Outlook is set up to work hand-in-hand with Office applications—Word, Excel, Publisher, and Access. You have already merged a Word document with Outlook contacts, written a letter in Word to a contact, and inserted existing Office documents as attachments to e-mail messages. You can also integrate Office applications and Outlook by sending a file as an e-mail message.

You can create e-mail messages using a file from any Office program installed on your computer as the message body. The message header with the recipients' addresses and the subject is the same as with other messages, but the body contains a Word document, a Publisher publication, an Excel worksheet, or an Access data page (called a data access page in Access). The Office program opens and its menus and toolbars give you complete access to all the selected program's features and commands. You can then create, edit, and format the message just as you would a stand-alone file in the program. The message is sent in HTML format. After you send the message, you can save the document, publication, worksheet, or data page as a file.

When recipients receive the message created with an Office program, the file appears as the message body, not as an attachment. Because the message is sent as HTML, all recipients can read it as long as their e-mail programs can read HTML. Recipients can read and respond to the message the same as any other message. If they have the appropriate Office program installed on their computer, they can open and edit the message body in the program. If the Office program is not installed, they can still view and edit the message body in Outlook, but they do not have access to any of the Office program's features.

For example, Cassandra can create an Excel worksheet with a mortgage analysis for the Kirnens, and then send it to them as an HTML e-mail message. If the Kirnens have Excel, they can edit the entire worksheet, including the formulas. If not, they can view and edit the worksheet data as they would text in the Message window. In addition, Cassandra can save the message body as an Excel workbook and continue to work on the file. The workbook is much more convenient than saving the data in a message format because Cassandra can add worksheets, formulas, and data as the analysis develops.

Mailing Office Files

- Display the Inbox.
- Click Actions on the menu bar, point to New Mail Message Using, point to Microsoft Office, and then click Microsoft Word Document, Microsoft Publisher Publication, Microsoft Excel Worksheet, or Microsoft Access Data Page.
- Enter the recipient addresses and a subject.
- Create the document, publication, worksheet, or data access page in the message body, using the commands and features of the selected Office program.
- Click the Send a Copy, Send this Sheet, or Send this Publication button, and then click the Send/Receive button on the Standard toolbar in the Inbox or Outbox, if necessary.
- If you want to save the Office file you created to your computer, click the Save button on the Office program's Standard toolbar, type a filename in the File name text box, change the Save in location as needed, and then click the Save button.
- Click the Close button in the program window title bar; click the No button to close the file without saving it, if necessary.

You'll e-mail an Excel worksheet with the mortgage calculation data rather than just listing the numbers in a document or message. This way, you or the Kirnens can change the numbers, and Excel will automatically recalculate the totals. No matter who updates the worksheet, you or the Kirnens, there will be accurate figures for analysis.

To create an Excel worksheet to send by e-mail:

1. Display the **Inbox** folder.

2. Click **Actions** on the menu bar, point to **New Mail Message Using**, point to **Microsoft Office**, and then click **Microsoft Excel Worksheet**. Excel opens with a worksheet and message headers. See Figure 5-18.

Figure 5-18 | **Excel with an open workbook and message headers**

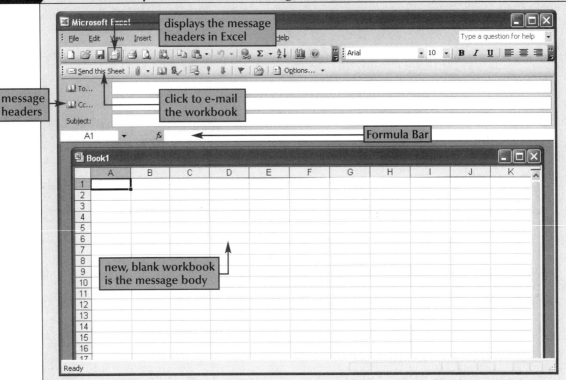

3. Type **Arlo Kirnen** in the To text box, and then press the **Tab** key. Arlo's name is underlined with a red wavy line. This means that Outlook found more than one entry in the Contacts folder for the name you typed.

4. Right-click **Arlo Kirnen** in the To text box. The shortcut menu that opens includes two entries: one for Arlo's e-mail address and one for his fax number.

5. Click the entry that does not include (Home Fax).

6. Type **Please confirm your debts** in the Subject text box.

   Next, you'll enter text, numbers, and formulas in cells within the Excel worksheet. You use text to create a label for the content of cells. A formula performs a calculation and can include numbers as well as references to cells. Cells are identified by their column letter and row number; for example, the first cell in the upper-left corner of the worksheet is cell A1.

To enter data in the Excel worksheet:

1. Click in cell **A1**, type **Debt**, press the **Tab** key to move to cell B1, type **Amount**, and then press the **Enter** key to move to cell A2.

2. Enter the following information in columns A and B. Remember to press the **Tab** key to move to the next cell and press the **Enter** key to move to the first cell in the next row. As you enter the information, not all the text will be visible in column A.

Car loan	6000
School loans	**15000**
Credit cards	**2000**

If all the content in a cell is not visible, such as in column A, you can widen the column to fit the longest entry.

3. Position the pointer over the column-heading border between column headings A and B so that it changes to ↔ , and then double-click. This action widens column A to fit the longest entry in the column—School loans. All the content in column A is visible.

You'll add a formula in cell B5 to total the values in the Amount column—the range of cells B2, B3, and B4.

4. Click in cell **B5**, click the **AutoSum** button Σ on the Standard toolbar, verify that the formula =SUM(B2:B4) appears in the Formula Bar, and then press the **Enter** key. The SUM formula calculates the sum of the selected range, B2:B4. The total amount in cell B5 is 23000.

The information in the worksheet would be easier to read if the values were formatted as currency and the column headings were boldface.

5. Drag to select cells **B2** through **B5**, and then click the **Currency Style** button $ on the Formatting toolbar. The amounts are formatted with dollar signs and decimal points.

6. Select cells **A1** and **B1**, and then click the **Bold** button B on the Formatting toolbar. The column headings change to boldface text.

7. Select cells **A4** and **B4**, click the **Borders** button list arrow ⊞ ▾ on the Formatting toolbar, and then click the **Bottom Border** button ⊞ on the palette. A border separates the total from the data above it.

8. Click in cell **A6** so you can see the changes you made. Your message should look like Figure 5-19.

Excel worksheet with data, formula, and formatting ◄ Figure 5-19

Now that the worksheet contains the data, you will send the worksheet. Once you send the message, Excel remains open so you can save the worksheet to your computer. You can open and edit the workbook file you saved in Excel at any time. If you don't want to keep a separate copy of the worksheet, you can close the file without saving changes. You can use the taskbar buttons to switch between Outlook and Excel.

To e-mail the worksheet, and then save it:

1. Click the **Send this Sheet** button on the message toolbar to send the message. The message is sent to the Outbox, and Excel stays open.

2. If necessary, click the **Inbox – Microsoft Outlook** button on the taskbar to switch to Outlook, send the message, and then click the **Microsoft Excel** button on the taskbar to switch back to the Excel program window.

3. Click the **Save** button 🖫 on the Standard toolbar in the Excel program window, and then save the file as **Debt Worksheet** in the **Tutorial.05\Tutorial** folder included with your Data Files.

4. Click **File** on the Excel menu bar, and then click **Exit**. The Excel workbook and program close.

The sent message appears in the recipients' Inboxes. They can read and respond to the message like any other message. The recipients can save a message created from an Office file in its original program format (for example, as an Excel workbook, Publisher publication, or Access database). They can then open and edit the file in that program, as long as they have the program on their computer.

You'll download the message with the debt data. Then you will respond to the message and save the data in an Excel workbook.

To respond to and save the e-mail with the Excel data:

1. If necessary, download your messages.

2. Double-click the **Please confirm your debts** message to open it, and then read the message. See Figure 5-20. The message was sent in HTML format to retain the formatting you added to the worksheet.

Figure 5-20 | Message with Excel data

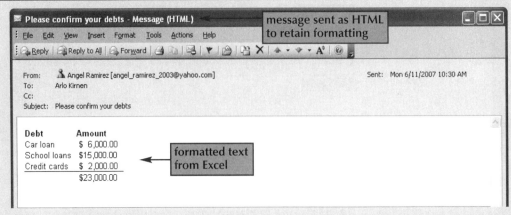

Trouble? If your message is in plain text format, your mail server or ISP may not allow HTML formatting. Continue with Step 3.

You can reply to the sender and save the worksheet data in Excel.

3. Reply to the message with the text **The car loan is actually $4000. Please update your records.** above the original message.

   Your reply may appear in colored type because of the HTML formatting.

4. Send the message. The InfoBar on the original received message lists the date and time of your reply.

   The window with the original message remains open. You'll save the workbook, and then update the car loan amount.

5. Right-click the message body, and then click **Open in Microsoft Excel 11** on the shortcut menu. The data from the workbook appears in an unsaved Excel workbook.

   Trouble? If the Open in Microsoft Excel 11 command is not on the shortcut menu or is grayed out and unavailable, skip Steps 5 through 7.

6. Click cell **B2**, type **4000**, and then press the **Enter** key. The car loan and total amounts are updated. The total becomes $21,000.

   You can save the worksheet in a variety of formats, including an Excel workbook, a Web page, and formats compatible with other spreadsheet programs. The available file formats are listed in the Save as type list in the Save As dialog box.

7. Save the worksheet with the filename **Debt Worksheet Revised** as a **Microsoft Office Excel Workbook** in the **Tutorial.05\Tutorial** folder included with your Data Files, and then close the file and exit Excel.

   Trouble? If you see Microsoft Office Excel Workbook (*.xls) in the dialog box, then your system is set up to show file extensions.

8. If necessary, download the reply message.

Because both Cassandra and the Kirnens have access to the worksheet, either can update the information right in Excel. Sometimes, you'll want to share document information without distributing a file that others can modify.

Sending and Receiving Faxes

Faxes are a popular way to send and receive information. Rather than printing a file and then sending it from a stand-alone fax machine, you can send and receive faxes right from Outlook.

The format of faxes you send from Outlook is similar to e-mail messages in that you need to enter a subject, a recipient name, and perhaps a short message. Instead of an e-mail address, however, you enter a fax number. You can send faxes to people and numbers you have already entered in your contact list, or you can type the name and number as you create the fax. If you are sending a fax internationally, you must precede the fax number with the appropriate country code. The country code stored in a contact card must begin with a plus sign (+)—for example, (+61)(402) 555-1234.

There are two ways to fax from Outlook. You can use a **fax service**, a free or commercial provider that sends (and sometimes receives) faxes from your Internet-connected computer using software that you install on your computer. To use a fax service with Outlook, you must also have Word installed on your computer. You can also use a fax modem on your computer to send faxes without using a fax service.

Sending Faxes from Outlook

- Click the New button list arrow on the Standard toolbar, and then click Internet Fax (*or* click File on the menu bar, point to New, and then click Internet Fax). A Message window opens.
- If you do not have a fax service, a dialog box opens, reminding you to sign up with a provider. Click the OK button, follow the instructions on the Web page that opens to sign up with a fax service provider, close the Web browser, and then repeat Step 1.
- Type the recipient's name and fax number in the Fax Recipient and Fax Number text boxes, and then type a subject in the Subject text box; for each additional recipient to whom you want to send the fax, click the Add More button and then enter that recipient's name and fax number.
- If necessary, attach the file you want to fax.
- Select the options you want in the Fax Service pane, and then complete the fax cover sheet in the message body.
- Click the Send button on the message toolbar in the Message window, and then click the Send/Receive button on the Standard toolbar in the Inbox or Outbox, if necessary.
  or
- Click the New button list arrow on the Standard toolbar, and then click Mail Message (*or* click File on the menu bar, point to New, and then click Mail Message). A Message window opens.
- Click the To button in the message header, double-click one or more names with fax number entries in your Contacts folder, and then click the OK button.
- Type a subject in the Subject text box.
- If necessary, attach the file you want to fax.
- Type the message text in the message area.
- Click the Send button on the message toolbar in the Message window, and then click the Send/Receive button on the Standard toolbar in the Inbox or Outbox, if necessary.

When you send a fax from Outlook using a fax service, the document you want to fax is converted to a TIFF image file and attached to an e-mail message. You enter each recipient's name and fax number in the To text box, and a subject in the Subject text box. You can type the recipient's fax number or select it from a contact card in the Contacts folder. You can include other information about the fax in the message body, which acts as the fax cover sheet. After you send the fax, your fax provider sends you an e-mail message to confirm that the fax was delivered (or not delivered).

The first time you try to send a fax from Outlook, you will be taken to Office Marketplace to sign up for a fax service provider. Or you can click Help on the menu bar, and then click Microsoft Office Online to go to that Web site; once you are on Microsoft Office Online, click the Office Marketplace link, and then click the Fax link to see a list of fax services available on Office Online. Step-by-step instructions for signing up with the fax service are available on the provider's Web site.

You can attach one or more documents to a fax, and you can send the fax to one or more recipients. Like with e-mail, if you are working offline, the fax is stored in your Outbox until the next time you connect to the Internet. Copies of all faxes you send are saved in the Sent Items folder.

If you don't want to sign up for a fax service, you can send faxes to contacts for whom you have entered a fax number just as you would send them e-mail messages. Open a new Message window, click the To button, show contacts from the appropriate Contacts folder, double-click fax recipients from those names followed by Business Fax, Home Fax, or Other Fax. Type a subject and message as usual, and then attach any files. When you're done, click the Send button.

If someone sends you a fax, you can use Outlook to receive faxes. When you set up Outlook to receive faxes, incoming faxes appear in your Inbox just like e-mail messages. You can open, read, and file these received faxes just as you would other messages.

Reviewing and Editing Journal Entries

Because you turned on the Journal to automatically record Office files, the Excel workbooks you have created for Cassandra to send to the Kirnens will appear as entries.

To view the entries in the Journal:

1. Display the **Journal** folder. The Journal opens in the main window.

2. Change the view to **By Type**, click the **plus sign** button ⊞ for any hidden group, and then review the journal entries you created so far. See Figure 5-21.

Journal entries with a Conversation   Figure 5-21

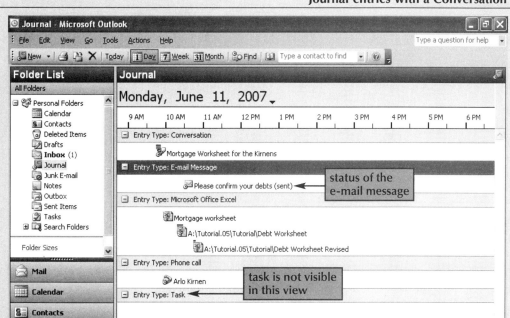

You want to change the journal entry for Mortgage Worksheet for the Kirnens from Conversation to Phone Call.

3. Double-click the **Mortgage Worksheet for the Kirnens** to open its Journal Entry window.

4. Click the **Entry type** list arrow, click **Phone call**, and then save and close the Journal Entry window. The journal entry moves into the Phone call group and the Conversation group disappears. See Figure 5-22.

Figure 5-22 | **Journal entries with two phone calls**

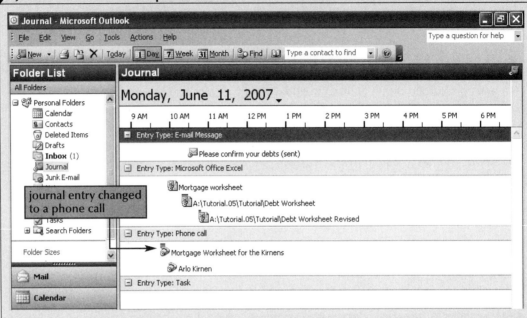

5. Review the modified journal entry in the main window.

Outlook not only gives you various options for creating and sending new files from different Office programs, you can also work with existing files. In Session 5.2, you'll import and export files, exchange instant messages, view Web pages, and print the journal entries.

Review

Session 5.1 Quick Check

1. What is the Journal?

2. Describe one benefit of using the Journal.

3. List the items you can record automatically in the Journal.

4. What are two ways to send an Office file as an e-mail message?

5. When recipients receive an Office file as the message body, what access do they have to the data?

6. How do you create an Office file from Outlook?

7. True or False: To create an Excel worksheet as an e-mail message, the Excel program must be installed on your computer.

8. True or False: You can send faxes from Outlook but you cannot receive faxes in Outlook.

Session 5.2

Importing and Exporting Files

Importing and exporting are two sides of the same coin. Both copy data created in one program and transform it into another program's format. The difference is whether you are copying data into a program (**importing**) or moving data out of a program (**exporting**). For example, you might import e-mail messages from another program, such as Netscape Mail or Lotus Organizer, into your Outlook Inbox so that you can store all your messages in one location. Or, you might export your Outlook Contacts folder into an Access database of names and addresses so that someone else can work with the list.

You can import information into Outlook from a Personal Folders file (for example, to restore an archived folder), from a Personal Address Book (for example, to add names, addresses, and phone numbers from a contact list), or from a file (for example, to bring existing information from another program file, such as an Access database). When you import information, you copy the contents of the file into the Outlook folder that you specify.

You can export items from Outlook to a Personal Folders file or another file type. Personal Folders files can be viewed only in Outlook. Other file types can be opened from or imported into other programs. If you plan to work with the exported data in Outlook, export to a Personal Folders file. If you plan to work with the data in another program, export to a file format that program can import. For example, if you wanted to work with your to-do list in Excel, you could export the Tasks folder into the Excel .xls file format.

You have already exported data into Outlook when you saved a contact as a vCard. The Save As command is a simple way to change the format of Outlook items. However, the file format options available with the Save As command are limited and depend on the type of item. The Import and Export Wizard provides a greater variety of file formats to choose from when exporting or importing. The wizard walks you through the steps for importing or exporting in Outlook. First, you choose the action you want to perform (import or export), then you select the file type you want to bring in or create, then you select the file you want to import or you select the folder items you want to export and the destination file, and finally you perform the import or export.

Importing from Other Mail Programs

When you've compiled an address book or messages in another program, such as Outlook Express, Eudora, or Netscape, you might want to import that information into Outlook. To import messages or addresses from another program, you must have that program installed on your computer.

One of the Ace assistants had been using Outlook Express to send and receive messages, and the address book contains a list of possible homebuyers that isn't stored elsewhere. Cassandra asks you to use the Import and Export Wizard to import this list from Outlook Express.

To import addresses from another mail program:

▶ **1.** If you took a break after the previous session, make sure Outlook is running and the Journal folder is open.

▶ **2.** Click **File** on the menu bar, and then click **Import and Export**. The Import and Export Wizard dialog box opens, so you can select what you want to do. See Figure 5-23.

Trouble? If Business Contact Manager is installed and in use with your profile, click File on the menu bar, point to Import and Export, and then click Outlook.

Figure 5-23 | Import and Export Wizard dialog box

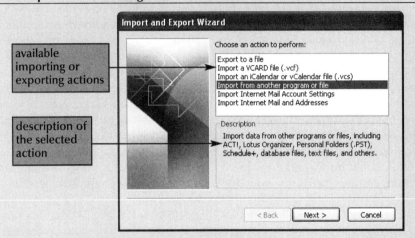

available importing or exporting actions

description of the selected action

3. Click **Import Internet Mail and Addresses** in the Choose an action to perform list box, and then click the **Next** button. You select which e-mail program you want to import from using the Outlook Import Tool dialog box. See Figure 5-24.

Figure 5-24 | Outlook Import Tool dialog box

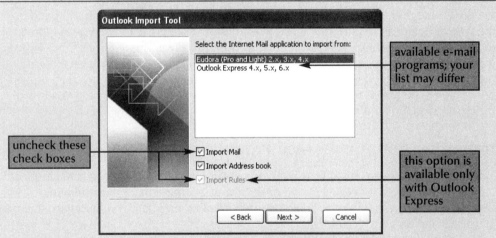

uncheck these check boxes

available e-mail programs; your list may differ

this option is available only with Outlook Express

Trouble? If your dialog box looks different, you might have selected the Import Internet Mail Account Settings action in the previous dialog box. Click the Back button, and then repeat Step 3, being careful to scroll down and click the correct option.

4. Click **Outlook Express 4.x, 5.x, 6.x** in the Select the Internet Mail application to import from list box. Because Outlook Express also uses rules, the selected Import Rules check box becomes active. You want to import only the address book.

5. Click the **Import Mail** and **Import Rules** check boxes to remove the check marks, and then click the **Next** button. The Import Addresses dialog box opens so you can specify where you want to place the imported addresses and how to handle addresses that duplicate those already in your Contacts folder. See Figure 5-25.

Import Addresses dialog box | Figure 5-25

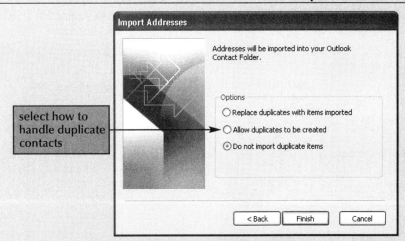

select how to handle duplicate contacts

Whether you replace duplicates, allow duplicates, or don't import duplicates depends on the list. If your list contains updated information, then you probably want to replace the duplicates with the items you are importing. If you know that you want to import all the items, regardless of duplicates, then you want to allow duplicates. If duplicate items are older than the existing items, then you probably don't want to import duplicates.

6. Click the **Do not import duplicate items** option button.

The wizard is all set up to import the addresses from Outlook Express into your Outlook Contacts folder. To copy the Outlook Express addresses into Outlook, you would click the Finish button. However, Cassandra remembers she has this data in another location, so you won't complete this action.

7. Click the **Cancel** button.

Instead, Cassandra asks you to import a contact list that is stored in an Office application.

Importing and Exporting with Office Applications

Cassandra has a list of current homebuyers that she created in an Access database. Rather than retyping the information into Outlook, risking typos and taking up time, you can import that list. The process for importing files is similar to importing from another mail program. The Import and Export Wizard walks you through the steps.

To import a contact list from Access:

1. Create a subfolder named **Ace** that contains **Contact Items** placed in the **Contacts** folder. You'll import the new contacts into this folder.

2. Click **File** on the menu bar, and then click **Import and Export**. The Import and Export Wizard dialog box opens.

3. Click **Import from another program or file** in the Choose an action to perform list box, if necessary, and then click the **Next** button. The Import a File dialog box shows a list of all the program files and formats from which you can import. See Figure 5-26.

| Figure 5-26 | Import a File dialog box |

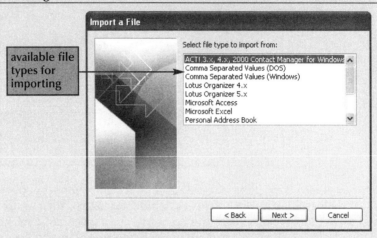

available file types for importing

4. Click **Microsoft Access** in the Select file type to import from list box, and then click the **Next** button. The next Import a File dialog box opens.

5. Click the **Browse** button, and then double-click the **Homebuyers** database file in the **Tutorial.05\Tutorial** folder included with your Data Files. The File to import text box shows the path, such as A:\Tutorial.05\Tutorial\Homebuyers.mdb.

6. Click the **Do not import duplicate items** option button. See Figure 5-27.

| Figure 5-27 | Second Import a File dialog box |

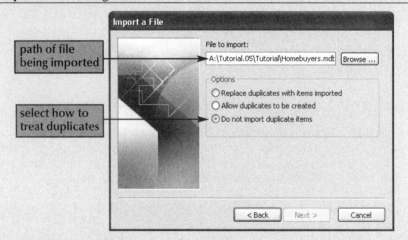

path of file being imported

select how to treat duplicates

7. Click the **Next** button, and then click the **Ace** folder in the Select destination folder list box. See Figure 5-28.

Third Import a File dialog box | Figure 5-28

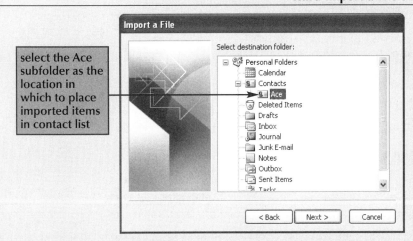

8. Click the **Next** button. The dialog box shows what actions will be performed. See Figure 5-29.

Fourth Import a File dialog box | Figure 5-29

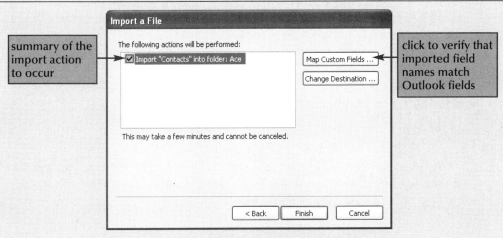

You are not quite done yet; you will complete the import process after you map fields.

Information you import must fit the structure of the Outlook folder you select. For example, the field names used in a database or worksheet must match the ones used in the Outlook folder. Different programs distinguish between fields in different ways. For example, Excel stores each field in a different worksheet cell and Access stores each field in table cells. Another way to distinguish between fields is to separate them with a comma or tab character, which is called **comma-delimited** or **tab-delimited**, as shown in Figure 5-30. This way, Outlook knows to place the following data into a new field each time a comma or tab appears.

Figure 5-30 **Comparison of delimited fields**

Comma-delimited

FirstName,LastName,Street,City,State
Harvey,Leiter,123 Main Street,Lindsay,ID

Tab-delimited

FirstName ⟶ LastName ⟶ Street ⟶ City ⟶ State
Harvey ⟶ Leiter ⟶ 123 Main Street ⟶ Lindsay ⟶ ID

Table or Worksheet

FirstName	LastName	Street	City	State
Harvey	Leiter	123 Main Street	Lindsay	ID

The first row in each example contains the field names, which label the columns. The data in each subsequent row is called a record and appears in the same order. The first field includes data until the comma or tab or cell border. Each column contains the data for the same field for all the records. For example, the first field is called FirstName; the first record in the second row begins with Harvey. If Outlook cannot determine how to insert information into the folder, an error message appears. If you know that field names in the imported file are different from what Outlook uses, you can **map**, or match, the imported fields to the appropriate Outlook fields.

You'll look at how the fields from the file you are importing will map into Outlook.

To map fields from an imported file to Outlook fields:

1. Click the **Map Custom Fields** button in the Import a File dialog box. The Map Custom Fields dialog box opens.

2. Click the **plus sign** button ⊞ next to Name in the To Microsoft Office Outlook Ace list to display the list of Name fields. As you can see, Outlook matches fields from the imported file to Outlook. See Figure 5-31.

Map Custom Fields dialog box Figure 5-31

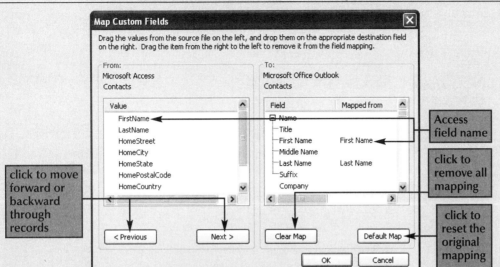

3. Click the **Next** button to view how the first imported record will appear in Outlook. See Figure 5-32.

First Access record mapped to Outlook Figure 5-32

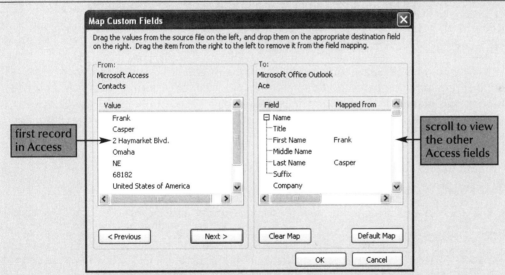

4. Scroll down in the To Microsoft Office Outlook Ace list on the right and expand the three Address fields to view the remaining mapping, and then click the **Previous** button to return to the field names in the From Microsoft Access Contacts list on the left.

If you needed to correct any field mapping, you would drag the field from the From list on the left and drop it onto the appropriate Microsoft Outlook field in the To group on the right. However, all the fields are mapping correctly.

5. Click the **Cancel** button to return to the Import a File dialog box. You are ready to complete the import process.

6. Click the **Finish** button. In a few moments, Outlook converts the records from the Access database and imports them into the Contacts folder.

7. Display the **Ace** folder and view the imported entries. See Figure 5-33.

| Figure 5-33 | Ace folder with imported Access records |

When you need to share some of your Outlook information with a person who uses another program, you can export the information into another format. Because you need to share this contact list with someone who uses only Excel, you'll export the Contacts folder to an Excel worksheet. You can also export the contact list to a Word, Access, comma-delimited, or tab-delimited file.

To export a contact list from Outlook:

1. Click **File** on the menu bar, and then click **Import and Export**.

2. Click **Export to a file** in the Choose an action to perform list box, and then click the **Next** button.

3. Click **Microsoft Excel** in the Create a file of type list box, and then click the **Next** button.

4. Click **Ace** in the Select folder to export from list box, if necessary, and then click the **Next** button.

5. Click the **Browse** button, change the Save in location to the **Tutorial.05\Tutorial** folder included with your Data Files, type **Homebuyer Addresses Worksheet** in the File name text box, and then click the **OK** button. The Save exported file as text box shows the path, such as A:\Tutorial.05\Tutorial\Homebuyer Addresses Worksheet.xls.

6. Click the **Next** button.

In this final dialog box, you confirm the actions that will be performed and have the opportunity to map fields. You do not need to map the fields this time because you are creating a new workbook and there are no field names to match. If you were exporting data to an existing worksheet, you would verify that the Outlook fields mapped correctly to the existing Excel field names.

7. Click the **Finish** button. In a few moments, Outlook converts the information from the contact list and exports it into an Excel worksheet. The original information remains in the Ace folder.

You want to check the Excel worksheet to see how the contacts look in the worksheet file.

To verify the list in Excel:

1. Start Excel, and then open the **Homebuyer Addresses Worksheet** file that you just created in the **Tutorial.05\Tutorial** folder included with your Data Files.

   The worksheet opens with the field names in the first row of the worksheet. Each column contains one field. Each row contains one record, starting in the second row.

2. Scroll down, if necessary, to view all the records.

3. Scroll to the right to review all the fields that were exported from Outlook.

4. Click **File** on the Excel menu bar, and then click **Exit** to close the worksheet and exit the program.

You can import or export to other applications using the same procedure.

Importing and Exporting Personal Folders Files

Recall that Outlook stores items in a Personal Folders file, a special file with a .pst extension, stored on your hard disk (not a network server) in which Outlook information, such as items, folders, and messages, are saved. You can import and export Personal Folders files just like other files. You might import and export Personal Folders files so you can share your Outlook items with other users. Another reason might be to create a backup copy of all your data. Unlike archiving, exporting a Personal Folders file creates a copy of your data and leaves the items intact in Outlook so you can continue to work. If you experienced computer problems, you could import your Personal Folders file into Outlook on another computer and continue to work. Be aware that a Personal Folders file is often too large to fit on a standard floppy disk, so you'll need to copy it on a larger storage medium, such as a network server, Zip disk, or CD-ROM.

You want to back up the Contacts folder.

To back up your Personal Folders file:

1. Click **File** on the menu bar, and then click **Import and Export**.

> **2.** Click **Export to a file** in the Choose an action to perform list box, and then click the **Next** button.

> **3.** Click **Personal Folder File (.pst)** in the Create a file of type list box, and then click the **Next** button. You can choose to export any or all of the folders and subfolders in Outlook. See Figure 5-34.

Figure 5-34	Export Personal Folders dialog box

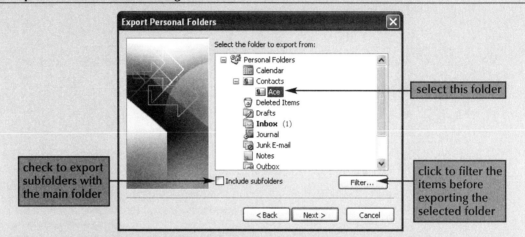

The Filter button enables you to specify a subset of items to export.

> **4.** Click **Ace** in the Select the folder to export from list box if it is not already selected, and then click the **Next** button.

> You will create and save a .pst file.

> **5.** Click the **Browse** button, and then set the exported file to save as **Ace Contacts Backup** in the **Tutorial.05\Tutorial** folder included with your Data Files.

> Because you are creating a new file, it doesn't matter which option you select for duplicated items.

> **6.** Click the **Finish** button. The Create Microsoft Personal Folders dialog box opens. See Figure 5-35.

Figure 5-35

Create Microsoft Personal Folders dialog box

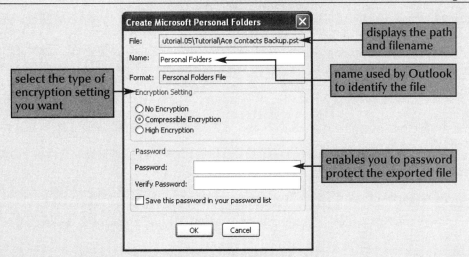

The Create Microsoft Personal Folders dialog box displays the path and filename you specified when you named the exported file. You cannot change this setting from this dialog box. The Name text box displays the name that appears in Outlook when you open the file. You'll leave the default, Personal Folders. Encryption settings cannot be changed after you create the Personal Folders file. Encryption encodes the file to make it unreadable by other programs. No Encryption does not encode your file. Compressible Encryption encodes the file in a format that allows compression; the file is compressed only if you have a compression program set up on your computer. High Encryption encodes the file in a format that offers the greatest degree of protection. If you have a disk-compression program, the file can be compressed but to a lesser degree than allowed by the Compressible Encryption option.

7. Click the **No Encryption** option button in the Encryption Setting group.

Password protecting your Personal Folders file is optional and provides added security. You will be prompted for the password when you start Outlook or connect to the Personal Folders file, unless you save the password in the password list. You will not set up password protection at this time.

8. Click the **OK** button. Outlook exports a copy of the folder as a Personal Folders file.

Even such a small number of items requires 265 KB of space on your disk. However, you could import this file into Outlook on your current computer or on another installation of Outlook.

Saving Items as Another File Format

An easy way to export Outlook items to another format is by using the Save As command. You have used the Save As command to save your calendar as a Web page in HTML format, which can be posted on intranets or the Internet. You can also use the Save As command to export other Outlook items, such as converting an Outlook item to an Office file (as you did earlier), an e-mail message into a Text Only (.txt) or a Rich Text Format (.rtf) file that most word-processing programs can read, or a contact into a vCard File (.vcf) format that most mail programs can read.

Reference Window

Saving Items in Another Format

- Select the item or items you want to save in another format.
- Click File on the menu bar, and then click Save As.
- Change the Save in location.
- Enter a new filename as needed.
- Click the Save as type list arrow, and then select the file format you want.
- Click the Save button.

You'll save one potential homebuyer entry from the Contacts folder as a Rich Text Format file.

To save a contact as a Rich Text Format file:

1. Display the **Ace** folder, if necessary, and then click the **Farnsworth, Luke** contact card to select it.

2. Click **File** on the menu bar, and then click **Save As**. The Save As dialog box opens, with the contact name in the File name text box.

3. Change the Save in location to the **Tutorial.05\Tutorial** folder included with your Data Files, if necessary.

4. Click the **Save as type** list arrow to display the file formats from which you can select. See Figure 5-36; your system may show file extensions.

Figure 5-36   Save As dialog box

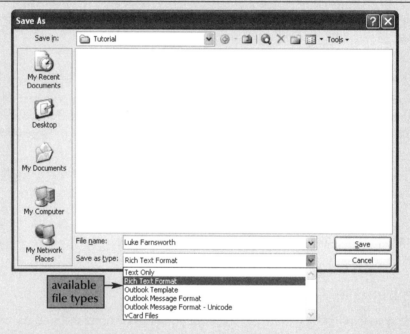

5. Click **Rich Text Format**, if necessary, to select that file format.

6. Click the **Save** button. The Luke Farnsworth contact card is saved as a Rich Text Format file with your Data Files.

You can share the exported file with others or open it in Word or any other program that can read Rich Text Format files.

To view the contact as a Rich Text Format file:

1. Start Word, and then open the **Luke Farnsworth** file that you just created in the **Tutorial.05\Tutorial** folder included with your Data Files. The Rich Text Format file opens in Word.

2. Verify that the information for Luke appears. See Figure 5-37.

Luke Farnsworth Rich Text file opened in Word — Figure 5-37

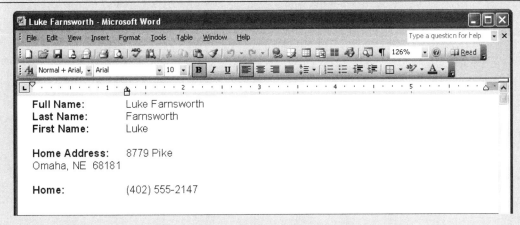

3. Close the document, and then exit Word.

Communicating with Instant Messages

You can use Outlook to send and receive instant messages over the Internet. **Instant messaging (IM)**, also called chatting, is an interactive communication tool you use to converse in real time with someone over the Internet. From Outlook, you can use Microsoft Windows Messenger or Microsoft MSN Messenger (or Microsoft Exchange Instant Messaging Service) to exchange instant messages with one to four people at a time. Any message you type appears almost instantly on the computer of the other person or persons you specify. Similarly, what they type appears on your computer. If your computer has a microphone and speakers, you can speak rather than type your messages. If you have a video camera set up on your computer, the other person can see you as you exchange messages. An indicator shows when someone is responding to your message.

Once you are logged onto Windows Messenger, you can see whether someone is online and his or her status (such as Free or Busy). You can change your status at any time based on your current availability. The service changes your status to "Away" when you've been inactive for several minutes or appear to be offline. You can select who can and cannot send you instant messages. You can also see who has added you to their contact list.

You can add the IM address of each person with whom you want to exchange instant messages on the General tab in the open Contact window for that contact. Whenever you open that person's contact card or receive an e-mail from that person, an icon with his or her online status appears next to the person's name. You can send an instant message by clicking the icon.

Cassandra wants the Ace team to be able to communicate instantly using instant messaging.

Using Windows Messenger

Instant messaging requires Windows Messenger. If you don't have the program installed on your computer, you must download the program from the MSN Messenger Web page. You need a .NET Passport account to use instant messaging.

Once you have Windows Messenger installed on your computer, you can start the program. A Windows Messenger icon appears at the right end of the taskbar when the software is installed and running. When you want to use Windows Messenger, you need to sign in by supplying the e-mail address and password you entered when you registered for a .NET Passport. You can then create your list of authorized users or contacts.

Reference Window	**Using Windows Messenger for Instant Messaging**

- Double-click the Windows Messenger icon at the right end of the taskbar (*or* click the Start button on the taskbar, point to All Programs, and then click Windows Messenger).
- Click the Click here to sign in link, type your Passport e-mail address in the E-mail address text box, type your Passport password in the Password text box, and then click the OK button.
- Click the Add a contact link in the Windows Messenger window, complete the Add a Contact Wizard to enter the contacts with whom you want to chat, and then click the Finish button.

You'll start by signing in to Windows Messenger and adding as a contact your classmate with whom you want to exchange instant messages.

To sign in to Windows Messenger:

1. Double-click the **Windows Messenger** icon ▨ at the right end of the taskbar. The Windows Messenger window opens.

   Trouble? If you do not see the Windows Messenger icon, then the program is probably not running. Click the Start button on the taskbar, point to All Programs, click Windows Messenger, and then continue with Step 2. If you don't have the program installed on your computer and you have access to install software on your computer, start Internet Explorer, go to *www.microsoft.com*, link to the Windows Messenger page, and then download and install the latest Windows Messenger program. If you do not have access to install software, you can read but not complete the rest of the steps in this section.

2. Click the **Click here to sign in** link. The .NET Messenger Service dialog box opens. See Figure 5-38.

.NET Messenger Service dialog box

Figure 5-38

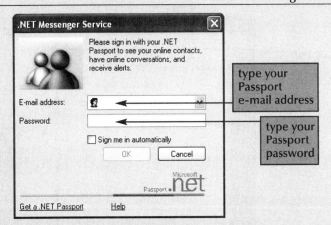

Trouble? If you do not see the Click here to sign in link, you are already connected. Skip Steps 3 and 4, and then compare your screen to Figure 5-39.

Trouble? If the.NET Messenger Service dialog box does not open and the Windows Messenger dialog box changes to indicate that you are online, skip Steps 3 and 4, and then compare your screen to Figure 5-39.

Trouble? If the .NET Passport Wizard opens, you do not have a .NET Passport added to your Windows XP user account. Click the Add a .NET Passport to your Windows XP user account option button, click the Next button, and then follow the wizard steps, making sure the Associate my Passport with my Windows user account check box is checked. Skip Steps 3 and 4, and then compare your screen to Figure 5-39.

You need to enter the e-mail address and password that you used when you registered for your Passport.

3. Type your Passport e-mail address in the E-mail address text box, and then type your Passport password in the Password text box.

4. Click the **OK** button. The IM features appear in the Windows Messenger window. See Figure 5-39.

Figure 5-39 | **Windows Messenger window**

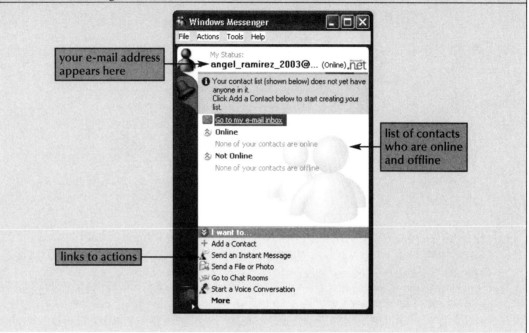

Next, you'll add an instant message contact for a classmate.

Adding an Instant Message Contact

The Windows Messenger window shows your current status and lists your contacts who are currently online and offline. It also provides a variety of links for adding contacts to your list, sending an instant message, sending a file or photo, creating or entering a chat room, starting a voice conversation, adding a group, sending e-mail, and starting a NetMeeting. For some of these activities, you'll need access to other files, programs, and equipment.

You'll add a classmate as a contact with whom you want to exchange instant messages.

To complete the steps in this section and the steps in the Sending and Receiving Instant Messages section, you'll need to work with a classmate. If you don't have a classmate to work with, ask you instructor for an e-mail address and create a contact card using that name and e-mail address. Otherwise, you should read but not complete the steps in this section and in the Sending and Receiving Instant Messages section.

To add a contact to Windows Messenger:

1. Click the **Add a Contact** link in the Windows Messenger window. The Add a Contact Wizard opens.

2. Verify that the **By e-mail address or sign-in name** option button is selected, and then click the **Next** button.

3. Type your classmate's e-mail address in the text box, and then click the **Next** button.

Trouble? If a dialog box opens telling you that your classmate has added you to his or her contact list, click the Allow this person to see when you are online and contact you option button, click the Add this person to my contact list check box to remove the check mark, and then click the OK button. Then click the Next button in the dialog box in which you typed your classmate's e-mail address.

The next dialog box tells you that your classmate was successfully added to your list. If you want, Windows Messenger will send an e-mail message to that e-mail address if that person is not already using Windows Messenger. You don't need this message sent.

4. Click the **Next** button. A dialog box opens telling you that You're Done! You could continue to add more contacts by clicking the Next button, which would bring you back to the first wizard dialog box. For now, you do not want to add another contact.

5. Click the **Finish** button. A message dialog box might open indicating that your classmate has added you to his/her contact list.

6. If necessary, click the **Allow this person to see when you are online and contact you** option button, click the **Add this person to my contact list** check box to remove the check mark, and then click the **OK** button. The contact you added appears in the Online or Not Online list in the MSN Messenger window.

Contacts must be online to exchange instant messages. If you are online and someone on your contact list signs in, a message window will briefly appear in the lower right corner of your screen so that you know that person is online.

Sending and Receiving Instant Messages

Like a telephone conversation, instant messaging is immediate, convenient, and often less formal than other types of communication. On the other hand, the speed of interaction means you often don't have the time for deeper thought or reflection. Be careful of what you say and how you say it. With a phone call, you have the benefit using your voice to convey emotions by varying your inflection, tone, pitch, and volume. When you're typing instant messages, the lack of emotion can cause misunderstandings. To make up for this, users rely on a growing list of abbreviations to convey their emotions and intent. They also use abbreviations as shortcuts to longer, often-used expressions, which reduces the amount of typing and speeds up the exchange. Figure 5-40 lists some common abbreviations used in instant messaging.

Figure 5-40 | **Common instant messaging abbreviations**

Abbreviation	Meaning
afk	away from the keyboard
brb	be right back
btdt	been there, done that
btw	by the way
cy	see ya'
imho	in my humble opinion
k	okay
lol	laughing out loud
rofl	rolling on the floor laughing
ttfn	ta ta for now
ttyl	talk to you later
ty or t/y	thank you
wb or w/b	welcome back
yw or y/w	you're welcome
<bg>	big grin
<bs>	big smile
<g>	grin
<s>	smile
<vbg>	very big grin
<vbs>	very big smile

Instant messaging is fast becoming a work tool similar to the telephone. Just as it is courteous to ask someone whether you have called at a convenient time, your first message might inquire whether the person has the time and the inclination to chat at that moment. Conversely, if you receive a message at an inopportune moment, you can ignore the message or tell the other person that you don't have time to chat at the moment. You might also want to change your status.

When you first sign in, Windows Messenger lists your status as Online. Your status will change to Away if you appear to be offline or haven't used the service in awhile. You can also change your status, choosing from a variety of descriptions, including Busy, Be Right Back, On the Phone, Out To Lunch, and Appear Offline. You should change your status to reflect your current availability. This way, people know whether you are available to exchange messages or occupied in another task. Similarly, respect the status of your contacts. Do not send a message to someone whose status is Busy or On the Phone, for example.

You'll exchange instant messages with your classmate.

To send an instant message:

1. Click the **Send an Instant Message** link in the Windows Messenger window. The Send an Instant Message dialog box opens.

2. Click your classmate's e-mail address on the My Contacts tab, and then click the **OK** button. The Conversation window opens. See Figure 5-41.

Conversation window | Figure 5-41

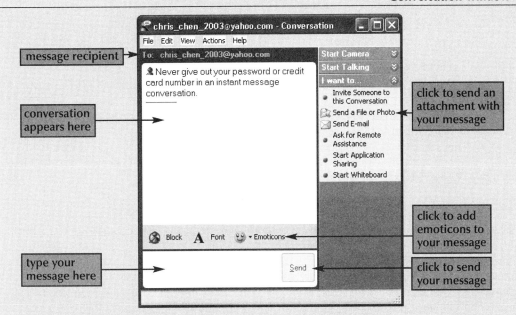

message recipient →

conversation appears here →

click to send an attachment with your message

click to add emoticons to your message

type your message here →

click to send your message

3. Type **Is this a convenient time for you to chat with me?**, and then click the **Send** button.

Both your classmate's and your messages should appear almost instantly. Now you reply to your classmate's message.

4. Type **Yes. What's up?**, and then click the **Send** button.

Again, the two messages appear in the Messenger window. As with an e-mail message, you can attach a file or photo to the instant message. If someone sends a file to you, you can choose to accept or decline the transfer. When you no longer want to exchange messages with someone, you close the Conversation window.

5. Click the **Close** button ☒ on the Conversation window title bar.

If you want to remove a person from your contact list, you can delete the person's contact from the list.

To remove a contact from the contact list:

1. Right-click your classmate's e-mail address in the Windows Messenger window, and then click **Delete Contact** on the shortcut menu. A message balloon opens in the taskbar or a dialog box opens asking you to confirm the deletion.

2. Click the **Yes** button. The contact is removed from the list.

When you're done exchanging messages and want to close Windows Messenger, you need to sign out.

To sign out of Windows Messenger:

1. Click **File** on the Windows Messenger menu bar, and then click **Sign Out**. In a moment, the Click here to sign in link appears, indicating that you have completed the sign-out process.

2. Click the **Close** button ☒ on the Windows Messenger window title bar. A message might open from the taskbar, indicating that the program will run in the taskbar.

3. If necessary, click the **Close** button ☒ in the message balloon.

When you close Windows Messenger, the program continues to run in the Windows taskbar so you can receive instant messages once you sign in again.

Viewing Web Pages

There are many ways to find information and collaborate with people on the Internet or on an intranet. The **Internet** is a worldwide collection of computer networks where users at one computer can access information on other computers. The most popular part of the Internet is the **World Wide Web (WWW** or **Web)**, an Internet service that stores and provides information that visitors navigate using graphical user interfaces and links. An **intranet** is a private internal corporate network that uses Internet and Web technology to enable employees in an organization to share computing resources and information. An intranet might be used to make a company policy manual available internally within the company but not to the general public. When access to the intranet is provided to people outside the organization, it is called an **extranet**.

People frequently rely on the Web to locate specific data. A **Web page** is an HTML document with text, graphics, sound, and links that is accessible on the Web or on an intranet. **HTML (Hypertext Markup Language)** is a standard coding system that specifies how to display the text, graphics, and links on a Web page for a viewer. Web pages provide a great way for individuals, organizations, and businesses to share information with people around the world or within the same building. Web pages are used to dispense information such as the price of a product, the latest news, or a description of a company's services. They can also provide a host of information—from family photo albums and happenings to the goals and memberships of associations, from businesses' catalogs of products or services to schools' programs, faculty, and syllabi. A collection of related Web pages is called a **Web site**.

Anyone who knows how to publish pages on the Web can do so. The content of the pages is neither regulated nor verified. Whenever you research information on the Web, you should assess data you find for:

- **Authorship.** Determine who wrote the information and assess whether the author has the credentials or expertise to write on the topic.
- **Currency.** Try to find out when the information was last updated; most Web pages include a last revision date at the bottom of the page. Consider whether timeliness affects the reliability of the information.
- **Validity.** Look at the source of the site to determine whether this is a trustworthy resource of information.
- **Accuracy.** Evaluate the content for relevancy and correctness. Confirm the information with a second source, like you would other research materials.

Web pages are viewed with a **Web browser**, a program such as Internet Explorer, Netscape Navigator, or Opera that enables you to access, display, and interact with the Web. You can use Outlook as a Web browser to open a Web page right from Outlook.

Using Outlook as a Web Browser

You can view Web pages in any Outlook main window. In this way, Outlook acts like a Web browser, similar to Internet Explorer. You move among Web pages in Outlook just as you do in a Web browser—by clicking links, clicking navigation buttons, or typing a URL. The Web toolbar provides all the buttons and features you need to navigate Web pages from Outlook. Many of the buttons are the same as the ones you use with Internet Explorer or on the Web toolbar in other Office programs. Figure 5-42 lists and describes these buttons.

Web toolbar buttons ◄ Figure 5-42

Button	Name	Description
⊕ Back	Back	Moves from the latest opened Web page to each earlier opened Web page.
⊙	Forward	Moves from earliest opened Web page to each later opened Web page.
✕	Stop	Halts the loading of a Web page.
▤	Refresh	Reloads the displayed Web page.
⌂	Start Page	Opens the default home page set for your computer.
⚲	Search the Web	Opens a search Web site, such as MSN Search.
outlook:today ▾	Address	Identifies the current Web page URL; use to open a specific Web page.

You'll use the Web toolbar to open Web pages in Outlook. When you know what Web page you want to view, you can enter its **URL (Uniform Resource Locator)**, the address or location of a Web page. A URL is split into several parts separated by slashes (/): the Web protocol, the Web server name, and possibly the path to a specific page. The **Web protocol** is HTTP (Hypertext Transfer Protocol), the communications system that enables Web browsers to access Web pages. Outlook assumes that all URLs begin with "http://" so you don't have to type these characters. A **Web server** is the name of the computer that stores the Web page. The Web server is also the home page for most Web sites. A **home page** is the main page of a Web site, and usually provides general introductory information with links to more specific content within the site. The term *home page* can also refer to the Web page that opens when you start a browser. The Web server can be followed by one or more folder names and a filename and extension that access a particular page. For example, look how each part makes up the Office of Federal Housing Enterprise Oversight (OFHEO) Web site URL shown in Figure 5-43.

Figure 5-43 ▶ Parts of a URL

$$\underbrace{\text{http://}}_{\text{Web protocol}}\underbrace{\text{www.ofheo.gov}}_{\text{Web server}}\underbrace{\text{/about.asp}}_{\substack{\text{specific HTML file} \\ \text{on the server}}}$$

You'll start by viewing the OFHEO home page from the Inbox. Web pages change frequently, so the headlines, content, and even design of the OFHEO home page you see might be different from those shown in the figures in the steps.

To view the OFHEO Web site in Outlook:

▶ 1. Display the **Ace** folder, right-click a blank area of the menu bar, and then click **Web** on the shortcut menu. The Web toolbar is displayed next to the Standard toolbar.

▶ 2. Connect to the Internet, if necessary, click the Address text box on the Web toolbar to select the current text, type **www.ofheo.gov** in the Address text box, and then press the **Enter** key. The loading progress of the Web page appears in the status bar. After a moment, the OFHEO home page finishes loading in the Inbox main window. See Figure 5-44.

Figure 5-44 ▶ OFHEO home page

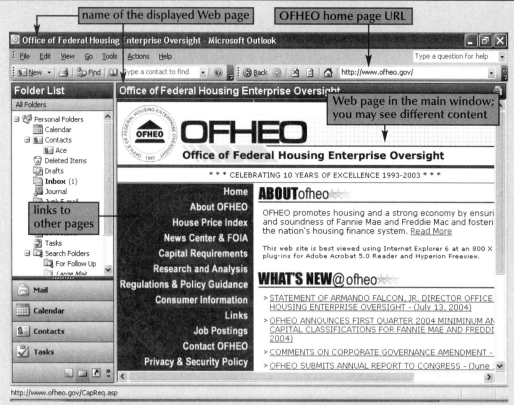

Trouble? If the Web page you see differs from the one shown in Figure 5-44, the content or layout of the page might have changed since this book was published. Web pages are constantly changing and being updated. However, the major links should still be available; continue with Step 3.

The home page contains some basic information along with many links to other pages on the site.

▶ **3.** Click the **About OFHEO** link on the Web page. A second page opens in the main window. This page contains links to specific topics about OFHEO. See Figure 5-45.

Web page with text ◀ Figure 5-45

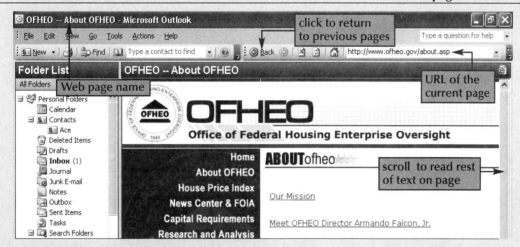

▶ **4.** Click the **Our Mission** link in the About OFHEO list. This page contains a document of text that you can read, scrolling as necessary to bring more text into view. The Address text box on the Web toolbar shows the full path of the page you are viewing.

Trouble? If you don't see the Our Mission link, the link might no longer be available. Click another link to view a third page on the OFHEO site.

Once you read this document, you might want to return to the previous page to select a different link. You can use the Web toolbar buttons to navigate between the pages you have already viewed. Because you have opened several pages, the Back button is active; the Forward button remains inactive until you back up one or more pages.

▶ **5.** Click the **Back** button on the Web toolbar. The previous page you loaded—the About OFHEO page—reappears in the main window.

Now that you have gone back one page, the Forward button is available. You can use it to return to the Our Mission page or you could continue back to the OFHEO home page.

▶ **6.** Click the **Forward** button 🔁 on the Web toolbar. The Our Mission page you loaded reappears.

▶ **7.** Click the **Back** button on the Web toolbar twice to return to the OFHEO home page.

When you're done viewing Web pages, you can switch to any Outlook folder. Before you view any more Web pages, Cassandra wants you to check the security zone settings.

Modifying Security Zone Settings

As you browse the Web or an intranet, you might expose your computer to viruses hidden within the scripts and active content programmed to run in HTML documents. To help protect your computer, you can set a security level for the HTML documents you open. For example, the Low security level allows all cookies, Active X controls, and plug-ins from Web sites to be saved on your computer and read by the Web site that created them, whereas the High security level blocks all potentially damaging content from Web sites. **Security zones** enable you to set what type of content you want to allow to run when viewing HTML documents. Outlook uses the same security zones as the Internet Explorer Web browser. You can set a different security level for each of four different zones, enabling you to customize your viewing experience.

The four security zones are:

- **Internet.** Anything not on your computer or an intranet, or assigned to another zone. Its default security level is Medium.
- **Local intranet.** Sites from your computer, network, and local intranet. Its default security level is Medium.
- **Trusted sites.** Sites you trust that you can download or run files from without damaging your computer or data. Its default security level is Low.
- **Restricted sites.** Sites you don't trust that you can download or run files from without damaging your computer or data. Its default security level is High.

You cannot assign a folder or drive on your computer to a security zone. Files already on your computer are assumed to be very safe and are assigned minimal security settings. Whenever you open or download content from the Web, Outlook checks the site against the security settings for that Web site's zone.

You can change the security level for a zone or you can customize the settings within a zone. You'll review the security settings for the Internet zone on your computer.

To review security settings:

1. Click **Tools** on the menu bar, click **Options**, and then click the **Security** tab in the Options dialog box.

2. Click the **Zone Settings** button. A dialog box opens, indicating that any changes you make affect the security zones for Internet Explorer, Outlook, Outlook Express, and any other programs on your computer that use security zones.

3. Click the **OK** button. The Security dialog box opens.

4. Click the **Internet** icon, and then click the **Default Level** button, if available. The default Internet zone is selected in the Security dialog box. See Figure 5-46.

Security dialog box Figure 5-46

available security zones

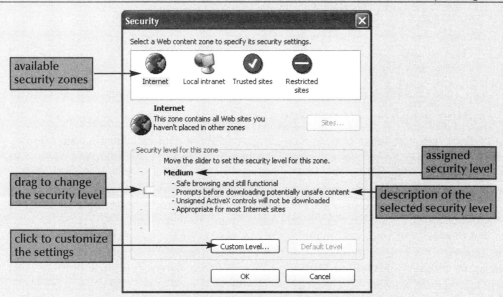

drag to change the security level

assigned security level

description of the selected security level

click to customize the settings

You select a zone and set security settings in the Security dialog box.

5. Drag the **Security level for this zone** slider up to display the High level, and then read the description of the security settings.

You can also change specific settings for each zone.

6. Click the **Custom Level** button. The Security Settings dialog box opens. See Figure 5-47.

Security Settings dialog box Figure 5-47

settings to customize; your list may differ

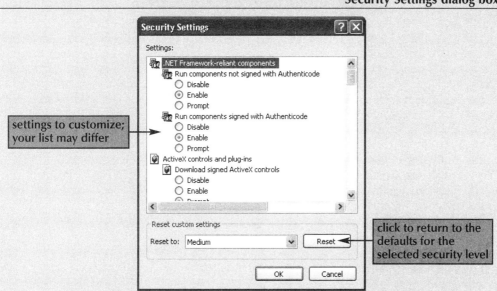

click to return to the defaults for the selected security level

7. Scroll to review the settings you can change.

You don't want to modify the security zone settings, so you'll close the dialog boxes without saving your changes.

8. Click the **Cancel** button in the Security Settings dialog box, click the **Cancel** button in the Security dialog box, and then click the **Cancel** button in the Options dialog box.

Cassandra wants you to regularly review the house price index, available on the OFHEO Web site.

Creating a Folder Home Page

In Outlook, you can assign one Web page to each Outlook folder, called a **folder home page**. Each time you display the folder, it displays the assigned Web page. You can assign a Web page to a default Outlook folder or create your own. Folder home pages are useful for creating links to Web pages that you view often, similar to storing a Web page in the Favorites folder of Internet Explorer or creating a bookmark to a Web page in other Web browsers.

The page being accessed as the folder home page can be located anywhere—on the Internet, on your local hard disk, or on a server on a corporate intranet. Folder home pages are most useful when the Web page is updated frequently to display the most current information, reminders, or messages. For example, an Internet Web page that lists the current membership of an association might be associated with a custom folder in the Contacts folder so you can see the latest list of members each time you open the folder. Or, you might associate an intranet Web page that displays the company's calendar to a custom folder in the Calendar folder so you can switch between your personal calendar and the corporate schedule.

If you use Microsoft Exchange Server and work remotely, you can store folder home pages for viewing offline.

Reference Window | **Creating a Folder Home Page**

- Right-click the folder to which you want to assign a folder home page, and then click Properties (or click the folder, click File on the menu bar, and then click Properties).
- Click the Home Page tab.
- Type the URL you want to associate with the folder in the Address text box (begin the URL with "http://").
- Click the Show home page by default for this folder check box to insert a check mark.
- Click the OK button.

Cassandra frequently asks you to visit the House Price Index Web page on the OFHEO Web site, which shows the current house price index for each state. If you assign this Web page to the Ace folder as its folder home page, you can view that Web page whenever you click the folder.

You'll assign the Home Price Index Web page as the default folder home page for the Ace folder you created earlier.

To assign a Web page to a folder:

1. Right-click the **Ace** folder in the Folder List, and then click **Properties** on the shortcut menu. The Ace Properties dialog box opens.

2. Click the **Home Page** tab. This tab contains information related to the selected folder's home page.

3. Type **http://www.ofheo.gov/HPI.asp** in the Address text box. This is the URL for the Web page you want to associate with the Ace folder.

4. Click the **Show home page by default for this folder** check box to insert a check mark. See Figure 5-48.

Home Page tab in the Ace Properties dialog box | Figure 5-48

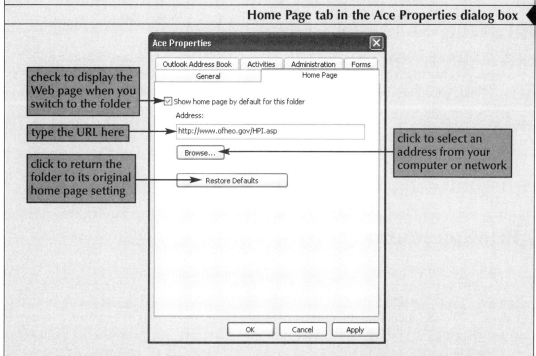

5. Click the **OK** button. The Web page associated with the folder—the House Price Index Web page, in this case—appears in the main window. See Figure 5-49.

Ace folder home page | Figure 5-49

Trouble? If the page you see on your screen differs from the one shown in Figure 5-49, it's because the Web is a dynamic environment where pages change constantly.

When you want to view the Web page, you need only to open the associated folder. However, you can no longer see the content in the Ace folder even though it's still there, so you'll remove the folder home page. To remove the folder home page from a folder, you delete the URL from the Home Page tab in the folder's Properties dialog box.

To remove the Ace folder home page:

1. Right-click the **Ace** folder in the Navigation Pane, click **Properties** on the shortcut menu, and then click the **Home Page** tab.

2. Delete **http://www.ofheo.gov/HPI.asp** from the Address text box. The check mark is automatically removed from the **Show home page by default for this folder** check box.

3. Click the **OK** button. No Web page is associated with the Ace folder.

4. Right-click either toolbar, and then click **Web** to close the Web toolbar.

Before you finish, you'll print the journal entries you created in this tutorial.

Printing Journal Entries

All the work you've done with Office files and e-mail is recorded in the Journal. This information is helpful if you want to see how you've spent your day, or locate the date and time you completed a specific activity. You'll review the journal entries that were created today, and then print them. When you print from the Journal, only selected items or groups print. If you want to print for a selected time frame, you must filter the Journal to display only items from that date.

To print journal entries:

1. Display the **Journal** folder, change the view to **By Type**, and then click the **Day** button on the Standard toolbar, if necessary.

2. Click the **Today** button on the Standard toolbar to make sure the current day is visible.

3. Click the **plus sign** button ⊞ for each category in the main window. See Figure 5-50.

Journal with entries for today | Figure 5-50

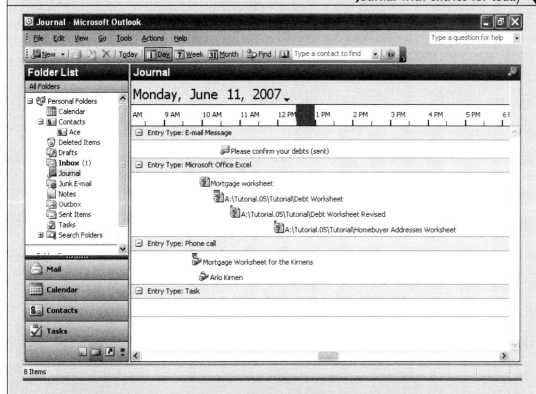

You'll filter the Journal to display only those items you created today.

4. Click **View** on the menu bar, point to **Arrange By**, point to **Current View**, and then click **Customize Current View**. The Customize View dialog box opens.

5. Click the **Filter** button in the Customize View dialog box. The Filter dialog box opens with options that enable you to select which Journal items you want to include in the view.

6. Click the **Time** list arrow, click **created**, click the right list arrow, and then click **today**. See Figure 5-51.

Filter dialog box | Figure 5-51

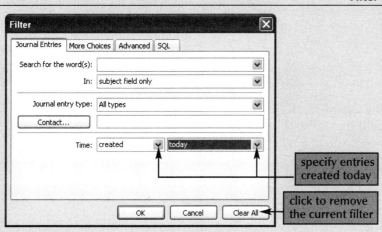

7. Click the **OK** button in the Filter dialog box, and then click the **OK** button in the Customize View dialog box. The Journal is filtered to show only those items you created today. The task still appears in the list because you filtered by the create date rather than the start date; the task's create date is today, and its start date is next Tuesday.

When you print the Journal, only the selected groups are included in the printout. You want all the groups included.

8. Press and hold the **Shift** key, click each entry in each group to select all the entries, and then release the **Shift** key. The entries you want to include are selected.

9. Click the **Print** button on the Standard toolbar. The Print dialog box opens.

10. If necessary, click the **Start each item on a new page** check box and the **Print attached files** check box to remove the check marks. You will print only the Journal timeline on continuous pages.

Trouble? If the Start each item on a new page check box is unavailable, then each journal entry will print on its own page; continue with Step 11.

11. Click the **OK** button in the Print dialog box. A dialog box opens, reminding you that the action will apply to all items in the selected groups.

12. Click the **OK** button. The entries you created today are printed.

Now that you've finished, you can remove the filter and turn off the automatic journal entries.

To remove the filter and turn off the Journal:

1. Right-click the background of the Journal main window, and then click **Customize Current View** on the shortcut menu that opens. The Customize View dialog box opens.

2. Click the **Filter** button, click the **Clear All** button in the Filter dialog box, click the **OK** button in the Filter dialog box, and then click the **OK** button in the Customize View dialog box. All the items are again visible in the Journal By Type view.

Next, you'll turn off the automatic recording of journal entries.

3. Click **Tools** on the menu bar, and then click **Options**. The Options dialog box opens.

4. Click the **Preferences** tab, if necessary, and then click the **Journal Options** button. The Journal Options dialog box opens.

5. Click the **E-mail Message**, **Microsoft Office Access**, **Microsoft Office Excel**, **Microsoft PowerPoint**, and **Microsoft Word** check boxes to remove the check marks.

6. Click the **Arlo Kirnen** check box to remove the check mark.

7. Click the **OK** button in the Journal Options dialog box, and then click the **OK** button in the Options dialog box.

Next, you'll delete the existing journal entries. Deleting journal entries removes only the entry. Any associated Outlook items, files, or documents remain intact. You can remove individual entries, pressing the Shift or Ctrl key to select more than one item at a time. Or, you can remove an entire group of entries by selecting the group heading.

To delete journal entries:

▶ 1. Click the **Please confirm your debts (sent)** e-mail message entry in the Journal folder, and then press the **Delete** key. The selected entry is moved to the Deleted Items folder.

▶ 2. Click the **Microsoft Office Excel** group heading to select it, if necessary, press and hold the **Shift** key, click the other group headings, and then release the **Shift** key. All the types of journal entries you created in this tutorial are now selected.

▶ 3. Press the **Delete** key. A dialog box opens to remind you that this action will apply to all items in the selected groups.

▶ 4. Click the **OK** button. All the selected journal entries are moved to the Deleted Items folder.

Before you empty the Deleted Items folder, you will delete all the other Outlook items you created for this tutorial.

▶ 5. Delete the items in the Inbox, Sent Items, Contacts, and Tasks folders that you created for this tutorial, and then delete the Ace subfolder.

Sometimes Outlook "remembers" a folder that contains contact items, even after you delete it.

▶ 6. Click **Tools** on the menu bar, click **E-mail Accounts**, click the **View or change existing directories or address books** option button, and then click the **Next** button.

▶ 7. Click **Outlook Address Book**, and then click the **Change** button. The Microsoft Office Outlook Address Book dialog box opens.

▶ 8. If **Ace: Personal Folders** appears in the Outlook Address Books list, click it, and then click the **Remove Address Book** button. *Important: If Ace: Personal Folders does not appear in the list, skip this step.*

▶ 9. Click the **Close** button, and then click the **Finish** button in the E-mail Accounts dialog box.

▶ 10. Empty the Deleted Items folder.

To completely remove the Ace folder from Outlook, you must exit and restart the program.

▶ 11. Exit Outlook, and then restart it.

As the Kirnens begin their search for a new home, you have sent and received e-mail messages with Office documents, created new Office documents within Outlook, and faxed information. In addition, you have imported and exported contact information for potential clients. Cassandra will be busy for the foreseeable future working with these homebuyers.

Review

Session 5.2 Quick Check

1. Briefly explain importing as it relates to Outlook.
2. Briefly explain exporting as it relates to Outlook.
3. Why would you want to import files into Outlook?
4. List four formats to which you can export Outlook items.
5. What is a tab-delimited file?
6. Why would you need to map fields?
7. Why would you want to export a Personal Folders file?
8. What is a folder home page?

Review

Tutorial Summary

In this tutorial, you used the Journal to record your activities both automatically and manually. You sent Office documents as e-mail messages and attachments. You learned how to send and receive faxes from Outlook. You imported data created in other Office programs and you exported Outlook data into file formats that programs other than Outlook can use. You communicated with instant messages and viewed Web pages from Outlook. Finally, you printed the journal entries that were created in this tutorial.

Key Terms

comma-delimited	import	URL (Uniform Resource
export	instant messaging (IM)	Locator)
extranet	Internet	Web browser
fax service	intranet	Web page
folder home page	map	Web protocol
home page	right-drag	Web server
HTML (Hypertext	security zone	Web site
Markup Language)	tab-delimited	World Wide Web (WWW)

Practice

Practice the skills you learned in the tutorial using the same case scenario.

Review Assignments

Data Files needed for the Review Assignments: Description.doc, Homesellers.xls

Ty Mumford, the listing agent for Ace Realty, works exclusively with seller clients. He handles all aspects of listing properties, preparing properties for showings, and procuring purchase offers. His latest client is Margie Tackett, who is selling her home in Omaha and relocating to North Platte due to a promotion at work. You will help Ty work on the listing for Margie's house and enter contact lists of other potential seller clients.

1. Create a task with the subject "Write listing for the Tackett house" and a due date of two days from now.
2. Create a contact for Margie Tackett, home phone number "402-555-7771," home fax "402-555-7782," address type Home, home mailing address "981 Lincoln Way, Omaha, NE 98182," and your e-mail address.
3. Turn on the Journal to automatically record e-mail messages for Margie Tackett and all Office files. (*Hint:* Use the Tools menu to open the Options dialog box.)
4. Create a new journal entry to record a five-minute conversation with Margie Tackett about the "Listing for the Tackett home" with the note "Margie called to request that we add information about the new roof she installed on her home to the listing." Assign Margie as the contact for this entry.

5. Right-drag the Write listing for the Tackett house task to the Journal folder, and then click Copy Here as Journal Entry with Attachment to create a journal entry for the task. Change the duration to 30 minutes.

6. Create a journal entry with the subject "Tackett house description" for the Microsoft Word entry type. Insert the **Description** document, located in the **Tutorial.05\Review** folder included with your Data Files, displayed as an icon. Open the Word document to view it, then close it, exit Word, and save and close the journal entry.

7. Create a new mail message using a Microsoft Word Document, addressed to Margie Tackett with the subject "Please review house highlights." Type "Tackett Home High- lights," press the Enter key, type "2 bedroom home with 1260 sq. ft. living space," press the Enter key, type "Basement, large family room, 2 car detached garage," press the Enter key, type "Large fenced yard with pleasant landscaping," press the Enter key, type "Large redwood deck and enclosed porch with swing," press the Enter key, and type "Available for immediate occupancy." Format all the lines except the first as a bulleted list using the Bullets button on the Formatting toolbar. Send a copy.

8. Close Word without saving the document you created.

9. Download the message, and then read it.

10. Right-click the message body, click Open in Microsoft Word 11, and then save the document as **Tackett Home Highlights** in the **Tutorial.05\Review** folder included with your Data Files. Close the file, and then exit Word. (If the Open in Microsoft Word 11 command in unavailable, then save the message in HTML format in the **Tutorial.05\Tutorial** folder included with your Data Files using the message subject as the filename.)

11. Create a new folder named "Ace" that contains Contacts Items, stored in the Con- tacts folder.

12. Import the list of home sellers stored in the Excel workbook **Homesellers**, located in the **Tutorial.05\Review** folder included with your Data Files, into the Ace folder using the Import and Export Wizard. Do not import duplicates.

13. Map custom fields between the Excel worksheet and Outlook. Expand the Name field category. Drag the First value in the Excel worksheet to the First Name field in Outlook, and then drag the Last value to the Last Name field. Confirm that the other fields map correctly, and then click the OK button.

14. Click the Finish button to import the Excel workbook data. Display the Ace folder and review the new cards.

15. Export the contact list from the Ace folder to an Access database. Save the database as **Home Seller Addresses Database** in the **Tutorial.05\Review** folder included with your Data Files; you do not need to map any custom fields.

16. Back up the Ace folder into a Personal Folders file saved as **Ty Contacts Backup** in the **Tutorial.05\Review** folder included with your Data Files with no encryption.

17. Save the Joe Dundst contact (stored in the Ace folder) as a vCard file; use the con- tact's name as the filename and save the file in the **Tutorial.05\Review** folder included with your Data Files.

For Steps 18 through 19, you need to work with a classmate.

18. Sign in to Windows Messenger, add a classmate to the contacts list, and then exchange instant messages with your classmate about selling a home, using appro- priate abbreviations.

19. Remove your classmate from your contacts list, sign out of Windows Messenger, and then close Windows Messenger.

20. Display the Web toolbar, then go to *www.fanniemae.com*, a Web site Ty references frequently. Click the About Fannie Mae link.

21. Create a new contact folder named "Fannie Mae" and assign the Fannie Mae home page (http://www.fanniemae.com) to the new folder, and then open it.

22. Review the journal entries you created for these assignments in Entry List view.

23. Filter the list to display only those entries you created today.

24. Print all the journal entries in Memo Style on one page; do not print any attached files. (*Hint:* Select all the entries before opening the Print dialog box.)

25. Remove the filter, and then turn off the Journal.

26. Delete all the items in the Journal, Inbox, Sent Items, Contacts, and Tasks folders that you created in these Review Assignments, including the Ace and Fannie Mae folders, and then empty the Deleted Items folder.

27. Remove the Ace and Fannie Mae contact folders as address books, if necessary, and then exit and restart Outlook.

Case Problem 1

Data Files needed for this Case Problem: Seminar.doc, Seminar Tasks.pst

Space du Jour   Space du Jour is a large open gallery that clients can rent for one- or multi-day events. The gallery has hosted all types of events, from art auctions to cooking demonstrations to small business workshops. Harriet Connors works with clients to arrange the open space as needed, whether split into partitioned rooms for seminars or divided by panels for hanging artwork. She uses Outlook to stay in touch with clients, record her daily activities, and organize her tasks.

1. Create a new contact for Mick Davis, using your home telephone number, home address, and e-mail address.

2. Turn on the Journal to automatically record all Outlook items for Mick Davis and all Office files.

3. Create a new tasks folder named "Training" within the Tasks folder. Create a new task with the subject "Arrange space for training seminar" and store it in the Training folder.

4. Create a new folder named "DOL" that stores task items placed within the Tasks folder, and then assign the Web page *http://www.doleta.gov* to the DOL folder.

5. Create a new journal entry from the task you created to record a 45-minute phone call with Mick about arranging the space for a customer service training seminar for a local chain of clothing stores. Enter appropriate notes and a contact.

6. Create a new e-mail message using Microsoft Word. Address the message to Mick Davis, and then type "Seminar Setup" as the subject.

7. Insert the **Seminar** document located in the **Tutorial.05\Cases** folder included with your Data Files as an attachment. (*Hint:* Click Insert on the menu bar, click File, change the Look in location, select the file, and then click the Insert button.)

8. Send the message, exit Word without saving changes to the document, and then download the message, if necessary.

9. Open the message, open the attachment, save the Word document as **Mick Davis Seminar Setup** in the **Tutorial.05\Cases** folder included with your Data Files, close the document and exit Word, and then close the Message window.

10. Switch to the Tasks folder in Outlook, and then import the tasks from the Personal Folders file **Seminar Tasks**, located in the **Tutorial.05\Cases** folder included with your Data Files, into the Outlook Tasks folder using the Import and Export Wizard. Do not import duplicates. (*Hint:* Select Tasks as the folder to import from.)

11. Create a journal entry for the two tasks that mention Mick's name. (*Hint:* Select the two tasks, drag them to the Journal folder in the Folder List, type "Mick Davis" as the subject, change the entry type to Task, and then save and close the journal entry.)

12. Display the Journal, and then change the view to Last Seven Days. Outlook applies a filter to display only the previous week's entries.

13. Sort the Journal in ascending order by Entry Type. (*Hint:* Click the Entry Type column heading.)

14. Print all rows of the journal entries for the last seven days in Table Style.

15. Delete all the journal entries you created in this Case Problem.

16. Change the Journal view to By Type, and then turn off the Journal.

17. Delete the e-mail in the Inbox and Sent Items folder, the contact, and all the tasks you created in this Case Problem, and then empty the Deleted Items folder.

Challenge

Extend what you learned in the tutorial to track activities for a gourmet catering business.

Case Problem 2

There are no Data Files needed for this Case Problem.

Janise's Vegetarian Table   Janise Kellar runs a vegetarian gourmet catering business in Raleigh, North Carolina. She and her staff of four provide catering for business and personal events, ranging from hand-passed appetizers to sit-down, multi-course meals. Janise uses Outlook to keep track of her clients and vendors and to record her daily activities.

1. Turn on the Journal to automatically record all Office files.

2. Create a contact for Janise Kellar, using your e-mail address, mailing address, and phone number.

3. Open the Journal Options dialog box, and set up the Journal to record items for Janise.

Explore

4. Create a new journal entry, and then click the Start Timer button to have Outlook determine the duration of the journal entry. The hands on the stopwatch rotate to indicate the passage of time.

5. For the open journal entry, enter "Fall mushroom supplies" as the subject, change the entry type to Conversation, and then type "Tanner expects a bountiful supply of wild mushrooms this autumn due to the unusual rainfall and temperature." in the notes text box.

Explore

6. The timer has been running as you created the journal entry. As each full minute passes, the time is recorded in the Duration text box. When the Duration text box reads at least 1 minute, click the Pause Timer button, and then save and close the entry.

7. Create a new e-mail message using Microsoft Excel Worksheet, addressed to Janise Kellar with the subject "Available mushroom types."

8. Type "Mushroom Type" in cell A1, type "Crimini" in cell A2, type "Oyster" in cell A3, type "Portobello" in cell A4, type "Shiitakes" in cell A5, type "Chanterelle" in cell A6, type "Hedgehog" in cell A7, and type "Morels" in cell A8.

9. Bold the text in cell A1, and then sort the column alphabetically by clicking the Sort Ascending button on the Excel Standard toolbar.

Explore

10. Send the sheet, and then save the workbook as **Mushroom Availability** in the **Tutorial.05\Cases** folder included with your Data Files; leave the workbook and Excel open.

11. Click the E-mail button on the Excel Standard toolbar to display the message headers, address the message to Janise Kellar, and then change the subject to "Mushroom order."

12. Expand the width of column A to the longest cell entry. Type "Pounds" in cell B1, type "20" in cell B2, type "10" in cell B4, type "10" in cell B5, and then type "2" in cell B8. Bold the text in cell B1. Send the sheet, save the revised workbook, and then exit Excel.

13. Download the messages, and then save the Mushroom order message as an HTML file named **Mushroom Order** in the **Tutorial.05\Cases** folder included with your Data Files.

14. Back up the Inbox into a Personal Folders file named **Mushrooms Messages Backup** in the **Tutorial.05\Cases** folder included with your Data Files.

15. Review the journal entries you created in this case in the By Type view, and then expand all the groups.

16. Change the view to show an entire month, and then click the Today button on the Standard toolbar.

17. Change the view to show a day, click the date banner, and then change the date to next Friday.

18. Click the Today button to display the entries you created in this case.

19. If necessary, filter the journal entries to display only those you created today.

20. Print all the journal entries in all categories on one page; do not print any attached files.

21. Remove the filter, if necessary, and then turn off the Journal.

22. Delete all the journal entries, the e-mail messages in the Inbox and Sent Items folders, and the contact you created in this Case Problem, and then empty the Deleted Items folder.

Apply

Apply what you learned in the tutorial by using the Journal to track communications with suppliers and customers of a frame shop.

Case Problem 3

Data File needed for this Case Problem: Frame.txt

Pete's Frame Shop   Pete Lazaro opened a frame shop in 1992 to provide Cincinnati residents with access to quality framing at rock-bottom prices. Pete is able to keep his prices lower than his competitors by buying frames and other supplies in bulk and cultivating artists and galleries with frequent framing needs as key customers—these savings are also passed along to customers with occasional framing needs. Pete uses Outlook to track his work with suppliers and customers.

1. Turn on the Journal to automatically record all Office files.

2. Create a new e-mail message using Microsoft Word Document. Click in the message area, and then type "Pete's Frame Shop provides the highest quality frames at the lowest cost. Our specially trained staff helps you select the frame, suggests complementary mats and borders, and then carefully frames your piece." Press the Enter key twice, and then type your name.

3. Send a copy of the document to your e-mail address, save the document as **Frame Shop Description** in the **Tutorial.05\Cases** folder included with your Data Files, and then close the document. Download the message, if necessary.

4. Import the list of customers and vendors stored in the tab-delimited text file **Frame** located in the **Tutorial.05\Cases** folder included with your Data Files into the Contacts folder using the Import and Export Wizard. (*Hint:* Use Tab Separated Values (Windows) as the file type to import.)

5. Map custom fields to ensure that all the fields import correctly. (*Hint:* Make sure Keywords maps to Categories in Outlook.)

6. Finish importing the text file to Outlook.

7. Turn on the Journal for all the contacts you imported.

8. Create mail merge Form Letters to a New Document, using all the imported contacts and the **Frame Shop Description** located in the **Tutorial.05\Cases** folder included with your Data Files as the existing document file. Enter the appropriate fields to address the letter, and then type an appropriate closing above your name at the bottom of the letter. Merge to a new document, and then save the merged document as **Frame Letter Merged** in the **Tutorial.05\Cases** folder included with your Data Files. Exit Word without saving the document file. (*Hint:* To start the mail merge, switch to the Contacts folder, click Tools on the menu bar, and then click Mail Merge.)

9. Export the contact list from the Contacts folder to an Excel workbook; save the file as **Frame Contact List** in the **Tutorial.05\Cases** folder included with your Data Files.

10. Back up the Outlook Contacts folder into a Personal Folders file saved as **Frame Shop Contacts Backup** in the **Tutorial.05\Cases** folder included with your Data Files.

11. Review the journal entries in the By Category view.

12. Filter the list to display only those entries you created today.

13. Print all the journal entries in the categories on one page; do not print any attached files.

14. Remove the filter, and then turn off the Journal.

15. Delete all the journal entries and the contacts you created in this Case Problem, and then empty the Deleted Items folder.

For Steps 16 through 20, you need to work with a classmate.

16. Sign in to Windows Messenger, and then add a classmate to the contacts list.

17. Exchange instant messages with your classmate about the frame shop. Use appropriate abbreviations and emoticons. (*Hint:* Click the Emoticon button in the Conversation window, and then click an emoticon button to insert that icon into your message at the location of the insertion point.)

Explore

18. Go to the Windows Messenger window, change your status to On The Phone, and then have your classmate send you an instant message to see what happens. (*Hint:* Click File on the menu bar, point to My Status, and then click On The Phone.)

Explore

19. Save your conversation as a text file with the filename **Pete IM Conversation** in the **Tutorial.05\Cases** folder included with your Data Files. (*Hint:* Click File on the Conversation window menu bar, and then click Save.)

20. Remove your classmate from your contact list, sign out of Windows Messenger, and then close the Windows Messenger window.

Create

Create and send invitations for an upcoming party.

Case Problem 4

There are no Data Files needed for this Case Problem.

Plan a Party You're going to plan a party for the event of your choice—a favorite holiday, your birthday, or even TGIF. You'll create a contact list, write an invitation, and then fax or e-mail the invitation to your guests.

1. Create a new folder named "Party" containing contact items, and then create contact cards in the Party folder for yourself and at least five other people (real or fictional); include names, addresses, phone numbers, and e-mail addresses (use your e-mail address if the other people are fictional).

2. Turn on the Journal to automatically record e-mail messages for all Office files.

Explore

3. Create a new journal entry with "Started party planning" as the subject by dragging your contact card to the Journal folder.

Explore

4. Create a new journal entry to record a 10-minute conversation about your upcoming party. Enter one of the contacts you created in the Contacts text box.

5. Create a new mail message using Microsoft Excel Workbook. Address the message to yourself, and type "Party Supplies" as the subject. In the message body, create the list of supplies that you'll need in column A and their estimated costs in column B. Use the AutoSum button on the Standard toolbar to total column B. Format the worksheet appropriately.

6. Send the message, save the workbook as **Party Supplies** in the **Tutorial.05\Cases** folder included with your Data Files, exit Excel, and then download your message, if necessary.

7. Create a new mail message from Microsoft Office using Microsoft Word Document. Address the message to the contacts you entered earlier and enter the subject "Party Invitation."

8. In the message body, type the text for your party invitation, including your name as the party host, and then format the text appropriately. Send the message, and then close Word without saving changes.

9. Download the message, if necessary, and then save the message as an HTML file with the filename **Party Invitation** in the **Tutorial.05\Cases** folder included with your Data Files.

10. Export the Party folder to a Microsoft Excel file; save the workbook as **Party Contacts Workbook** in the **Tutorial.05\Cases** folder included with your Data Files.

Explore

11. Import the **Party Contacts Workbook** from the **Tutorial.05\Cases** folder included with your Data Files into the Party folder, but do not allow duplicates.

12. Back up the Inbox folder into a Personal Folders file saved as **Party Messages Backup** in the **Tutorial.05\Cases** folder included with your Data Files.

Explore

13. If you have the ability, fax the **Party Invitation** in the **Tutorial.05\Cases** folder included with your Data Files to yourself or a classmate.

14. Search the Web for a Web site with party theme ideas, and then assign the home page for that Web site to a new contacts folder you create named "Party Themes."

15. Review the journal entries you created for this case in Entry List view.

16. Filter the list to display the entries you created today.

17. Print all rows of the journal entries in Table Style.

18. Remove the filter, and then turn off the Journal.

19. Delete all the journal entries, the e-mail messages in the Inbox and Sent Items folders, and the Party and Party Themes contact folders you created in this Case Problem, and then empty the Deleted Items folder. Remove the Party and Party Themes folders from the Address Book, if necessary, and then exit and restart Outlook.

Review

Quick Check Answers

Session 5.1

1. A diary that records the date, time, and duration of your actions with Outlook items, Office documents, and other activities

2. The Journal enables you to look back at your activities on a timeline and locate a specific document or recall the events of a certain day.

3. E-mail messages; meeting requests, responses, and cancellations; task requests and responses; files you create, open, close, and save in Access, Excel, PowerPoint, and Word

4. As an e-mail attachment or as the message body

5. Recipients can save a message created from an Office file in its original program format, which they can then open and edit in that program, as long as they have the source program on their computer.

6. You can send the file as an e-mail attachment or you can save the file to your computer.

7. True.

8. False. You can send and receive faxes with Outlook.

Session 5.2

1. Copying data created in another program into Outlook

2. Moving data out of Outlook into another program's format

3. To bring into Outlook address books or messages you or someone else created in other programs

4. Personal Folder files, vCards, .rtf files, .txt files

5. A file of data in which fields for a record are separated by a tab character

6. To let Outlook know where to store imported data that is set up with field names different from those used in Outlook

7. To create a backup of an Outlook folder without removing the items from Outlook, as occurs when archiving

8. A Web page you can assign to an Outlook folder

Objectives

Session 6.1
- Customize the New Contact form
- Create and use custom fields
- Develop and use a mail template

Session 6.2
- Customize views using fields
- Explore and customize Outlook Today
- Configure Calendar options
- Customize the Navigation Pane
- Create custom menus and toolbars

Customizing Outlook

Creating Forms, Using Outlook Today, and Configuring Options

Case

Lumine

Lumine is a small nonprofit theater group that performs six original shows each year. The shows range from comedy to drama to experimental theater. Past shows have included singing jugglers, musical readings of poetry collections, dramatizations of children's tales, and environmental parables. The four founders—Fred O'Riordan, Ada Shubin, Bette Wattis, and Brian Cummings—write, direct, and act in all the shows. They hire a small staff to help with costumes, lights, and sound during productions. In addition, the staff manages the office and handles ticket sales, advertising, and promotion.

Although the shows are regularly sold out, ticket sales alone do not bring in enough money to support the group. This independent theater relies on outside funding to help pay its rent, utilities, and salaries, to purchase costumes and props, and to hire visiting musicians and guest actors. To supplement its ticket sales, the group organizes an annual fundraiser. Brian wants to be able to collect the contributor information in Outlook. He needs to store each contributor's name, the contribution amount, and whether the contributor wants to be credited in the program that is handed out at each performance. You can customize Outlook to track this kind of information for Brian to better match the specific needs and working style of the Lumine team.

In this tutorial, you will create a custom Contact form based on the built-in Contact form. You will use the form you created to enter contact information. Then you will create a mail template based on the built-in Mail form. Next, you will customize Outlook by adding fields to views, modifying Outlook Today, changing the Calendar options, adding groups and shortcuts to the Navigation Bar, and creating a toolbar.

Student Data Files

There are no student Data Files needed for this tutorial.

Session 6.1

Customizing Forms

Each time you write an e-mail message, schedule an appointment, record details about a contact, or create any other Outlook item, you type the appropriate data in a special window. The window in which you enter and view information about an item in Outlook is called a **form**. Every Outlook item is based on a form. Outlook provides standard forms for each item, such as creating and viewing messages, appointments, and contact information. Forms are used to gather the required data in fields. For example, you have used the standard built-in New Message form to compose e-mail messages and the New Contact form to enter information for a contact. You can modify some of the built-in forms or create custom ones.

Reference Window **Customizing a Form**

- Open a blank item with the form you want to modify.
- Click Tools on the menu bar, point to Forms, and then click Design This Form.
- Customize the form by adding and deleting fields, options, tabs, and controls.
- Click Tools on the menu bar, point to Forms, and then click Publish Form.
  or
- Open the folder or item for which you want to create a new form.
- Click Tools on the menu bar, point to Forms, and then click Design a Form.
- Customize the form by adding and deleting fields, options, tabs, and controls.
- Click Tools on the menu bar, point to Forms, and then click Publish Form.

The four basic steps for customizing a form are:

1. Open an existing form in design mode.
2. Modify the form.
3. Test the form.
4. Publish the form.

Opening a Form in Design Mode

Custom forms are based on existing Outlook forms. When you want to modify a form, you need to switch the form to design mode. **Design mode** (also called the Outlook Form Designer) is the environment in Outlook in which you create and customize forms. You know a form is in design mode because "(Design)" appears in the form's title bar, a dotted grid pattern appears in the background, and additional tabs appear in the window.

The form you choose to customize depends on what you want to accomplish. Select the existing form that best matches your goals for the custom form. For example, Brian wants you to create a custom form that collects information about people who make financial contributions to Lumine. The existing form that has fields with information about individuals is the New Contact form. Therefore, you'll start by opening the New Contact form, to which you can add fields to collect contributor information.

To open an Outlook form in design mode:

1. Open a new Contact window as if you were creating a new contact. The Contact window is the form you want to modify.

2. Click **Tools** on the menu bar, point to **Forms**, and then click **Design This Form**. The form switches to design mode.

3. If necessary, maximize the form window. See Figure 6-1.

New Contact form in design mode ◀ Figure 6-1

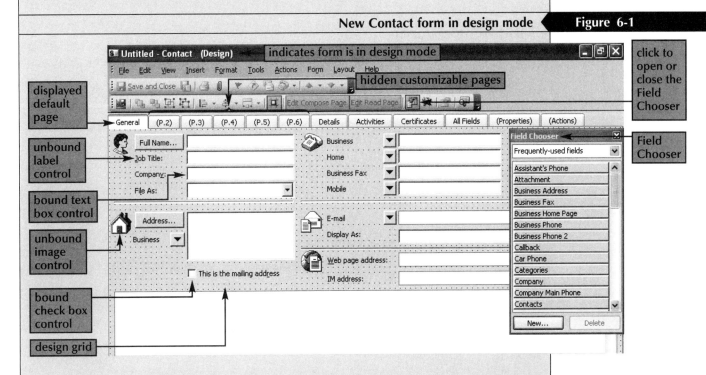

Trouble? If the Field Chooser doesn't appear, click the Field Chooser button [icon] on the Form Design toolbar.

Trouble? If the dotted grid background doesn't appear, click Layout on the menu bar, and then click Show Grid.

Each form is made up of pages. Each page appears on a separate tab in the item's window. The first page contains the fields and organization you've seen before. On some forms, including the New Message and New Contact forms, you can modify this first page. For all forms, you can modify the next five pages, which are blank by default. These unused pages are hidden in the published form, as indicated by the parentheses around their names, but they appear in design mode. When you modify a form, you can customize the existing fields, options, and layout on the default pages or you can display a blank page to create the layout you want.

Layout refers to the organization of the controls on the page. A **control** is an object on a form, such as a text box, button, list box, check box, or option button, that is used to collect user input or display data. A **bound control** is an object on a form in which a user enters information that Outlook displays. Some common bound controls are check boxes, list boxes, and text boxes. An **unbound control** is an object that displays text, an image, or another design element for informational or decorative purposes that a user cannot edit (change). Some common unbound controls are text labels, lines, and pictures. Figure 6-1 identifies some of the controls on the General page of the New Contact form.

From design mode, you customize form pages by adding fields to collect and store information. Fields are made up of bound and unbound controls. The simplest way to add fields to a form is with the **Field Chooser**, a list of available fields that is available in design mode whenever a customizable page of a form is displayed. Not all the default fields in Outlook appear on a form; some default fields, such as the Customer ID and Referred By fields, are available in the Field Chooser but are not used. When you add a field to a form page with the Field Chooser, it appears as a bound control with a text label.

Modifying a Form

You add fields to a form page by dragging them from the Field Chooser to the location on the page where you want them to appear. The grid helps you to accurately position the fields on a form. The Field Chooser organizes all the available fields into field sets to make it easier for you to find the ones you want. Not all the built-in fields appear on the default forms. If you repeat a field from another page or on the same page, the same information appears in all locations when data is entered in one location.

Brian asks you to add fields to one of the blank form pages, rather than modify the standard General page of the form. You'll display a blank page for the contributor information, and then rename the page with a descriptive name: Contributions.

To display and rename a page:

1. Click the **(P.2)** tab on the form. This is the hidden page you want to display and customize. The grid fills the page.

2. Click **Form** on the menu bar, and then click **Display This Page**. The parentheses disappear from the tab name, indicating the page will appear in the finished form.

3. Click **Form** on the menu bar, and then click **Rename Page**. The Rename Page dialog box opens.

4. Type **Contributions** in the Page name text box, and then click the **OK** button. The tab is renamed on the form.

The next step for creating a form is to add fields to the layout. As you place fields on the grid, two features help you align them neatly. Snap to Grid positions fields along the closest line of dots to where you drag them. AutoLayout aligns the fields in a column no matter where you drop the fields on the form.

To add fields to a form:

1. Click the list arrow in the Field Chooser, and then click **All Contact fields** to display the built-in Contact fields in the Field Chooser.

2. Scroll down the alphabetical list until you see Customer ID in the Field Chooser list.

3. Drag the **Customer ID field** from the Field Chooser to the page. No matter where you release the mouse button, Outlook places the field in the upper-left corner of the page and inserts the appropriate controls for the field—a label (Customer ID:) and a text box.

Trouble? If the field doesn't move to the upper-left corner of the form, AutoLayout is probably turned off. Click Layout on the menu bar, and then click AutoLayout. You'll reposition the Customer ID field shortly.

4. Drag the **Referred By field** from the Field Chooser to below the Customer ID field, as shown in Figure 6-2.

Contributions page with two fields ◄ **Figure 6-2**

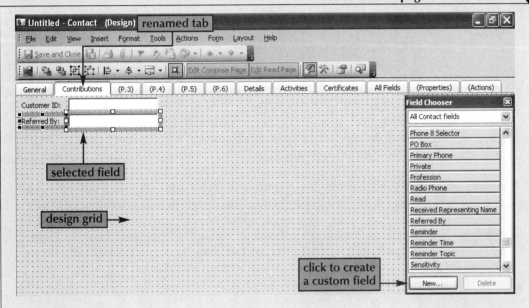

Trouble? If your fields don't align exactly as shown, you'll fix the alignment later in this tutorial.

The other fields Brian wants on the form—Contributor, Donation, and Pledged—don't exist in any field set. You'll create these as custom fields in Outlook to meet your needs.

There are three types of fields—simple, combination, and formula. A **simple field** holds a basic piece of data, such as a name, amount, or date. A **combination field** combines existing fields into a single field, as you've seen with the Full Name field, which includes the Title, First Name, Middle Initial, Last Name, and Suffix fields. A **formula field** performs a calculation on data in other fields, such as the number of days until a specific date.

When you create a custom field, you'll need to supply three things: the custom field's name, type, and format. Each field is based on a specific data type, which is the kind of information you want to enter and display in that field. Figure 6-3 describes the field types available in Outlook. The format specifies how the data appears in that field; most data types have several format options. For example, a field with percentage data can be formatted to show all digits (32.8938%), two decimals (32.89%), one decimal (32.9%), or no decimals (33%). You enter the field's name, type, and format in the New Field dialog box.

Figure 6-3 ▶ Field types for custom fields

TYPE	DESCRIPTION	EXAMPLE
Combination	multiple fields and/or text	Harry and Sue Cozzel
Currency	numbers shown as money amounts	$123.45 ($123.45) £123.45
Date/Time	date and time	12/15/03 10 AM
Duration	numbers shown as minutes, hours, or days	10 hours 1.5 days
Formula	calculations based on fields	number of days until a contact's birthday
Integer	nondecimal (whole) numbers	123
Keywords	user-defined fields for grouping related items; similar to categories	Benefactor,Patron,Contributor
Number	nonfinancial numbers	323.313
Percent	numbers expressed as percentages	98%
Text	alphanumeric characters, up to 255 characters	987 Main Street (888) 555-1234
Yes/No	Data that is restricted to one of two values; often shown as a check box	Yes or No, True or False, On or Off

You'll create three new fields for the custom form. The Contributor field has a text type and a text format; Brian will use it to list the name that contributors want to appear in the program, such as Anonymous, The Tiger Corporation, or The Worthnell Family. The second new field is named Donation and has a Currency field type without cents in the format; this field will be used to identify the amount of the financial contribution. The third new field is Pledged and has a Yes/No type with an Icon format; the pledged field will be checked when the contributor has not yet submitted the promised donation. A custom field is available only in the folder in which you create it. Therefore, the custom fields you'll create will be available only in the Contacts folder.

To create a new field:

▶ 1. Click the **New** button in the Field Chooser. The New Field dialog box opens. See Figure 6-4.

Figure 6-4 ▶ New Field dialog box

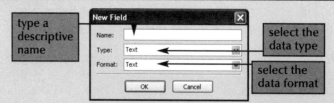

▶ 2. Type **Contributor** in the Name text box.

You want to leave the Type and Format list boxes set to Text.

3. Click the **OK** button. The Field Chooser switches to show User-defined fields in folder and displays the custom field. See Figure 6-5.

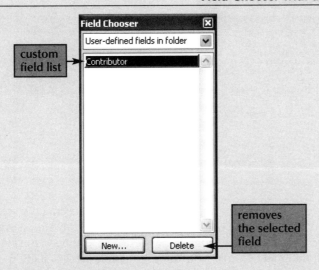

Trouble? If you see any other fields in the list, someone has defined Contact user fields in your Outlook installation.

4. Click the **New** button in the Field Chooser, and then type **Donation** in the Name text box.

5. Click the **Type** list arrow to display the available field types, and then click **Currency**.

6. Verify that the format is **$12,345.60 ($12,345.60)**.

7. Click the **OK** button. The Donation field appears as a user-defined field on the Field Chooser.

8. Create a new field named **Pledged** with the **Yes/No** type and **Icon** format. You should have three new fields in the User-defined fields in folder list.

The custom fields you created are placed on a page the same way as the default fields—by dragging them from the Field Chooser to the grid. You'll place the custom fields you created on the page. The fields are located in the User-defined fields in folder field set.

To place custom fields on a form page:

1. If necessary, click the list arrow in the Field Chooser, and then click **User-defined fields in folder**. The fields you created appear in the Field Chooser.

2. Drag the **Contributor field** from the Field Chooser to below the Referred By field. The field remains in the field list for you to use again on this form or another page.

3. Drag the **Donation field** from the Field Chooser to below the Contributor field. The text box displays a default value of $0.00, showing the selected currency format.

4. Drag the **Pledged field** from the Field Chooser to the right of the Donation field. The Pledged label and check box are grouped into one unit. See Figure 6-6.

Figure 6-6

Custom fields on Contributions page

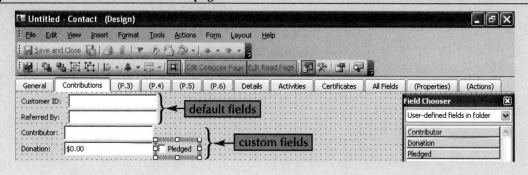

If you want to reposition a control for any reason, you can drag the selected control to a new position. To select a single control, you can click it. However, if you want to move an entire field, which includes the label and its text box, you need to select both controls. To select multiple controls, you can use the following selection methods:

• Press and hold the Ctrl key as you click controls to select nonadjacent ones.
• Select the first control, press and hold the Shift key, and then click the last control to select a group of adjacent ones.
• Drag a selection box around a group of controls, boxing in the ones you want to select.

You know a control is selected when sizing handles and a hatched border surround it. **Sizing handles** are small squares around the border of a selected object that you can drag to resize an object. You'll use the sizing handles to reduce and expand fields later.

To reposition fields:

1. Click the **Referred By label** to select it.

2. Press and hold the **Ctrl** key, click the **Referred By text box** to select it, and then release the **Ctrl** key.

3. Position the pointer over the border of one of the selected Referred By controls so that it changes to ✛, and then drag the selected controls to below the **Donation** field. See Figure 6-7.

Repositioned field ◀ Figure 6-7

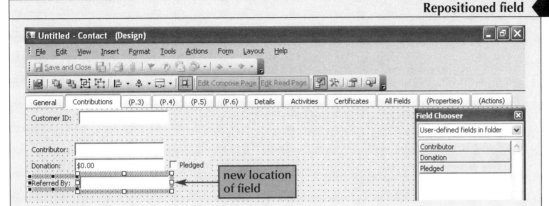

4. Select the **Contributor label** and **text box**, and then drag these selected controls to the right of the **Customer ID** field. Don't worry if you can't position the control exactly as you want; you will learn how to align controls later in this tutorial.

5. Select the **Pledged** field, and then drag it to below the **Customer ID** label.

6. Select the **Donation label** and **text box**, and then drag them to the right of the **Pledged** field.

7. Select the **Referred By label** and **text box**, and then drag them up to fill the empty space. See Figure 6-8.

Fields reorganized on the Contributions page ◀ Figure 6-8

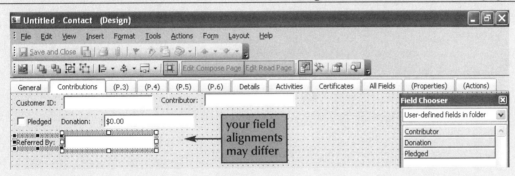

Trouble? If your fields are not in the same basic positions as shown in Figure 6-8, continue to select and reposition controls to approximate the placement in the figure.

This placement is a logical order for users to enter information in the fields. However, the order that fields are selected when users press the Tab key may not be logical. **Tab order** specifies the sequence that users move through fields on a form when they press the Tab key. Outlook matches the tab order to the sequence in which you selected fields from the Field Chooser. However, as you add, move, and replace fields, the tab order remains the same. As a result, pressing the Tab key may bounce users all over the page.

To test the tab order:

1. Click the **Customer ID label** to select it.

2. Press the **Tab** key. The Customer ID text box is selected, which makes sense, as it is the adjacent control.

3. Press the **Tab** key. The Referred By label is selected at the end of the page, which is not what users will expect.

4. Continue to press the **Tab** key, noticing the order controls are selected, until the Customer ID label is selected again.

As you can see, the current tab order is not a logical sequence for the location of the controls. You can reset the tab order to better match the placement of the fields on the form page.

To set the tab order:

1. Click **Layout** on the menu bar, and then click **Tab Order**. The Tab Order dialog box opens. See Figure 6-9.

Figure 6-9 ▶ Tab Order dialog box

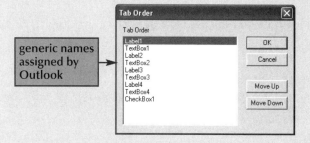

The controls are listed by the default generic names given by Outlook—Label, TextBox, and CheckBox—and are numbered in the order you originally placed them on the form. Because you have repositioned the controls, it is difficult to know which is which.

2. Click the **Cancel** button. The Tab Order dialog box closes.

You can rename each control by changing its properties. A descriptive name enables you to quickly identify each control. For each control, you can enter a descriptive name that Outlook will use internally and modify the caption that users see. The simplest identification is to name the control using the same text as the caption. Avoid typing any spaces or punctuation in field names, which can cause problems if you later export the data in these fields from Outlook to other Office applications. If your field name has two or more words, begin the second word with a capital letter to make it easier to read. For example, use FirstName rather than First Name or Firstname.

You can also determine how each control looks and functions by setting its properties. The Display tab in the Properties dialog box shows how the selected control is referenced by Outlook and how it looks on the form. The position settings show the current size and location of the selected control; you can specify precise numbers here or modify the control on the form with the mouse and let Outlook fill in these numbers. The font and color settings let you modify the typeface and foreground and background colors of the control. For even greater flexibility, you can modify the Settings options, which are described in Figure 6-10.

Control properties settings options ◄ | Figure 6-10

SETTING	CHECKED	UNCHECKED
Visible	Displays the control on the finished form.	Hides the control on the finished form.
Enabled	Allows users to enter data in the control.	Prevents users from entering data in the control; control appears grayed out.
Read only	Allows users to only select or copy data in the control.	Allows users to edit the data in the control.
Resize with form	Enlarges or reduces the control proportionally with the form window.	Keeps the control the same size no matter how the form window is resized.
Sunken	Makes the control look three-dimensional.	Makes the control look two-dimensional.
Multi-line	Starts a new line within the control when users press the Enter key.	Selects next control when users press the Enter key.

You'll set the display properties for each of the fields you placed on the Contributions page.

To set a control's display properties:

1. Verify that the **Customer ID label** control is selected. Sizing handles and a hatch pattern appear around a selected control.

2. Click the **Properties** button 🔲 on the Form Design toolbar. The Properties dialog box opens. See Figure 6-11.

Properties dialog box for the Customer ID label ◄ | Figure 6-11

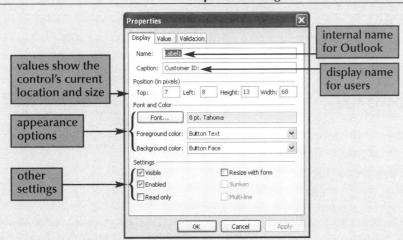

3. Type **CustomerIDLabel** in the Name text box; do not type any spaces between the words.

4. Verify that the **Visible** and **Enabled** check boxes contain check marks. The other check boxes should be unchecked.

5. Click the **OK** button.

The properties you set for this control did not change how it appears in the form, although they do affect how the control appears and works in the finished form. You need to set the properties for each of the other controls.

To set the display properties for the other controls:

▶ 1. Click the **Customer ID text box** to select it, and then click the **Properties** button 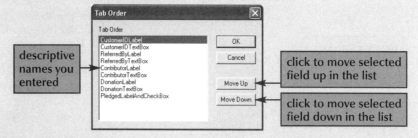 on the Form Design toolbar. The Properties dialog box opens for the text box.

▶ 2. Type **CustomerIDTextBox** in the Name text box. There is no caption for the text box because it will display the text you enter, not default text like a label.

▶ 3. Verify that the **Visible**, **Enabled**, and **Sunken** check boxes contain check marks and the other check boxes are unchecked.

▶ 4. Click the **OK** button.

▶ 5. Set the properties for each of the remaining controls: **Contributor label**, **Contributor text box**, **Pledged label and check box** (the Pledged label and check box are grouped so you can select them as one unit), **Donation label**, **Donation text box**, **Referred By label**, and **Referred By text box**, using the caption name followed by the control type without spaces as the Name and verify that the Visible, Enabled, and, if necessary, Sunken check boxes are selected. (Make sure you use an uppercase letter at the beginning of each word to make reading the property label easier.)

Now that the controls all have descriptive names, you can rearrange the tab order.

To set the tab order:

▶ 1. Click **Layout** on the menu bar, and then click **Tab Order**. The Tab Order dialog box opens. See Figure 6-12.

Figure 6-12	Tab Order dialog box with descriptive names

▶ 2. Click **ReferredByLabel** in the Tab Order list box.

▶ 3. Click the **Move Down** button until ReferredByLabel appears at the end of the list.

▶ 4. Click **ReferredByTextBox** in the Tab Order list box, and then click the **Move Down** button until it appears at the end of the list.

▶ 5. Click **PledgedLabelAndCheckBox**, and then click the **Move Up** button twice so that it appears fifth in the list. See Figure 6-13.

Completed Tab Order dialog box **Figure 6-13**

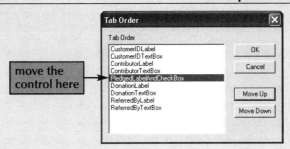

6. Click the **OK** button.

You'll check the tab order on the page to ensure that the order is sequential and logical.

To test the revised tab order:

1. Click the **Customer ID label**, and then press the **Tab** key. The Customer ID text box is selected.

2. Press the **Tab** key to select the Contributor label.

3. Press the **Tab** key to select the Contributor text box.

4. Press the **Tab** key five times to verify that the selection moves in the following order: Pledged check box, Donation label, Donation text box, Referred By label, and Referred By text box.

Trouble? If your tab order differs, you need to reorder the controls in the Tab Order dialog box. Click Layout on the menu bar, and then click Tab Order to open the Tab Order dialog box. Move fields up and down as needed until the controls in the Tab Order list box match the order shown in Figure 6-13.

The Referred By field isn't really appropriate with the contribution information. You'll delete it from the form.

To delete a field:

1. Select the **Referred By label** and the **Referred By text box**.

2. Press the **Delete** key. The two controls disappear from the form.

The form includes the appropriate fields in a logical arrangement with a tab order that will move users sequentially through the page. However, the fields may not be aligned precisely.

Professional forms carefully group related fields and align and size controls to make the form look neat and organized for users. For example, fields on the same row should be aligned horizontally. Fields in a column should be spaced equal distances apart. Figure 6-14 describes some of the layout tools available for forms.

Figure 6-14　**Layout tools for forms**

TOOL	DESCRIPTION
Alignment	Lines up selected controls along their left, right, center, middle, top, or bottom edges to the dominant control or to the grid.
Center in Form	Centers selected controls between the top and bottom or the left and right edges of the form.
Make Same Size	Resizes two or more controls to the same height, width, or height and width as the dominant control.
Spacing	Increases, decreases, removes, or makes even the horizontal or vertical spacing between selected controls.
Grouping	Combines two or more selected controls into one object so they can be moved or changed as one.

In many cases, the movement of selected controls depends on which control is dominant. The dominant control is determined by how you select controls. If you Shift-click to select controls, the first selected control is dominant. If you Ctrl-click to select controls, the last control selected is dominant. If you draw a rectangle around the controls you want to select, the control nearest the pointer when you started dragging the rectangle is dominant. No matter which selection method you used, you can Ctrl-click twice the control you want to be dominant. You can always tell which control is dominant because it has white selection handles; the other controls have black selection handles.

You'll use some of these tools to align the fields on your form. If any alignment changes have an unexpected result, you can press and hold the Ctrl key as you press the Z key to undo your previous action. *You can undo only one action*, so carefully look at your results before trying another option.

To align controls:

1. Click the **Customer ID label** to select it, press and hold the **Shift** key, click the **Contributor text box**, and then release the **Shift** key. The four controls in the first row are selected.

   The Customer ID label has white selection handles and is the dominant control, so any alignment changes will reference that control's current placement.

2. Click the **Align Left** button list arrow ![icon] on the Form Design toolbar. Left, Center, and Right provide vertical alignment options. Top, Middle, and Bottom provide horizontal alignment options. To Grid moves the control to the nearest dots on the design grid.

3. Click **Middle**. The controls horizontally align at their center points to match the center point of the Customer ID label. See Figure 6-15.

Horizontally aligned controls ◄ **Figure 6-15**

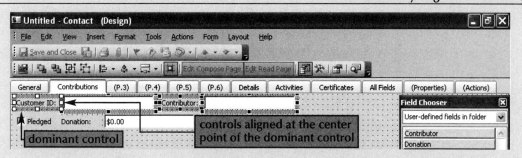

Trouble? If your controls do not align as shown in Figure 6-15, press the Ctrl+Z keys to undo the action and carefully repeat Steps 1 through 3.

4. Click the **Pledged control** to select it, press and hold the **Shift** key, click the **Donation text box**, and then release the **Shift** key. The controls on the second row are selected. Pledged is the dominant control.

5. Click the **Align Left** button list arrow [≡▾] on the Form Design toolbar and then click **Middle**. Again, the controls align horizontally by their centers.

Next, you'll resize some of the text boxes. The Customer ID text box has a lot of extra space, as does the Donation text box.

To resize the text boxes:

1. Click the **Customer ID text box** to select it, and then point to the right-center sizing handle. The pointer changes to ◄—►.

2. Drag the right-center sizing handle to the left until the text box is about one-quarter its original size, and then release the mouse button.

3. Select the **Contributor label** and **text box**, and then drag the controls left until they are close to the Customer ID text box (approximately three dots apart on the grid). See Figure 6-16.

Each row of controls aligned horizontally ◄ **Figure 6-16**

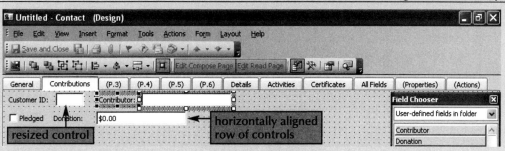

Trouble? If necessary, middle-align the controls in the first row again.

4. Click the **Donation text box**, press and hold the **Ctrl** key, click the **Contributor text box**, and then release the **Ctrl** key. The Contributor text box is the dominant selected control.

Trouble? If a copy of the Donation text box appears, you dragged the control while holding the Ctrl key. Press the Ctrl+Z keys to undo the copy action, and then repeat Step 5.

5. Click the **Align Left** button list arrow 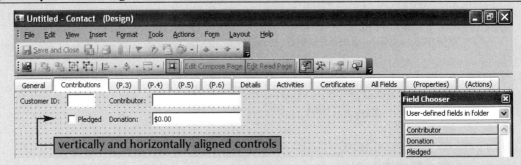 on the Form Design toolbar, and then click **Right**. The Donation text box aligns vertically with the Contributor text box along its right edge.

6. Click the **Donation label**, hold the **Ctrl** key, click the **Contributor label**, and then release the **Ctrl** key. The Contributor label is the dominant selected control.

7. Click the **Align Left** button list arrow on the Form Design toolbar, and then click **Left**. The Donation label aligns vertically along the left edge of the Contributor label.

8. Align the **Pledged control** with the left edge of the Customer ID text box, and then deselect the controls. See Figure 6-17.

Figure 6-17 **Completed rearrangement of controls**

Trouble? If the Donation label is covered by the Pledged label, select the Contributor and Donations controls and text boxes and drag them to the right.

In addition to setting properties for individual controls, you can set properties for the form itself. The form properties enable you to assign various elements to the form, including:

- **Category and Sub-category.** Classifications to group forms to make it easier to find and open a specific form.
- **Contact.** The name of the person whom users can contact for help or more information about the form.
- **Description.** Comments about the form, its purpose, or how to use the form.
- **Version and Form Number.** An alphanumeric classification you create to track forms.
- **Send form definition with item.** Saves the form's design information with the form so the layout is included when you share the form with others, such as by e-mail; uncheck if you plan to save the form in a forms library. (See below for more details about forms libraries.)

You can enter all this information on the hidden Properties page of the form. The information is displayed in the Choose Form dialog box, which is used to open a form, but is hidden in the opened form. Some of the information also appears in the form's Properties dialog box and in the About dialog box that opens from the Help menu.

To enter form properties:

1. Click the **(Properties)** tab in the form. The form Properties page opens.

2. Type **Contributions** in the Category text box.

3. Type **1** in the Version text box.

4. Type **CNTRB** in the Form Number text box.

5. Type your name in the Contact text box.

6. Type **This form is used to collect information about contacts and their current contributions.** in the Description text box. See Figure 6-18.

Form Properties page ◀ Figure 6-18

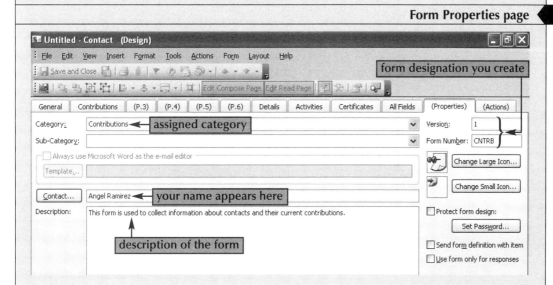

Once you are done modifying and documenting the form, you need to test it.

Testing a Custom Form

Before you finish creating a custom form, you need to test it to ensure that the fields and controls you added work as expected. You test the form in **run mode**, which shows the form as it will appear when it is used. From run mode, you can enter information in the form, send or post it, and then open the form to make sure it appears correctly. If any aspect of the form is not correct, you can return to design mode and make changes to it.

To test the form:

1. Click **Form** on the menu bar, and then click **Run This Form**. The form switches from design mode to a new form in run mode. At first glance, the form looks like the same New Contact form you have been using; however, this version includes the new Contributions tab.

   You didn't modify the General page, so you'll switch to the Contributions tab and test that page.

2. Click the **Contributions** tab. The custom page of the form opens. See Figure 6-19.

Figure 6-19 | **Blank Contributions page**

3. Click in the **Customer ID** text box, type **D-12**, and then press the **Tab** key. The insertion point moves to the Contributor text box.

4. Type **Bill Parker** in the Contributor text box, and then press the **Tab** key to move to the Pledged check box.

5. Press the **spacebar** to insert a check mark in the Pledged check box. When a check box is selected, pressing the spacebar inserts or removes a check mark from the box. The general rule for check boxes is that a check mark indicates yes, true, or on.

6. Press the **Tab** key, type **2500.9** in the Donation text box, and then press the **Tab** key. Outlook formats the amount as currency, inserting the necessary dollar sign, comma, and extra zero. See Figure 6-20.

Figure 6-20 | **Completed Contributions page**

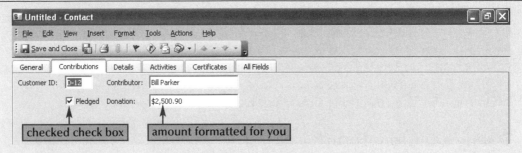

The form works as you expect, so you'll close it.

7. Click the **Close** button [X] on the form's title bar. A dialog box opens, asking whether you want to save changes. You don't want to save any changes because this is test data.

8. Click the **No** button in the dialog box. The test form closes and you return to the form in design mode.

If you needed to make changes, you could revise the form as necessary. After any revisions, you should retest the form to ensure that you have achieved the results you intended.

Publishing a Form

After the form is complete, you can **publish** the form, which saves the form so it can be used in Outlook. If you make changes to a published form, you must republish the form to be able to use the updated form. There are three ways to publish a form. You can save the form in the Outlook folder where you want to use it, you can save the form in a forms library so that others can also use it, or you can save the form as a file so you or others can use it as a template or in other programs. These three options are detailed below:

- **Outlook folder.** The form is saved in the open Outlook folder. Use this option when you don't want to share the form or when you want to send a form to someone by e-mail. The form is available from the Actions menu of that folder.
- **Forms library.** The form is saved to the forms library you specify. A **forms library** is the location where Outlook stores published forms. Outlook has three forms libraries. The Personal forms library is stored on your computer and is accessible only to you. The Outlook Folders forms library saves the form to a public folder that is accessible to others or to a private folder that is accessible only to you. The Organizational forms library is stored on a corporate server and is accessible to everyone in an organization. The form is available from the Tools menu and Forms submenu.
- **File.** The form is saved in another file type so you can work with it in another program or the form is saved as a template so you can create new items from it. Use this option when you don't want to share the form or when you want to send a form to someone by e-mail.

Once you select the location to save the form, you need to enter the display name and form name. The display name is the caption that appears at the top of the form as well as in the Forms menu and Choose Forms dialog box (from which you select a form to start a new item). The display name you enter also appears as the form name, unless you change the form name. The form name is the filename you assign to the form. You'll use Lumine Contacts as the display name and Contributions as the form name.

The last item in the Publish Form As dialog box is the Message Class field. The **message class** is the internal identifier used by Outlook (and Microsoft Exchange) to locate and activate a form. Outlook generates the message class from the form name and assigns it to the form. The message class of all Outlook items begins with IPM, which is an acronym for interpersonal message. The second part of the message class specifies the type of form being used, such as Contact. The third part of the message class is the form name (or filename) you entered for the form. For example, the message class of the form you created will be IPM.Contact.Contributions.

Reference Window

Publishing a Form

- Click the Publish Form button on the Form Design toolbar (*or* click Tools on the menu bar, point to Forms, and then click Publish Form or Publish Form As).
- Change the Look in location.
- Type a caption for the form in the Display name text box.
- Type a filename for the form in the Form name text box.
- Click the Publish button.

You'll publish the form in the Contacts folder, the open Outlook folder. Then you'll assign the display name "Lumine Contributors" and the form name "Contributions."

To publish a form:

1. Click the **Publish Form** button 🖼 on the Form Design toolbar. The Publish Form As dialog box opens. You'll store the form in the open Outlook folder.

2. Click the **Browse** button, click the **plus sign** button ➕ next to Personal Folders, if necessary, click **Contacts**, and then click the **OK** button. The Outlook folder in which you want to store the form is selected.

3. Type **Lumine Contacts** in the Display name text box. The name is repeated in the Form name text box.

4. Press the **Tab** key, and then type **Contributions** in the Form name text box. Outlook generates the message class, IPM.Contact.Contributions, from the information you entered. Outlook uses the message class to locate and load the form. See Figure 6-21.

Figure 6-21	Publish Form As dialog box

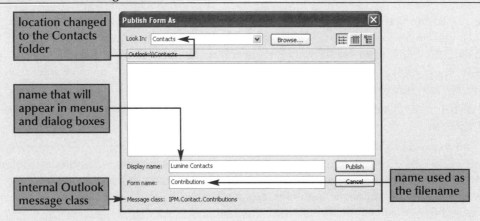

5. Click the **Publish** button. The form is saved to the specified location.

You'll close the finished, published form. When you save a custom form based on a contact form without entering a name in the File As field (even if the field doesn't appear on the form), Outlook notifies you that the field is empty. You can then save the blank form or return to the form to enter information. If you enter data in the form, then that data will appear each time you create a new item based on that form. You'll want to save the form without any data.

To close the form:

1. Click the **Close** button ❌ on the Contact window title bar. A dialog box opens, asking whether you want to save changes.

   If you save changes, then a blank contact card is saved in the Contacts folder.

2. Click the **No** button.

The process for creating custom mail forms is similar to the process you used to create a custom contact form. To create a custom mail form, you must change your options, if necessary, to use Outlook as the mail editor. To customize all the pages of the mail form, open a Message window, and then switch to design mode. The major difference is that each page of the mail form can have separate Compose and Read versions. The Compose page version shows what senders see when they create and send outgoing messages. The Read page version shows what recipients see when they open and read incoming messages. You switch between the Compose page version and the Read page version by clicking the appropriate button on the Form Design toolbar. Each version can be customized with different controls. If you want the Compose and Read versions of a page to be identical, you can disable the Separate Read Layout option.

You'll use the contact form you created to enter new contacts for Brian.

Opening a Custom Form

You enter information in a custom form the same way as you do a standard form. The only difference between using a custom form and using a standard form is how you open the form. The process for opening a custom form varies, depending on where you saved the custom form, as described earlier.

Opening a Custom Form
Reference Window

- Click Tools on the menu bar, point to Forms, and then click Choose Form (or click File on the menu bar, point to New, and then click Choose Form or click the New button list arrow, and then click Choose Form or switch to the Outlook folder in which you saved the form, click Actions on the menu bar, and then click the form name at the bottom of the menu).
- Click the Look In list arrow, and then click the location where you published the form you want to open.
- Click the form you want to open.
- Click the Details button to display or hide the description, contact, and message class of the selected form.
- Click the Open button.

You'll open the custom contact form and enter general contact information in the default page. Then you'll use the custom page you created to enter the contribution information for each contact.

To open the custom form:

1. Click **Tools** on the menu bar, point to **Forms**, and then click **Choose Form**. The Choose Form dialog box opens, showing the forms stored in the Standard Forms Library. You'll switch to the folder in which you stored the new form.

2. Click the **Look In** list arrow, and then click **Contacts**. Any forms available in that folder are listed in the dialog box.

3. Click the **Lumine Contacts** form.

4. If necessary, click the **Advanced** button to display the description, contact, version, and message class of the selected form. See Figure 6-22.

Figure 6-22 ▶ **Choose Form dialog box**

location of the form

descriptive form name you entered

information from the form's Properties page

click to show or hide details

5. Click the **Open** button. A new Lumine Contacts window opens based on your custom form.

You enter information in the contact card as usual. The General page looks exactly as you would expect from your previous experience entering contact information. The Contributions page has the custom fields.

To enter information in the contact card:

1. Enter the following contact information on the General tab: full name **John Ravenfoot**, home phone **401-555-7526**, address type **Home**, home mailing address **12 Lake Shore Drive, Kingston RI 02852**, and your e-mail address (fix the Display as name). See Figure 6-23.

Figure 6-23 ▶ **General tab completed for new contact**

2. Click the **Contributions** tab to switch to the custom page you created.

3. Enter the following information: Customer ID **D-172**, Contributor **The Ravenfoot Family**, Pledged **unchecked**, Donation **2500**, and then press the **Enter** key. See Figure 6-24.

Contributions tab completed for new contact ◀ Figure 6-24

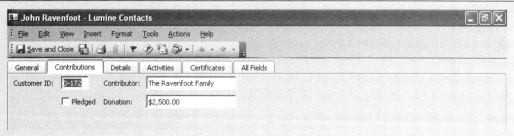

4. Save and close the contact card.

You'll enter a few more contacts for Brian. You can create a new contact card based on the form from the Actions menu, which is a bit faster than using the Choose Form dialog box.

To enter additional contacts:

1. Display the **Contacts** folder, click **Actions** on the menu bar, and then click **New Lumine Contacts**. A new Lumine Contacts window based on the custom form opens.

2. Enter the following contact information: full name **Kara Martin**, home phone **401-555-1197**, address type **Home**, home mailing address **792 Oak Lane, Kingston RI 02852**, Customer ID **D-173**, Contributor **Anonymous**, Pledged **checked**, and Donation **1750**.

3. Click the **Save and New** button 🔳 on the Standard toolbar to close the Kara Martin contact card and open a new contact card based on the custom form.

4. Enter the following contact information: full name **Mitch Elkin**, home phone **401-555-4967**, address type **Home**, home mailing address **11 Shady Brook Road, Kingston RI 02852**, Customer ID **D-174**, Contributor **In memory of Lillian Elkin**, Pledged **unchecked**, Donation **8575**.

5. Save and close the contact card.

The contacts you created appear in the Contacts main window, although you cannot see the information you entered on the Contributions page.

Creating Mail Templates

Rather than publish a custom form in Outlook, you might want to save the form as a template. A **template** is similar to a form in that both provide a blueprint of the fields and layout for an item. When you save a form as a template, Outlook creates a separate file with the .oft extension. In addition to customizing a form with fields, you can enter specific data in a field, and then publish or save the form. Any new items based on the form will include that data.

Brian wants to send an e-mail message to everyone who contributes to Lumine, acknowledging the receipt of the contribution. Because Brian will use the same subject and message for each e-mail, you'll create a new e-mail, enter the standard subject and message body, and then save the e-mail as a template. You'll leave the To text box blank, so that Brian can address the e-mail when he sends the message.

To create a mail template:

1. Click **Tools** on the menu bar, click **Options**, click the **Mail Format** tab, click the **Use Microsoft Office Word 2003 to edit e-mail messages** check box to remove the check mark, if necessary, click the **Compose in this message format** list arrow, click **Plain Text**, if necessary, and then click the **OK** button.

2. Create a new e-mail message, do not enter any addresses in the To or Cc text boxes, type the subject **Thank you for your support**, type the message **The curtain will continue to rise on our stage thanks to your generous support. As a token of our appreciation, we are sending you a commemorative program with highlights from our past ten years. Thank you.**, press the **Enter** key twice, type your name, press the **Enter** key, and then type **Lumine**.

3. Click **File** on the menu bar of the Message window, and then click **Save As**. The Save As dialog box opens.

4. Type **Lumine Mail Template** in the File name text box.

5. Click the **Save as type** list arrow, and then click **Outlook Template**.

    Trouble? If you don't see Outlook Template in the Save as type list, then you are probably using Microsoft Word as your mail editor. Click the Cancel button in the Save As dialog box, close the Message window without saving changes, and then repeat Steps 1 through 5, being sure to uncheck the Use Microsoft Word to edit e-mail messages check box in Step 1.

6. Change the Save in location to the **Tutorial.06\Tutorial** folder included with your Data Files.

7. Click the **Save** button. The mail form is saved as a template with your Data Files.

8. Click the **Close** button ☒ on the Message window title bar to close it.

9. Click the **No** button to close the message without saving changes.

The template can be used several ways. You can create a new message from the template. You can e-mail the template to other users, who can then open the attachment from their computer. You can save the template to a disk, which is a convenient way to transfer the form to another computer or to create a backup of the form.

You'll use the mail template form to send a message to John Ravenfoot, one of the contacts who donated financial support to the theater group.

To send a message using the mail template:

1. Display the **Inbox**, click **Tools** on the menu bar, point to **Forms**, and then click **Choose Form**. The Choose Form dialog box opens.

   You need to change the Look In location to the folder included with your Data Files where you saved the template.

2. Click the **Look In** list arrow, click **User Templates in File System**, click the **Browse** button to open the Browse for Folder dialog box, navigate to the **Tutorial.06\Tutorial** folder included with your Data Files, and then click the **OK** button. The Lumine Mail Template appears in the Choose Form dialog box.

   Trouble? If you have trouble locating the Tutorial.06\Tutorial folder included with your Data Files, scroll to the top of the list in the Browse for Folder dialog box to see the My Documents folder, or scroll to the bottom of the list to see other disk drives.

3. Click **Lumine Mail Template** in the list box in the Choose Form dialog box, and then click the **Open** button. A new Message window opens based on your mail template. See Figure 6-25.

Message based on mail template ◄ **Figure 6-25**

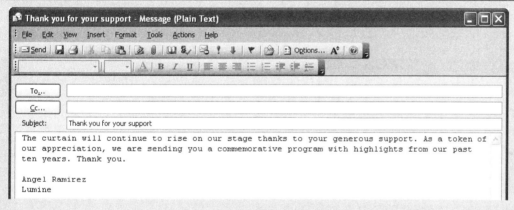

4. Address the message to **John Ravenfoot**, and then send the message.

   Trouble? If you type John's name in the To text box and then press the Tab key and the name does not become underlined to indicate that Outlook found an e-mail address associated with the name, delete the name you typed, click the To button, click the Show Names from the list arrow, select Contacts, click John Ravensfoot in the list, click the To button, and then click the OK button.

   Notice that your Outbox contains one unread mail message. This is the template that you opened. The template remains in your Outbox until you delete it.

5. Download the message, if necessary, and then read the message.

So far, you have customized the Contact form for Lumine and used the custom form to create new contacts with specific data. You have also created a mail template with standard body text and then used the template to send an e-mail message. In Session 6.2, you'll learn other ways to view your items and customize Outlook.

Review

Session 6.1 Quick Check

1. What is a form?
2. List the four basic steps for customizing a form.
3. Explain the difference between a bound control and an unbound control.
4. Describe a simple field.
5. Define tab order.
6. What does it mean to publish a form?
7. Explain the difference between the Compose page and Read page in a mail form.
8. How does a form differ from a template?

Session 6.2

Customizing Views with Fields

The default views that are available for each folder provide a good starting point for looking at items. But the ability to add or remove fields to any view as well as to select the order in which those fields appear is part of what makes Outlook so powerful. You can use the Show Fields dialog box or the Field Chooser to customize the views to show exactly the fields you want in the main window for each Outlook folder.

Reference Window | **Customizing Views with Fields**

- Switch to the view you want to customize.
- Click View on the menu bar, point to Current View, click Customize Current View, and then click the Field button in the Customize View dialog box (or right-click the column headings, click Customize Current View, and then click the Fields button in the Customize View dialog box or right-click the main window background, and then click Show Fields).
- To display additional fields in the current view, select one or more fields in the Available fields list box, and then click the Add button.
- To remove displayed fields from the current view, select one or more fields in the Show these fields in this order list box, and then click the Remove button.
- To reorder fields displayed in the current view, select a field in the Show these fields in this order list box, and then click the Move Up or Move Down button as needed.
- When all fields you want to display in the current view are listed in the appropriate order, click the OK button.
- Click the OK button in the View Summary dialog box, if necessary.
  or
- Switch to the view you want to customize.
- To remove a field from the current view, drag the field from the column headings into the main window.
- To add a field to the current view, right-click column headers, click Field Chooser, drag a field from the Field Chooser to the appropriate location within the column headings using the red arrows to position the field, and then click the Close button on the Field Chooser title bar to close the Field Chooser.
- To reorder column headings, drag a column heading to a new location within the column headings, using the red arrows to position the field.

The contacts you created include data for four fields that do not appear in any of the standard Contacts folder views. You'll customize Address Cards view to display these fields.

To customize the Contacts folder view:

1. If you took a break after the last session, make sure Outlook is running.

2. Display the **Contacts** folder, and then verify that the current view is **Address Cards**.

3. Right-click the background (not a contact card) of the Contacts main window, and then click **Show Fields** on the shortcut menu. The Show Fields dialog box opens. See Figure 6-26.

Show Fields dialog box  **Figure 6-26**

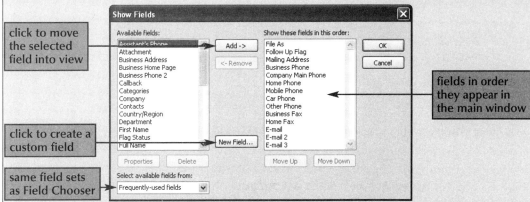

4. Click the **Select available fields from** list arrow, and then click **User-defined fields in folder**. The three custom fields you created earlier appear.

   You'll add the Donation and Contributor fields below the File As name.

5. Click **Donation** in the Available fields list box to select it, and then click the **Add** button. The field moves to the end of the Show these fields in this order list box.

   You want to move up the fields to below the File As name.

6. Click the **Move Up** button until Donation appears as the second field in the list below File As.

7. Add the **Contributor** field to the Show these fields in this order list box. The field is added below the selected item, third in the list.

   Trouble? If the Contributor field is not the third item in the list, select the field and then use the Move Up and Move Down buttons to position it.

8. Click the **OK** button. The Donation and Contributor fields appear at the top of each contact card. See Figure 6-27.

Figure 6-27 | **Customized Address Cards view**

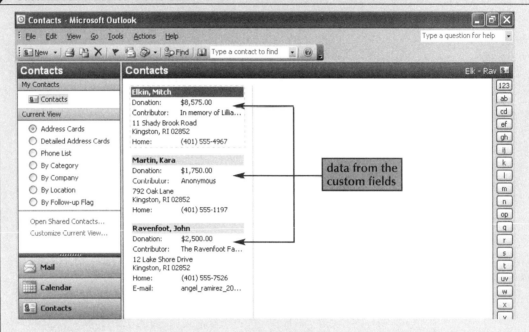

Next, you'll create an appointment with Mitch Elkin.

To create an appointment with a contact:

1. Click the **Elkin, Mitch** contact card to select it.

2. Click **Actions** on the menu bar, and then click **New Appointment with Contact**. A new Appointment window opens with Mitch listed at the bottom of the window as the contact.

3. Set up an appointment with the subject **Funding a workshop for young actors** for **tomorrow** starting at **10 AM** and ending at **11 AM**.

4. Save and close the appointment.

With all your work on creating custom forms, you haven't updated your task list. You also want to create a folder in which to store the messages related to Lumine contributions. You'll do both now.

To create tasks and a folder:

1. Create a new task with the subject **Confirm details of opening season gala**, a due date of **tomorrow**, a **High** priority, and no reminder.

2. Create a new task with the subject **Arrange audition with actor Aaron Geom**, a due date of **tomorrow**, a **Normal** priority, and no reminder.

3. Create a new task with the subject **Check on printing of program**, a due date of **yesterday**, a **Normal** priority, and no reminder.

4. Create a new folder named **Lumine Mail** that contains **Mail and Post Items** placed within the **Inbox**.

You could view all these items you created by opening the appropriate folders, but this doesn't give you the "big picture" that Outlook Today provides.

Using Outlook Today

Each Outlook folder has a variety of views you can use to review the folder's active or overdue items. For example, you can view your incoming messages in the Inbox, display your active appointments in the Calendar, and show any in-progress or overdue to-do items in the Tasks folder. Although the information in each folder is helpful, you need to do a lot of clicking around to attain a complete summary of the items. Outlook Today provides an overview of your current schedule, tasks list, and new e-mail messages.

Navigating with Outlook Today

From Outlook Today, you can quickly jump to any item or folder. Each task or appointment item or any listed folder in Outlook Today is a hyperlink that you can click to open the item's window or display the folder's main window.

You'll use Outlook Today to view the calendar, task, and e-mail items in Outlook.

To view the Outlook Today page:

1. Click **Personal Folders** either in the All Mail Folders pane in the Mail pane or in the All Folders pane in the Folders List to switch to Outlook Today. The Outlook Today page in the main window displays Calendar, Tasks, and Messages. See Figure 6-28.

Outlook Today **Figure 6-28**

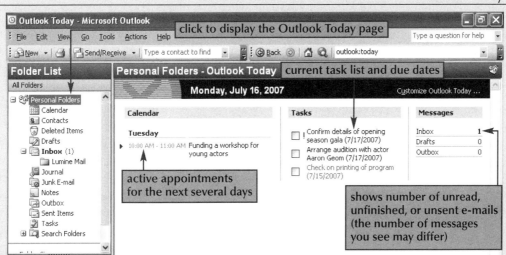

Trouble? If your Outlook Today page looks different than in Figure 6-28, continue with Step 2. You will learn about changing the Outlook Today style shortly.

2. Point to **Inbox** in the Messages area. The pointer changes to 🖑, which indicates that the Inbox is a hyperlink you can click to jump to the folder.

3. Click **Inbox**. The Inbox main window opens, so you can begin sending, replying to, and receiving e-mail messages.

4. Click **Personal Folders** in the Navigation Pane to return to Outlook Today.

5. Click the **Check on printing of program** task (not the check box). The Task window opens so you can review and modify the details as needed.

6. Change the task's due date to **tomorrow**, change the priority to **High**, and then save and close the task. The task information is updated in Outlook Today. See Figure 6-29.

Figure 6-29	Updated task list in Outlook Today

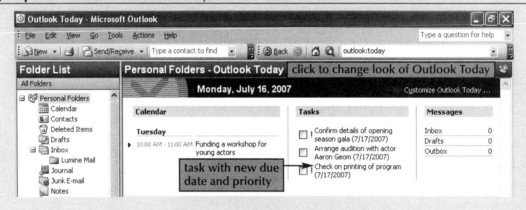

Many people start their day from Outlook Today. After reviewing this snapshot of their upcoming appointments and most pressing tasks, they begin working on their top priority item.

Customizing Outlook Today

Rather than manually opening Outlook Today when you begin working, you can set this page to open each time you start Outlook. This way, you can preview your activities before moving to a specific folder. You can also change how much information appears on the page and what the page looks like. For example, you can view appointments for the next one to seven days, see a count of unread messages for the e-mail folders you select, choose which tasks to view and in what order, and even decide on the layout you prefer.

You'll customize Outlook Today to better meet your needs.

To customize Outlook Today:

1. Click the **Customize Outlook Today** button in the upper-right corner of the main window (below the folder banner). The Outlook Today Options page opens in the main window. See Figure 6-30.

Customize Outlook Today page ◄ Figure 6-30

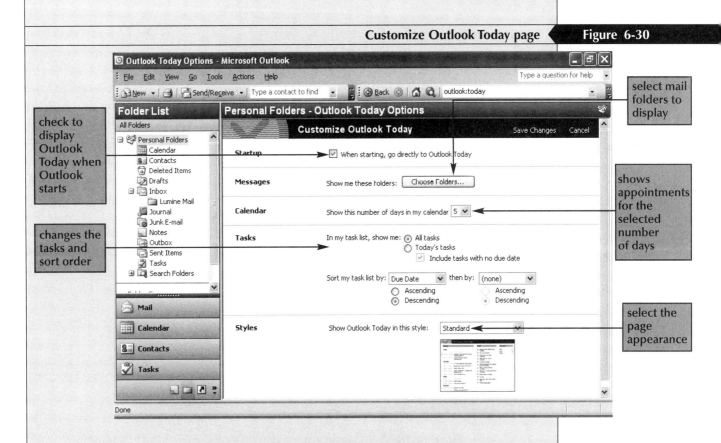

Trouble? If you can't locate the Customize Outlook Today button, then your Outlook Today page is probably in a different style, and the button is located elsewhere in the main window. Try looking in the lower-right corner of the window.

2. Verify that the **When starting, go directly to Outlook Today** check box contains a check mark. Each time you start Outlook, Outlook Today will open in the main window.

    You can select which mail folders appear in the Messages area. If you display a folder that does not store mail items, then the messages count on the Outlook Today page will always be 0.

3. Click the **Choose Folders** button. The Select Folder dialog box opens; checked message folders appear on the Outlook Today page.

4. Expand the **Inbox** folder, if necessary, and then click the **Lumine Mail** folder check box to insert a check mark. See Figure 6-31.

Figure 6-31 | Select Folder dialog box

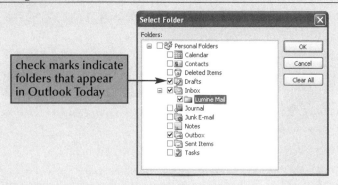

check marks indicate folders that appear in Outlook Today

▶ 5. Click the **OK** button. The folder will appear on the Outlook Today page when you save the options.

You can organize your task list to better reflect the way you work by setting the two sort criteria.

▶ 6. If necessary, click the **Sort my task list by** list arrow, click **Due Date**, and then click the **Descending** option button. You can select a second criterion by which to sort the task on the Outlook Today page.

▶ 7. Click the **then by** list arrow, and then click **Importance**. Tasks will be sorted in descending order by their priority level within due date groups.

The default three-column layout is functional, but you may prefer another style.

▶ 8. Click the **Show Outlook Today in this style** list arrow, and then click **Summer**. The graphic shows how the Outlook Today page will appear.

▶ 9. Change the Outlook Today style to **Standard (two column)**.

When you finish customizing Outlook Today options, you must save your selections to have them take effect.

▶ 10. Click the **Save Changes** button near the top of the window. The customized Outlook Today page appears with the changes you specified. See Figure 6-32.

Figure 6-32 | Customized Outlook Today

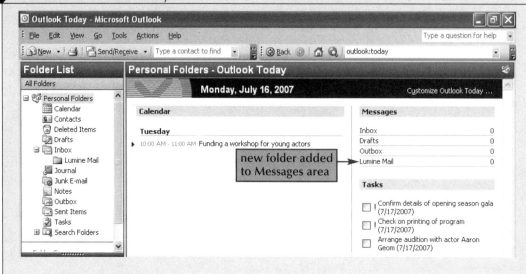

new folder added to Messages area

You'll switch to the Calendar, display the TaskPad, and then customize the TaskPad to show the Priority field. This time you'll use the Field Chooser to customize the view.

To customize the Calendar TaskPad:

1. Click the **Calendar** link in Outlook Today to open that folder, and then, if necessary, change the current view to **Day** within the **Day/Week/Month** view.

2. Display tomorrow in the planner to review the appointment with Mitch.

3. Click **View** on the menu bar, and then click **TaskPad**. The TaskPad appears below the Date Navigator, which moves from the Navigation Pane to the right side of the main window.

   The TaskPad shows the Icon, Complete, and Subject fields. You want to display the Priority field.

4. Right-click the **TaskPad** column heading, and then click **Field Chooser** on the shortcut menu. The Field Chooser opens, displaying the Frequently-used fields list.

5. Drag the **Priority** field from the Field Chooser to the right of the TaskPad column heading, using the red placement arrows to position the field. The field is inserted at the right side of the TaskPad column heading.

   The field would be better if it were to the left of the TaskPad field.

6. With the Field Chooser still open, drag the **Priority** column heading to between the Complete and TaskPad column headings. The field is inserted as the third column.

7. Drag the **Due Date** field from the Field Chooser to the right of the Priority field. The final order of fields in the TaskPad is Icon, Complete, Priority, Due Date, TaskPad.

8. Click the **Close** button ☒ on the Field Chooser title bar. The Field Chooser closes.

   You'll sort the TaskPad by the fields you added so you can better prioritize each day's tasks.

9. Click the **Due Date** field, press and hold the **Shift** key, click the **Priority** field, and then release the **Shift** key. The TaskPad is sorted by due date and then by priority. See Figure 6-33.

TaskPad displayed and sorted by added fields   **Figure 6-33**

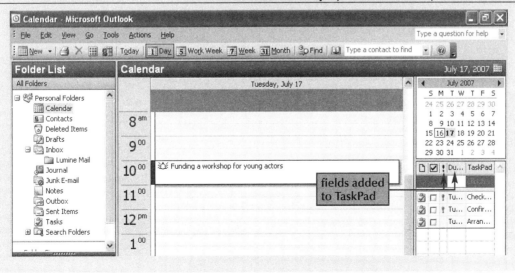

You'll find that this flexibility for adding and removing fields makes Outlook more useful. In addition to Outlook Today, you can configure other Outlook options.

Configuring Outlook Options

Outlook is quite functional with its default settings. However, it also has many optional settings. At some point, you may want to fine-tune some of these settings to better fit the way you work. There are options available for each Outlook folder and function. The complete list of options available depends on which Add-Ins are installed.

Configuring Calendar Options

The Options dialog box provides access to most of the customization options for Outlook. They are organized by categories and subcategories within the tabs. You'll open the Options dialog box and change some of the Calendar options.

You'll start by modifying the times Outlook displays as the workday, or usual business hours. Because of its evening shows, the theater group starts its day at 10 a.m. and closes its office at 6 p.m.—an hour later than usual business hours. You can change the Calendar options to reflect this shifted workday.

To configure Calendar options:

▶ 1. Click **Tools** on the menu bar, click **Options**, and then, if necessary, click the **Preferences** tab. The Preferences tab in the Options dialog box opens.

▶ 2. Click the **Calendar Options** button. The Calendar Options dialog box opens. See Figure 6-34.

Figure 6-34 ▶ **Calendar Options dialog box**

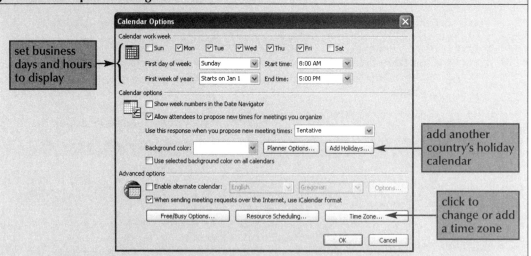

You can change the days considered part of the workweek, specify the standard hours counted as the workday, and set which days at the start of the year are counted as workdays. You can also add another country's holidays to the Calendar.

▶ 3. Click the **Sat** check box to insert a check mark.

▶ 4. Click the **Start time** list arrow, and then click **10:00 AM**.

5. Click the **End time** list arrow, and then click **6:00 PM**.

6. Click the **OK** button in the Calendar Options dialog box, and then click the **OK** button in the Options dialog box. The light and dark yellows, indicating the workday, are shifted to reflect your changes.

7. Click the **Today** button on the Standard toolbar. See Figure 6-35.

Customized workday **Figure 6-35**

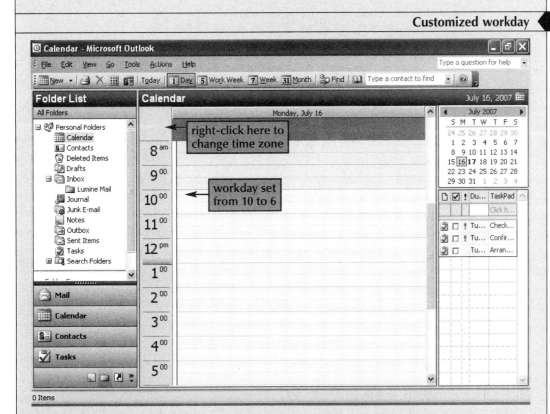

Trouble? If you don't see the change in the planner, then you might be looking at Sunday. Click another day in the Date Navigator.

In addition to these daily settings, there are some settings you can change based on your location.

Changing Time Zones

If you regularly work with others in another time zone, you can set up Outlook to display both zones. In addition, if you travel, you can swap the time zones so your calendar and messages are converted to the time zone you're currently visiting.

Ada will be teaching a theater class in Athens for the next six months. Because she will remain active in the theater's planning and activities, the group will need to pay attention to time zone differences when setting up conference calls. You'll add the Athens time zone to the Calendar. Rather than reopening the Options dialog box, you can go directly to the Time Zone dialog box using a shortcut menu.

To change the time zone settings:

1. Right-click the square space above the times in the daily planner, and then click **Change Time Zone** on the shortcut menu. The Time Zone dialog box opens. See Figure 6-36.

Figure 6-36 | Time Zone dialog box

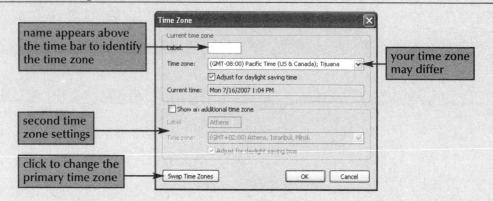

2. Type **Here** in the Label text box. This identifies your current time zone. Your time zone, daylight savings time, and current time are set for your location.

3. Click the **Show an additional time zone** check box to insert a check mark.

4. Type **Athens** in the Label text box. This identifies Ada's time zone.

5. Click the **Time zone** list arrow, and then click **(GMT+02:00) Athens, Istanbul, Minsk**.

6. Click the **OK** button in the Time Zone dialog box. The two time zones appear in the daily planner. See Figure 6-37.

Figure 6-37 | Calendar with two time zones

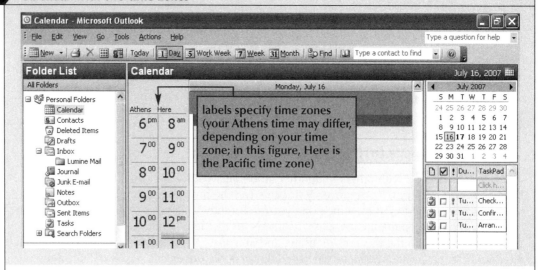

There are many other options you can use to customize Outlook to match your personal work style and preferences.

Customizing the Navigation Pane

As you've seen, the Navigation Pane is the main navigation tool in Outlook. The default buttons on the Navigation Pane give you access to all the Outlook folders. You can customize the Navigation Pane to display more or fewer buttons, resize the buttons, or change the order in which the buttons appear. You can resize the width of the Navigation Pane by dragging its right border to the left or right. You can also create additional groups and can add more icons to any group in the Shortcuts pane on the Navigation Pane to more quickly access Outlook folders and items you create. These customizations affect only the computer on which they were made.

Earlier you created a subfolder within the Inbox and added the folder to Outlook Today. You want to move the e-mail messages related to Lumine from the Inbox into that folder.

To move e-mail messages from the Inbox to the Lumine Mail folder:

▶ **1.** Display the **Folder List**, if necessary, display the **Inbox**, and then expand the **Inbox** in the Folder List to display the Lumine Mail folder.

▶ **2.** Drag the **Thank you for your support** message from the Inbox to the **Lumine Mail** folder.

Some people prefer to use the Folder List to navigate Outlook because you can see all the Outlook folders and any subfolders you created in one list.

Resizing the Navigation Pane Buttons

Even with only the default buttons displayed on the Navigation Pane, some of the folders and subfolders may move out of view. Although you can scroll to see these out-of-view icons, you can also resize the Navigation Pane buttons so you see more folders and subfolders at once in the Navigation Pane. Then you can access any folder without scrolling through a long list. You can quickly resize the Navigation Pane buttons by dragging the horizontal splitter bar that appears above the buttons. Drag the splitter bar down to reduce the large buttons displayed vertically in the Navigation Pane to small button icons displayed horizontally at the bottom of the pane, or drag the splitter bar up to change the small button icons to large buttons. If you drag the splitter bar to the bottom of the Navigation Pane, all the buttons are displayed as small button icons. You can also click the Configure Buttons button at the bottom of the Navigation Pane, and then click Show More Buttons or Show Fewer Buttons to change the display between the large and small buttons.

To resize the Navigation Pane buttons:

▶ **1.** Note how many large buttons appear on the Navigation Pane, and then point to the horizontal splitter bar above the large buttons on the Navigation Pane. The pointer changes to $\updownarrow$.

▶ **2.** Drag the splitter bar down to move the lowest large button to a button icon at the bottom of the Navigation Pane. See Figure 6-38.

Figure 6-38 **Resized Navigation Pane buttons**

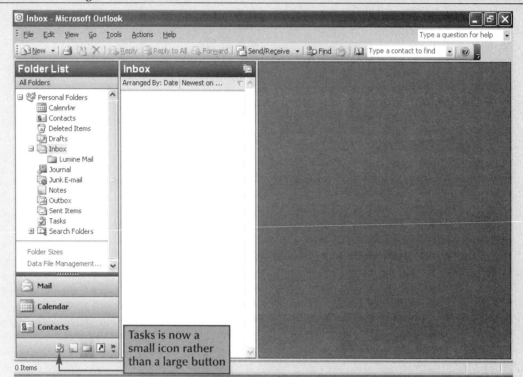

3. Continue to drag the splitter bar down until all the large buttons are small icons at the bottom of the Navigation Pane. There is much more display space for the All Folders pane. See Figure 6-39.

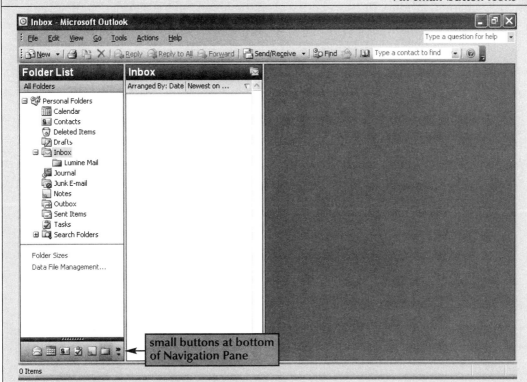

small buttons at bottom of Navigation Pane

4. Click the **Configure Buttons** button ⁑ at the bottom of the Navigation Pane, and then click **Show More Buttons**. The leftmost small button icon moves from the bottom of the Navigation Pane to become a large button.

5. Repeat Step 4 until the same number of large buttons you noted in Step 1 appear on the Navigation Pane.

Use the large and small icons in whichever way works best for you.

Adding, Removing, and Reordering Navigation Pane Buttons

As you work, you may find that you use some folders quite frequently and others rarely. To accommodate your working style, you can add or remove buttons from the Navigation Pane to streamline the view, and you can reorder the buttons you leave displayed so that they appear in the order most useful for you. To add or remove buttons and reorder buttons, you can open the Navigation Pane Options dialog box, and then select the buttons you want to display and move selected buttons up or down to change the order. You can also add or remove a button from the Navigation Pane by clicking the Configure Buttons button at the bottom of the Navigation Pane, pointing to Add or Remove Buttons, and then clicking the button you want to add or remove. A check mark precedes the names of buttons that are displayed in the Navigation Pane.

To add, remove, and reorder the Navigation Pane buttons:

▶ **1.** Click the **Configure Buttons** button ⬍ at the bottom of the Navigation Pane, and then click **Navigation Pane Options**. The Navigation Pane Options dialog box opens. See Figure 6-40.

Figure 6-40 ▶ **Navigation Pane Options dialog box**

▶ **2.** Click the **Notes** check box to remove the check mark. The Notes button will no longer appear in the Navigation Pane.

▶ **3.** Note the location of Folder List in the Display buttons in this order list box (it's usually below Notes), click **Folder List** in the Display buttons in this order list box, and then click the **Move Up** button until the Folder List appears as the first item.

▶ **4.** Click the **OK** button. The Navigation Pane Options dialog box closes, the Notes button is removed from the Navigation Pane, and the Folder List button appears at the top of the Navigation Pane buttons. See Figure 6-41.

Figure 6-41 ▶ **Reordered Navigation Pane buttons**

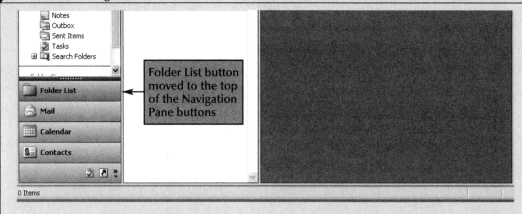

▶ **5.** Click the **Configure Buttons** button ⬍ at the bottom of the Navigation Pane, point to **Add or Remove Buttons**, and then click **Notes**. The Notes button again appears on the Navigation Pane.

▶ **6.** Click the **Configure Buttons** button ⬍ at the bottom of the Navigation Pane, and then click **Navigation Pane Options**. The Navigation Pane Options dialog box opens.

▶ **7.** Click **Folder List** in the Display buttons in this order list box, and then click the **Move Down** button until the Folder List appears in the location you noted in Step 3 (usually below Notes).

▶ **8.** Click the **OK** button. The Navigation Pane returns to its original display.

Groups and shortcuts are another way to customize the Navigation Pane.

Adding and Renaming Shortcut Groups and Shortcuts

You can add groups and shortcuts to the Shortcuts pane in the Navigation Pane. A **group** is a named list of shortcuts to folders. A **shortcut** provides one-click access to a default or custom folder. You can create shortcuts to folders you use frequently; however, this list can quickly become long and unwieldy. One way to manage the list is to create groups to organize the shortcuts into related categories. For example, you might create a group in the Shortcuts pane to store shortcut icons related to a particular project, company, or person. To add a group, click the Add New Group link in the Shortcut pane, and then type the group name. To create a shortcut, click the Add New Shortcut link.

You'll create a new group for Lumine in the Shortcuts pane.

To add a group to the Shortcuts pane:

1. Click the **Shortcuts** button ▣ at the bottom of the Navigation Pane to display the Shortcuts pane, and then click the **Add New Group** link near the top of the Navigation Pane. The new group appears as a text box in the Shortcuts pane, ready for you to type a name. See Figure 6-42.

New shortcut group added to Shortcuts pane ◀ Figure 6-42

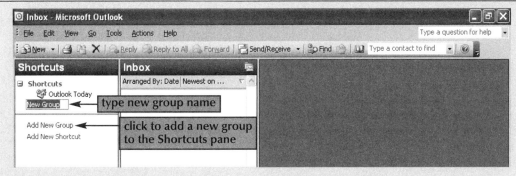

2. Type **Contributors** as the name for the group, and then press the **Enter** key. The new group is added, ready for you to add shortcuts.

You can change the name of a group in the Shortcuts pane at any time to better describe the shortcut items it contains. You'll change the Contributors group to "Lumine" because you'll be adding shortcuts related to the company in the group.

To rename a group in the Shortcuts pane:

1. Right-click the **Contributors** group, and then click **Rename Group** on the shortcut menu. The group name becomes a text box with the text selected so you can type a new name.

2. Type **Lumine** as the new name for the group, and then press the **Enter** key. The group is renamed.

You can reorder the groups in the Shortcuts pane so that groups you use more frequently appear at the top of the list and groups you use less frequently appear lower down. To shift a group up or down, right-click the group in the Shortcuts pane, and then click Move Up in List or Move Down in List. Each time you click the command, the group shifts up or down one group in the pane. You'll move the Lumine group to the top of the list in the Shortcuts pane to make it easier to find.

To move a group in the Shortcuts pane:

1. Right-click the **Lumine** group, and then click **Move Up in List** on the shortcut menu. The group shifts higher in the Shortcuts pane.

2. Repeat Step 1 until the Lumine group is the top group listed in the Shortcuts pane.

You can add shortcuts to any group in the Shortcuts pane.

Adding Shortcuts to Shortcuts Pane

You can create shortcuts to any existing folders, whether they are default or custom folders. To add a new shortcut, click the Add New Shortcut link in the Shortcuts pane, click the folder for which you want to create a shortcut, and then click the OK button. The new shortcut is placed at the end of the first group in the Shortcuts pane. You can move the shortcut up or down in the current group, or you can drag the selected shortcut into another group.

You'll create a shortcut to the Lumine Mail folder to provide easy access to that folder.

To create a shortcut to an existing Outlook folder:

1. Click the **Add New Shortcut** link in the Shortcuts pane. The Add to Navigation Pane dialog box opens.

2. Click the **Lumine Mail** folder within the Inbox. You want to add a shortcut to this folder. See Figure 6-43.

Figure 6-43 ▶ Add to Navigation Pane dialog box

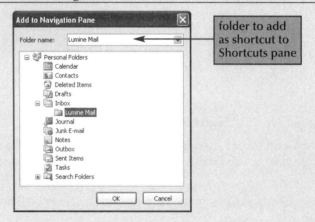

> **3.** Click the **OK** button. A shortcut to the Lumine Mail folder is added to the Lumine group in the Shortcuts pane. The shortcut reflects the type of item that the folder stores, in this case, messages. See Figure 6-44.

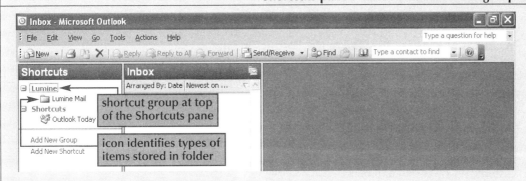

Even though you want to be certain to name the shortcuts with descriptive labels, the icons can help you to quickly identify the type of shortcut in the Shortcut pane.

Shortcuts can be moved between groups as well. To move a shortcut to a new group, drag the shortcut to the group, and then continue to drag the shortcut to the location you want. You can scroll to a position out of view by pointing to the top or bottom of the group.

Sometimes the shortcut names are not descriptive enough or are so long that only part of the name is visible. In either case, just as you renamed the group, you can rename the shortcut. Right-click the shortcut you want to rename, click Rename Shortcut on the shortcut menu, type a new name in the text box that opens, and then press the Enter key. Only the shortcut is renamed; the file or folder to which the shortcut points retains the original name.

Customizing the Favorite Folders Pane in the Mail Pane

The Mail pane contains two panes for viewing folders that store Mail and Post items—the Favorite Folders pane and the All Mail Folders pane. The Favorite Folders pane, located at the top of the Mail pane, displays a list of folders that store Mail and Post items that you select placed in the order you want. The All Mail Folders pane shows an alphabetical listing of all the folders that store Mail and Post items. Although the two panes might seem to be similar at first glance, the Favorite Folders pane usually shows a subset of the folders in the All Mail Folders pane, although you can choose to add all the folders from the All Mail Folders pane to the Favorite Folders pane. Conversely, you can decide to display no folders in the Favorite Folders pane, although you cannot remove the pane entirely. To add a folder to the Favorite Folders pane, you drag it from the All Mail Folders pane and drop it in the location you want using the horizontal placement bar as a guide. The folder is then listed in both panes. You can drag any folder in the Favorite Folders pane to a new location in the list. To remove a folder from the Favorite Folders pane, you right-click the folder and then click Remove from Favorite Folders on the shortcut menu. If you were to delete the folder from the Favorite Folders pane, the folder and all the items it contained would be moved into the Deleted Items folder, and would no longer appear in either the Favorite Folders pane or the All Mail Folders pane.

The Favorite Folders pane can be useful if you have many custom folders that you use frequently. For example, Brian might create a folder to store e-mail correspondence with each actor, staff member, and supplier (such as office supplies, lumber for set construction, and fabrics for costume design). Over time, this list can become fairly extensive. Rather than scrolling through the entire list of folders, Brian can create a custom list of the folders he uses most frequently in the Favorite Folders pane, and change the order in which they appear, depending on his current projects. During preproduction, he might place the suppliers at the top of the list, and during a production, he might want the current actors at the top.

You'll add the Lumine Mail folder to the Favorite Folders pane.

To add a folder to the Favorite Folders pane:

1. Click the **Mail** button in the Navigation Pane. The Favorite Folders pane and the All Mail Folders pane appear in the Navigation Pane.

2. Drag the **Lumine Mail** folder from the All Mail Folders pane to the bottom of the Favorite Folders pane, using the horizontal placement bar as a guide. Your folder now appears in both panes. See Figure 6-45.

Figure 6-45 ▶ **Customized Favorite Folders pane**

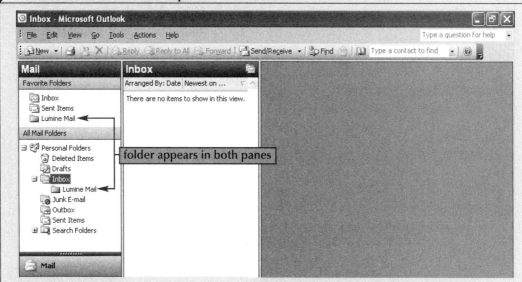

3. Drag the **Lumine Mail** folder in the Favorite Folders pane up to the top of the Favorite Folders pane. The Lumine Mail folder is now the first item in the Favorite Folders pane, though its placement hasn't changed in the All Mail Folders pane.

You can see how the Favorite Folders pane gives you the flexibility to arrange your mail folders in the exact order that suits your needs at the moment.

Customizing Menus and Toolbars

As you work with Outlook, you'll find that some menus and buttons you use frequently; others you'll use rarely, if at all. In addition, sometimes, you'll wish that certain commands would appear on a specific menu or toolbar. In these cases, you can customize the menus and toolbars.

Most menus are located on the menu bar, which is considered a toolbar. Toolbars can contain buttons, menus, or both. You can add and remove buttons and menus on the built-in toolbars or custom toolbars you create. You can customize the menu bar the same way you customize toolbars, adding or removing commands and menus; however, unlike toolbars, you cannot hide the menu bar nor can you add a second menu bar.

Creating a Custom Menu or Toolbar

You can create additional menus and toolbars for Outlook. You might create a custom menu or toolbar to keep the list of commands and buttons on a built-in menu or toolbar a manageable length. Or, you might want to group commands or buttons related to a specific task in one location.

You'll create a new toolbar named "Navigate" that contains buttons for moving around in Outlook.

To create a toolbar:

1. Right-click any toolbar, and then click **Customize** on the shortcut menu. The Customize dialog box opens.

2. Click the **Toolbars** tab, if necessary. Check marks next to the toolbar names indicate that the toolbar is visible. See Figure 6-46.

Toolbars tab in the Customize dialog box ◀ Figure 6-46

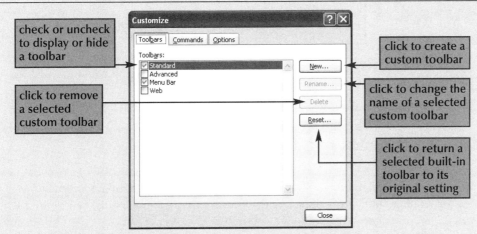

check or uncheck to display or hide a toolbar

click to remove a selected custom toolbar

click to create a custom toolbar

click to change the name of a selected custom toolbar

click to return a selected built-in toolbar to its original setting

3. Click the **New** button. The New Toolbar dialog box opens so you can enter a descriptive name for the toolbar.

4. Type **Navigate** in the Toolbar name text box, and then click the **OK** button. The new, descriptive toolbar name appears in the Toolbars list box with a check mark, and the empty toolbar appears in the Outlook window. See Figure 6-47.

Figure 6-47 New, empty toolbar

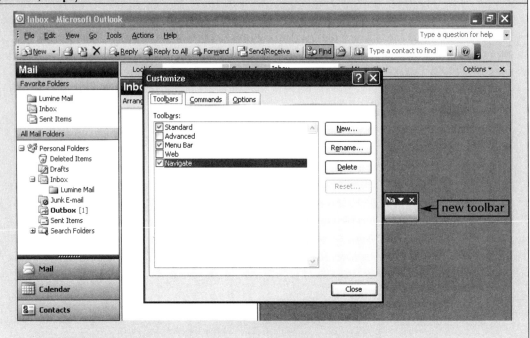

Once you create a toolbar, you can add buttons to it.

Adding Commands to a Toolbar or Menu

Opening the Customize dialog box enables you to edit the toolbars. You can add or remove a command from any toolbar or menu that is visible in the main window. The process for adding commands is the same whether you're adding them to a built-in menu or toolbar, menu bar, or a custom menu or toolbar.

You'll add two buttons to the Navigate toolbar. One button will open or close the Navigation Pane so you can quickly make more room on the screen. The second button will open the Go to Folder dialog box so you can easily switch to a folder when the Folder List is closed.

To add commands to a toolbar:

1. Click the **Commands** tab in the Customize dialog box. Commands are organized by logical categories so you can quickly find the ones you need. See Figure 6-48.

Figure 6-48

Commands tab in Customize dialog box

Categories list

Commands list

2. Click **View** in the Categories list box. The various tools available in that category appear in the Commands list box.

3. Scroll down until you see Navigation Pane, and then drag **Navigation Pane** from the Commands list box to the Navigate toolbar. The command appears on the toolbar.

   If you closed the dialog box, you could click the command on the toolbar. As long as the Customize dialog box is open, you can drag the command to a new location or continue to add other commands.

4. Click **Go** in the Categories list box, scroll through the Commands list box until you see Folder. . ., press and hold the mouse button, drag **Folder** from the Commands list box to the right of the Navigation Pane button on the Navigate toolbar, but do not release the mouse button. A placement bar appears, indicating the drop location. See Figure 6-49.

Adding buttons to a custom toolbar

Figure 6-49

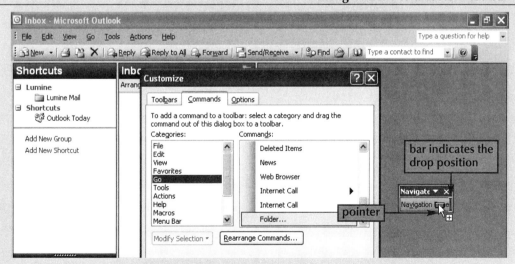

bar indicates the drop position

pointer

5. Release the mouse button. The command appears on the toolbar to the right of the Navigation button.

You could repeat this process to add other commands to the toolbar. The process is similar for adding commands to a menu, except that you drag the command onto the menu, pause until the menu opens, drag the command to the location you want, and then release the mouse button.

If you closed the Customize dialog box, you could use the new toolbar and its buttons. However, you want to make one more change.

Customizing Command Names and Icons

Right now, the Folder button on the Navigate toolbar shows text rather than an icon on the button. You can modify the icon for any button or the text for any menu.

To customize a toolbar button icon:

▶ **1.** Verify that the Customize dialog box is open and that the Folder button on the new Navigate toolbar is selected (there is a dark border around the button).

▶ **2.** Click the **Modify Selection** button in the Customize dialog box. The Modify Selection menu provides information about the command's name, image, and style, and provides a variety of commands you can use to modify the selected command.

▶ **3.** Click **Image and Text**. The Folder button increases in width to make room for an icon to the left of the text.

▶ **4.** Click the **Modify Selection** button in the Customize dialog box, and then point to **Change Button Image** on the Modify Selection menu. A palette of icons opens from which you can select an image for the button. See Figure 6-50.

Figure 6-50	Changing a button icon

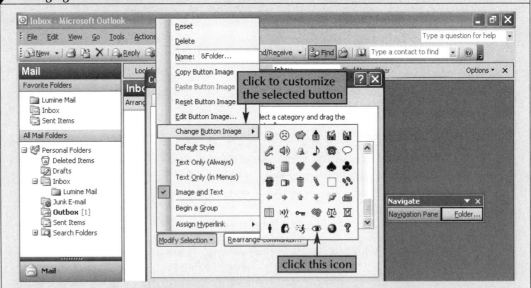

You can use the eye image to remind you that this button will enable you to see another folder.

▶ **5.** Click the **eye** icon on the image palette. The image appears next to the text.

To make the toolbar button more consistent with other buttons, you'll set the button text to appear only in menus.

6. Click the **Modify Selection** button in the Customize dialog box, and then click **Text Only (in Menus)**. The icon shows only the eye image because the button is located on a toolbar rather than in a menu. See Figure 6-51.

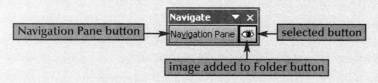

7. Click the **Close** button in the Customize dialog box.

Once the Customize dialog box is closed, you can no longer add commands to the toolbars and menus. You hide and display and move the custom toolbar the same way as you would any other toolbar.

To use the custom toolbar:

1. Drag the **Navigate toolbar** up and to the right of the Standard toolbar. The toolbar docks next to the existing toolbars and behaves just like the other toolbars.

2. Right-click the toolbar area. The Navigate toolbar is listed with the other available toolbars.

3. Press the **Esc** key, and then point to each button on the Navigate toolbar. ScreenTips appear for each button just like on the other toolbars.

4. Click the **Navigation Pane** button on the Navigate toolbar. The Navigation Pane closes. The button works as a toggle to open and close the Navigation Pane.

5. Click the **Folder** button 🔘 on the Navigate toolbar. The Go to Folder dialog box opens. You can use this to navigate the Outlook folders instead of the Navigation Pane.

6. Click the **Folder name** list arrow in the Go to Folder dialog box, click **Contacts**, and then click the **OK** button. The Contacts main window appears.

7. Click the **Navigation Pane** button on the Navigate toolbar. The Navigation Pane opens.

You can customize any toolbar or menu to match the way you work or the tasks you perform regularly.

Removing a Menu or Toolbar Button

If you want to delete a toolbar button, you must display the toolbar from which you want to delete the button. You can then press and hold the Alt key as you drag the button off the toolbar. Once the button is off the toolbar, you can release the Alt key and the button is removed from the toolbar. To delete a menu and all the items it contains from the menu bar, you would use the same procedure. *You cannot undo this procedure nor will a dialog box open to ask you to confirm your action.*

Removing Customizations from Outlook

Before you finish, you'll remove all the customizations you made to Outlook. This includes removing the contact and mail forms you created and deleting the custom fields. You'll also return Address Cards view, Outlook Today, Calendar, and the TaskPad to their default settings, and delete any messages, contacts, and toolbars you created in this tutorial.

To save a form and remove it from a forms library:

1. Click **Tools** on the menu bar, and then click **Options**. The Options dialog box opens.

2. Click the **Other** tab, and then click the **Advanced Options** button. The Advanced Options dialog box opens.

3. Click the **Custom Forms** button, and then click the **Manage Forms** button. The Forms Manager dialog box opens. The form has two identical list boxes so you can manage forms in two locations and copy or move forms between locations.

4. Click the **Set** button above the list box on the left in the dialog box. The Set Library To dialog box opens.

5. Expand the folders as needed, select **Contacts** in the Folder Forms Library list box, and then click the **OK** button. The Lumine Contacts form appears in the left list box.

6. Click **Lumine Contacts**, click the **Copy** button, click **Lumine Contributors** in the right list box, click the **Save As** button, switch the Save in location to the **Tutorial.06\Tutorial** folder included with your Data Files, type **Lumine Contacts** as the filename, verify that **Form Message** is the file type, and then click the **Save** button.

   Now that the form is saved with your Data Files, you can delete it from the Outlook folders.

7. Click the **Delete** button, click the **Yes** button to confirm that you want to delete the form, click **Lumine Contacts** in the left list box, click the **Delete** button, and then click the **Yes** button to confirm that you want to delete the form.

8. Click the **Close** button in the Forms Manager dialog box, and then click the **OK** button in each of the remaining dialog boxes to close them.

Next, you'll remove the fields from Address Cards view, and then delete the custom fields you created. When you return to Address Cards view, you'll delete the contact cards you created in this tutorial.

To remove fields from a view, delete custom fields, and delete contact cards:

1. Right-click the Contacts main window background, and then click **Show Fields**. The Show Fields dialog box opens.

You can remove the fields you added to Address Cards view and delete the custom fields.

▶ **2.** Click the **Donation** field in the Show these fields in this order list box, press and hold the **Shift** key, click the **Contributor** field, and then release the **Shift** key. Both custom fields are selected.

▶ **3.** Click the **Remove** button to place the fields back into the Available fields for User-defined fields in folder.

▶ **4.** Click the **Contributor** field in the Available fields list, press and hold the **Shift** key, click the **Pledged** field, and then release the **Shift** key. All three custom fields are selected.

▶ **5.** Click the **Delete** button, and then click the **OK** button in the dialog box to confirm the deletion.

▶ **6.** Click the **OK** button to close the Show Fields dialog box.

▶ **7.** Delete the contact cards for **Mitch Elkin**, **Kara Martin**, and **John Ravenfoot** from the Contacts main window.

Next, you'll return the Calendar and TaskPad to their default views. You can quickly remove unwanted fields from a table view, such as the TaskPad, by dragging the fields off the table by their column headings.

To remove customizations from the TaskPad:

▶ **1.** Display the **Calendar** folder.

▶ **2.** Drag the **Priority** field by its column heading out of the TaskPad until a big X appears over the field, and then release the mouse button. The field is removed from the TaskPad.

▶ **3.** Drag the **Due Date** field off the TaskPad.

▶ **4.** Delete the tasks you created.

▶ **5.** Click **View** on the menu bar, and then click **TaskPad**. The TaskPad is no longer displayed and the Date Navigator moves back into the Navigation Pane.

Next, you'll remove the extra time zone and labels from the planner, and return the workday to its default setting of Monday through Friday, 8 a.m. to 5 p.m.

To remove the Calendar customizations:

▶ **1.** Click **Tools** on the menu bar, click **Options**, and then, if necessary, click the **Preferences** tab.

▶ **2.** Click the **Calendar Options** button. The Calendar Options dialog box opens.

▶ **3.** Click the **Sat** check box to remove the check mark.

▶ **4.** Click the **Start time** list arrow, and then click **8:00 AM**.

▶ **5.** Click the **End time** list arrow, and then click **5:00 PM**.

6. Click the **Time Zone** button. The Time Zone dialog box opens.

7. Delete **Here** from the top Label text box, and then delete **Athens** from the additional time zone Label text box.

8. Click the **Show an additional time zone** check box to remove the check mark.

9. Click the **OK** button in the Time Zone dialog box, click the **OK** button in the Calendar Options dialog box, and then click the **OK** button in the Options dialog box.

10. Delete the appointment you created for 10 AM tomorrow.

The Calendar is returned to its default settings. Next, you'll reset the default Outlook Today options.

To reset the Outlook Today defaults:

1. Display the **Outlook Today** page, and then click the **Customize Outlook Today** button.

2. Click the **Choose Folders** button, click the **Lumine Mail** check box to remove the check mark, and then click the **OK** button.

3. Sort the task list by **Due Date** in **Descending** order and then by **(none)**.

4. Click the **Show Outlook Today in this style** list arrow, and then click **Standard**.

5. Click the **Save Changes** button. Outlook Today returns to its default settings.

You'll remove the shortcuts and group you added to the Shortcuts pane in the Navigation Pane. When you remove a shortcut icon, only the shortcut is removed, not the file or folder to which it pointed. The process is the same to remove a group or shortcut. If you remove a group, all the shortcuts it contains are also deleted.

To remove a shortcut and group from the Shortcut pane:

1. Click the **Shortcuts** button ⬚ at the bottom of the Navigation Pane.

2. Right-click the **Lumine Mail** shortcut icon in the Lumine group, and then click **Delete Shortcut** on the shortcut menu. A dialog box opens, asking you to confirm the deletion.

3. Click the **Yes** button to confirm that you want to remove the shortcut.

4. Right-click the **Lumine** group, and then click **Remove Group** on the shortcut menu.

5. Click the **Yes** button to confirm that you want to remove the group. The group is deleted.

You can delete a toolbar button or menu command without opening the Customize dialog box. However, when you want to delete a custom toolbar, you must do so from the dialog box. You'll delete the custom Navigate toolbar. When you delete the toolbar, you delete all of its buttons as well, although the commands are still available from their original categories in the Customize dialog box.

To delete a custom toolbar:

1. Right-click any toolbar, click **Customize** on the shortcut menu to open the Customize dialog box, and then click the **Toolbars** tab.

2. Click **Navigate** in the Toolbars list box, and then click the **Delete** button.

3. Click the **OK** button in the dialog box to confirm that you want to delete the Navigate toolbar.

4. Click the **Close** button. The Customize dialog box closes and the toolbar no longer exists.

Your final task is to delete the Lumine Mail folder you created as well as any messages you sent in this tutorial from the Sent Items folder. Then you'll empty the Deleted Items folder.

To remove the mail folder and e-mail items:

1. Display the Folder List.

2. Right-click the **Lumine Mail** folder, and then click **Delete "Lumine Mail"** on the shortcut menu.

3. Click the **Yes** button to confirm the deletion and move all of its contents to the Deleted Items folder.

4. Delete any messages you sent from the **Sent Items** folder.

5. Delete the template from the **Outbox** folder.

6. Empty the **Deleted Items** folder.

The custom forms and fields you created will make it easier for Brian to keep track of current contributors and their donations and to respond with an appropriate message. In addition, the customization options ensure that Brian is working most efficiently in Outlook.

Session 6.2 Quick Check

Review

1. Why would you add a field to a view?
2. Describe the two ways you can add fields to a view.
3. What is Outlook Today?
4. Give two reasons why you might display two time zones in the Calendar planner.
5. What are three ways you can customize the Navigation Pane?

6. What is the difference between the All Mail Folders pane and the Favorite Folders pane?
7. Why would you create a custom toolbar or menu?
8. True or False: Toolbars can only contain buttons with images, and menus must always have only text.

Review

Tutorial Summary

In this tutorial, you learned how to customize forms and create fields. You modified the built-in New Contact form by displaying a hidden page and adding default and custom fields. You also created a custom mail template. You used the custom forms to create contacts and send a message. Then you used fields to customize which data appeared in the main window. You reviewed items in Outlook Today, and customized Outlook by modifying the Calendar time zone, adding groups and shortcuts to the Navigation Pane, and creating a new toolbar.

Key Terms

bound control	forms library	simple field
combination field	formula field	sizing handle
control	layout	tab order
design mode	message class	template
Field Chooser	publish	unbound control
form	run mode	

Practice

Practice the skills you learned in the tutorial using the same case scenario.

Review Assignments

There are no Data Files needed for the Review Assignments.

Lumine records information about its series subscribers in the Outlook Contacts folder. The group has been running an early-bird promotion that gives series subscribers an additional 25 percent off the regular prices. Many people have responded, and Brian wants you to create a form to record the data. The information collected includes whether the subscription is new or a renewal, which series package the subscriber wants (categorized as Series A through Series G), and the number of tickets the subscriber is purchasing.

1. Open a new Contact window, click Tools on the menu bar, point to Forms, and then click Design This Form to create a new form based on a blank Contact window.
2. Use the Form menu to display page 2 and rename the page "Subscription."
3. Display All Contact fields in the Field Chooser, and then add the Customer ID field and the Account field to the form.
4. Create the following three new fields, and then drag the custom fields to the form: "Series" with a Text data type and a Text format; "Renewal" with a Yes/No data type and an Icon format; and "Tickets" with an Integer data type and a 1,234 format.
5. Arrange the fields on the form so that Customer ID and Renewal appear on the first row, Tickets and Series appear on the second row, and Account appears on the third row.
6. For each control, open the Properties dialog box and rename the control, entering its caption name plus control type without any spaces as the Name and verifying that the Visible, Enabled, and, if appropriate, Sunken check boxes are checked.

7. Rearrange the tab order so the controls appear in the following sequence: CustomerIDLabel, CustomerIDTextBox, RenewalCheckBox, TicketsLabel, TicketsTextBox, SeriesLabel, SeriesTextBox, AccountLabel, and AccountTextBox.

8. Reduce the Customer ID text box to ¼ its width, reduce the Tickets text box to ¼ its width, and then align the fields using an organized, attractive, and logical layout.

9. Delete the Account field from the form.

10. Switch to the form's Properties page, and then enter "Subscriptions" as the Category, "1.0" as the Version, "Series" as the Form Number, your name as the Contact, and the description "This form is used to collect information about series subscribers."

11. Test the form, and then close the test form without saving it. Make any changes needed.

12. Publish the form in the Outlook Contacts folder with the display name "Lumine Subscribers" and the form name "Subscribers."

13. Save the form as a template with the name **Lumine Subscribers Contact Template** in the **Tutorial.06\Review** folder included with your Data Files, and then close the form without saving changes.

14. Create a new folder named "Lumine Contacts" that contains Contact Items and is placed within the Contacts folder.

15. Create a new contact in the Lumine Contacts folder based on the custom form for the following information: full name "Pam Shephard"; home phone "401-555-3457"; address type "Home"; home mailing address "41 Larkin Street, Kingston RI 02852"; Customer ID "S-544"; Renewal checked; Tickets "4"; and Series "A."

16. Create a new contact in the Lumine Contacts folder based on the custom form for the following information: full name "Ralph Salvas"; home phone "401-555-3778"; address type "Home"; home mailing address "112 Quenton Street, Kingston RI 02852"; Customer ID "S-545"; Renewal unchecked; Tickets "1"; and Series "C."

17. Create a new contact in the Lumine Contacts folder based on the custom form for the following information: full name "Garret Bruneau"; home phone "401-555-7431"; address type "Home"; home mailing address "981 Center Road, Kingston RI 02852"; Customer ID "S-546"; Renewal checked; Tickets "2"; and Series "A."

18. Display the contacts you created in Address Cards view in the Lumine Contacts main window, and then customize Address Cards view to display the Customer ID, Renewal, Tickets, and Series fields below the File As name.

19. Sort the cards in ascending order by Customer ID.

20. Filter the cards to display only those that have a check mark in the Renewal check box. (*Hint:* In the Advanced tab of the Filter dialog box, create a criterion for the Renewal field that equals yes.)

21. Print the cards in Card Style and then remove the filter, sort, and custom fields you added to the view.

22. Use the Actions menu to create a half-hour appointment with Pam Shephard for tomorrow at 10 a.m. with a Normal importance to confirm the number of tickets she requested, show time as Free, add the label Phone Call, and do not set a reminder.

23. Create a half-hour appointment with Garret Bruneau for tomorrow at 11 a.m. with a High importance to confirm that he wants Series A, show time as Free, add the label Phone Call, and do not set a reminder.

24. Create a new mail message with the subject "Series rates increase on Monday" and the message text "Friday is the last day to receive the 25% early-bird discount for the series subscription for the new season. Subscribe today to lock in the best rates. Thank you." Press the Enter key twice and then type your name. Save the message as a draft by clicking the Save button, and then close the message.

25. Display the Outlook Today page, and then print the view.

26. Customize Outlook Today to use the Winter style and show three days in the Calendar.

27. Click the link for the appointment with Pam tomorrow at 10 a.m., and then click the Delete button on the Standard toolbar in the Appointment window. The window closes, and in a moment the appointment is removed from Outlook Today and your calendar. (If this were a recurring appointment, the entire series would be deleted.)

28. Click the Drafts link to open the Drafts folder.

29. Save the message as an Outlook Template with the filename **Early Bird Discount** in the **Tutorial.06\Review** folder included with your Data Files.

30. Create a new message based on the Early Bird Discount template, address the message to your e-mail address, send and receive the message, and then print the received message.

31. Display the Shortcuts pane in the Navigation Pane, add a new shortcut to the Lumine Contacts folder, add a new group named "Lumine," and then drag the Lumine Contacts folder shortcut from the Shortcuts group to the Lumine group.

32. Save the Lumine Subscribers form from the forms library in the Outlook Contacts folder as **Lumine Subscribers** in the **Tutorial.06\Review** folder included with your Data Files, remove the form from the forms library, and then delete the custom fields you created for the form.

33. Open the Customize dialog box, click the Commands tab, click the Go category, drag the Folder command to View on the menu bar, pause until the menu expands, and then drop the Folder command below the Navigation Pane command.

34. Change the Button Image of the Folder command to the shoe steps icon, and then change the property of the Folder command on the Go menu that you just added to Image and Text so that the shoe steps icon appears to the left of the text on the menu. Close the Customize dialog box.

35. Click View on the menu bar, and then click Folder to use the command you just added to the View menu to open the Go to Folder dialog box.

36. Use the Go to Folder dialog box to go to folders with items you created in these assignments and delete them, including the contacts, the appointments, and the e-mail messages from the Inbox, Drafts, and Sent Items folders. Go to Outlook Today and return the page to the Standard style and show five days in the Calendar.

37. Open the Customize dialog box, drag the Folder command off the View menu, and then close the Customize dialog box.

38. Delete the Lumine group and the shortcut from the Shortcuts pane, and then empty the Deleted Items folder.

Apply

Apply the skills you learned in the tutorial to create a custom Contact form to track client conversations for a jewelry designer.

Case Problem 1

There are no Data Files needed for this Case Problem.

Sexton Jewels   Beverly Sexton makes and sells custom jewelry, from high-quality costume jewelry to high-end gemstone and precious metals jewelry. Her clients include individuals as well as boutiques and independent shops. Beverly contacts her regular clients once each month to solicit new orders. She asks you to create a custom Outlook form she can use to track her last conversation with contacts.

1. Create a new form based on a Contact window.
2. Delete the Business phone label, button, and text box controls from the second column on the General tab in the Contact form.
3. Create a new field named "Last Talked To" with a Date/Time data type in the Tues 12/12/2007 4:30 pm format.
4. Drag the Last Talked To custom field to the space you created above the phone fields on the General tab.
5. Change the field's properties so that each control's name reflects the field caption and control type.
6. Adjust the tab order so that the Last Talked To field is selected after the File As field. (*Hint:* Press and hold the Shift key as you click each control to select and move both controls at one time.)
7. Adjust the size and alignment of the field you added to the form as needed.
8. Display the form's Properties page, and then enter "Follow up" as the Category, your name as the Contact, and the description "This form is used to record the date and time of the last conversation with the contact."
9. Test the form by entering "yesterday 10 AM" in the Last Talked To text box, and then close the test form without saving it. Make any changes needed.
10. Publish the form in the Outlook Contacts folder with the display name "Contact Follow Up" and the form name "Follow Up." Close the form without saving changes.
11. Create a new contact based on the custom form with the following information: full name "Claire Wagstaffe"; last talked to "yesterday 7 AM"; home phone "407-555-2117."
12. Create a new contact based on the custom form for the following information: full name "Wesley Rider"; last talked to "one month ago 3 PM"; home phone "407-555-8718."
13. Create a new contact based on the custom form with the following information: full name "Florence Peterson"; last talked to "four Wed ago noon"; home phone "407-555-5534."
14. Create a new contact based on the custom form with the following information: full name "Margaret Wong"; last talked to "yesterday noon"; home phone "407-555-4719."
15. Create a new folder named "Follow Up" that contains Contact Items placed within the Contacts folder. Move the four contacts you created to the Follow Up folder.
16. Create a shortcut to the Follow Up folder in the Shortcuts group in the Shortcuts pane. Use the shortcut you created to open the Follow Up folder.

xplore

17. Click View on the menu bar, point to Arrange By, point to Current View, and then click Define Views. The Custom View Organizer dialog box opens. You'll use this dialog box to create a new custom view.

Explore

18. Click "Phone List" in the Views for folder list box, click the Copy button to open the Copy View dialog box, type "Last Called" in the Name of new view text box, click the All Contact folders option button, if necessary, and then click the OK button.

19. Click the Fields button in the Customize View dialog box, and then use the Show Fields dialog box to display only the following fields in this order: Icon, Attachment, Flag Status, Full Name, Home Phone, and Last Talked To. (*Hint:* You'll need to re-create the Last Talked To Date/Time field in this folder.)

20. Click the OK button in the Show Fields dialog box, click the OK button in the Customize View dialog box, review the new view in the Custom View Organizer dialog box, and then click the Apply View button.

21. Sort the fields in descending order by the Last Talked To field, and then print all rows of the view in Table Style.

Explore

22. Delete the Last Called view. Open the Custom View Organizer dialog box, select the Last Called view, click the Delete button, click the OK button to confirm the deletion, and then click the Close button.

23. Save the Contact Follow Up form from the forms library in the Outlook Contacts folder as **Contact Follow Up** in the **Tutorial.06\Cases** folder included with your Data Files, remove the form from the forms library, and then delete the custom fields you created for the form in both the Contacts folder and Follow Up folder.

24. Delete any items or customizations you created in this case, including the contacts, the Follow Up folder, and the Shortcuts pane shortcut, and then empty the Deleted Items folder.

Apply

Apply the skills you learned in the tutorial to create a custom Task form to organize the staff's responsibilities for a bed and breakfast.

Case Problem 2

There are no Data Files needed for this Case Problem.

Zafforini Bed & Breakfast   Zafforini Bed & Breakfast organizes its staff into three teams—Red, Yellow, Blue—to foster a sense of commitment and community among employees. Each team is responsible for a variety of jobs, and selects a different team leader (or contact) for each task. In addition, Vicki Zafforini, owner of the B&B, rotates the tasks among the three teams. She asks you to create a custom Task form to help organize the team's responsibilities.

1. Create a new form based on a Task window.

2. Display page 2 and rename the tab "Teamwork."

3. Display All Task fields in the Field Chooser, and then add the Contact field (be sure you don't use the Contacts field), the Role field, the Sensitivity field, and the Team Task field to the form.

4. Rearrange the fields so that they appear in one column in the following order: Team Task, Role, Contact, Sensitivity.

5. Change the field's properties so that each control's name reflects the field caption and control type.

6. Adjust the tab order so that pressing the Tab key moves users consecutively through the controls.

7. Center align the text boxes and left align the labels and the check box on the form.

8. Display the form's Properties page, and then enter your name as the contact, and the description "This form is used to record information about the tasks being completed by the team."

9. Test the form, and then close the test form without saving it. Make any changes needed.

10. Delete the Sensitivity field from the Teamwork page.
11. Publish the form in the Outlook Tasks folder with the display name "Team Tasks" and the form name "Team Tasks." Close the form without saving changes.
12. Create a new folder named "Red Team" that contains task items placed within the Tasks folder; create a shortcut to the folder in the Shortcuts group in the Shortcuts pane.
13. Create a new group in the Shortcuts pane named "Red," and then move the Red Team folder shortcut to the new group.
14. Use the shortcut to open the Red Team folder, and then switch to the Simple List view.
15. Use the Field Chooser to add the Team Task, Role, and Contact fields to the Simple List view after the DueDate field.
16. Create the following new tasks from the custom Simple List view with the following information:

Subject	Due Date	Team Task	Role	Contact
Housecleaning	next Monday	checked	Primary	Simone Turner
Dining Room Setup	next Monday	checked	Secondary	Irving Shenk
Guest Check-in	next Monday	unchecked	Primary	Gayle Sufy
Guest Check-out	next Monday	unchecked	Primary	Gayle Sufy
Room Service Delivery	next Monday	checked	Primary	Irving Shenk

17. Sort the tasks in ascending order by Team Task (unchecked will appear before checked), and then Role. (*Hint:* Click the Team Task column heading, press and hold the Shift key, click the Role column heading, and then release the Shift key.)
18. Print all rows of the task list in Table Style.
19. Save the Team Tasks form from the forms library in the Outlook Tasks folder as **Team Tasks** in the **Tutorial.06\Cases** folder included with your Data Files, and then remove the form from the forms library.
20. Delete any items or customizations you created in this case, including the tasks, the Red Team folder, and the Shortcuts pane shortcut and group, and then empty the Deleted Items folder.

Case Problem 3

There are no Data Files needed for this Case Problem.

Steindler Travel Newsletter   Steindler Travel Newsletter provides travel and destination information to budget vacationers. The weekly newsletter includes information about little-known sales from airlines, hotels, and tour packagers. New subscribers are given a choice of promotional welcome gifts—a tote bag, a travel alarm clock, or a sleep mask. Barry Steindler, the founder of the newsletter, uses Outlook to store contact information about subscribers. He asks you to create a custom combination field that displays both partners' names and to create a list box (called combo box) from which he can select the promotional gift the new subscribers requested.

Challenge

Extend the skills you learned in the tutorial by creating custom fields to track subscriber promotions for a travel newsletter.

Explore

1. Add the Design This Form command to the Standard toolbar in a new item window. Open a new Task window, open the Customize dialog box, and then drag the Design This Form command from the Tools category on the Commands tab to the leftmost position on the Standard toolbar. Close the Customize dialog box, and then close the Task window.

2. Open a new Contact window, and then click the Design This Form button on the Standard toolbar to switch to design mode. (*Hint:* The button may not be in the left-most position.)

3. On the General tab of the Contact window, delete the Job Title and Company fields.

4. Insert the Spouse field from the Personal fields list below the Full Name field, and then change the fields' names and captions appropriately. Left-align each control with the appropriate control above it, and then horizontally align the Spouse controls with the Home controls in the next column.

Explore

5. Expand the Spouse text box so that it is the same width as the Full Name text box. (*Hint:* Make the Full Name text box the dominant control, click Layout on the menu bar, point to Make Same Size, and then click Width.)

Explore

6. Click the Control Toolbox button on the Form Design toolbar to open the Toolbox, click the TextBox button, and then click below the Spouse text box to add a text box to the form.

7. Resize and align the text box to match the dimensions and left-alignment of the Spouse text box. Middle-align the text box with the Business Fax field.

Explore

8. Open the new text box control's Properties dialog box, and then click the New button on the Value tab. Create a new field with the name "Household" and the type Combination, and then click the Edit button to open the Combination Formula Field dialog box.

Explore

9. Click the Field button, point to Name fields, click Spouse, type "and" in the Formula text box after "[Spouse]" (without the quotation marks), press the spacebar, click the Field button, point to Name fields, and click Full Name. The text "[Spouse] and [Full Name]" appears in the Formula text box.

10. Click the OK button in the Combination Formula Field dialog box, click the OK button in the New Field dialog box, click the Display tab, change the name to "HouseholdTextBox," and then click the OK button to close the Properties dialog box. The value will appear by default in the blank form.

Explore

11. Click the Label button in the Toolbox, click below the Spouse label to add a label to the left of the Household text box; open the label's Properties dialog box, and then change the name to "HouseholdLabel" and the caption to "Household:."

12. Resize and align the label to match the dimensions and left-alignment of the Spouse label box. Middle-align the label with the Household text box.

13. Test the form in run mode; type "Lisa Taylor" in the Full Name text box, type "Mark Quince" in the Spouse text box, verify that "Mark Quince and Lisa Taylor" appear in the Household text box, and then close the test form without saving changes.

14. Delete the Business Fax and Mobile fields from the right side of the form page.

Explore

15. Click the ComboBox button in the Toolbox, click the form below the Home field, and then open the combo box control's Properties dialog box.

Explore

16. Click the New button on the Value tab, create a custom field named "Promo" with Text as its type and format, and then click the OK button.

Explore

17. Click in the Possible values text box, and then type "Tote bag;Travel clock;Sleep mask" to enter the list box options. A semicolon separates each selection in a list.

18. On the Display tab, type "PromoComboBox" as the name, and then click the OK button.

Explore

19. Click the Label button in the Toolbox, and then add a label to the left of the Promo combo box with the caption "Promo Gift:" and the name "PromoLabel."

20. Resize and align the Promo controls appropriately on the form, and change the tab order as needed.

21. Test the form in run mode using fictitious data to verify the three selections in the list box, and then close the test form without saving changes.

Explore

22. Hide the Details tab in the form. (*Hint:* Click the Details tab, click Form on the menu bar, and then click Display This Page to remove the check mark.)

23. Save the form as a template with the name **Promotions Contact Template** in the **Tutorial.06\Cases** folder included with your Data Files, and then close the form without saving changes.

24. Open a new window using the form template you created, and then enter the following contact: full name "Lisa Taylor"; spouse "Mark Quince"; Promo list "Travel clock"; address type "Home"; and home mailing address as your address.

25. Print the contact, and then close the contact card without saving it.

26. Open a new Task window, remove the Design This Form button from the Standard toolbar, and then close the form without saving. (*Hint:* Press and hold the Alt key, drag the Design This Form button off the Standard toolbar, and then release the mouse button and Alt key.)

27. Delete the custom Promo and Household fields you created in the Contacts folder.

Case Problem 4

Create

Create a custom Contact form to track children and counselor interests for a camp.

There are no Data Files needed for this Case Problem.

Urban Camp Services Urban Camp Services (UCS) is a volunteer organization in Vancouver, Washington, that provides camp activities to children ages 5 through 18. UCS matches children with adult volunteers who have similar interests. In many cases, the children's parents or guardians request an adult counselor of a specific gender. UCS wants to track all this information in Outlook, and asks you to create a custom form.

1. Create a new form based on a Contact window.

2. Drag the Gender field and the Hobbies field from the Personal fields in the Field Chooser to page 2 of the form.

3. Rename the page 2 tab "Counselors."

4. Press the Ctrl+A keys to select all the fields on the form.

Explore

5. Click the Group button on the Design Form toolbar to combine the controls into one group. Now you can move the two fields as one group.

6. Drag the grouped fields down to make room for two fields above them.

Explore

7. Click the Ungroup button on the Design Form toolbar to separate the fields.

8. Show the Name fields in the Field Chooser, drag the Full Name field to the empty space you created at the top of the page, and then drag the Nickname field to the space below the Full Name field.

9. Change the fields' properties so that each control's name reflects the field caption and control type.

10. Adjust the tab order so that the user moves consecutively through the fields you added to the form.

11. Fix the alignment of the fields you added to the form as needed.

12. Display the form's Properties page, and then enter "Volunteers" as the Category, your name as the Contact, and the description "This form is used to record the gender and the interests of volunteer counselors."

13. Test the form, and then close the test form without saving it. Make any changes needed.

14. Publish the form in the Outlook Contacts folder with the display name "UCS Volunteer Counselors" and the Form name "Counselors." Close the form without saving changes.

15. Create a new contact based on the custom form, and then enter the following information on the Counselors tab: full name "Matthew Riker"; nickname "Matt"; gender "Male"; and Hobbies "football."

Explore ▶

16. Display the General tab, and then verify that Matt's full name appears on the page.

17. Create the following new contacts based on the custom form, and then enter the following information on the Counselors tab:

Full Name	Nickname	Gender	Hobbies
Marilyn Rosow	Rosie	Female	softball and archery
Susan Parvin	none	Female	soccer
Jesse Haskins	Jess	Male	computer games and chess

18. Customize Address Cards view to show the following fields below the File As field: Full Name, Nickname, Gender, and Hobbies. (You can leave the other fields in the view.)

19. Filter the contact list to show only the male counselors in the custom Address Cards view, and then print all items in the filtered contact list in Card Style.

20. Remove the filter, and then print all the contacts in the custom Address Cards view in Card Style.

21. Remove the fields you added to Address Cards view, and then delete the contacts you created.

22. Save the UCS Volunteer Counselors form from the forms library in the Outlook Contacts folder as **UCS Volunteer Counselors** in the **Tutorial.06\Cases** folder included with your Data Files, and then remove the form from the forms library.

23. Delete the contacts you created in this Case Problem, and then empty the Deleted Items folder.

Review

Quick Check Answers

Session 6.1

1. A form is a window in which you enter and view information about an item electronically.

2. (1) open an existing form in design mode; (2) modify the form; (3) test the form; (4) publish the form

3. A bound control is an object on a form in which a user enters information that Outlook displays (check boxes, list boxes, and text boxes); an unbound control is an object that displays text or images that users cannot edit (change) for informational or decorative purposes (text labels, lines, and images).

4. A simple field holds basic pieces of data, such as a name, amount, or date.

5. Tab order is the sequence that users move through fields on a form when they press the Tab key.

6. Publishing a form saves the form so you or others can use it in Outlook.

7. The Compose page shows what senders see when they create and send outgoing messages; the Read page shows what recipients see when they open and read incoming messages.

8. A template and a form both provide a blueprint of the fields and layout for an item, but a template is a separate file with the .oft extension.

Session 6.2

1. Adding a field to a view enables you to see the exact data you want in a folder's main window.

2. (1) Drag fields from the Field Chooser in any table view; (2) open the Show Fields dialog box, and select and order the fields that will be displayed in any view.

3. Outlook Today provides an overview of your current schedule, task list, and unread e-mail messages.

4. (1) If you regularly work with others in another time zone, displaying both time zones enables you to see the time differences without mental calculations. (2) If you regularly travel between time zones, you can swap time zones so your calendar and messages are converted to the time zone you're in.

5. Any three of the following: (1) resize the Navigation Pane buttons; (2) add, remove, and/or reorder the Navigation Pane buttons; (3) add and/or rename groups and shortcuts in the Shortcuts pane; (4) reorder shortcuts in the Shortcuts pane; (5) add and reorder folders in the All Mail Folders pane.

6. The All Mail Folders pane shows folders in alphabetical order; the Favorite Folders pane shows any mail folders you want in the order you want them to appear.

7. to group commands or buttons related to a specific task in one location

8. False. Toolbars can contain buttons with images, images and text, or only text. Menus can have text and images, or only text.

Objectives

- Set up an Exchange Server e-mail account
- Grant delegate access
- Generate an out of office message
- Create an Offline Folder file and offline folders
- Synchronize offline folders

Using Outlook with Microsoft Exchange Server

Microsoft Exchange Server (or just **Exchange**) is a mail server used for corporate messaging and collaboration systems that run under Windows 2000, Windows NT Server, and Windows XP. People who have access to the mail server are said to be on the Exchange for that server. If you use Outlook with Exchange, you have access to most capabilities of Outlook, including such features as:

- Group scheduling to plan a meeting, using the free/busy times of attendees, locations, and equipment (see Tutorial 3)

- Message recall to retrieve or replace messages that recipients have not yet opened (see Tutorial 4)

- Voting buttons to gather and track responses about topics by polling recipients through e-mail (see Tutorial 4)

- Public folders to share files and Outlook items among a group

- Delegate access permission to allow another person to work in your folders

- Out of Office Assistant to send an automatic response to incoming messages

- Offline folders to work remotely and synchronize folder contents with those on the Exchange Server computer

- Web access to Exchange for remote access to e-mail, calendar, and contacts

Exchange saves information on the server in **stores**. The Public store is used for shared information. Any user on the Exchange can create a public folder within the store, and then allow a specific group of people to access it, such as a workgroup, department, or entire organization. For example, human resources might post the company's calendar of upcoming events and holiday schedule for the year in a public folder so all employees can read it. The Private store is used for your e-mail messages and other personal information. If you'd like, you can grant specific people access to folders in your Private store. You can also choose to save your e-mail messages and other information in a Personal Folders file on your computer's hard drive.

Student Data Files

There are no student Data Files needed for this appendix.

Setting Up an Exchange Server E-Mail Account

If you are working in a corporate environment and have an Exchange Server e-mail account, your network administrator has likely set up Outlook to work with that e-mail account for you. However, you can also easily set up an Exchange Server e-mail account in Outlook yourself.

To set up an Exchange Server e-mail account:

1. Exit Outlook if necessary, click **Start**, click **Control Panel**, click the **Mail** icon, and then click the **E-mail Accounts** button. The E-mail Accounts dialog box opens.
2. Click the **Add a new e-mail account** option button, and then click the **Next** button.
3. Click the **Microsoft Exchange Server** option button, and then click the **Next** button. See Figure A-1.

Figure A-1 E-mail Accounts dialog box

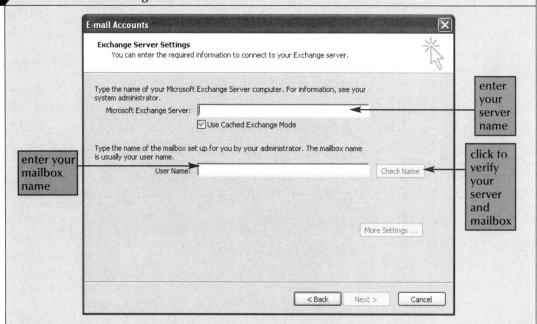

4. Enter the appropriate information provided by your network administrator.
5. Click the **Check Name** button. Outlook verifies that Exchange Server recognizes your name and server, and then underlines them to indicate that the verification was successful.

   Trouble? If the check is unsuccessful, double-check the information you entered in Step 4 and verify that your computer is connected to your network, and then repeat Step 5. If the check is still unsuccessful, ask your network administrator or technical support person for help.

6. Click the **Next** button, and then click the **Finish** button. The Exchange Server e-mail account is set up.

   Trouble? If a dialog box opens warning that Mail from this Microsoft Exchange Server account will be delivered to the existing Personal folder on your local computer, click the Yes button.

7. Close any open dialog boxes.

After your Exchange Server e-mail account it set up, you can work with all the features of Outlook.

Setting Permissions for Delegate Access

If you have a secretary, an assistant, or anyone else who sends your e-mail messages or schedules your appointments and meetings for you, then you can make that person a delegate so he or she can perform these actions on your behalf right from Outlook. A **delegate** is a person who has permission to access someone else's folders on the Exchange. You can have many delegates. Depending on the assigned permissions level, a delegate may read, create, modify, and delete items from folders you designate. The folder owner determines which folders the delegates can access and what permissions level the delegates have. You can grant delegate access to your Calendar, Tasks, Inbox, Contacts, Notes, and Journal folders, choosing one of the following permissions level for each folder:

- **None.** No permission; delegates cannot open a folder and cannot read, create, or modify items.
- **Reviewer.** Delegates can read items, but cannot create, modify, or delete items.
- **Author.** Delegates can read and create items, and can modify and delete only items they created.
- **Editor.** Delegates can read, create, modify, and delete any items.

If you assign more than one delegate to the same folder, each delegate can receive a different permissions level. For example, you might give an administrative assistant Editor delegate access to your Inbox, Calendar, Tasks, and Contacts folders, which enables that person to manage your messages, your schedule, send and reply to meeting and task requests, and update your contact list. You then might want to allow a colleague only Reviewer access to your Inbox so that person can read (but not create, modify, or delete) your messages while you are out of the office. You decide how much you want delegates to be able to do for you and from which folders.

The **Global Address List** is an address book created and maintained by a network administrator that contains all user, group, and distribution list e-mail addresses in your organization. Exchange users see the Global Address List in addition to their Contacts folder. The Global Address List is available from the list of address books in Outlook.

The Delegate Access feature is available only when you have an Exchange Server e-mail account. You must be connected to the server, and the Delegate Access add-in must be installed.

To complete the steps in this section, you'll need to work with a classmate who is on your Exchange. Otherwise, you should read but not complete these sections.

To set sharing permissions for a delegate:

1. Click **Tools** on the menu bar, click **Options** to open the Options dialog box, and then click the **Delegates** tab. See Figure A-2.

Figure A-2 | **Delegates tab in the Options dialog box**

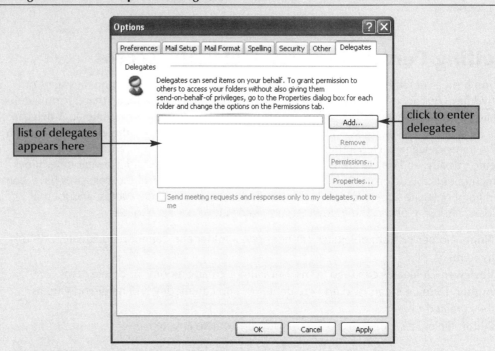

list of delegates appears here

click to enter delegates

Trouble? If the Delegates tab is not available, then you need to install the Delegate Access add-in. Click the Other tab in the Options dialog box, click the Advanced Options button, and then click the Add-In Manager button in the Advanced Options dialog box. Click the Delegate Access check box to insert a check mark, and then click the OK button. If the Delegate Access check box is not available, click the Install button, and then set up the add-in. Click the OK button in the Add-In Manager dialog box, and then click the OK button in the Advanced Options dialog box. If you still have trouble, ask your instructor or technical support person for help.

▶ **2.** Click the **Add** button. The Add Users dialog box opens. See Figure A-3.

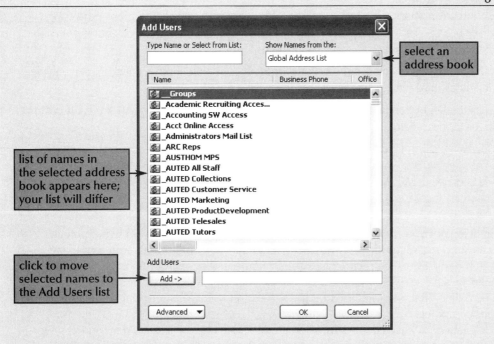

The Add Users dialog box shows the contacts in the selected address book; you can change this to another address book if needed.

3. Click the **Show Names from the** list arrow, and then click the address book you want.

4. Click your classmate's name (the name of the person for whom you want to set delegate permissions) in the Type Name or Select from List box, and then click the **Add** button. If you wanted to add more than one delegate, you would press the Ctrl key as you click multiple names.

5. Click the **OK** button in the Add Users dialog box. The Delegate Permissions dialog box opens, enabling you to assign a permissions level for the users you selected. See Figure A-4.

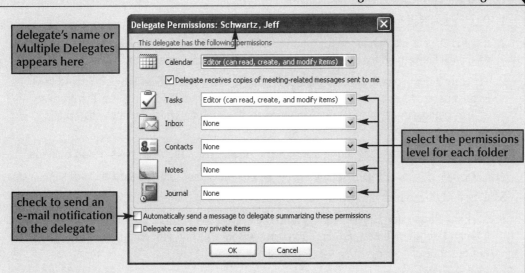

Trouble? If a dialog box opens, prompting you to set permissions levels for the delegates, click the OK button.

6. For each Outlook item, click the list arrow, and then select the appropriate permissions level.

7. Click the **Automatically send a message to delegate summarizing these permissions** check box to insert a check mark. Outlook will send a message to the delegates notifying them of their delegate status and permissions.

8. Click the **Delegate can see my private items** check box to insert a check mark if you want delegates to be able to view your private items.

9. Click the **OK** button in the Delegate Permissions dialog box, and then click the **OK** button in the Options dialog box.

10. Download your messages, if necessary, open and read the message sent by your classmate informing you that you have delegate status in his or her private folders, and then close the Message window.

The delegates you specified now have **send-on-behalf-of permission**, which means they can send messages for you. Messages sent this way contain both your name and the delegate's name. Message recipients see your name in the Sent On Behalf Of text box and the delegate's name in the From text box in the Message window. In addition, your e-mail must be delivered to your mailbox on the server and not into a Personal Folders file stored on your computer.

A delegate must have Editor permission for your Calendar or Tasks folder and Reviewer permission in your Inbox to accept meeting or task requests for you. If you check the Send meeting requests and responses only to my delegates, not to me check box on the Delegates tab in the Options dialog box, then the delegate does not need Reviewer permission for the Inbox. The delegate receives any meeting requests and responses directly in his or her Inbox.

Sending an E-Mail for Someone Else

Before someone can send an e-mail for you, you must grant that person Author or Editor delegate permission. You must also share your Exchange mailbox with the delegate. You have already set the delegate access. Next, you'll share your Exchange mailbox.

To share your Exchange mailbox:

1. Display the **Mail** folder.

2. Right-click your **Exchange** mailbox in the All Mail Folders pane in the Navigation Pane, and then click **Sharing** on the shortcut menu. The Properties dialog box for Outlook today opens.

   Trouble? If you already see the delegate's name, then you clicked Inbox in the All Mail Folders pane rather than your Exchange mailbox. Close the dialog box, and then repeat Step 2, being careful to click your Exchange mailbox folder, which is usually listed as "Mailbox – *user name.*"

3. Click the **Permissions** tab, and then click the **Add** button. The Add Users dialog box opens.

4. Click your classmate's name in the Name list box, and then click the **Add** button.

5. Click the **OK** button in the Add Users dialog box to return to the Properties dialog box.

6. Click the **Permission Level** list arrow, and then select the appropriate permissions level (Owner, Publishing Editor, Editor, Publishing Author, Author, Nonediting Author, Reviewer, or Contributor).

7. Click the **OK** button.

In order to send an e-mail, the delegate must then set up an e-mail account for your mailbox on his or her computer, and then send the e-mail message specifying you as the sender.

To set up an e-mail account for someone else's mailbox:

1. Click **Tools** on the menu bar, and then click **E-mail Accounts** to open the E-mail Accounts dialog box.
2. Click the **View or change existing e-mail accounts** option button, and then click the **Next** button.
3. Select your Exchange account, and then click the **Change** button.
4. Click the **More Settings** button to open the Microsoft Exchange Server dialog box, and then click the **Advanced** tab.
5. Click the **Add** button in the Mailboxes area. The Add Mailboxes dialog box opens.
6. Type the name of your classmate's mailbox in the Add Mailbox text box (the mailbox name is usually the person's full name), and then click the **OK** button.
7. Click the **OK** button, click the **Next** button, and then click the **Finish** button. The other person's mailbox appears in the All Mail Folders pane or the Folder List in the Navigation Pane.

Sending an e-mail on behalf of someone else is then very similar to sending one from yourself. The main difference is that you enter the other person's name in the From text box in the message header. Although you can click the From button and select any name in the Global Address List, you cannot send a message for that person unless they have granted you permission to do so.

To send an e-mail for someone else:

1. Click the **New** button list arrow on the Standard toolbar, and then click **Mail Message**. A new Message window opens.
2. Type your classmate's name (the person for whom you are sending the message) in the From text box. If you do not enter a name in the From text box, the message will be sent from you.

    Trouble? If you don't see the From text box, you'll need to display it. If you are using Word as your e-mail editor, click the Options button list arrow on the message toolbar, and then click From. If you are using the Outlook mail editor, click View on the menu bar and then click From Field.
3. Type the message in the message area and then send the message as usual.

    The recipient will see the name of the person you entered as the sender.
4. Download your messages, if necessary, and then read the message you received from your classmate. Note the name of the sender.

Setting Delegate Access to Share Tasks

If you have received delegate access with Editor permission to someone else's Tasks folder, you in effect have a shared task list and can read, create, and modify that person's tasks. In addition, you can send and respond to task requests.

Assigned delegates can open the folders you specified. Any items created by a delegate who has Author or Editor permission while the shared folder is active are stored in your folder.

To open another person's folder:

1. Click **File** on the menu bar, point to **Open**, and then click **Other User's Folder**. The Open Other User's Folder dialog box opens. See Figure A-5.

2. Click the **Name** button to open the Select Name dialog box, click your classmate's name, and then click the **OK** button.

3. Click the **Folder type** list arrow, and then click **Tasks** (or the name of the folder you want to open).

4. Click the **OK** button. The Tasks main window opens in a separate window.

Trouble? If a dialog box opens with the message "Unable to display folder," then you probably have not received delegate permission from the folder owner.

Once the folder is open, you can create an item for that person. The item's window, such as a Task window or Contact window, has the same options as when you create that item in your own folder. The task would appear on the task list in the owner's Tasks folder; a contact would appear in the owner's Contacts folder.

To create a task in another person's Tasks folder:

1. Click the **New** button list arrow on the Standard toolbar, and then click **Task**. A new Task window opens.

Trouble? If a dialog box opens, saying that you cannot create a task for the other person, then the folder owner probably did not assign you an adequate delegate permissions level.

2. Type a task name in the Subject text box, and then set a due date.

3. Set any other task options, just as you would for a task you create from your own Tasks folder.

4. Save and close the task. The task appears on the task list in your classmate's Tasks folder.

When you're done working in the other person's folder for which you have delegate access, you should close the folder.

To close the other person's Tasks folder and view a task created for you:

1. Click the **Close** button on the Standard toolbar. The other person's folder closes.

2. Open your Tasks folder, and then open and read the task your classmate created for you.

3. Close the Task window.

If you don't have an assistant or someone else who can review your messages as a delegate when you're out of the office, then you might want to create an out of office message.

Setting an Out of Office Message

When you are on vacation or don't have access to your e-mail for a time, anyone who sends you a message and doesn't receive a timely response might think that you are either ignoring the message or never received it—either scenario is bad business practice. Rather than leave senders wondering, you can set up the Out of Office Assistant to respond to messages that arrive during your absence. The activated **Out of Office Assistant** sends an automated reply message that you specify to all the senders of incoming messages, even when your computer is turned off. Before you leave, turn on the Out of Office Assistant, type the message you want sent, and then set up rules for any exceptions. While you're enjoying time away, Outlook replies automatically to every message with your preset response.

To use the Out of Office Assistant, you must be using Outlook with Exchange Server and have the Exchange Extensions add-in installed.

To set up the Out of Office Assistant:

1. Display the **Inbox**.
2. Click **Tools** on the menu bar, and then click **Out of Office Assistant**. The Out of Office Assistant dialog box opens. See Figure A-6.

Out of Office Assistant dialog box   **Figure A-6**

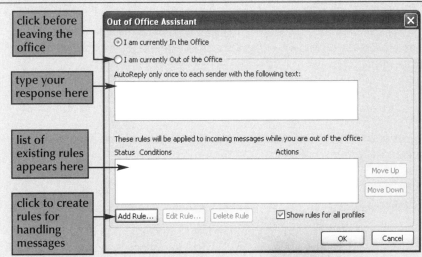

Trouble? If you don't see Out of Office Assistant on the Tools menu, the feature may not be available. Make sure you are using Outlook with Exchange Server and have the Exchange Extensions add-in installed. If you need further assistance, ask your instructor or technical support person for help.

3. Click the **I am currently Out of the Office** option button to turn on the Out of Office Assistant.
4. Click in the **AutoReply only once to each sender with the following text** text box, and then type **I am out of the office until Tuesday. I will respond to your message when I return.**
5. Click the **Add Rule** button to open the Edit Rule dialog box.

You could set up rules to have some messages handled differently, such as deleting messages from a certain e-mail address or forwarding them to another person. Each rule you add slows down the processing of your mail, so you might consider responding to all messages with the same generic reply without exception.

6. Click the **Cancel** button to close the Edit Rule dialog box without adding any rules, and then click the **OK** button in the Out of Office Assistant dialog box.

If you are enrolled in any listservs, be aware that the Out of Office Assistant will respond to every posting you receive, which in turn will be distributed to the entire group. Some listserv moderators will drop you from the list if you do this, even if you do it unintentionally. Instead, don't use the AutoReply, add the listservs to your exception list, or manage the listserv subscriptions by setting them to NOMail or unsubscribe.

When you return to the office and start Outlook and connect to your e-mail server, a dialog box opens to remind you that the Out of Office Assistant is turned on. You can then choose to leave the Out of Office Assistant on or turn it off. If you turn it off, the AutoReply and any rules you created remain intact (but inactive) so you can reuse them next time. All the messages that arrived while the Out of Office Assistant was turned on appear in the Inbox or in folders according to the rules you set up.

To turn off the Out of Office Assistant:

1. Click **Tools** on the menu bar, and then click **Out of Office Assistant**. The Out of Office Assistant dialog box opens.

2. Click the **I am currently In the Office** option button to turn off the Out of Office Assistant.

3. Delete any rules and the text you typed in the AutoReply text box, as needed. Any text or rules that you leave in the dialog box will be available the next time you use the Out of Office Assistant.

4. Click the **OK** button.

You can also access your messages and calendar as well as the public folders on the server when you are away from your office.

Working Remotely

If you often spend time at various locations, you might find it convenient to be able to use a laptop computer to send and receive messages and schedule upcoming events on your calendar. By setting up Outlook to work offline (disconnected from a server), you can manage e-mail messages and other items while you are away from your office.

Working with Offline Folders

The simplest way to work offline with Exchange is with offline folders, which enable you to keep identical information on the server and your remote computer. **Offline folders** are folders on your remote computer's hard drive that duplicate the contents of Outlook folders stored on the server, including the Inbox, Outbox, Deleted Items, Sent Items, Calendar, Contacts, Tasks, Journal, Notes, and Drafts folders. You work with the contents of these offline folders just as you do with folders on Exchange Server. For example, you can edit and move items in your offline Inbox and send messages that are placed in your offline Outbox. Offline folders are stored in the **Offline Folder file** on your computer's hard disk.

The basic process for setting up offline folders for a remote computer to work with Exchange Server is:

1. Install Outlook on the remote computer, and then set up an Exchange Server e-mail account.
2. Create an Offline Folder file.
3. Select the custom folders you want available.
4. Specify the dial-up connection you want to use.
5. Download the Global Address List.
6. Synchronize the offline folders with the Exchange folders.
7. Set Outlook to start offline.
8. Exit Outlook, and then start Outlook from a remote location.

After you have Outlook set up on your remote computer and set up an Exchange Server e-mail account, you can create the Offline Folder file. An Offline Folder file can be created automatically when you set up Outlook, or you can create one when you first make a folder available offline. You must have an Exchange Server e-mail account to create and use an Offline Folder file. The following steps assume you have an existing Exchange Server e-mail account.

To create an Offline Folder file:

1. Click **Tools** on the menu bar, and then click **E-mail Accounts**. The E-mail Accounts dialog box opens.

2. Click the **View or change existing e-mail accounts** option button, and then click the **Next** button.

3. Click **Microsoft Exchange Server** in the list box, and then click the **Change** button.

4. Click the **More Settings** button to open the Microsoft Exchange Server dialog box, and then click the **Advanced** tab. See Figure A-7.

Advanced tab in the Microsoft Exchange Server dialog box ◄ **Figure A-7**

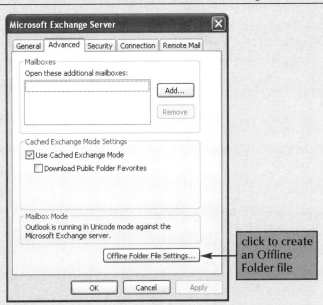

click to create an Offline Folder file

5. Click the **Offline Folder File Settings** button. The Offline Folder File Settings dialog box opens. See Figure A-8.

| **Figure A-8** | **Offline Folder File Settings dialog box** |

6. Type the path for your Offline Folder file in the File text box (or click the **Browse** button, navigate to the folder, type the filename, and then click the **Open** button).

Encryption encodes the file to make it unreadable by other programs. The encryption settings are the same as those for the Personal Folders file (see Tutorial 5). No Encryption does not encode your file. Compressible Encryption encodes the file in a format that allows compression; the file is compressed only if you have a compression program set up on your computer. Best Encryption encodes the file in a format that offers the greatest degree of protection; if you have a disk-compression program, the file can be compressed but to a lesser degree than allowed by the Compressible Encryption option. Be aware that you cannot change the encryption setting later.

7. Click the **No Encryption** option button.

Trouble? If the No Encryption option button is not available, leave the default option selected.

8. Click the **OK** button to close the Offline Folder File Settings dialog box. A dialog box opens with the message that the file couldn't be found and asks whether you want to create the file

Trouble? If a dialog box opens warning that the next time you log in you will not be able to work with offline folders, click the Yes button.

9. Click the **Yes** button to return to the Microsoft Exchange Server dialog box, and then click the **OK** button to return to the E-mail Accounts dialog box.

10. Click the **Next** button, and then click the **Finish** button. Your remote computer includes an Offline Folder file that contains a copy of the folders in your Exchange store.

The Inbox, Outbox, Deleted Items, Sent Items, Calendar, Contacts, Tasks, Journal, Notes, and Drafts folders are automatically available offline when you set up offline folders. If you want to use any other folders offline, you must set them up for offline use.

To set a custom folder for offline use:

1. Display the **Folder List**, if necessary, and then click the custom folder you want to use offline in the Folder List.

2. Click **Tools** on the menu bar, point to **Send/Receive**, point to **Send/Receive Settings**, and then click **Make This Folder Available Offline**.

You can set more than one folder at a time for offline use.

To set custom folders for offline use:

1. Select the custom folders you want to use offline in the Folder List.

2. Click **Tools** on the menu bar, point to **Send/Receive**, point to **Send/Receive Settings**, and then click **Define Send/Receive Groups**. The Send/Receive Groups dialog box opens. See Figure A-9.

Send/Receive Groups dialog box | Figure A-9

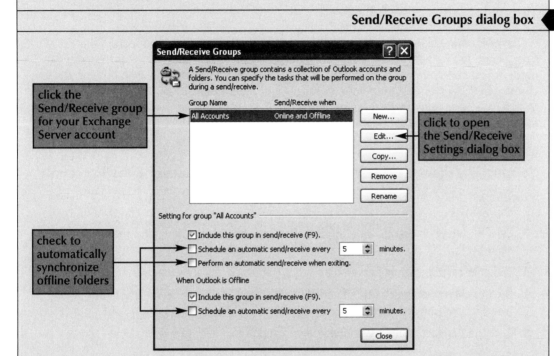

click the Send/Receive group for your Exchange Server account

click to open the Send/Receive Settings dialog box

check to automatically synchronize offline folders

3. Click a Send/Receive group with an Exchange Server account, and then click the **Edit** button. The Send/Receive Settings dialog box opens. See Figure A-10.

Send/Receive Settings dialog box | Figure A-10

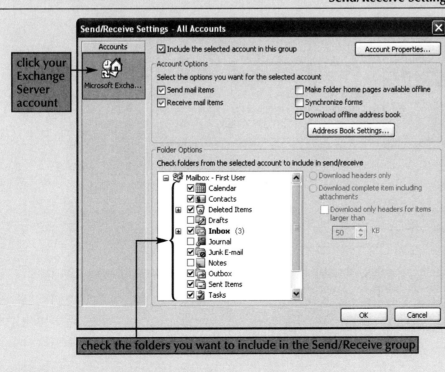

click your Exchange Server account

check the folders you want to include in the Send/Receive group

4. Click your Exchange Server account in the Accounts list.

5. Click the check boxes of the folders that you want to use offline in addition to your default folders.

6. Click the **OK** button in the Send/Receive Settings dialog box, and then click the **Close** button in the Send/Receive Groups dialog box.

To work offline using a modem, you'll need to select the dial-up connection on the Connection tab in the Microsoft Exchange Server dialog box. Your computer must have a modem and dial-up networking software, and be connected to a telephone line for you to connect to the server and send your messages and other items. If you are working offline from a local area network (LAN) with a dial-up, DSL, cable, or other type of connection, then you just select the LAN option in the dialog box.

To specify a dial-up connection for your Exchange Server e-mail account:

1. Click **Tools** on the menu bar, and then click **E-mail Accounts**. The E-mail Accounts dialog box opens.

2. Click the **View or change existing e-mail accounts** option button, and then click the **Next** button.

3. Click **Microsoft Exchange Server** in the list box, and then click the **Change** button.

4. Click the **More Settings** button to open the Microsoft Exchange Server dialog box, and then click the **Connection** tab.

5. Click the **Connect using my phone line** option button. See Figure A-11.

| Figure A-11 | Connection tab in the Microsoft Exchange Server dialog box |

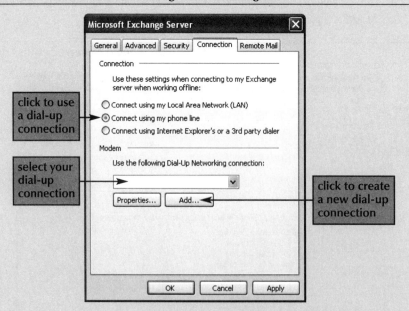

6. In the Modem group, click the **Use the following Dial-Up Networking connection** list arrow, and then click the appropriate dial-up connection.

7. Click the **OK** button to return to the E-mail Accounts dialog box.

8. Click the **Next** button, and then click the **Finish** button.

If you plan to send e-mail while you are working remotely, you'll need to copy the Global Address List to your remote computer.

To copy the Global Address List to a remote computer:

1. Click **Tools** on the menu bar, point to **Send/Receive**, and then click **Download Address Book**. The Offline Address Book dialog box opens. See Figure A-12.

Offline Address Book dialog box ◀ **Figure A-12**

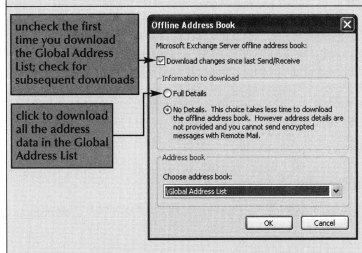

uncheck the first time you download the Global Address List; check for subsequent downloads

click to download all the address data in the Global Address List

2. Click the **Download changes since last Send/Receive** check box to remove the check mark if this is the first time you are downloading the Global Address List; otherwise, verify that the check box contains a check mark.

3. Click the **Full Details** option button. The download time is longer for this option, but you have access to the address details.

4. Click the **OK** button. The Global Address List is downloaded onto your remote computer.

The next step is to synchronize the folders on your remote computer with those on your desktop computer.

Synchronizing Folders

Once you have determined which folders will be available offline, you synchronize the offline folders with the Exchange folders. **Synchronizing** is the process of updating the folders on your remote computer and the corresponding folders on the server so their contents are identical. You can choose to manually synchronize a selected offline folder, a group of offline folders, or all of your offline folders. You need to synchronize your folders when you set up your offline folders, and then periodically as you work offline to ensure that the folders on both your remote computer and the server contain the same items and information.

To manually synchronize offline folders:

▶ **1.** If necessary, select the offline folder you want to synchronize.

▶ **2.** Click **Tools** on the menu bar, point to **Send/Receive**, and then click **This Folder** to synchronize the selected folder or click **Send/Receive All** to synchronize all your offline folders.

Outlook copies the changes made in each folder to the other folder, and then disconnects. Any item that is deleted from either the offline folder or the corresponding Exchange folder is deleted from both.

If you prefer, you can set up a specific interval in which Outlook automatically synchronizes the folders on your remote computer and the Exchange server. From the Send/Receive Groups dialog box, you can set up Outlook to synchronize your offline folders when you disconnect and/or during specified time intervals while you are working. You can set an interval from 1 to 1440 minutes for when your remote computer is online as well as for when your remote computer is offline; the default time is every 5 minutes. You can also have Outlook synchronize the folders whenever you exit Outlook while working online from your remote computer.

To automatically synchronize offline folders:

▶ **1.** Click **Tools** on the menu bar, point to **Send/Receive**, point to **Send/Receive Settings**, and then click **Define Send/Receive Groups**. The Send/Receive Groups dialog box opens.

▶ **2.** Click your Exchange Server account in the Group Name list.

▶ **3.** Under Setting for group "All Accounts," click the **Schedule an automatic send/receive every** check box to insert a check mark, and then type **5** in the minutes text box.

▶ **4.** Click the **Perform an automatic send/receive when exiting** check box to insert a check mark.

▶ **5.** In the When Outlook is Offline group, click the **Schedule an automatic send/receive every** check box to insert a check mark, and then type **5** in the minutes text box.

▶ **6.** Click the **Close** button.

You can save space and downloading time by synchronizing your offline folder in Cached Exchange Mode. In **Cached Exchange Mode**, a copy of your mailbox is stored on your computer and is frequently updated with the mail server.

You can also prevent large messages from downloading when you synchronize by setting a message size limit. If you use a dial-up connection with your remote computer, large messages can take a long time to download, tying up your computer and phone line. Instead, you can create a Large Messages folder on your server and create a rule that moves large messages to this folder. The Large Messages folder is not included when you synchronize your Inbox, but its contents are still available on the mail server the next time you work online. You can add exceptions to the Large Message rule; for example, you might specify that messages from specific clients be delivered regardless of their size.

The last step before working from a remote location is to select the startup setting of Outlook on your remote computer. You can have Outlook automatically detect your connection state, or you can manually control the connection state each time you start. If you select the automatic option, Outlook determines whether you are online or offline when you start; if available, it connects to the server so you have access to the Exchange store. The automatic detection option is most appropriate if you sometimes start your remote computer connected to the server and sometimes start it not connected. If you select the manual option, you can select from three options: (1) choose whether to connect to the server or work offline each time you start Outlook; (2) always connect to the server; or (3) work offline and use dial-up networking. You'll set Outlook to always start offline.

To set Outlook to start offline:

1. Click **Tools** on the menu bar, and then click **E-mail Accounts**. The E-mail Accounts dialog box opens.

2. Click the **View or change existing e-mail accounts** option button, and then click the **Next** button.

3. Click **Microsoft Exchange Server** in the list box, and then click the **Change** button.

4. Click the **More Settings** button to open the Microsoft Exchange Server dialog box, and then click the **General** tab in the Microsoft Exchange Server dialog box.

5. Click the **Manually control connection state** option button in the When starting group. See Figure A-13.

General tab in the Microsoft Exchange Server dialog box ◀ **Figure A-13**

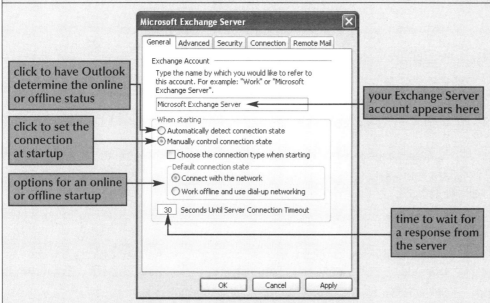

6. Click the **Work offline and use dial-up networking** option button. This sets Outlook to always start offline.

7. Click the **OK** button in the Microsoft Exchange Server dialog box.

8. Click the **Next** button, and then click the **Finish** button. The E-mail Accounts dialog box closes.

When you exit Outlook, you can start Outlook from an offline location. As you work offline, Outlook connects to the server at the interval you specified so you can periodically synchronize your folders. As you did above, you can also manually synchronize an individual offline folder or all your offline folders at one time.

When you are done working remotely, you can reset Outlook to work online, and then either disable or delete the Offline Folder file you created.

To set Outlook to start online:

1. Click **Tools** on the menu bar, and then click **E-mail Accounts**. The E-mail Accounts dialog box opens.
2. Click the **View or change existing e-mail accounts** option button, and then click the **Next** button.
3. Click **Microsoft Exchange Server** in the list box, and then click the **Change** button.
4. Click the **More Settings** button to open the Microsoft Exchange Server dialog box, and then click the **General** tab in the Microsoft Exchange Server dialog box.
5. Click the **Automatically detect connection state** option button.
6. Click the **OK** button in the Microsoft Exchange Server dialog box.
7. Click the **Next** button, and then click the **Finish** button. The E-mail Accounts dialog box closes.

At some point, you may no longer have the ability or need to work remotely. If you are passing the laptop to someone else in your organization, you may want to remove your personal files and folders from the computer. You can delete the Offline Folder file you created.

To delete an Offline Folder file:

1. Click **Tools** on the menu bar, and then click **E-mail Accounts**. The E-mail Accounts dialog box opens.
2. Click the **View or change existing e-mail accounts** option button, and then click the **Next** button.
3. Click **Microsoft Exchange Server** in the list box, and then click the **Change** button.
4. Click the **More Settings** button to open the Microsoft Exchange Server dialog box, and then click the **Advanced** tab.
5. Click the **Offline Folder File Settings** button. The Offline Folder File Settings dialog box opens.
6. Click the **Disable Offline Use** check box to insert a check mark, and then click the **Browse** button to open the New Offline File Folder dialog box.
7. Click the Offline Folder file you created, and then press the **Delete** key.
8. Click the **Yes** button to confirm the deletion.
9. Click the **Cancel** button to close the New Offline Folder File dialog box.
10. Click the **OK** button in the Offline Folder File Settings dialog box, and then click the **OK** button in the Microsoft Exchange Server dialog box.
11. Click the **Next** button, and then click the **Finish** button.

When you use Outlook with Exchange Server, you have the flexibility to work uninterrupted even from a remote location. If you don't have Exchange Server and want to be able to manage your e-mail, contacts, tasks, and calendar remotely, you might consider using a personal digital assistant (PDA) and then synchronizing that information with Outlook. Appendix C reviews options available to you with PDAs and Outlook.

Review

Appendix A Quick Check

1. What is Microsoft Exchange Server?
2. Exchange saves information on the server in _____.
3. What is a delegate?
4. What does the Out of Office Assistant do?
5. Define offline folders.
6. Where are offline folders stored?
7. What is the Global Address List?
8. Explain synchronizing.

Review

Appendix Summary

In this appendix, you learned about how to use Outlook with Exchange Server. You set up an Exchange Server e-mail account. You granted delegate access, and then sent an e-mail message and set up a task for someone else. You set up an Out of Office message. You also created an Offline Folder file and offline folders, and learned to synchronize them.

Key Terms

Cached Exchange Mode	Microsoft Exchange Server	send-on-behalf-of permission
delegate	offline folder	store
Exchange	Offline Folder file	synchronize
Global Address List	Out of Office Assistant	

Practice

Practice the skills you learned in the appendix.

Review Assignments

There are no Data Files needed for the Review Assignments.

When you use Outlook with Exchange, you have greater flexibility and additional options for managing your folders and items. In these Review Assignments, you'll grant a class-mate delegate access to your Inbox and Contacts folder. Then you'll set an out of office message. Finally, you'll create an Offline Folder file and set up Outlook for offline use from a remote computer.

1. Assign a classmate Editor delegate access to your Inbox and Contacts folders. Send a notification message to the delegate about his or her delegate status and permissions. (Your classmate should assign you the same access.)
2. Download the notification message, and then open your classmate's Contacts folder.
3. Create a contact card with your name and your e-mail address in the other person's Contacts folder.
4. Close the other person's Contacts folder.
5. Confirm that the contact card your classmate created appears in your Contacts folder.
6. Use the Out of Office Assistant to set the AutoReply message "Thank you for your message. I am out of the office until next Monday. I will respond to your message then. Thank you." and then type your name.
7. Send a message to your e-mail with the subject "Need a reply" and the message "Are you available for lunch tomorrow?"

8. Download the AutoReply message and the message you sent, and then turn off the Out of Office Assistant and delete the AutoReply message.
9. Create an Offline Folder file, using your name as the filename.
10. Create a subfolder named "Offline" that contains Mail and Post Items placed within the Inbox.
11. Set the custom Offline Folder file for offline use.
12. Specify a dial-up connection for your Exchange Server e-mail account.
13. Set Outlook to automatically synchronize your offline folders every three minutes when online or offline. Do not synchronize when exiting.
14. Set Outlook to work offline and use your dial-up connection.
15. Send a message to your e-mail address with the subject "Working Remotely" and the message "This message should arrive from your offline location." Download the message, if necessary.
16. Exit Outlook, and then restart Outlook from an offline location.
17. Synchronize your offline folders. The Working Remotely message should appear in your offline Inbox.
18. Set Outlook to start online.
19. Delete the Offline Folder file you created.
20. Delete the contact card, messages, and folder you created, and then empty the Deleted Items folder.

Review

Quick Check Answers

1. a mail server used for corporate messaging and collaboration systems that runs under Windows 2000, Windows NT Server, and Windows XP
2. stores
3. A delegate is a person who has permission to access someone else's folders.
4. The activated Out of Office Assistant sends an automated reply message that you specify to all the senders of incoming messages even when your computer is turned off.
5. Offline folders are folders on your remote computer's hard drive that duplicate the contents of Outlook folders stored on the server, including the Inbox, Outbox, Deleted Items, Sent Items, Calendar, Contacts, Tasks, Journal, Notes, and Drafts folders.
6. Offline folders are stored in the Offline Folder file on your computer's hard disk.
7. The Global Address List is an address book created and maintained by a network administrator that contains all user, group, and distribution list e-mail addresses in your organization.
8. Synchronizing is the process of updating the folders on your remote computer and the corresponding folders on the server so their contents are identical.

Objectives

- Install Business Contact Manager
- Associate a new or existing database with Business Contact Manager
- Add business contacts and accounts
- Create an opportunity
- Update the History list for business contacts and accounts
- Track progress with reports

Using Business Contact Manager

Business Contact Manager is an add-in program for Outlook that enables you to track customer and account data from Outlook. The data you collect for these customers and accounts are stored in a database on your computer. A **database** is a collection of related records stored in one file. A **record** is a collection of related fields of data stored as a unit. For example, all the data related to one contact can be considered a record. Recall that a field is an individual unit of data, such as a first name, a last name, or a job title.

After you install Business Contact Manager, the Business Contact Manager folder appears in the Folder List. It contains subfolders to store contacts, tasks, and a journal with the actual data you collect. The Business Tools menu, which you can use to navigate the Business Contact Manager folders, appears on the menu bar.

Business Contact Manager can be used with HTTP-based and POP e-mail accounts, Microsoft Small Business Server, and hosted Microsoft Exchange servers only. If you are using a different version of Exchange, you can create one profile with your Exchange Server e-mail account, and a second profile for the Business Contact Manager database.

Student Data Files

There are no student Data Files needed for this appendix.

Starting Business Contact Manager

Business Contact Manager is an add-in program for Outlook 2003. If it is not already installed, then you'll need to use the Business Contact Manager Setup Wizard on the Business Contact Manager for Microsoft Office Outlook 2003 CD to install the program. (If you do not have access to the Business Contact Manager for Microsoft Office Outlook 2003 CD, ask your technical support person for help.) After Business Contact Manager is installed, you can select the profiles with which it will run.

To start Business Contact Manager for the first time:

1. Start Outlook, and then select the profile with which you want to use Business Contact Manager. The Microsoft Outlook with Business Contact Manager dialog box opens. See Figure B-1.

| Figure B-1 | Microsoft Outlook with Business Contact Manager dialog box |

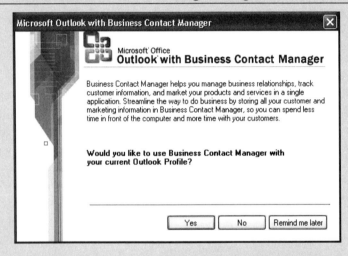

Trouble? If the Microsoft Outlook with Business Contact Manager dialog box does not open, compare your screen to Figure B-2. If Business Tools appears on the menu bar, Business Contact Manager has already been set up for this Outlook profile. Skip Steps 2 and 3.

2. Click the **Yes** button. After a few moments, Outlook Today appears. A new menu, the Business Tools menu, is on the menu bar, a new toolbar appears below the Standard toolbar, and Business Contact Manager appears at the bottom of the Folder List. The Welcome to Microsoft Outlook with Business Contact Manager message appears in your Inbox. See Figure B-2.

Business Contact Manager added to profile | **Figure B-2**

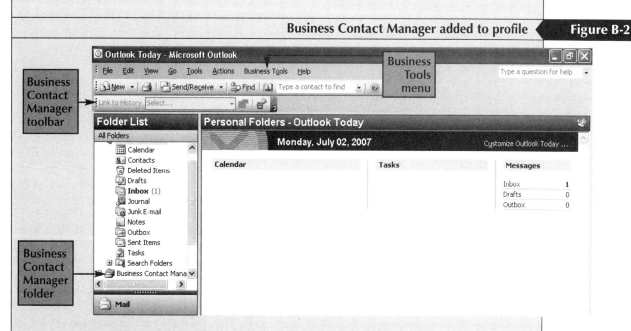

> **3.** Read the **Welcome to Microsoft Outlook with Business Contact Manager** message in your Inbox, and then delete it.

Business Contact Manager is set up and ready to use with your profile.

Associating a New or Existing Database

Although Business Contact Manager installs with a new database associated with the Business Contact Manager folder, sometimes you may want to associate it with another database or create a new database. For example, you might use an existing database someone else created that already contains the records you need, or you might want to create a new database to use for a specific purpose and keep it separate from other databases. In either case, you can associate Business Contact Manager with a new or different database using the Associate Database Wizard. After you complete the steps to associate the database you need to exit and restart Outlook in order to see the new database.

You can associate only one database at a time with each user profile. If you want to use multiple databases, then you could create another profile for each database or change the database association each time you work. You can also associate the same database in Business Contact Manager for different user profiles. This enables two or more users to work with the same database.

To associate a database with Business Contact Manager:

> **1.** Click **File** on the menu bar, and then click **Data File Management**. The Outlook Data Files dialog box opens. See Figure B-3.

Figure B-3 | Outlook Data Files dialog box

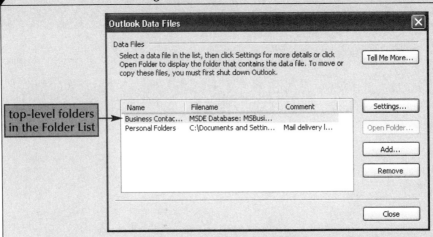

top-level folders in the Folder List

Each top-level item in the Folder List is listed in the Data Files list in the Outlook Data Files dialog box. For example, if any archive folders are open, they would be listed here. The Business Contact Manager folder with "MSDE Database" in the filename is the current database.

2. Click the **Business Contact Manager** folder in the list box, and then click the **Settings** button. The Associate Database Wizard dialog box opens. See Figure B-4.

Figure B-4 | Associate Database Wizard dialog box

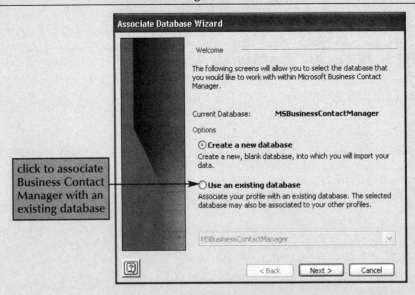

click to associate Business Contact Manager with an existing database

You can choose to create a new database or use an existing database. If you wanted to create a new database, you would click the Create a new database option button, click the Next button, and then name the database and click the Next button to move through the wizard, entering the appropriate information in each step, finally clicking the Finish button after the last step. You will use an existing database.

3. Click the **Use an existing database** option button. The list box at the bottom of the dialog box becomes active.

4. Click the list box arrow, and then click **MSBusinessContactManager**, if necessary. This is the database that will be associated with the current profile.

5. Click the **Next** button. The next screen informs you that the Business Contact Manager database for this profile has been successfully changed.

6. Click the **Finish** button, and then click the **Close** button in the Outlook Data Files dialog box. When you change the database associated with an Outlook profile, you must exit Outlook and restart it.

7. Exit Outlook, restart Outlook, display the Folder List, scroll to the bottom of the list, and then click **Business Contact Manager** in the Folder List in the Navigation Pane. A Welcome to Business Contact Manager message appears in the main window.

8. Click the **plus sign** button ⊞ next to Business Contact Manager. A list of subfolders available in the Business Contact Manager folder appears. See Figure B-5.

Welcome message in Business Contact Manager main folder	Figure B-5

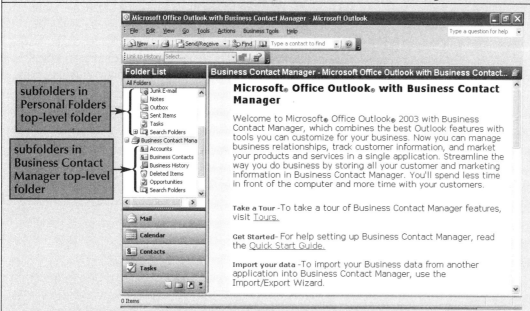

Trouble? If you don't see all the subfolders in the Business Contact Manager folder in the Navigation Pane, you can use a menu command to view the folders. Click Go on the menu bar, and then click Folder to open the Go to Folder dialog box. Click the plus sign button ⊞ next to Business Contact Manager to display the list of subfolders. Click the Cancel button.

The database is created and associated with your Outlook profile.

Adding Business Contacts and Accounts

Business Contact Manager enables you to keep detailed records of all your interactions with customers and accounts that you can view and update right from Outlook. Business Contact Manager uses the terms *business contact* and *account* to refer to customers and accounts. A **business contact** is any individual with whom you work at an account. An **account** is a company, department, or person with whom you do business. Each account you create will have at least one business contact associated with it. If you work with several people at one account, you can associate all these business contacts with that account and specify which business contact is your primary contact. Conversely, each business contact can be associated with only one account.

There are several ways to enter business contacts and accounts into Business Contact Manager. You can create a new business or account directly in Business Contact Manager. You can move or copy contacts already in your Contacts folder into Business Contact Manager. Or, you can import contacts from another database or file into Business Contact Manager.

Creating New Business Contacts and Accounts

When you create a new business contact or account in Business Contact Manager, a window opens in which you can enter the appropriate information. The window is similar to the Contact window you have already used in Outlook, as are the methods for entering data and moving between fields.

To create a new account:

1. Click **Accounts** in the Business Contact Manager folder in the Folder List in the Navigation Pane. The Accounts main window appears.

   Trouble? If you don't see the Accounts subfolder in the Business Contact Manager folder in the Navigation Pane, you need to use the Go to Folder dialog box to navigate to the subfolder. Click Go on the menu bar, and then click Folder to open the Go to Folder dialog box. Click the plus sign button ⊞ next to Business Contact Manager, click Accounts, and then click the OK button. Use this same process to navigate to the Business Contact subfolders in the rest of the steps in this appendix.

2. Click the **New** button list arrow on the Standard toolbar, and then click **Account**. A new Account window opens. See Figure B-6.

Figure B-6 ▸ **Account window**

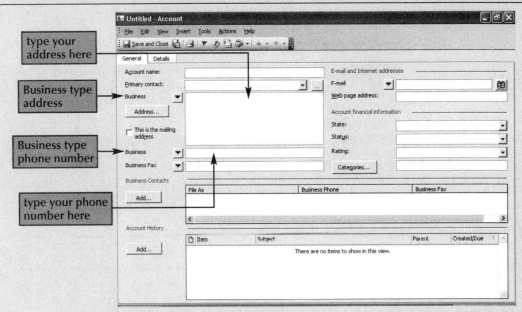

3. Type **My Account** in the Account name text box.
4. Type your address in the Business text box next to the Address button. (Keep Business as the address type.)
5. Type your phone number in the text box next to Business (below the text box in which you typed your address).
6. Click the **Save and Close** button on the Standard toolbar. The account is saved in Business Contact Manager and appears in the Accounts main window.

You'll need to create an account for each company with which you do business. If you work with many people within the same company, you might want to create a different account for each department or group with which you work. Remember, each account can have multiple business contacts associated with it.

To create a business contact:

1. Click the **New** button list arrow on the Standard toolbar, and then click **Business Contact**. A new Business Contact window opens. See Figure B-7.

Business Contact window | **Figure B-7**

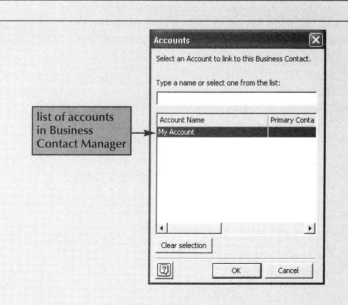

2. Type your name in the Full Name text box, type **Sales Rep** in the Job Title text box, and then type your e-mail address in the E-mail text box.

   Next, you'll specify with which account the business contact should be associated.

3. Click the **Account name** button ⋯ to the right of the Account name text box. A menu opens, offering you the choice of selecting an existing account or creating a new account. If the account with which you want to associate the contact already exists, then you need only to select the appropriate account. If the account does not yet exist, then you need to create a new one.

4. Click **Add Existing Account**. The Accounts dialog box opens. See Figure B-8.

Accounts dialog box | **Figure B-8**

5. Click **My Account** in the list box, and then click the **OK** button. The account you selected appears in the Account name text box.

6. Click the **Details** tab. You can add quite a bit of helpful information for each contact on this tab.

7. Click the **Source of lead** list arrow, and then click **Trade Show**.

8. Click the **Method of contact** list arrow, and then click **Email**.

   You have finished entering the business contact data.

9. Click the **Save and Close** button on the Standard toolbar, and then click **Business Contacts** in the Business Contact Manager folder in the Folder List in the Navigation Pane. The new contact card appears in the Business Contacts main window.

If the contacts you want to enter already exist in the Contacts folder, you can reuse contacts without retyping the information.

Using Outlook Contacts

You can move or copy any existing contact cards in the Contacts folder or any custom Contacts folder you have created. Contacts you move from the Contacts folder into Business Contact Manager are permanently deleted from the Contacts folder. However, you cannot move any contact that contains attachments, such as an e-mail message, an appointment, or a file. In this case, you'll need to copy the contact from the Contacts folder into Business Contact Manager. The attachments are still listed in the History list but no longer are linked to the appropriate items; you'll need to re-associate the attachments (as you'll learn in the "Using the History List" section). When you copy a contact from the Contacts folder into Business Contact Manager, the contact appears in both places, but the two items are not linked. This means that if you update the contact card in Business Contact Manager, you must make the same change manually in the Contacts folder, and vice versa.

Conversely, you can also move a business contact from Business Contact Manager into the Contacts folder. This creates a copy of the contact in the Contacts folder, although the information in the History area is not retained. As when you copy a contact from the Contacts folder into Business Contact Manager, the contact appears in both locations but the two items are not linked.

Reference Window	**Adding Contact Items to Business Contact Manager**

- Display the Contacts main window, and then select the contacts you want to move or copy to Business Contact Manager.
- Drag the contacts from the Contacts main window to the Business Contacts subfolder in the Business Contact Manager folder in the Folder List (*or* press and hold the Ctrl key as you drag to copy the contacts).

Importing Contacts

You can import contacts stored in another database or file into the Business Contacts subfolder in the Business Contact Manager folder. File types you can import include: Act! 4.0, 5.0 database (.dbf); QuickBooks 8.0, 9.0 data (.iif); Comma Separated Values (.csv; also called comma-delimited); Microsoft Access database (.mdb); Microsoft Office Excel workbook (.xls); Microsoft bCentral List Builder Contacts (.bcm) or Customer Leads (.bcm); and Business Contact Manager data (.bcm). You use the Business Data Import/Export Wizard to import the contact data from these file types into Business Contact Manager. The process is similar to using the Import/Export Wizard, which you did in Tutorial 5. If you import data from an Act! database, some of the history information will also be imported with the contacts. If you are using a database or file type that is not included in the list, you can usually save the file in the Comma Separated Values format and then import this version into Business Contact Manager.

Reference Window

Importing Data as New Business Contacts or Accounts

- Click File on the menu bar, point to Import and Export, and then click Business Contact Manager to start the Business Data Import/Export Wizard.
- Click the Import a file option button, click the Next button, select the file type you want to import, and then click the Next button.
- Click the Browse button next to the File to import text box, navigate to the file you want to import, and then double-click that file.
- In the Options section, click the appropriate option button to select whether or not you want to import duplicate contacts, and then click the Next button.
- Click the check box next to the data you want to import in the Import Data list, and then click the Business Contacts or Accounts option button, depending on how you want the imported data classified.
- Click the Map button to open the Map Fields dialog box, drag values from the left side (the field names used in the file from which you are importing) to their corresponding fields on the right side (the field names in Business Contact Manager), and then click the OK button when you are done.
- Click the Next button to see the message that you are ready to import, and then click the Next button to begin the importing process.
- When the importing process is complete, click the Close button to confirm that the data has been imported successfully.

The new accounts or business contacts appear in Business Contact Manager.

Creating Opportunities

Business Contact Manager is primarily a sales tool. Instead of just a list of tasks, you can create a list of **opportunities**, which are records of chances to sell your product or services.

To create a new opportunity and link it to a contact or account:

▶ **1.** Click the **New** button list arrow, and then click **Opportunity**. A new Opportunity window opens. See Figure B-9.

Figure B-9 | Opportunity window

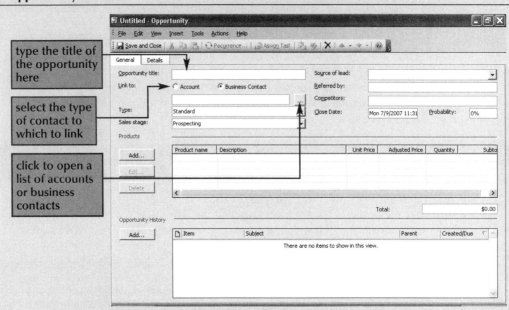

2. Type **Sell my product** in the Opportunity title text box.

3. Click the **Business Contact** option button, if necessary, click the [...] button next to the text box below the option button, and then click **Add Existing Contact**. The Business Contacts dialog box opens.

4. Click your name in the list, and then click the **OK** button. Your name appears below the Business Contact option button in the Opportunity dialog box.

   You could add information about the product you are trying to sell, and you can add items to the History list. For example, you can add the source of your lead, the names of your competitors, the target date by which you want to close the deal, and the probability of doing so. You could also click the Details tab and add more information in the Comments text box.

5. Click the **Save and Close** button on the Standard toolbar. The Opportunities window closes and the opportunity appears in the Opportunities main window. See Figure B-10.

Figure B-10 | Opportunity in the Opportunities window

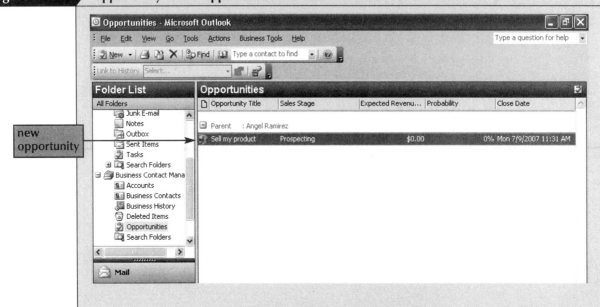

Using the History List

The History list in the Business Contact window and in the Account window shows all your interactions with that business contact or account. You can enter and review the information for each interaction in the Business Contact History or Account History area. You can create and link to notes, e-mail messages, tasks, appointments, a record of phone calls (a phone log), opportunities, or files on your computer. Then, whenever you open a business contact or account, you can quickly review a list of all the interactions you have had with that person or company.

To add a new item to the History list:

1. Click **Business Contacts** in the Business Contact Manager folder in the Folder List in the Navigation Pane, and then double-click the contact card with your information.

2. Click the **Add** button in the Business Contact History area. You can create a record of a variety of items in this list. See Figure B-11.

Add menu in the Business Contact window | **Figure B-11**

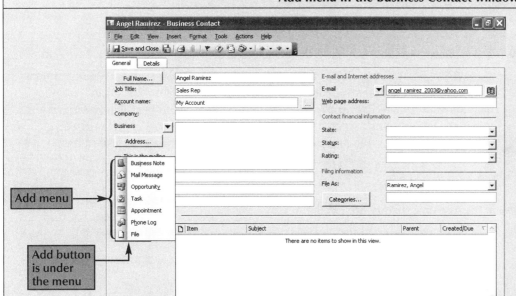

3. Click **Task**. A new Task window opens.

4. Type **Read about opportunities in Business Contact Manager Help** in the Subject text box.

5. Click the **Contacts** button. The Select Contacts dialog box opens.

6. Scroll to the bottom of the Look in list box, click the **plus sign** button ⊞ next to Business Contact Manager, and then click **Business Contacts**. The Items list box at the bottom of the dialog box changes to show the contents of the Business Contacts folder.

7. Click your name in the Items list, and then click the **OK** button. You are assigned as the contact for this task.

8. Click the **Save and Close** button on the Standard toolbar. The Task window closes and the task is added to your contact card in the Business Contact History area. See Figure B-12.

Task in the Business Contact History area in the Business Contact window

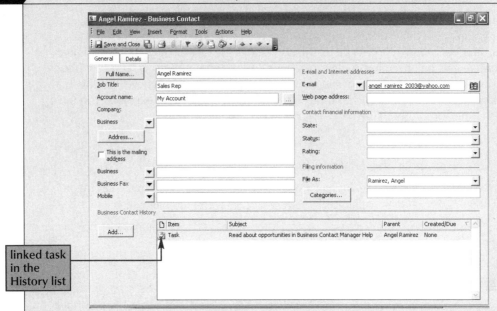

linked task in the History list

> **9.** Click the **Save and Close** button on the Standard toolbar. Your contact card is saved with the updated History list.

> **10.** Click **Accounts** in the Business Contact Manager folder in the Folder List in the Navigation Pane, and then double-click the **My Account** card in the Accounts main window. You are listed in the Business Contacts area because when you created your contact card, you linked it to this account. The task you added to your contact card also appears in the Account History area on the My Account card because your contact card is linked to this account. See Figure B-13.

Task in the Account History area in the Account window

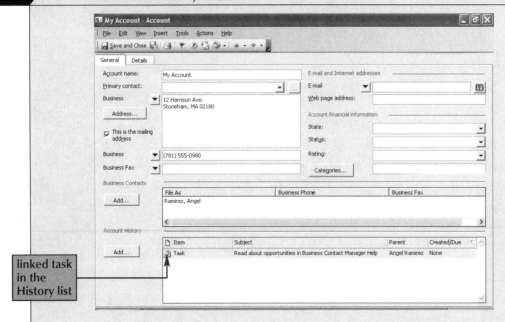

linked task in the History list

> **11.** Click the **Save and Close** button on the Standard toolbar. The My Account card closes.

You can also link existing appointments, tasks, or e-mail messages to a specific business contact or account. You simply open the appointment, task, or e-mail message that you want to link to a business contact or account, and then use the Business Contact Manager toolbar to select the business contact or account to which you want to link. The item will then appear in the History area of the Business Contact or Account window, depending on whether you linked to a business contact or an account.

You can also link any e-mail messages you sent to or received from your business contacts and accounts to the appropriate business contact or account. You can do this both for your existing messages and for new messages you send and receive. Business Contact Manager matches the sender or receiver addresses from your incoming and outgoing e-mails to the e-mail addresses you entered for your business contacts and accounts. As with linked appointments, the messages appear in the History area of the Business Contact or Account window. You can set Business Contact Manager to automatically look for new incoming and outgoing messages in the folders you specify to link to your business contacts and accounts. You can also set Business Contact Manager to link existing e-mail messages in the folders you specify to your business contacts and accounts.

To link existing or new e-mail messages to business contacts or accounts:

1. Click the **New** button list arrow on the Standard toolbar, and then click **Mail Message**. A new Message window opens.

2. Click the **To** button. The Select Names dialog box opens. See Figure B-14.

Select Names dialog box ◀ **Figure B-14**

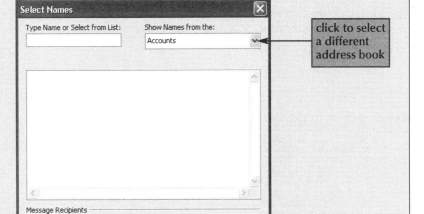

3. Click the **Show Names from the** list arrow, click **Business Contacts** to select that address book, click your name in the list, if necessary, click the **To** button, and then click the **OK** button.

4. Type **Linked e-mail message** in the Subject text box, and then send the message.

5. Download your message, if necessary. The Linked e-mail message appears in your Inbox.

6. Click **Business Tools** on the menu bar, point to **Link E-mail**, and then click **Link Existing E-mail**. The Link Existing E-mail dialog box opens. If you wanted to automatically link all incoming and outgoing messages to the appropriate business contact and account, you would click Auto Linking to open the Link E-mail Automatically dialog box. See Figure B-15.

Figure B-15 Link Existing E-mail dialog box

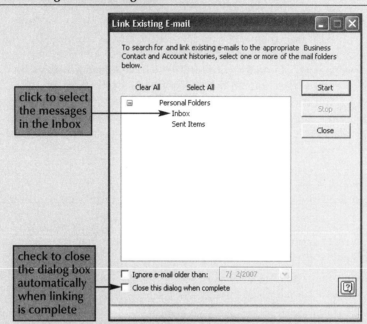

click to select the messages in the Inbox

check to close the dialog box automatically when linking is complete

7. Click **Inbox** in the list, click the **Close this dialog when complete** check box to check it, and then click the **Start** button. After a moment, the dialog box closes.

8. Click **Business History** in the Folder List in the Navigation Pane. All the items that have a business history appear in the Business History main window grouped by date. See Figure B-16.

Figure B-16 History items in the Business History folder

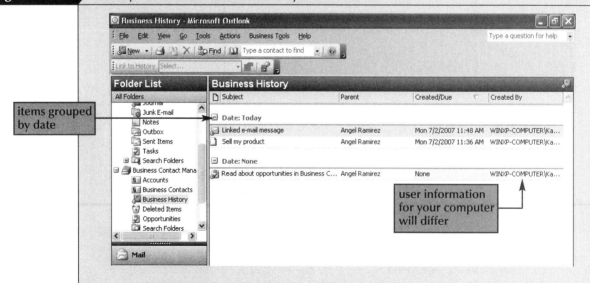

items grouped by date

user information for your computer will differ

9. Double-click the **Linked e-mail message** item. The e-mail message you sent opens.

10. Close the e-mail message. All e-mail messages you send and receive related to your business contacts and accounts will be listed in the History area for those business contacts and accounts.

Using Reports

Business Contact Manager comes with a variety of reports that you can use to monitor and evaluate your effectiveness with your business contacts and accounts. These include reports in the following categories: Business Contacts, Accounts, Opportunities, and Other. Once you create a report, you can click the Modify Report button on the toolbar in the Report window to change the way the information is displayed.

To create a report:

1. Click **Business Tools** on the menu bar, point to **Reports**, point to **Business Contacts**, and then click **Neglected Business Contacts**. After a moment, the report opens in a new window. See Figure B-17.

Neglected Business Contacts report ◀ Figure B-17

There are no contacts listed because you entered activity on your business contact today.

2. Click **File** on the menu bar, click **Save As**, navigate to the **Appendix.B\Tutorial** folder included with your Data Files, type **Sample Business Report** in the File name text box, and then click the **Save** button. The report is saved as a Word document.

3. Click the **Close** button to close the report.

Business Contact Manager reports make it simple to keep track of all your business contacts and accounts as well as track your progress and success.

Removing Customizations and Deleting Items

Before you end your Outlook session, you should delete the items you created in this appendix. It is easy to delete all the items associated with an account. When you delete the account, any items linked only to that account are automatically deleted as well.

To delete the contact, account, opportunity, and history:

► **1.** Click **Accounts** in the Business Contact Manager folder in the Folder List in the Navigation Pane, click **My Account** in the Accounts main window, and then click the **Delete** button ✕ on the Standard toolbar.

► **2.** Click **Business Contacts** in the Business Contact Manager folder in the Folder List in the Navigation Pane. Your contact card is not in the Business Contacts folder. It was automatically deleted when you deleted the account you created because it was linked to that account.

► **3.** Click **Business History** in the Business Contact Manager folder in the Folder List in the Navigation Pane, note that there are no items in this folder, and then click **Opportunities** to verify that the item in this folder was deleted as well.

► **4.** Click **Inbox** in the Folder List in the Navigation Pane. The e-mail message is still there. Although it was linked to My Account, it is not part of Business Contact Manager.

► **5.** Delete the **Linked e-mail message** in the Inbox and in the Sent Items folder.

► **6.** Empty the **Deleted Items** folder in the Personal Folders folder, and then empty the **Deleted Items** folder in the Business Contact Manager folder.

Business Contact Manager is a robust program with many functions and capabilities. This brief appendix covered only the most basic tasks. To learn more about Business Contact Manager, click Help on the menu bar, and then click Business Contact Manager Quick Start Guide, Business Contact Manager Tours, or Business Contact Manager Help.

Review

Appendix B Quick Check

1. What is Business Contact Manager?
2. Where are the data you enter in Business Contact Manager stored?
3. True or False: You can associate two or more databases with Business Contact Manager at the same time.
4. What is the difference between a business contact and an account?
5. True or False: Each business contact can be associated with multiple accounts.
6. What happens when you move an existing contact card from Outlook into Business Contact Manager?
7. What is the History list?
8. True or False: Business Contact Manager comes with built-in reports you can use to track your success with business contacts and accounts.

Review

Appendix Summary

In this appendix, you learned how to use Outlook with Business Contact Manager. First, you learned how to associate a new or existing database with Business Contact Manager. Then, you added an account and a business contact. You also learned how to use contacts from the Outlook Contacts folder, and how to import contacts from another database or file. You learned how to create an opportunity. You updated the History list for business contacts and accounts to include new interactions or link to existing Outlook items, such as e-mails and appointments. Finally, you used the built-in reports to track your progress and success with your business contacts and accounts.

Key Terms

account

business contact

Business Contact Manager

database

opportunity

record

Practice

*Practice the skills you
learned in the appendix.*

Review Assignments

There are no Data Files needed for the Review Assignments.

When you use Outlook with Business Contact Manager, you can compile, organize, and analyze your business contacts and accounts. This can be a great help in keeping your customers or clients satisfied and identifying opportunities for future sales. In these Review Assignments, you'll use Business Contact Manager to create and manage an account and business contact, and create a report.

1. Set up Business Contact Manager to run with your profile, if necessary.
2. Associate the existing database with Business Contact Manager.
3. Create an account using a fictitious business name and your address and phone number.
4. Create a business contact using a fictitious name and job title, associate the business contact with the account you created, and then select a lead source and contact method on the Details tab.
5. Create a new opportunity with a title related to the business you selected for the account, and then link the opportunity to the business contact you created.
6. Add a new task to the History list; use an appropriate subject and assign the task to the business contact you created.
7. Automatically link all incoming and outgoing messages to the business contact and account you created.
8. Create a report of your choosing, and then save the report as **Business Report** in the **Appendix.B\Review** folder included with your Data Files.
9. Delete the account you created, confirm that the business contact, opportunity, and History list were also deleted, and then empty the Deleted Items folders.

Review

Quick Check Answers

1. an add-in program for Outlook that enables you to track customer and account data from Outlook
2. in a database on your computer
3. False. Only one database can be associated at a time with each user profile.
4. A business contact is any individual with whom you work at an account. An account is a company, department, or person with whom you do business.
5. False. Each business contact can be associated with only one account, although each account can have multiple business contacts associated with it.
6. The contact is deleted permanently from the Contacts folder.
7. a list of all your interactions with that business contact or account
8. True

Objectives

- Review the history of PDAs
- Learn the components of PDAs
- Review synchronizing PDAs with Outlook
- Consider virus issues

Synchronizing Outlook with Personal Digital Assistants

Personal digital assistants (PDAs) are small, portable, handheld devices that offer data input, processing, storage, and retrieval capabilities similar to computers. Specially designed software give PDAs the power to offer many functions, applications, and tools. People carry these convenient portable devices everywhere. You can use your PDA to enter contacts, send and receive e-mail messages, schedule appointments, create tasks, and jot down notes at any time, and then, when you return to the office, you can **sync** (synchronize) the Outlook folders on your PDA with the Outlook folders on your desktop or laptop computer. **Synchronizing** is the process of updating the folders on your computer and the corresponding folders on the PDA so their contents are identical. Any new items in either location are duplicated in the other location, ensuring that the entries on both the portable device and the desktop contain identical information. Because microprocessor technology has made such rapid advances and chips continue to become smaller and more versatile, many cellular telephones now also include the same features and functions as PDAs.

When first introduced, PDAs were intended to be electronic pocket organizers that could store addresses, phone numbers, appointments, to-do lists, and notes. Today's PDAs do all these things plus send and receive e-mail, create word-processing documents and spreadsheets, set alarms, perform calculations, access information on the Internet, and play music (MP3 files), games, and movies (MPEG files). Some PDAs even integrate other devices and features, such as digital cameras and global positioning satellite (GPS) receivers. The features available on a PDA vary by model and manufacturer.

Student Data Files

There are no student Data Files needed for this appendix.

History of Portable Devices

Handheld computer organizers originated in the 1980s to enable people to store phone numbers and addresses, take notes, and track appointments. The Psion Organiser, introduced in 1984, is considered the first personal digital assistant. It stored addresses and phone numbers, kept a calendar, and included a clock and a calculator. However, the early devices were expensive, complex to use, and were too large to fit in a pocket comfortably. Newton MessagePad, introduced by Apple Computer in 1993, was one of the first commercially available PDAs to accept handwriting as input. The early handwriting recognition programs used for inputting data were ineffective and error-prone. These programs attempted to "learn" the user's handwriting and convert the handwritten letters and numbers into digital characters. These first PDAs did not capture a large number of users.

The release of the PalmPilot by Palm Computing in 1996 changed the world of PDAs. The PalmPilot was the fastest selling computer product in history—it sold faster than the VCR, the color TV, the cell phone, and even the personal computer. Small and light enough to be carried in a pocket or purse, these new PDAs ran for weeks on AAA batteries, were easy to use, and could store thousands of contacts, appointments, and notes. The PDA became an indispensable tool for both business and personal use.

With the success of the PalmPilot came advances in the technology and newer models that made PDAs more than simple digital calendars and address books. Depending on the brand and model, PDAs now provide spreadsheet capabilities, Web access, e-mail exchange, text messaging, digital photography, games, and music playback. Today, most computer manufacturers sell PDAs, including Apple, Dell, Hewlett-Packard, Sony, and IBM, as do some dedicated PDA companies, including palmOne and Research in Motion (RIM). In addition, companies such as palmOne, Motorola, Kyocera, Nokia, and Audiovox are manufacturing PDA/cell phones (called "smartphones"), which combine cell phone, Web browsing, and traditional organizer technologies in one small device. Figure C-1 shows two popular PDAs.

Figure C-1 ▶ **Common PDAs**

Today, people of all vocations and interests rely on PDAs. Everyone who spends time away from his or her desktop or laptop computer and relies on scheduling or contact management software will find a PDA useful. PDAs can greatly improve the efficiency of technicians making service calls, sales representatives calling on clients, professors teaching classes and monitoring students, and parents tracking children's activities. Specialized programs designed to be used with PDAs are available for use in many fields. For example, truckers may use PDAs to track their expenses and mileage, refer to maps, and even e-mail the dispatcher at set times; physicians may use PDAs to enter notes for patient charts, write prescriptions, and look up information in reference manuals, such as the *Physician's Desk Reference*. The potential for PDAs grows daily as developers and manufacturers continually provide new ways to integrate other functions and features. An important function of a PDA is its ability to link or synchronize this information back to a main computer, in many cases, using Outlook.

Reviewing PDA Components

All PDAs feature the same basic components, regardless of brand or model: a microprocessor, an operating system, memory, storage, a power supply, a display screen, an input device, an input/output device, and software.

Microprocessor

Just like desktop and laptop computers, PDAs require microprocessors to manage data flow. A **microprocessor** performs arithmetic and logical operations that process data. But unlike current desktop and laptop computers, PDAs use smaller, less expensive, slower microprocessors. However, the slower speeds are made up for by the smaller sizes and lower prices of PDAs, which are usually not used to perform the large and complex operations expected of desktops and laptops.

Operating System

The **operating system** contains preprogrammed instructions that tell the microprocessor how to input, process, store, and output the data. PDAs use simpler operating systems than PCs, so they require less memory. The two most commonly used PDA operating systems are Palm OS and Microsoft's Pocket PC (based on Microsoft Windows CE). The operating system determines how your PDA synchronizes with a laptop or desktop computer, how it sends and receives data and files through beaming technology, how it sends and receives e-mail, what type of handwriting or character recognition input it supports, and whether it supports voice input.

Memory

A PDA stores its standard programs (address book, calendar, memo pad, and operating system) in a **read-only memory (ROM)** chip, the contents of which remain intact even when you shut off the device. Data and any programs you install are stored in the **random access memory (RAM)**. With this system, your programs are available immediately when you turn on the PDA. Any data you add or change is saved automatically. When you turn off the PDA, your data is stored because the PDA continues to draw a small amount of power from the batteries. The amount of memory in a PDA varies by brand, model, and customization, but is currently between 8 MB and 64 MB of RAM. You want to be sure that you have enough memory to install the programs you want and store sufficient data. In general, 1 MB of memory can store up to 4,000 addresses and 100 e-mail messages.

Storage

Unlike personal computers, PDAs don't save data to a floppy disk or a hard disk. However, removable storage is available for PDAs in the form of memory cards. Some products for storing images, document files, or other data from a PDA include MemPlug, SmartMedia, Memory Stick, and Compact Flash cards.

Power Supply

PDAs are powered by batteries or an AC adapter. Some PDAs use alkaline batteries; others use rechargeable batteries. How long the batteries last depends on the brand and model of your PDA and how you use it. Some batteries currently available can operate the PDA for as long as 14 hours without recharging. If you drain all the power from the batteries, you'll lose any data stored in the PDA. For this reason, you should synchronize your PDA with your desktop or laptop computer and you should be vigilant about recharging your PDA by plugging it into a charger on a regular basis. In addition to chargers that plug into a standard wall outlet, other chargers plug into the power outlet in a car. You can also purchase chargers that adapt to different voltages for international travel.

Display Screen

PDAs use a liquid crystal display (LCD) screen for both displaying and entering data. Depending on the brand and model, the LCD screens vary in color, size, and resolution. PDAs use either passive or active matrix technology; active matrix screens are easier to see at different angles and in lower-light environments. Most PDAs have settings that you can change to adapt to the current light conditions. If you set your PDA to dim the backlight, you will use less battery power. You can also choose between monochrome and color screens. If you plan to use your PDA for viewing images, such as drawings or photographs, you might consider buying one with a color screen.

Input Device

PDAs have small buttons that open screens and issue commands so that you can enter and access the data. However, you'll use the buttons in conjunction with one of five basic methods to enter data: onscreen keyboard and keypad, handwriting recognition, external keyboard, synchronization, or importing.

The LCD screen on every PDA is also a touch screen that you can tap or write on with a stylus to issue commands and enter data (never use a pen or sharp objects that could damage the screen). Some styluses look like pens; others have rings that you slip on your finger. Most are highly flexible, made of nylon, and slip into a slot on the PDA. Styluses have become a fashion accessory, and are available to purchase from many vendors in a variety of colors and styles. When you tap an onscreen icon, the PDA responds by issuing that command, similar to when you use the mouse to click a toolbar button in a program on a desktop or laptop computer. You can also display an onscreen character keyboard or numeric keypad and enter data by tapping the appropriate keys either character by character or number by number.

A faster input method than the onscreen keyboard and keypad is **character recognition**, a program that converts characters you draw one at a time into letters, symbols, and numbers. An outgrowth of the earlier handwriting recognition programs, character recognition programs require you to write with a modified alphabet (somewhat like shorthand symbols) or standard block printing that the character recognition programs recognize. Palm OS, for example, uses Graffiti, which is a character recognition program that recognizes a modified alphabet. Pocket PC includes Transcriber, Letter Recognizer, and Block Recognizer handwriting recognition programs, which recognize your natural handwriting as well as block characters. It can take some practice to become proficient with either recognition-input method. If you prefer, you can connect your PDA to an external keyboard and type your data directly into the PDA. As voice recognition technology advances, it will become more common to speak to your PDA to enter data.

If data is already entered in a personal information manager such as Outlook or another application on your computer or PDA, you can synchronize or import the data rather than reentering it. Importing transfers the data from another program or PDA into your PDA without requiring you to type it manually. You can usually import data from a database, spreadsheet, comma-delimited, or tab-delimited file. You can also synchronize from one PDA to another.

Input/Output Device

PDAs are intended to complement your desktop or laptop computer, not replace it. Synchronizing the data between devices requires a connection between the PDA and your computer. You can connect the PDA to the computer with a cable and a serial or USB port. Some PDAs can sit in a cradle or docking station that connects to the computer. Many PDAs have an infrared (IR) communications port that uses IR light to beam information, files, and applications to another computer or PDA. Some PDAs can exchange data with a network through an Internet service provider or use a modem to transfer files.

Software

PDAs require special software installed on your laptop or desktop computer to synchronize the data between the two machines. You'll also need a personal information manager, such as Outlook or the applications that come with your PDA, to access the address book, calendar, tasks, and so forth on your computer. You can also install versions of common programs, such as Word and Excel, on a PDA. PDA software is available in many categories, including games, productivity, and business and finance.

Synchronizing Outlook with a PDA

All PDAs help you to manage personal information. When you walk away from your desktop or laptop computer, you may want to take some of the information stored in Outlook on your computer with you on your PDA. Or, you may have collected some information on your PDA that you want to transfer to Outlook on your laptop or desktop computer. For example, if you make appointments in Outlook for a day of out-of-office meetings, you can transfer those to your PDA for portability. If you add some entries to your task list or collect a new contact's information while at those meetings, you can transfer that data to Outlook on your computer for permanent storage. In addition, it's a good practice to synchronize the information you saved on the PDA to your computer as a backup in case of a power failure on the PDA. If your PDA loses power because, for example, the batteries die prematurely or you forget to charge them, you might lose all the stored data. If the information is complete on your desktop, you simply synchronize back to the PDA. In addition, because PDAs are light and portable, there is a possibility that you might misplace or lose yours. The loss of an expensive device is exacerbated by the permanent loss of all the data contained on the PDA, unless you have a backup in another location.

You can transfer much of the data you collect and store in Outlook to a PDA, including items from the Inbox, Outbox, Contacts, Calendar, Tasks, Notes, and Drafts folders. However, depending on the version of the software you are using, the items may have fewer fields available on the PDA. Outlook reminders can be converted to audible alarms on PDAs. Some PDAs provide categories for grouping items, although not all the standard Outlook categories are included in the default list on the PDAs. The terminology used to refer to these items and functions may differ from Outlook and from PDA to PDA. Though much of your Outlook information is transferable to PDAs, you will find that the interface for displaying and entering data will look different on the PDA, depending on the software you are using to link or synchronize the data.

Synchronization Software

As mentioned earlier, there are a variety of ways to "physically" connect your PDA with your computer: PDA cradle or docking station, cable, IR port, and modem. Once your computer and PDA have a way to connect, you'll need a special program to perform the synchronization. Outlook does not have its own synchronization utility, but many are available through third-party vendors. DataViz Beyond Contacts, Intellisync, Microsoft ActiveSync, palmOne HotSync, and RealINSIGHT SyncUp are just a few of the many synchronization utilities available.

No matter which software you use, you'll need to make a few standard decisions when you synchronize. You should plan how you use your PDA with your computer before synchronizing them. Use this list of questions as a guide:

- What items do I want to synchronize? Do I want all Outlook items, such as contacts, notes, tasks, and e-mail, available on both my computer and the PDA?
- Which version overwrites, or takes priority? Do Outlook items overwrite PDA data, or vice versa? Do most recent items always update older items?
- What happens to the deleted items? Do they get stored in an archive file or deleted?
- Does the PDA have enough memory to store the selected data?

As you perform the synchronization, the software compares items on the PDA to those stored on your computer, looking for additions, modifications, and deletions. Depending on the preferences you set, data will be copied from the computer to the PDA or from the PDA to the computer. If a record was modified on both the PDA and the computer, a duplicate record can be made on both devices so you can manually intervene at a later time. Once the synchronization process is complete, Outlook and the PDA should have the same data for those items.

Synchronization is a simple way to back up the data on your PDA. You should make a habit of synchronizing at regular intervals to keep your data current. The few minutes you spend become invaluable if your PDA breaks, is stolen, or runs out of power.

Protecting from Viruses

PDAs are becoming just as susceptible to viruses as laptop and desktop computers. As PDAs gain popularity, they also risk increased security issues. The Liberty Crack program discovered in August 2000, which could delete all the applications on a PDA with the Palm OS, was the first Trojan horse targeted specifically to PDAs. A **Trojan horse** is a supposedly harmless program or data that contains malicious or harmful code that damages a computer or data in some way. Fortunately, users whose PDAs were invaded by this Trojan horse could simply synchronize their PDAs with the backup they created on their desktop or laptop computer. Although the damage by Liberty Crack was fairly minimal, it did call attention to the need for virus protection on PDAs. Besides being a target of virus infection, PDAs can also transfer viruses to other devices, including computers.

Although personal information management tools such as address books and calendars are fairly secure, more advanced features pose serious security risks. The limited memory of PDAs led early developers to focus on features rather than security measures. Consider the following common features and their attendant risks. E-mail, Web access, and instant messaging have almost no security on PDAs. IR light enables you to beam data, applications, and files between your PDA and a computer or another PDA; however, viruses can be beamed just as easily. During synchronization, a virus transferred from an unprotected PDA to a computer can compromise the security of that computer or its network. While downloading any of the myriad of freeware, shareware, or other applications widely available for PDAs, you could also be downloading a virus or Trojan horse.

Protecting PDAs and Computers

So how do you protect your PDA and your computer from viruses? Following a few basic guidelines can minimize your exposure and risk to viruses and Trojan horses, making the data and programs on your PDA—and thus your computer—more secure.

- **Use antivirus software.** Install and run antivirus software on both your computer and your PDA (there are specialized versions for PDAs). Be sure to run the software regularly and download updated virus definitions frequently to ensure that you are protected from the latest viruses. Symantec and McAfee are two well-known companies that specialize in virus protection, detection, and inoculation.
- **Exchange data and files only with people you trust.** Ask about someone's antivirus procedures before exposing your PDA to potential infections. Remember, your goal is to protect your PDA from viruses.
- **Download from trustworthy Web sites.** Consider whether a Web site from which you plan to download data, files, or applications is trustworthy. In general, Web sites of well-known PDA manufacturers, suppliers, or software companies are safe. Evaluate shareware and freeware sites carefully before starting to download.
- **Synchronize often.** Frequent synchronization of your PDA and computer ensures that you can retrieve all your current contacts, appointments, address books, and other items should a virus wipe out your PDA's memory.
- **Back up regularly.** A regular backup ensures that you have a complete copy of the data and applications on your PDA stored on your computer. If necessary, you can reinstall the PDA operating system and use the backup to reset your PDA.

Follow these guidelines to help ensure that your PDA and your computer or your network (if you have one) remain secure and virus-free.

Review

Appendix C Quick Check

1. What does synchronizing mean?
2. True or False: PDAs are used only to manage personal information, such as appointments and contact lists.
3. What are the two most common operating systems used in PDAs?
4. Where does a PDA store its standard programs?
5. True or False: You do not need a keyboard to enter information into a PDA.
6. True or False: PDAs cannot be infected by viruses.

Review

Appendix Summary

In this appendix, you reviewed the history of PDAs. You then learned about the components of PDAs and you reviewed how to synchronize PDAs with Outlook. You also learned about guidelines for protecting your PDA from viruses.

Key Terms

character recognition	personal digital	read-only memory (ROM)
microprocessor	assistant (PDA)	sync
operating system	random access	synchronize
	memory (RAM)	Trojan horse

Quick Check Answers

1. the process of updating the folders on your computer and the corresponding folders on the PDA so their contents are identical
2. False
3. Palm OS and Pocket PC
4. in ROM
5. True
6. False

Glossary/Index

Glossary/Index

Outlook Feature Guide

This Outlook Feature Guide provides full-color screenshots of the most popular features of Microsoft Outlook as well as some of the new features in Outlook 2003. Outlook uses color to help you organize items, determine their levels of importance or priority, and navigate among folders and items. You can also use color to enhance your e-mail messages. In the following pages, you'll see some color-coding features in the Calendar, how Outlook uses color in Quick Flags and the Navigation Pane, and how you can use color to enhance and organize e-mail messages and notes.

Figure 1

A new feature of Outlook 2003 is a preview of messages if your options are set to download messages automatically. The preview contains the sender's name, subject line and the first few lines of text. This preview appears if Outlook is open, regardless of what application you are working in.

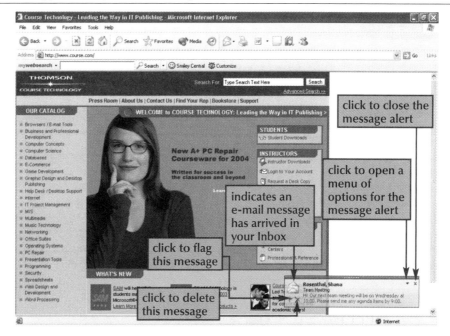

Figure 2

Color is used when spelling and grammar are checked in an e-mail message. Possible misspelled words are flagged with a red, wavy underline and the possible misspelled word is highlighted in red in the Spelling and Grammar dialog box.

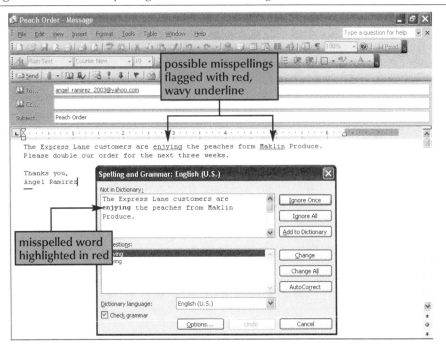

Figure 3

Using stationery is one way to make your e-mail messages more visually interesting. You can also format text in an e-mail message using commands on the Formatting toolbar.

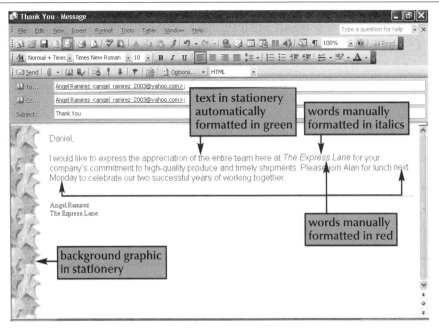

Notes can be customized by changing the color to indicate different topics. You can also assign categories and contacts to notes by clicking the Note icon in the upper-left corner.

Figure 4

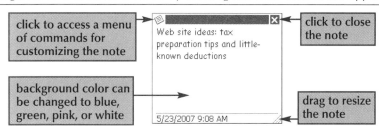

click to access a menu of commands for customizing the note

click to close the note

background color can be changed to blue, green, pink, or white

drag to resize the note

Web site ideas: tax preparation tips and little-known deductions

5/23/2007 9:08 AM

The current folder is highlighted in yellow in the new Navigation Pane. Colored icons provide information about the messages in your mail folders.

Figure 5

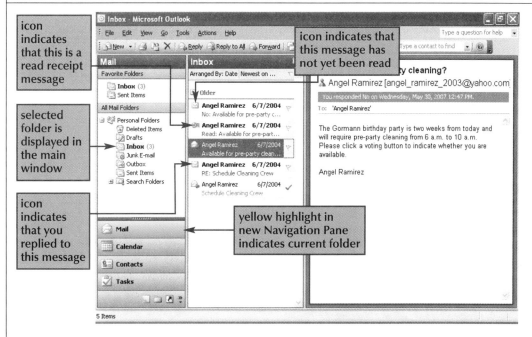

icon indicates that this is a read receipt message

icon indicates that this message has not yet been read

selected folder is displayed in the main window

icon indicates that you replied to this message

yellow highlight in new Navigation Pane indicates current folder

| **Figure 6** | Quick Flags are useful for quickly identifying items that need follow-up. Outlook colors items that are overdue for follow-up red. |

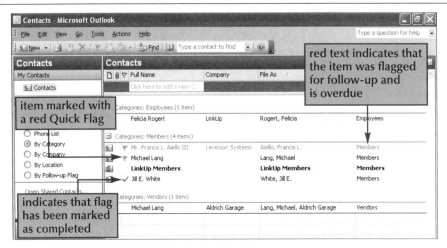

| **Figure 7** | Quick Flags can be color-coded to help you organize items in your Outlook folders. |

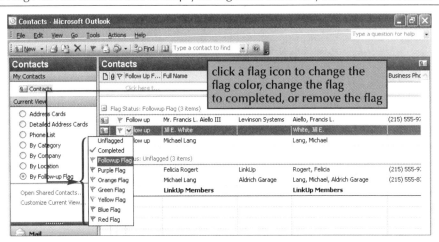

| **Figure 8** | Items in folders can be viewed in a variety of ways, including filtering items for follow-up (items that have been flagged) and grouping them by their flag colors. |

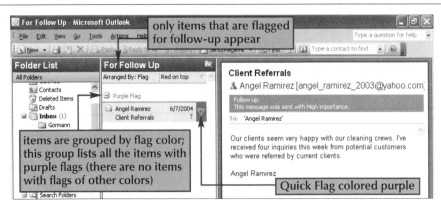

Outlook uses red exclamation points to indicate High importance and blue downward pointing arrows to indicate Low importance. You can also create rules to handle messages in your Inbox. A rule was created here to color all messages that are marked as High importance in blue and to make them boldface.

Figure 9

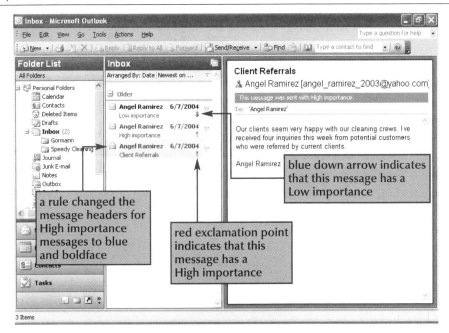

You can customize Outlook Today to show you the information you want to see when you start Outlook. Overdue items are highlighted in red text.

Figure 10

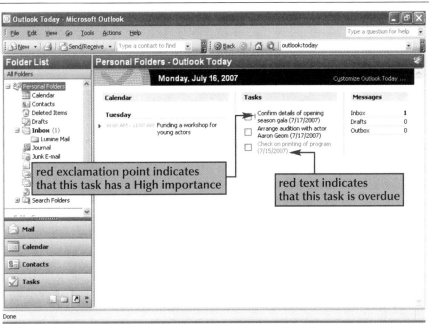

Figure 11 ▶ Outlook's Calendar items are color-coded to make it easier to identify them.

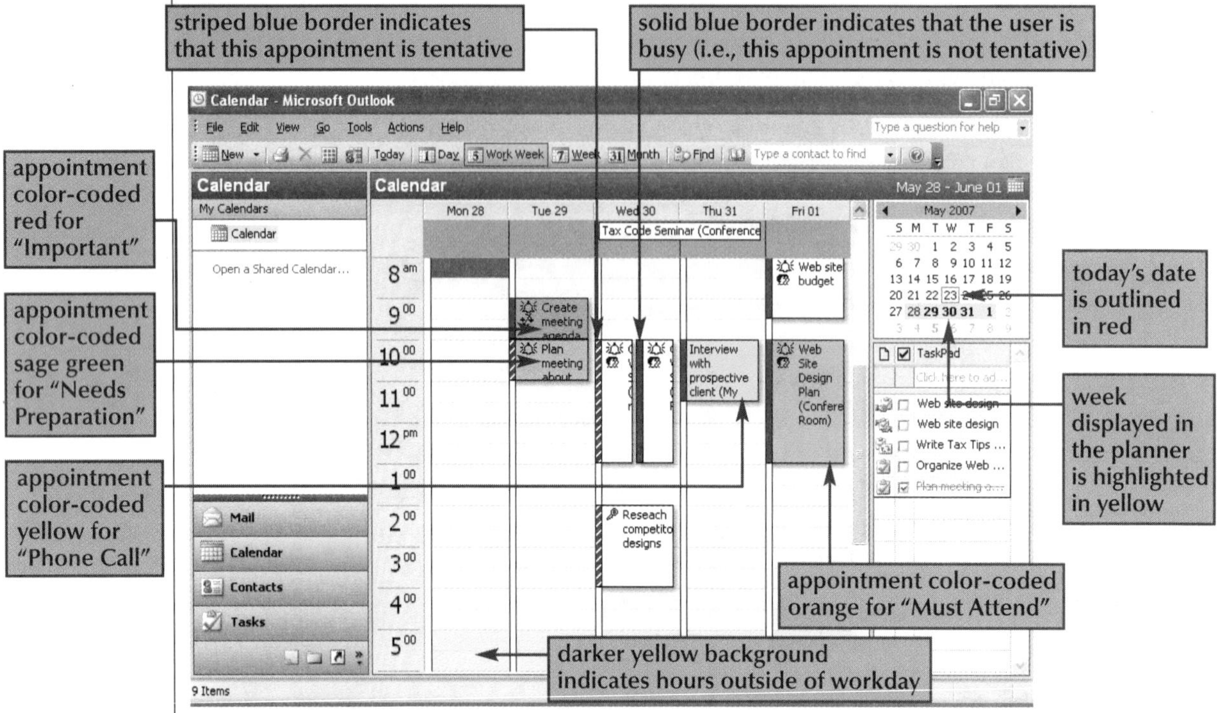

striped blue border indicates that this appointment is tentative

solid blue border indicates that the user is busy (i.e., this appointment is not tentative)

appointment color-coded red for "Important"

appointment color-coded sage green for "Needs Preparation"

appointment color-coded yellow for "Phone Call"

today's date is outlined in red

week displayed in the planner is highlighted in yellow

appointment color-coded orange for "Must Attend"

darker yellow background indicates hours outside of workday

Figure 12 ▶ You can save a calendar as a Web page and then post it for others to view. The user's name is automatically added at the top of the calendar. Details about each appointment or event appear on the right.

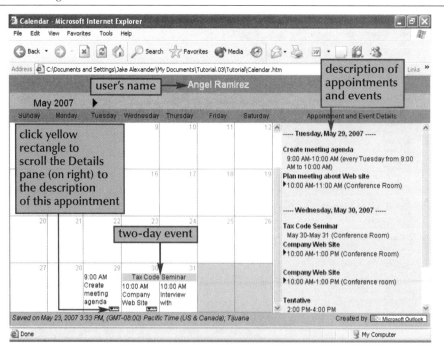

user's name → Angel Ramirez

description of appointments and events

click yellow rectangle to scroll the Details pane (on right) to the description of this appointment

two-day event

Task Reference

TASK	PAGE #	RECOMMENDED METHOD
activity, link to contact	OUT 97	See Reference Window: Linking an Activity to a Contact
activity, view for contact	OUT 97	Open Contact window, click Activities tab
appointment, create from task	OUT 156	Drag task from Tasks folder or TaskPad to Calendar in Navigation Pane or Calendar main window
appointment, create private	OUT 174	Open Appointment window, click Private check box, click the Save and Close button
appointment, delete	OUT 181	Click appointment in Calendar to select it, click ☒ or press Delete key; if appointment is recurring, click option to delete the series or just this occurrence, click OK
appointment, schedule	OUT 155	See Reference Window: Scheduling an Appointment
appointment, schedule recurring	OUT 160	Create appointment, click the Recurrence button, select recurrence pattern and range, click OK
appointment or meeting, schedule with contact	OUT 97	Select contact, click Actions, click New Meeting Request to Contact or New Appointment with Contact
archive, create automatically	OUT 234	See Reference Window: Setting Up AutoArchive
archive, create manually	OUT 237	Click File, click Archive, select folders, enter date, select Archive file location, click OK, click Yes
archive files, retrieve	OUT 238	Click File, click Open, click Browse, navigate to file location, click Open, click OK
attachment, add to e-mail	OUT 50	In Message window, click 📎, select file location, double-click file
attachment, open	OUT 52	Double-click attachment in Message window or Reading Pane, click Open
attachment, save	OUT 52	Right-click attachment in Message window or Reading Pane, click Save As, select save in location, type filename, click Save
AutoArchive, turn off	OUT 246	Click Tools, click Options, click Other tab, click AutoArchive, uncheck Run AutoArchive check box, click OK, click OK
Business Contact Manager, associate a new database with	OUT B3	Click File, click Data Management, click Business Contact Manager in the list box, click Settings, follow steps in wizard
Business Contact Manager, create new account	OUT B6	Click Accounts in Business Contact Manager folder, click New button list arrow, click Account, fill-in information, click the Save and Close button
Business Contact Manager, create new business contact	OUT B7	Click New button list arrow, click Business Contact, fill-in information, click ⌞...⌟, click Add Existing Account, click account name in list box, click OK, click the Save and Close button
Business Contact Manager, create report	OUT B15	Click Business Tools, point to Reports, point to desired report category, click desired report
Business Contact Manager, delete account	OUT B16	Click Accounts in Business Contact Manager folder, click account to delete, click ☒
Business Contact Manager, import data as new business contacts or accounts	OUT B9	See Reference Window: Importing Data as New Business Contacts or Accounts
Business Contact Manager, link all e-mail messages automatically	OUT B14	Click Business Tools, point to Link E-mail, click Link Existing E-mail, click AutoLinking, click folder in list, click Start, click Close if necessary
Business Contact Manager, move and copy contacts into	OUT B8	See Reference Window: Moving and Copying Contacts from the Contacts Folder into Business Contact Manager

TASK	PAGE #	RECOMMENDED METHOD
Calendar, configure options	OUT 354	Click Tools, click Options, click Preferences tab, click Calendar Options button, make changes as needed, click OK
calendar, print	OUT 163	In Calendar folder, display view and dates, click 🖨, select print style and range, click OK
calendar, save as Web page	OUT 179	See Reference Window: Saving a Calendar as a Web Page
category, add to Master List	OUT 78	Click Categories in item's window, click Master Category List, type category name, click Add, click OK
category, assign to e-mail message	OUT 200	Create e-mail, click the Options button, select or create category, click Close, send message
category, assign to item	OUT 77	See Reference Window: Assigning a Category
category, delete from Category List	OUT 115	Click Edit, click Categories, click Master Category List, click Master category to remove, click Delete, click OK, click OK
category, remove from item	OUT 79	Select category, including comma, in item's windows, press Delete key
category, view items by	OUT 102	In item's folder, click By Category option button or click View, click Arrange By, click Current View, click By Category
command, add to toolbar or menu	OUT 366	Right-click toolbar, click Customize, click Commands tab, click category, drag command to toolbar or menu
conditional formatting, apply to items	OUT 218	See Reference Window: Applying Conditional Formatting to Items
contact, accept duplicate name	OUT 74	Click Add this as a new contact anyway option button in Duplicate Contact Detected dialog box, click OK, click File as list arrow to save with different File as name
contact, add to Windows Messenger	OUT 296	Click Add a Contact in Windows Messenger window, click By e-mail address or sign-in name option button, click Next, type contact's e-mail address, click Next, click Next, click Next to enter a new contact or click Finish
contact, create	OUT 65	See Reference Window: Creating a Contact
contact, create from e-mailed contact card	OUT 89	Drag attached contact card from Reading Pane to Contacts in Navigation Pane
contact, delete	OUT 116	In Contacts folder, select contact, press Delete key
contact, delete from Windows Messenger	OUT 299	Right-click contact's e-mail address, click Delete Contact, click Yes
contact, edit	OUT 84	Switch to Address Cards or Detailed Address Cards view, click in contact card, edit text as usual, click outside contact card
contact, flag for follow up	OUT 99	See Reference Window: Flagging a Contact for Follow-Up
contact, schedule appointment, meeting, or task with	OUT 97	Drag contact from Contacts main window to Calendar or Tasks folder or select contact in Contacts main window, click Actions, click New Appointment, New Meeting Request, or New Task for Contact
contact, send by e-mail	OUT 88	See Reference Window: Sending Contact Information by E-mail
contact list, print	OUT 85	Select contact or contacts, click 🖨, select print style and range, click OK
contacts, change views	OUT 82	In Contacts folder, click desired view option button
contacts, view by flag	OUT 100	In Contacts folder, click By Follow-up Flag option button

TASK	PAGE #	RECOMMENDED METHOD
control, delete from form	OUT 333	Select control, press Delete
control, resize	OUT 335	Select control, drag sizing handles
control properties, set	OUT 331	Select control, click 🔲, set properties, click OK
controls, align on form	OUT 334	Select controls, click 🔲 ▾, click option
Deleted Items folder, empty	OUT 54	Right-click Deleted Items folder, click Empty "Deleted Items" Folder, click Yes
Deleted Items folder, restore	OUT 183	Display Deleted Items folder, drag item from Deleted Items main window back to item's original folder
dial-up connection, specify for Exchange Server e-mail account	OUT A14	Click Tools, click E-mail Accounts, click View or change existing e-mail accounts option button, click Next, click Microsoft Exchange Server, click Change, click More Settings, click Connection tab, click Connect using my phone line option button, click Use the following Dial-Up Networking connection list arrow and select a dial-up connection, click OK, click Next, click Finish
distribution list, create	OUT 80	See Reference Window: Creating a Distribution List
e-mail account, create new	OUT 13	Click Tools, click E-mail Accounts, click Add a new e-mail account option button, lick Next, select mail server type, click Next, enter user, logon, and server information as needed, click More Settings, type E-mail account name on General tab, click Outgoing Server tab, enter options as needed, click Connection tab, click the option button next to the type of connection you will use, click OK, test account settings, click Next, and then click Finish
e-mail account, set up for someone else's mailbox	OUT A7	Click Tools, click E-mail Accounts, click View or change existing e-mail accounts option button, click Next, select your Exchange account, click Change, click More Settings, click Advanced tab, click Add in Mailboxes area, type the person's mailbox name in the Add Mailbox text box, click OK, click OK, click Next, click Finish
e-mail message, check spelling and grammar	OUT 19	Click 🔲 (or click Tools, click Spelling), change or ignore highlighted words to correct spelling, click OK to confirm spelling check is complete
e-mail message, create and send	OUT 18	See Reference Window: Sending an E-mail Message
e-mail message, create from note	OUT 135	Drag note to Inbox in Navigation Pane
e-mail message, delete	OUT 54	Select message in Inbox, click ✖
e-mail message, format	OUT 43	Select message text, click appropriate buttons on Formatting toolbar
e-mail message, forward	OUT 36	Select message, click the Forward button, enter e-mail address, type message, click the Send button
e-mail message, print	OUT 37	Select message or messages, click File, click Print, select print style, click OK
e-mail message, recall	OUT 202	Open message from Sent Items folder, click Actions, click Recall This Message, select recall options, click OK
e-mail message, reply	OUT 35	Select message, click the Reply button, type reply message, click the Send button
e-mail message, save in another format	OUT 45	Select message, click File, click Save As, type filename, select save in location, click Save as type list arrow, click file format, click Save
e-mail message, send for someone else	OUT A7	click New button list arrow, click Mail Message, type person's name in the From text box, type message in message area, send message

TASK	PAGE #	RECOMMENDED METHOD
e-mail messages, send or receive from mail server	OUT 27	Display Inbox or Outbox, click the Send/Receive button
e-mail message, send to contact or distribution list	OUT 91	Select contact or distribution list, click 🔲, create and send message as usual
e-mail message, track delivery	OUT 199	In Message window, click Options button, check Request a delivery receipt for this message and Request a read receipt for this message check boxes
event, delete	OUT 116	Click event in Calendar to select it, click ✕ or press Delete key; if event is recurring, click option to delete series or just this occurrence, click OK
event, schedule	OUT 162	See Reference Window: Scheduling an Event
Exchange mailbox, share	OUT A6	Display Mail folder, right-click Exchange mailbox, click Sharing, click Permissions tab, click Add, click person's name, click Add, click OK, click Permission Level list arrow, click permission level, click OK
Exchange Server e-mail account, set up	OUT A2	Click Tools, click E-mail Accounts, click Add a new e-mail account option button, click Next, click Microsoft Exchange Server option button, click Next, enter appropriate information, click Check Name, click Next, click Finish
Favorite Folders, add folder to	OUT 364	Drag folder to Favorite Folders pane
fax, create and send from Outlook	OUT 278	See Reference Window: Sending Faxes from Outlook
field, add to form	OUT 324	Drag field from Field Chooser to form
field, create new	OUT 326	Click New in Field Chooser, type name, select type, select format, click OK
field, delete	OUT 370	Right-click main window background, click Show Fields, click field in Available fields list box, click Delete, click OK, click OK
field, remove from view	OUT 370	Right-click main window background, click Show Fields, click field in Show these fields in this order list box, click Remove, click OK
field, reposition on form	OUT 328	Select field, drag to new location
fields, map imported fields Outlook fields	OUT 286	Click Map Custom Fields in Import a File dialog box, drag fields to as needed between From group and To group, click OK
files, import or export	OUT 281	Click File, click Import and Export, select action and other options as needed in wizard
filter, apply to view	OUT 103	See Reference Window: Filtering a View
filter, remove	OUT 115	Click Customize Current View in Navigation Pane, click Filter, click Clear All, click OK, click OK
folder, set for offline use	OUT A12	Display Folder List, click folder, click Tools, point to Send/Receive, point to Send/Receive Settings, click Make This Folder Available Offline
folder home page, create	OUT 306	See Reference Window: Creating a Folder Home Page
folder home page, remove	OUT 308	Right-click folder, click Properties, click Home Page tab, delete text from Address text box, uncheck Show home page by default for this folder check box, click OK
folders, set for offline use	OUT A13	Select folders in Folder List, click Tools, point to Send/Receive, point to Send/Receive Settings, click Define Send/Receive Groups, click a Send/Receive group with an Exchange Server account, click Edit, click Exchange Server account, check the folders you want to use offline, click OK, click Close
form, customize	OUT 322	See Reference Window: Customizing a Form
form, open	OUT 341	See Reference Window: Opening a Custom Form

TASK	PAGE #	RECOMMENDED METHOD
form, publish	OUT 339	See Reference Window: Publishing a Form
form, remove from library	OUT 370	Click Tools, click Options, click Other tab, click Advanced Options, click Custom Forms, click Manage Forms, click Set above left list box, select library location, click form, click Delete, click Yes, click Close, click OK in each dialog box
form, save to a new location	OUT 370	Click Tools, click Options, click Other tab, click Advanced Options, click Custom Forms, click Manage Forms, click Set above right list box, select library location, click form, click Save As, select Save in location, type filename, select file type, click Save, click Close, click OK in each dialog box
form, test	OUT 337	Click Form, click Run This Form, enter data and select options as usual, click ⊠, click No
form page, display or hide	OUT 324	Click tab, click Form, click Display This Page
form page, rename	OUT 324	Click tab, click Form, click Rename Page, type name, click OK
form properties, enter	OUT 337	Click (Properties) tab on form, enter form properties as needed
Global Address List, copy to remote computer	OUT A15	Click Tools, point to Send/Receive, click Download Address Book, uncheck for first download or check for subsequent downloads the Download changes since last Send/Receive check box, click Full Details option button, click OK
Help, get using Type a Question for Help box	OUT 24	See Reference Window: Getting Help from the Type a Question for Help Box
Help, get using the Outlook Help task pane	OUT 29	See Reference Window: Getting Help Using the Outlook Help Task Pane
History list, use in Business Contact Manager	OUT B11	Open a contact or account card, click Add in History area, click item type, fill-in information, click OK, click the Save and Close button, click the Save and Close button in the contact or account card
importance level, set	OUT 44	In Message window, click ❗ or ⬇
instant message, send	OUT 298	Click Send an Instant Message in Windows Messenger window, click contact's e-mail address, click OK, type message, click Send
instant messaging, sign out	OUT 300	Click File in Windows Messenger window, click Sign Out
instant messaging, using Windows Messenger	OUT 294	See Reference Window: Using Windows Messenger for Instant Messaging
item(s), delete	OUT 54	Select item or items, click ⊠ or press Delete key
items, group	OUT 231	See Reference Window: Grouping Items
items, move between folders	OUT 209	See Reference Window: Moving Items Between Folders
items, save in another file format	OUT 292	See Reference Window: Saving Items in Another Format
items, sort by field	OUT 106	See Reference Window: Sorting by Fields
Journal, delete entries	OUT 311	Select entries or group headings, press Delete
Journal, filter entries	OUT 308	Right-click Journal folder background, click Customize Current View, click Filter, specify filter options, click OK, click OK
Journal, print entries	OUT 308	Select entry or entries, click 🖨, select print style and range, click OK
Journal, record entries automatically	OUT 260	See Reference Window: Recording Journal Entries Automatically
Journal, record entry manually for existing items	OUT 264	Right-drag item from main window to Journal folder, click desired option, complete Journal window, click the Save and Close button

TASK	PAGE #	RECOMMENDED METHOD
Journal, record entry manually for new items	OUT 262	Click the New button in the Journal folder, type subject, select entry type, set duration, enter notes, insert file, click the Save and Close button
Journal, turn off automatic recording	OUT 310	Click Tools, click Options, click Preferences tab, click Journal Options, uncheck check boxes, click OK, click OK
Journal, view entry	OUT 269	Display Journal folder, select view, expand or collapse groups
Junk E-mail Filter, set up	OUT 240	See Reference Window: Setting the Junk E-Mail Filter
letter, write to contact or distribution list	OUT 94	See Reference Window: Writing a Letter to a Contact
mail editor, select default	OUT 17	Click Tools, click Options, click Mail Format tab, check or uncheck Use Microsoft Office Word 2003 to edit e-mail messages check box, click OK
mail template, create	OUT 344	Click the New button in a Mail folder, select message format, type text, click File, click Save As, type filename, select Outlook Template as Save as type, change Save in location, click Save, close Message window without saving changes
mail template, open	OUT 345	Switch to Inbox, click Tools, point to Forms, click Choose Form, change Look in location, select template, click OK
Mailbox Cleanup, use	OUT 239	Click Tools, click Mailbox Cleanup
meeting, delete	OUT 181	Click meeting in Calendar to select it, click ☒ or press Delete key; if you organized meeting, click option to send or not send cancellation notice, if you were invited to meeting, click option to send or not send a response; click OK
meeting, schedule	OUT 166	See Reference Window: Planning a Meeting
meeting attendees, add or remove	OUT 174	Select meeting in Calendar, click Actions, click Add or Remove Attendees, add or remove attendees, click OK or open Meeting window, click Actions, click Add or Remove Attendees, select attendee to add and click Required or Optional, select attendee to remove and press Delete key
meeting attendees, review status	OUT 173	Double-click meeting in Calendar, click Tracking tab or open Meeting window, review InfoBar, click Tracking tab
meeting request, respond to	OUT 171	In meeting request Message window or in Reading Pane, click the Accept, Tentative, Decline, or Propose New Time button, change meeting time or enter message as needed, send message
message delivery options, set	OUT 24	Click Tools, click Options, click Mail Setup tab, click desired options, click OK
message format,	OUT 17	Click Tools, click Options, click Mail Format tab, click Compose in this message format list arrow, select default message format, click OK
message options, set	OUT 198	See Reference Window: Setting Message Options
message security, set	OUT 48	Click Tools, click Options, click Security tab, select or deselect options in Encrypted e-mail area, click OK
messages, find	OUT 222	See Reference Window: Finding Messages
messages, sort by one field	OUT 231	Click column heading
messages, sort by two or more fields	OUT 230	Click column heading, hold down Shift, click additional column headings, release Shift
Microsoft Office Online, using	OUT 31	Click 🕮, click Connect to Microsoft Office Online
Navigation Pane, add new group	OUT 361	Click 🔲, click Add New Group, type name, press Enter

TASK	PAGE #	RECOMMENDED METHOD
Navigation Pane, add, remove, and reorder buttons	OUT 360	Click ▾, click Navigation Pane Options, check or uncheck check boxes, select button, click Move Up or Move Down to reorder, click OK
Navigation Pane, add shortcuts	OUT 362	Click Add New Shortcut in Shortcuts pane, select folder, click OK
Navigation Pane, hide	OUT 8	Click View, click Navigation Pane
Navigation Pane, rearrange shortcuts	OUT 362	Drag shortcut to new location
Navigation Pane, remove group	OUT 372	Right-click group, click Remove Group, click Yes
Navigation Pane, remove shortcut	OUT 372	Right-click shortcut, click Delete Shortcut, click Yes
Navigation Pane, rename group	OUT 361	Right-click group, click Rename Group, type name, press Enter
Navigation Pane, reorder group	OUT 362	Right-click group, click Move Up in List or Move Down in List
Navigation Pane, reorder shortcuts	OUT 363	Drag shortcut to new location
Navigation Pane, resize buttons	OUT 357	Drag horizontal splitter in Navigation Pane up or down
Navigation Pane, view	OUT 8	Click View, click Navigation Pane
NetMeeting, schedule	OUT 175	See Reference Window: Scheduling a NetMeeting
note, assign contact	OUT 129	Open note, click 🖉, click Contacts, click Contacts, click a contact, click OK, click Close, click ✖
note, attach to e-mail message	OUT 135	Right-click note, click Forward
note, change color	OUT 133	Right-click note, point to Color, click desired color
note, create	OUT 128	Click the New button in the Notes folder, type text, click ✖
note, customize look	OUT 132	See Reference Window: Customizing a Note
note, delete	OUT 138	Select note, click ✖
note, insert into meeting request	OUT 169	In meeting request, click Insert, click Item, click Notes in Look in list, click Text only option button, select notes, click OK
note, open and edit	OUT 132	Double-click note, edit as usual
note, resize	OUT 133	Double-click note, drag corner or edge of note
notes, organize	OUT 135	In Notes folder, click desired option button in Navigation Pane
notes, print	OUT 136	Select note or notes, click 🖨, select print style and other options, click OK
Office file, send as e-mail	OUT 273	See Reference Window: Mailing Office Files
offline folder, synchronize manually	OUT A16	Click offline folder, click Tools, point to Send/Receive, click This Folder to synchronize selected folder or click Send/Receive All to synchronize all offline folders
Offline Folder file, create	OUT A11	Click Tools, click E-mail Accounts, click View or change existing e-mail accounts option button, click Next, click Microsoft Exchange Server, click Change, click More Settings, click Advanced tab, click Offline Folder File Settings, type path for Offline Folder file path, select an encryption option, click OK, click Yes, click OK, click Next, click Finish

TASK	PAGE #	RECOMMENDED METHOD
Offline Folder file, delete	OUT A18	Click Tools, click E-mail Accounts, click View or change existing e-mail accounts option button, click Next, click Microsoft Exchange Server, click Change, click More Settings, click Advanced tab, click Offline Folder File Settings, check the Disable Offline Use check box, click Browse, click Offline Folder file, press Delete, click Yes, click Cancel, click OK, click OK, click Next, click Finish
offline folders, synchronize automatically	OUT A16	Click Tools, point to Send/Receive, point to Send/Receive Settings, click Define Send/Receive Groups, automatically, click Exchange Server account, set options, click Close
opportunity, create in Business Contact Manager	OUT B9	Click New button list arrow, click Opportunity, fill-in information, click [...], click Add Existing Contact or Add Existing Account, click contact or account in list box, click OK, click the Save and Close button
Out of Office message, set	OUT A9	In Inbox, click Tools, click Out of Office Assistant, click I am currently Out of the Office option button, type message in AutoReply text box, click Add Rule, set up rules and exceptions as needed, click OK, click OK
Out of Office message, turn off	OUT A10	In Inbox, click Tools, click Out of Office Assistant, click I am currently In the Office option button, delete message from AutoReply text box as needed, delete rules as needed, click OK
Outlook, set to start offline	OUT A17	Click Tools, click E-mail Accounts, click View or change existing e-mail accounts option button, click Next, click Microsoft Exchange Server, click Change, click More Settings, click General tab, click Manually control connection state option button, click Work offline and use dial-up networking option button, click OK, click Next, click Finish
Outlook, set to start online	OUT A18	Click Tools, click E-mail Accounts, click View or change existing e-mail accounts option button, click Next, click Microsoft Exchange Server, click Change, click More Settings, click General tab, click Automatically detect connection state option button, click OK, click Next, click Finish
Outlook, start	OUT 6	Click Start, point to All Programs, point to Microsoft Office, click Microsoft Office Outlook 2003
Outlook Today, customize	OUT 350	Click Customize Outlook Today in Outlook Today main window, select options, click Save Changes
profile, set up	OUT 5	Click User Accounts in Control Panel, click Mail icon, click Show Profiles, click Add, type a profile name, click OK, click Close, click OK, click OK
QuickFlag, change	OUT 196	Right-click flag icon, click a different color, Flag Complete, or Clear Flag
Quick Flag, create	OUT 194	In Message window, click [▼], select preset text or type custom text in Flag to box, set due date and time, click OK
rule, create	OUT 211	See Reference Window: Creating a Rule with the Rules Wizard
rule, delete	OUT 245	Click Tools, click Rules and Alerts, select rule, click Delete, click Yes, click OK
rule, export	OUT 217	Click Tools, click Rules and Alerts, click Options button, click Export Rules, enter filename and save location, click Save, click OK, click OK
rule, run	OUT 216	Click Tools, click Rules and Alerts, click Run Rules Now button, check rule(s) to run, select folder(s) to apply rule to, and what to apply rules to, click Run Now, click Close, click OK
Search Folders, view	OUT 226	Click [+] next to Search Folders in Navigation Pane, *or* right-click Search Folders, click New Search Folder, click folder in list, click OK

TASK	PAGE #	RECOMMENDED METHOD
security zone settings, modify	OUT 304	Click Tools, click Options, click Security tab, click Zone Settings, click OK, click Internet icon, drag slider to change level, click Custom Level, change settings, click OK in each dialog box
sensitivity level, set	OUT 45	In Message window, click Options button, click Sensitivity list arrow, select desired level, click OK
shared folder, open	OUT A8	Click File, point to Open, click Other User's Folder, click Name, click folder owner, click OK, click Folder type list arrow, click folder name, click OK
sharing permissions, set for delegate	OUT A3	Click Tools, click Options, click Delegates tab, click Add, click Show Names from the list arrow, click address book, click name of person or persons, click Add, click OK, click each item list arrow and click permissions level, select options, click OK, click OK
signature, create	OUT 39	See Reference Window: Creating a Signature
signature, delete	OUT 54	Click Tools, click Options, click Mail Format tab, click Signatures, select signature, click Remove, click Yes to confirm deletion, click OK in each dialog box
sort, remove	OUT 115	Click Customize Current View in Navigation Pane, click Sort, click Clear All, click OK, click OK
stationery, use	OUT 41	See Reference Window: Creating an E-mail with Stationery
subfolder, create	OUT 207	Click the New button list arrow, click Folder, type folder name, select item you want folder to contain, select new folder location, click OK
subfolder, delete	OUT 246	Click subfolder in Folder List, press Delete
tab order, set	OUT 330	Click Layout, click Tab Order, click control, click Move Up or Move Down to reposition, click OK
task, assign to others	OUT 145	See Reference Window: Assigning a Task
task, check off completed	OUT 174	Click task's completed check box
task, create	OUT 137	See Reference Window: Creating a Task
task, create from note	OUT 137	Drag note to Tasks in Navigation Pane
task, create recurring	OUT 140	See Reference Window: Creating a Recurring Task
task, delete from TaskPad	OUT 182	Click task to select it, press Delete; if it's a task you accepted, click option to decline and delete or just delete; if it's a recurring task, click option to delete all occurrences or just this occurrence; click OK
task, update accepted task	OUT 150	Open accepted task, click Status list arrow, click option, click Details tab, select options, save and close task
task request, respond to	OUT 147	Open task request message or view in Reading Pane, click the Accept or Decline button, click option for sending response with or without adding message, send message
TaskPad, customize	OUT 353	Display Calendar, right-click TaskPad column heading, click Field Chooser, drag fields from Field Chooser to TaskPad, drag fields to reposition on TaskPad, click column headings to sort TaskPad, drag fields off TaskPad to remove
time zone, change in Calendar planner	OUT 356	Right-click gray space above times in daily planner, click Change Time Zone, type current time zone label, click Show an additional time zone check box, if desired, type a label, select time zone, click OK
toolbar, create custom	OUT 365	Right-click a toolbar, click Customize, click Toolbars tab, click New, type name, click OK

TASK	PAGE #	RECOMMENDED METHOD
toolbar, delete custom	OUT 373	Right-click a toolbar, click Customize, click Toolbars tab, click toolbar name, click Delete, click OK, click Close
toolbar buttons, customize	OUT 368	Right-click toolbar, click Customize, click Commands tab, click button on toolbar, click Modify Selection, point to Change Button Image, click desired icon, click OK
view, customize with fields	OUT 346	See Reference Window: Customizing Views with Fields
view, switch	OUT 229	Click View, point to Arrange By, point to Current View, click desired view
votes, track	OUT 204	Open original message in Sent Items folder, click Tracking tab, close message
voting buttons, use	OUT 203	Click voting button in Message window or Reading Pane, edit response if necessary, send message
voting buttons, create	OUT 199	In Message window, click Options button, click Use voting buttons check box, select standard buttons or type custom buttons in the Use voting buttons box, set options as needed, click Close
Web page, view in Outlook	OUT 302	Type URL in Address text box on Web toolbar, press Enter